Graphic Novels and Comics
in Libraries and Archives

Also By Robert G. Weiner

Captain America and the Struggle of the Superhero: Critical Essays (McFarland, 2009)

Marvel Graphic Novels and Related Publications: An Annotated Guide to Comics, Prose Novels, Children's Books, Articles, Criticism and Reference Works, 1965–2005 (McFarland, 2008)

Graphic Novels and Comics in Libraries and Archives

Essays on Readers, Research, History and Cataloging

EDITED BY ROBERT G. WEINER

*Forewords by Elizabeth Figa
and Derek Parker Royal;
Afterword by Stephen Weiner*

McFarland & Company, Inc., Publishers
Jefferson, North Carolina, and London

LIBRARY OF CONGRESS CATALOGUING-IN-PUBLICATION DATA

Graphic novels and comics in libraries and archives : essays on readers, research, history and cataloging / edited by Robert G. Weiner ; forewords by Elizabeth Figa and Derek Parker Royal ; afterword by Stephen Weiner.
p.   cm.
Includes bibliographical references and index.

ISBN 978-0-7864-4302-4
softcover : 50# alkaline paper ∞

1. Libraries— Special collections— Graphic novels.   2. Graphic novels— History and criticism.   3. Libraries— Special collections— Comic books, strips, etc.   4. Comic books, strips, etc.— History and criticism.
I. Weiner, Robert G., 1966–
Z692.G7G7   2010   025.2'77415 — dc22   2010004218

British Library cataloguing data are available

Front cover ©2010 Shutterstock

Manufactured in the United States of America

*McFarland & Company, Inc., Publishers
Box 611, Jefferson, North Carolina 28640
www.mcfarlandpub.com*

I dedicate this book to
My father, Dr. Len Weiner, and to Susan,
Sara Dulin, Larry and Vicki, and Marilyn May.
Thank you for your help, your love, and your patience.
And to
the memory of LeRoy (my best buddy) and Shelia,
my first two prairie dogs,
and my constant companions for seven years.
Thank you for all the Yahoos and cuddles.

Acknowledgments

This book is also dedicated to Randall Scott, Stephen Weiner, Lizzie Figa, Parker Royal, John Lent, Michael Rhode, Jerry Bails, Gene Simmons, Asa Berger, Steve Raiteri, Thomas Inge, Peter Sanderson, Les Daniels, and every librarian, writer and academic who saw and fought for the value of graphic novels and comics.

I dedicate this book in part to Sara Dulin. Thank you so much for being my "big sister" and for ALL YOUR HELP. I know I am not always easy to be around, so thank you for putting up with me.

Larry and Vicky. I wish you all the happiness in the world.

Thanks to Brian Quinn for suggesting I work on this project to begin with. I appreciate all your advice.

Special thanks to Dr. Elizabeth Figa for her fun sequential art foreword. Thanks to Derek Royal for the other foreword (great working with you), and thanks to Stephen Weiner (no relation) for the afterword. You have been inspirations to me.

Thanks to Dr. Cynthia Miller (you rock), S.E. Ward, Tom Gonzales, Joe Ferrer, Geraldine, Scott, and Anthony Q. Thanks to KV for being the best cook in the world and for your editing help. Thanks KD for the peer reviewing and help.

Thanks to CK, for finding that article for me, and to Joe Duke, Chris Caddel, Jim and Erica Johnson, and the Louise Underwood Center for the Arts.

Thanks to KD for your help and encouragement, and to Susan Schafer, Dr. Sam Dragga, Dr. Jim Bush, Sheriff J.W. Pepper, Simon Garth, James Howlett, Hank McCoy, Matches Malone, Megan Fox, Asia Argento, Kate Beckensale, and Cory Chandler.

Thanks to the dean of the Texas Tech Library, Dr. Donald Dyal, and all the associate deans—Jennifer Spurrier, Bob Sweet, Shelia Hoover, and Ernestine Dukes. Thanks to all the staff of the TTU libraries, but especially Shelley Barba, Joy Perrin (my right hand), Jim Brewer, Chris Starcher, Mr. Mark Key, Justin McDonald, Louise Sanders, Susan Hidalgo (my mentor), Lance King, Kenny Ketner, Kevin Jones, Shannon Adams, Kristen Young, Traci Havens, Kaley Daniel, Heather Jackson, Lisa Gonzales, Justin Daniel, Raphael, Marina Oliver, John, Maria, Margie, Pam Hight, Kathrin Dodds, Julie Toland, Zack, Liz Applin, Melanie Clark, Teri B, Christina Thomas, Bill and Donna McDonald, Matthew McKinney, Donna O, Jason T, and everyone else. If there is anyone I missed, I thank you too.

Thanks to all the folks in document delivery: Rene, Kory, Crystal, Conni, Penny, Justin and everyone else there. Thanks for being my lifeblood.

Thanks to all my colleagues in the information services department. A special thanks to Laura Heinz for always having good advice! Dr. Jon R. Hufford, Tom Rohrig, Cynthia Henry, Kim Vardman, Esmeralda Rodriguez, Susan Hidalgo, Shelia Hoover, Sam Dyal, Jake

Syma, Innocent Awasom, Carrye Syma, Shelia Hoover, Arlene Paschal, Jack Becker, Minerva Alaniz, Brian Quinn, Donell Callender, and Sandy River.

Thanks to all my little critters and Linda Watson who has been there whenever there have been problems. Special thanks to Blanche, Grant, Gable, Persia, and Spike and to all my little babies who are always there with a Yahoo and who make me smile.

Table of Contents

Foreword

ELIZABETH FIGA

Foreword

DEREK PARKER ROYAL

Of Panels and Patrons

In 2005, James Turner created *Rex Libris*, a comic book series featuring the thrilling adventures of a public librarian with Coke-bottle glasses and an arsenal of high-tech weaponry. As revealed in the first issue, the comic chronicles "the tumultuous tales of the public library system and its unending battle against the forces of evil." But this isn't mundane evil we're talking about. As Turner puts it, Rex Libris's struggle is "not just confined to our terrestrial sphere, but extends out into the furthest reaches of the cosmos ... *and beyond!*" Beginning his career in the original Library of Alexandria, Rex is over a thousand years old and a member of the Ordo Biblioteca, a secret international society of librarians. In his exploits he confronts dangers that every librarian must face, "patrons so terrible, so horrific, that they cannot be described ... without the risk of driving readers *mad*." In Turner's apt hands, career librarians are freed from their debilitating stereotypes (no uptightness or prissiness here) and are transformed into something hip and heroic. It's like Billy Batson uttering the wizard's name, "*Shazam!*" and turning into Captain Marvel.

There is a similar transformation taking place in our contemporary libraries. As one contributor to this volume asks, alluding to the power of nomenclature, "What's in a name?" For many librarians, that name is *graphic novels*, and the answer to the question is becoming increasingly undeniable. No longer are teachers, researchers, and catalogers wrestling with the seriousness or value of comics—well, some still do, although I would guess that those unenlightened few aren't thumbing through these pages—but instead, they have taken their prominence as a given and are moving on to more significant inquiries. Many of those questions, and the answers they provide, can be found in the book you now hold in your hands. What you are about to read is a series of conversations on the readership, the history, the categorization, the research, the promotion, and the organizational strategies surrounding graphic novels and their place in our libraries today. The authors initiating these conversations are all researchers and librarians, individuals keenly attuned to the tastes of the reading public, the needs of students, and the demands of a growing body of scholars who are making comics their critical focus. They understand the impact of graphic novels in our contemporary culture. What is more, these contributors are conversant in the language of comics—its use of images and words, the frames on the page, and the blank spaces or "gutters" that lie in-between. In the fullest sense of the word, what we have here is a full-fledged *panel* discussion.

And the significance of paneled narrative is what this book is all about. Robert G. Weiner has pulled together a variety of perspectives on graphic novel catalogs, and there is something here for librarians and educators of every stripe. Those with nascent graphic novel collections will find a wealth of information on how to develop and organize their holdings. Librarians at larger research institutions can uncover strategies for complementing the work of comics' scholars. Archivists have in this book a series of dialogues on the benefits and costs of graphic collections. Educators will discover a number of revealing surveys and studies concerning the demographics and reading habits of student populations. Those in secondary education as well as public libraries can learn of methods for expanding youth-friendly environments. And researchers interested in the history of graphic novels will discover the undeniable role libraries have played in the medium's success.

When it comes to comics and catalogers, Rob Weiner knows his stuff. Like Rex Libris, he has undertaken battles against menacing patrons whose ignorance of graphic novels extends well beyond the realm of the stacks. The author/editor of several books on popular culture (including *Marvel Graphic Novels and Related Publications* [2008] and *Captain America and the Struggle of the Superhero* [2009]), Weiner understands the possibilities within the medium and the promise that they bring to libraries. His approach is inclusive. Unlike those found in other recent studies of graphic narrative, the contributors to this volume are not only interested in the impact of "literary" or non-generic comics ... you know, titles like *Maus*, *Blankets*, and *Persepolis*, the kind of comics that have come to define "the graphic novel" for so many educators. They are also concerned with the more popular genres (superhero, manga, crime, and horror comics) and how librarians take full advantage of readers' expansive tastes. Weiner makes sure that his approach is democratic. What you will find in the pages that follow is nothing less than a transformation of expectations, a series of essays that can change the way you envision your online catalog. Read on, and you'll see that lying behind the mild-mannered façade of our libraries is a graphic adventurer just waiting to get out. *Oh Mighty Isis!*

Introduction

To say that graphic novels, sequential art, comics, photo-novels, graphics, paperback comics novels (whatever name one wants to use) have become a major part of popular culture in the first part of the 21st century would be an understatement. More books, films, articles, and websites related to sequential art are being produced than ever before. In fact, in a world that is going more and more with digital content, graphic novels are one of the last varieties of the printed form that are gaining in popularity as each year goes by. Graphic novels are now an established part of the library and academic worlds, despite those who may still thumb their nose at them. This book *Graphic Novels and Comics in Libraries and Archives* is proof of that. Now more than ever, there are theses and dissertations being written about graphic novels, and the number of college courses related to sequential art is at an all time high. In fact, for the university/college world to survive and remain relevant they have to offer courses which students will be interested in taking (e.g., sequential art, film, gaming, sports and other forms of popular culture). Librarians and scholars have written hundreds of books and articles since 2000 that discuss the role of libraries and the academy in studying and using sequential art. Yet there has never been a book which collects various librarians' and scholars' ideas related specifically to graphic novels in the library and archive world. This book attempts to help fill some of that gap.

As we know, the current interest in sequential art as a legitimate form has not always been open for discussion in academia and libraries. For the last half century librarians, educators, and academics have "pooh-poohed" sequential art as a throwaway form of entertainment with little or no value. To be sure there have always been those forward thinking scholars and librarians who cried out in the wilderness, arguing for its legitimacy as a form as though they were lone coyotes surrounded by angry gun-toting cattlemen. That sequential art has been thought of as just bad children's literature has been well documented. However, one must remember that as writer and editor Tom Defalco pointed out almost twenty years ago, "Comics were originally not intended for kids" (quoted in Daniels, 1992: 225). Witness the fact that early Batman and Captain America books depicted these superheroes either killing other characters directly, or allowing them to die. Early comics in newspapers were certainly aimed at adult audiences as well.

One of the first attempts at legitimizing the form for educators and librarians was the appearance of the strip *Texas History Movies*, which first appeared in the *Dallas Morning News* in 1926 and subsequently in a hardback book printed in 1928 (one of the first real sequential art novels published in the United States, Lynd Ward notwithstanding?), and in numerous booklets/books appearing in the 1930s and beyond. Beginning in 1935, educators and librarians used *Texas History Movies* as a way to teach Texas history. One might be tempted to say that the difference here is that the series was called *Texas History Movies* as a way to distance itself from the word comics, which was still coming into its own. However, this would be an inaccurate assessment; as Steven Williams (2008) points out, "The inclusion of the word 'movies' in the name is somewhat puzzling to modern readers, but in the late 1920s comics were frequently referred to as 'movies in print' and this association is the most likely reason for the inclusion of the word 'movies' in the title for the new comic strip series." There were also numerous attempts over the years to collect various serious strips into book form, long before many graphic novels were published. One example of this is the soap-opera–like Steve Canyon, by Milton Caniff, who published numerous paperback versions of his strips in 1959 (e.g., *Steve Canyon Operation Snowflower*). This coincided with his appearance as a television series. Canyon is not really aimed at a children's audience *per se* so, for all practical purposes, this is an example of publishing a graphic novel long before its time. Other works of note include the *Illustrated Roger Zelazny* (1979) and the winner of the Shazam Award for Special Recognition (one of the first sequential art awards), Gil Kane's *Black Marc* (1971). One can find other similar works published throughout the years by comic book writers and artists that could feasibly have the term graphic novel attached long before the popularization of the term.

That sequential art (comic book storytelling) is a way to get reluctant readers to read and learn is something often debated and discussed (including in this book). Resident demon and Kiss songwriter, millionaire, and bassist Gene Simmons states, "My love of comic books ... is how I learned to speak English.... My graduating term paper in college (in the early nineteen seventies) was *The Social Significance of the Panel Graphic Art Form*." Simmons received an A+ for this paper. Right after college, he started teaching sixth grade in Spanish Harlem. The kids Simmons taught were from "broken homes" and "very destitute." He couldn't get them to read *Jane Eyre* but when he brought in *Spider-Man* comics, they "grabbed onto it right away." Spidey was a character the kids (even the girls) could relate to. The administration of the school did not like it at all, but the "kids got it." Thus Simmons' career as a schoolteacher was ended before it really began. But he still acknowledges that he owes a "great debt" to Superman, Spider-Man, and comics in general (Simmons 2004).

One of the biggest problems facing scholars, librarians, and researchers is that since the 1960s there have been so many ephemeral publications related to sequential art (e.g., fan publications and magazines which could be used for research). Even today sequential art publications like that could provide excellent research for scholars. While publications like *Wizard, Alter-Ego Comic News Digest*, and *Comics Journal* are not indexed in any standard database much less with full text, this is true in film, sports, and gaming studies as well. However, there are numerous databases on the Internet such as Michael Rhodes and John Bullough's fantastic *Comics Research Bibliography* (http://www.rpi.edu/~bulloj/comxbib.html). It is hoped some of the major database providers like Ebsco or Wilson Web will get into the act and start indexing this type of material. Alexander Street Press now has a comic database. Certainly Michigan State's Collection of material is a boon to the scholar, but in most cases one has to travel there. The time for research today is exciting because of the Internet and the proliferation of various commercial databases, yet there is still a long way to go. Perhaps more full text digitization will occur, if not commercially, then privately — if we ever get over the dreaded copyright question.

Numerous essays make mention of works like *Maus: Contract with God, Watchmen, Understanding Comics*, and *Persepolis* which is a testament to their being pivotal works in the field. There is also much discussion of the work of scholars/librarians such as Allen Ellis, Doug Highsmith, Michelle Gorman, Fredric Wertham, Francesca Goldsmith, Randall Scott, Steve Miller, Michael Lavin, Stephen Weiner, and Scott McCloud among others. This is not only a testament to their pioneering studies and work, but also to the fact that true sequential art scholarship is really in its infancy. The good news is that each author in this book uses these sources in their own unique way. The editor would like to think that some key works are also contained in this volume.

The essays in this book cover a wide variety of issues and perspectives representing the spectrum of library collecting from academic, public, and school libraries, including an interview with pioneer librarian Randall Scott. Oddly, the academic libraries section is the biggest section in this book. This surprised the editor because major collecting of graphic novels and sequential art is a fairly recent development in academic libraries. But there are essays here that give matter-of-fact advice to academic librarians as well as to librarians who staff public and school libraries. There are essays that deal with the "graphic novel name" and its interpretations. There also is a section on the history of comics and how librarians have dealt with them in the past (mostly negatively). Of particular note is an essay about the relationship between manga and Japanese libraries in which the author translated a number of Japanese texts in order to tell the tale. To my knowledge this is one of the first publications in English that relates this story. There are essays looking at library outreach to particular audiences (including adults) using graphic novels, and there is a piece on the aesthetic value of sequential art. One essay looks at a particular state library archive (in this case Pennsylvania) and reveals how they deal with comics and sequential art. We have very detailed evaluations of graphic novels in Canadian and Association of Research libraries, and the editor did not leave out any essays on Web or Meta comics. And finally, Stephen Weiner (no relation) provides an afterword which relates his personal experiences with graphic novels.

These articles contain a wide variety of information and viewpoints for the reader to draw on and learn from. Rather than provide a detailed description of each essay, the editor would like readers to jump in and read (in Stan Lee hyperbole) the "Amazing, Astounding works of Academic Wonderment and Useful Pronouncements." Sequential art is a form of storytelling and the library of the future must become (and always should have been) storytellers. Or as Peter Brantley says in the March/April 2008 issue (43) of *EDUCAUSEreview*: "Libraries must tell stories." While Brantley is arguing for the integration of various technologies (such as games and "media based learning" beyond the book form), the graphic novel and comic fits right into this concept. Although many are still printed, there are digital sequential art stories. The point is to engage the patron, student, faculty member, youth, adult (the audience is wide open). Through the combination of pictures/text or purely graphic storytelling without words one uses both sides of the brain. For libraries and librarians to tell stories, the sequential art form must be a part of that equation along with all the emerging technological advances and digital content.

It is my hope that this book or parts of it can be used as a textbook for Library and Information Science classes (whether in printed form or digitally), but more importantly that librarians, scholars, and archivists can find value in the essays presented here. Librarians and academics share some of their experiences offering, in addition to theoretical constructs, some practical solutions in dealing with graphic novels in the library world. While *Graphic Novels and Comics in Libraries and Archives* is not the last word on graphic novels in libraries, it should come pretty close to being a starting point for discussion, education, and solutions. Optimistically, this work will be also be used for years to come.— R.G.W.

References

Brantley, Peter. March/April 2008. "Architectures for Collaboration: Roles and Expectations for Digital Libraries." *EDUCAUSEreview*. 43: 2: 30–38. http://www.educause.edu/EDUCAUSE+Review/EDUCAUSE ReviewMagazineVolume43/ArchitecturesforCollaborationR/162676.

Caniff, Milton Arthur. 1959. *Steve Canyon: Operation Snowflower*. New York: Grosset & Dunlap.

Daniels, Les. 1992. *Marvel: Five Fabulous Decades of the World's Greatest Comics*. New York: Henry Abrams.

Kane, Gil. 1971. *Black Marc*. New York: Bantam.

Simmons, Gene. 2004. *Speaking in Tongues*. UK: Sanctuary Records Group/Simmons Records (audio CD).

Williams, Stephen. February 13, 2008. "Texas History Movies, its publishing history and reincarnations." *Book Marcs*. http://bookmarcsonline.blogspot.com/2008/01/texas-history-movies.html.

Zelazny, Roger. 1979. *The Illustrated Roger Zelanzy*. New York: Ace.

1

A Librarian's Guide to the History of Graphic Novels

ALICIA HOLSTON

Let me start by telling you how it was in the beginning. In the beginning, God made comics, and we drew on the walls of caves trying to tell everybody how we captured a mastodon that afternoon.

— Will Eisner

At this juncture, it is not a question of whether to include graphic novels in libraries, but where to begin. Many librarians have grown up with comics and graphic novels and have an idea what to include in a collection and what not to include. Other librarians are new to the format and are overwhelmed by the choices and genres and the sheer quantity of graphic novels that come out in a year. The American Library Association and the Texas Library Association both have graphic novel lists that guide librarians to age appropriate materials (American Library Association, 2009; Texas Library Association, 2009). However, it behooves librarians who carry graphic novels in their collections to understand what they are purchasing, beyond a list of recommended titles.

In order to understand something, one has to study its history. Likewise, understanding the history of graphic novels and how they developed is key to understanding the medium in its current form, and its cultural impact. Graphic novels are being included in library collections and school curricula more frequently as time passes (Ellis & Highsmith, 2002). This is in part due to changes in the way children are receiving and interpreting information and learning from that information (*Publishers Weekly*, 2007). With the increase in visual stimuli in everyday surroundings, single focus information sources, such as text-only books, don't have the wide appeal that multimedia information sources do. Reluctant readers find graphic novels a good way to ease into more advanced reading. Graphic novels have made the move into mainstream literature, and in order to make wise collection choices, it benefits librarians to learn more about this medium and what it has to offer. To do so, an overall view of the graphic novel field — its origins and journey to its current existence — offers a comprehensive picture that aids librarians in selecting appropriate materials for their users.

This guide is by no means an exhaustive list of all the great and important graphic novels throughout the history of the medium; it is a collection of some of the more important works that shaped the face of the graphic novel industry in the United States in the late 20th century. This treatise focuses on later graphic novels rather than the comic strips and books that preceded them, and a few non-fiction works that have been written on the subject itself. Since the most profound developmental progress occurred from the 1970s forward, that is the time frame this list centers on.

History

Librarians are experiencing part of a relatively recent renaissance of graphic novels and their mass appeal. Traditionally, comic books, the precursor to graphic novels, were not considered literature or even worthy of adding to a library's collection. They were found on newsstands with the other ephemeral publications like newspapers and magazines. They weren't meant to be collected like books and yet the children who read them saved them to read over and over. The original American comic books, or funny books, were collections of comic strips from newspapers. In 1934, Max Gaines of Eastern Color Printing put together what would come to be known as the first modern comic book, a collection of comic strips in two books called *Funnies on Parade* and *Famous Funnies: a Carnival of Comics*. Cartoons had been published in book form before, but *Famous Funnies*, published by Eastern Color Printing at the time, was the first to use comic strips where the characters spoke in word balloons in each panel rather than in lines of text under the illustrations like children's picture books of today (*Comic Art And Graphix Gallery*, 1992). Shortly after these first comic compilations were published, comics creators started telling stories beyond the bounds of their 4 panel strips. The stories were adventures and intrigue like the pulp novels of the day. Those pulp comics made way for the first superhero comics. The characters were two-dimensional, black and white, good and bad. Often the storylines were allegory for World War II or the social climate of the time, and characters were portrayed as good guys or bad, us or them. In the second half of the 20th century, a generation of comic book readers grew up and effectively brought their toys and childhood pursuits with them (Jackson & Arnold, 2007). Graphic novels had to grow up too. Heroes and protagonists became grittier, the universes became darker and more dangerous—dystopias of sorts. Spider-Man marked the advent of the humanized hero, and Frank Miller's *Dark Knight* gave that hero depth through mental torment and ethical quandaries.

Graphic novels are typically categorized chronologically by time period. Golden Age, Silver Age, Bronze Age and the Modern Age are the common classifications, although the Atomic Age (1952–1965) and the Modern Age (aka the Iron Age) are also used in some references. The ages of comics/graphic novels are commonly delineated as follows:

Golden Age (1938–1944). The Golden Age begins with the appearance of Superman in 1938 and ends with World War II. *Superman (1938)*, *Batman*, and *Wonder Woman* were the popular superheroes of the time.

Atomic Age (1944–1956). Post-war comics were a little more tongue in cheek, more lighthearted to lighten moods after the war. The Atomic Age ended with the publication of *Seduction of the Innocent* by Frederic Wertham and the subsequent Senate Subcommittee on Juvenile Delinquency, leading to the advent of the Comics Code Authority.

Silver Age (1956–1972). The Silver Age began just after the Senate Subcommittee on Juvenile Delinquency and the creation of the Comics Code Authority (CCA) as comic companies began self-regulating in response to the 1953 Senate hearings on the connection between juvenile delinquency and the reading of comic books. A rise in superhero comics marks the age, with DC and Marvel Comics gaining more acceptance and commercial success. Underground comics developed during the Silver Age in response to the Comics Code Authority. Artists who felt restrained by the limitations set on their work found outlets in self-published magazines. These usually self-published magazines were dubbed "comix" with an "x" to differentiate them from mainstream comics and to indicate a racier subject matter not bound by the restrictions of the CCA.

Bronze Age (1972–1986). The Bronze Age is marked by artist/writer Jack Kirby's move from Marvel to DC and a period when darker elements were introduced into the typically bright comic books. During the Bronze Age the Comics Code Authority allowed drug use to be portrayed in comics as long as it was shown in a negative light. There was resurgence in horror comics due to the CCA relaxing the rules on use of monsters, ghouls, vampires, etc. in comics, allowing for such titles as *Swamp Thing* and reprints of EC Comics' *Tales from the Crypt.*

Modern Age (1986–present). This was also called the Dark Age or Iron Age of Comics with publication of Frank Miller's *Year One, Dark Knight,* Alan Moore's *Watchmen,* and the rebirth of gritty hard-boiled hero and anti-hero comics. In 1992, Todd McFarlane, Rob Liefeld, Jim Lee and a group of other comic creators left Marvel Comics and began Image Comics, an independent publisher, to fight for retention of creators' rights to their own works.

Within the chronological classifications, there are genres of graphic novels as well. Some, like the autobiographical stories, do not show up with any frequency or depth until the 1970s. Gay/Lesbian/Bi/Trans genre is also a late arrival, showing up closer to the 1980s. Influential biographical and autobiographical novels include *Maus*, by Art Spiegelman, *American Splendor,* by Harvey Pekar, and *Persepolis*, by Marjane Satrapi. An annotated list of these and other seminal titles is found below.

First and foremost, graphic novels and the comic books that preceded them are not a genre. Graphic novels are a medium in which many genres are represented. There are science fiction and fantasy graphic novels, graphic novels about heroes and villains, often in Spandex costumes and sometimes with capes, and stories about the human condition, love and loss; there are graphic novels in any genre found in books without pictures.

Some of the early comic books depicted graphic violence due to the nature of the stories. Crime novels were very popular in the 1940s and so were crime comics. William Gaines, son of Max Gaines and publisher of EC Comics, discovered a new niche in horror comics in the 1950s. Originally publishing crime comics, Gaines and the company noticed that the more horrific stories sold much better than other titles. These horror titles stopped being printed after the creation of the Comics Code Authority.

Manga, or comics and cartoons printed in Japan, have become popular in the United States in the past 20 years, but they have been around in Japan for much longer. The current form of manga has been in existence since just after World War II (Kinsella, 2000). Traditional manga has played a minor role in the development of American graphic novels until its popularity soared in the 1980s. Titles like *Lone Wolf and Cub,* translated and published in the United States by First Comics, and *Akira,* from Marvel Comics, marked the beginning of the manga craze in America — one that continues in full force with books like *Bleach, Yu-Gi-Oh,* and *Fruits Basket.* Manga influenced comic creators in the U.S. to produce manga-styled books. *Ronin,* by Frank Miller, and *Usagi Yojimbo,* by Stan Sakai, were both products of the new wave of manga in America.

Annotated List

Graphic novels and comic books in this section are listed chronologically by original publication date, with a discussion on the storylines and their influence in the field. Comic books are included in the list because of their historical relevance to the medium and its development; however, in the case of comic books, the collection into a few volumes is listed in the bibliography for ease of acquiring and reading the books. The list begins with books published in the 1970s, when the most drastic changes in storylines and artwork started to appear.

PEKAR, HARVEY. *AMERICAN SPLENDOR:*
THE LIFE AND TIMES OF HARVEY PEKAR.
NEW YORK: D.C. COMICS, 2006–2008.

Harvey Pekar's *American Splendor* is difficult to place in the timeline of comics and graphic novels solely because it has been published erratically since 1976 in one form or another. *American Splendor* is not the first autobiographical comic published, but it epitomizes the underground comic movement, a major part of which were comic memoirs, or autobiographies. The early 1970s saw the beginning of "slice of life" comics, which influenced creators to branch out and produce stories about real people rather than superheroes and anti-heroes.

EISNER, WILL. *A CONTRACT WITH GOD*
AND OTHER TENEMENT STORIES.
NEW YORK: W.W. NORTON & CO., 2006.

A Contract with God, originally published in 1978 by Baronet Books, deemed one of the most important graphic novel works by industry professionals, is considered to be the first example of a true graphic novel. Eisner used the term "graphic novel" to describe the book to publishers to give the work weight and to separate it from the lesser regarded "comic book."

A Contract with God and Other Tenement Stories is a collection of four stories, semi-autobiographical, about life in a Bronx tenement in the 1930s. In each tale, the immigrants who live in the building are in one way or another trying to find a better life, to lift themselves and their families up from the tenements.

SIM, DAVE. *CEREBUS VOL.1. KITCHENER,*
ONTARIO: AARDVARK-VANHEIM, 1991.

Cerebus the Aardvark started in 1977 as a funny animal parody of barbarian comics such as *Conan the Barbarian*. Two years into the series, creator Dave Sim announced that *Cerebus* would go to issue 300. After that point, Sim and background artist Gerhard started producing more serious storylines covering politics, religion, and gender issues. *Cerebus* is an influential work in its longevity, its scope of themes, and the fact that the entire series was self-published by Sim's company, Aardvark-Vanaheim. *Cerebus* also holds the honor of being the longest running American comic by a single writer and artist. The individual issues have been collected into 16 story arcs. The complete list follows:

1. *Cerebus* Collects issues 1–25 (1977–1981).
2. *High Society* Collects issues 26–50 (1981–1983); this was published before the "phone book" *Cerebus.*
3. *Church and State I* Collects isses 52–80 (1983–1985).
4. *Church and State II* Collects issues 81–111 (1985–1988).
5. *Jaka's Story* Collects issues 114–136 (1988–1990).
6. *Melmoth* Collects issues 139–150 (1990–1991).
7. *Flight* ("Mothers and Daughters" vol. 1) Collects issues 151–162 (1991–1992).
8. *Women* ("Mothers and Daughters" vol. 2) Collects issues 163–174 (1992–1993).
9. *Reads* ("Mothers and Daughters" vol. 3) Collects issues 175–186 (1993–1994).
10. *Minds* ("Mothers and Daughters" vol. 4) Collects issues 187–200 (1994–1995).
11. *Guys* Collects issues 201–219 (1995–1997).
12. *Rick's Story* Collects issues 220–231 (1997–1998).
13. *Going Home* ("Going Home" vol. 1) Collects issues 232–250 (1998–2000).
14. *Form and Void* ("Going Home" vol. 2) Collects issues 251–265 (2000–2001).
15. *Latter Days* ("Latter Days" vol. 1) Collects issues 266–288 (2001–2003).
16. *The Last Day* ("Latter Days" vol. 2) Collects issues 289–300 (2003–2004).

WOLFMAN, MARV; PEREZ, GEORGE. *CRISIS ON INFINITE EARTHS.* NEW YORK: DC COMICS, 1985; REPRINT EDITION JANUARY 1, 2001

With many writers working in the DC universe, deviations from original storyline are inevitable. In the *Crisis on Infinite Earth* series, DC brought the disparate storylines together with an explanation of multiple universes, or a multiverse, and used it to explain why Superman used to only be a super-strong, super-fast man and later he could fly. This *deus ex machine* technique would be utilized years later by Marvel Comics in their *Secret Invasion* series on a much larger scale.

MOORE, ALAN; GIBBONS, DAVE. *WATCHMEN.* NEW YORK: DC COMICS, APRIL 1, 1995 (REPRINT).

Moore and Gibbon's *Watchmen* is one of a few graphic novels originally published in 1986 that are considered to have started the Modern Age of Comics. Storylines became darker, heroes became grittier than before. The story follows the lives of a group of superheroes called The Watchmen after their crime-fighting years are behind them. Set in the 1980s in an alternate universe in which the United States won the Vietnam War, Richard M. Nixon is still president, and vigilante superheroes are no longer revered, *Watchmen* focuses on the struggles of heroes as humans with problems and obstacles.

MILLER, FRANK. *BATMAN: DARK KNIGHT RETURNS.* NEW YORK: DC COMICS, 1986.

Frank Miller was one of the forefathers of the Modern Age of comics, with books like *Year One* and *Batman: Dark Knight Returns*, among others. Not only did Miller redefine superheroes with dark sides, he took advantage of the new format in graphic novels, square backed echoing the format of trade paperbacks. In *Dark Knight*, Miller re-imagines the Batman saga, giving Bruce Wayne and the Batman more depth and angst, and adding more adult themes into the stories.

SPIEGELMAN, ART. *THE COMPLETE MAUS: A SURVIVOR'S TALE.* NEW YORK: PANTHEON, 1996 (REPRINT).

Originally published in 1986 in two volumes, Art Spiegelman's *Maus* is an epic telling of Spiegelman's father's life as a Polish Jew before and during World War II and his survival of Auschwitz. One of a few seminal bio- and autobiographical graphic novels, *Maus* has won a Pulitzer Prize Special Award, an Eisner award, a Harvey award, and many others. It is used in school curricula as a teaching aid in the study of the Holocaust.

GAIMAN, NEIL. *SANDMAN,* NEW YORK: VERTIGO, 1989–1996.

For many Gen X-ers, *Sandman* by Neil Gaiman was their introduction to graphic novels not featuring spandex-clad superheroes. Gaiman's *Sandman* was originally set to be a reprisal of Jack Kirby's *Sandman*, published by DC Comics in the 1970s; however, the story ended up following its predecessor in name only. Gaiman took the lead character and changed him from a trenchcoat and gas-mask wearing mystery man to an anthropomorphized personification of dreams, with siblings embodying other archetypes— Death, Desire, Despair, Destruction, Destiny and Delirium. Characters include mythological personas such as Calliope the muse of poetry, Orpheus (son of the title character in his Morpheus guise) and his short-lived bride Eurydice, as well as historical figures like Dr. John Dee and William Shakespeare. *Sandman* defies categorization, although Norman Mailer did his best when he dubbed it "a comic for intellectuals"(Anderson, 2001). The individual *Sandman* comics are collected in 10 volumes as follows:

1. *Preludes and Nocturnes* (collecting *The Sandman 1–8*, 1988–1989): The first 8 books follow Dream after capture by ceremonial magicians trying to capture and control Dream's older sister, Death. Consequences include people around the world falling into dreamless sleep and dreams escaping to the waking world.
2. *The Doll's House* (collecting *The Sandman 9–16*, 1989–1990): Dream/Morpheus cleans up the mess made while he was imprisoned by collecting errant dreams that threaten the waking world.
3. *Dream Country* (collecting *The Sandman 17–20*, 1990): Books 17–20 are four standalone stories with minor appearances by Dream and Death.
4. *Season of Mists* (collecting *The Sandman 21–28*, 1990–1991): Dream travels to Hell to visit a former lover; Lucifer has abandoned Hell and left the key to Morpheus, who has factions from various dimensions and realities vying for the key and control of Hell.
5. *A Game of You* (collecting *The Sandman 32–37*, 1991–1992): Barbie, from *The Doll's House* travels to the Dreaming and a dreamscape from her childhood and fights to keep it intact.
6. *Fables and Reflections* (collecting *The Sandman 29–31, 38–40, 50, Sandman Special 1* and *Vertigo Preview 1*, 1991, 1992, 1993): A collection of short stories revisiting stories from Morpheus' past. These stories are standalone, giving depth to characters but not promoting the main storyline. Stories include Morpheus' dealings with kings and leaders from mythological and ancient places. One book handles the Morpheus/Orpheus story cycle.
7. *Brief Lives* (collecting *The Sandman 41–49*, 1992–1993): Books 41–49 introduce the reader to the rest of the Endless family when Delirium wants to search for her missing brother, Destruction.
8. *Worlds' End* (collecting *The Sandman 51–56*, 1993): This is an introduction of Fiddler's Green. Travelers gather at an inn and exchange stories while waiting for a "reality storm" to pass.

9. *The Kindly Ones* (collecting *The Sandman 57–69* and *Vertigo Jam 1*, 1994–1995): An ancient feud between Morpheus and the Furies comes to a climax.
10. *The Wake* (collecting *The Sandman 70–75*, 1995–1996): Death of Morpheus, followed by the next Morpheus taking on the mantle of the Dream King.

These are also collected in four beautiful hardback volumes as *The Absolute Sandman*.

MILLER, FRANK. *RONIN*. NEW YORK: DC COMICS, 1995.

Originally published in 1983, Miller's *Ronin* was one of the early American graphic novels to be influenced by Japanese manga. Miller combines feudal Japan with gritty, modern day New York in a story of a samurai and a demon geisha cursed to inhabit the sword that killed them both until they are resurrected in New York in the 20th century. Like most of Miller's work, *Ronin* is a complex story juxtaposed to the clean lines of Miller's art. *Ronin* is worth reading to see how American comic creators assimilated the manga style and made it their own.

SMITH, JEFF. *BONE*. COLUMBUS, OHIO: CARTOON BOOKS; 1991–2004. REVISED COMPILED EDITION 2004.

Bone is the story of the Bone family, cousins who are run out of their hometown of Boneville and set off to find adventure and trouble along the way. The Bone cousins, Phoncible P. "Phoney" Bone, Smiley Bone, and Fone Bone, are drawn deeper into the world outside Boneville when they meet Thorn and Gran'ma Ben. In Smith's prequel series, *Rose,* the reader discovers just who Gran'ma Ben really is. The lighthearted series appeals to all ages.

Jeff Smith self-published *Bone* under his publishing company Cartoon Books. The entire series has recently been reprinted in color and re-released by Scholastic. Collected volumes are listed below:

1. *Out from Boneville* (originally released as *The Complete Bone Adventures* volume 1) 1995 *Bone #1–6*. The Bone cousins are ousted from Boneville. They reunite in Barrelhaven and meet Thorn and Gran'ma Ben, as well as Lucius, and the Red Dragon.
2. *The Great Cow Race* 1996 *Bone #7–11*. After spending time in Barrelhaven, Phoney Bone devises a cow race, with Smiley as the cow.
3. *Eyes of the Storm* 1996 *Bone #12–19*. Fone Bone has unusual Moby Dick dreams and shares them with Gran'ma Ben, who shares secrets of her own.
4. *The Dragonslayer* 1997 *Bone #20–27*. Gran'ma Ben and the Bones fight off rat creatures. Introduction of The Hooded One. Phoney appoints himself leader of Barrelhaven and promises to protect the citizens from dragons ... for a price.
5. *Rock Jaw: Master of the Eastern Border* 1998 *Bone 28–32*. Fone and Smiley set a baby rat creature free and it befriends them. They meet Rocque Ja, who takes them to a cave to deliver them to the Hooded One. Locust magic causes ghost circles that erase reality.
6. *Old Man's Cave* 1999 *Bone 33–37*. Thorn goes to save Fone and Smiley. The true identity of the Hooded One is discovered.
7. *Ghost Circles* 2001 *Bone 38–43*. The Bones, Gran'ma Ben, Thorn and Bartleby fight their way past rat creatures and through ghost circles to get to Atheia.
8. *Treasure Hunters* 2002 *Bone 44–49*. In Atheia, the troupe look for Gran'ma Ben's old mentor and discover how to fight the Hooded One.
9. *Crown of Horns* 2004 *Bone 50–55*. Thorn and the Bones are imprisoned. After escape, Thorn, Gran'ma Ben and the Bones traverse the land of ghost circles again, with Thorn in the lead. The Crown of Horns is found and used to defeat the Hooded One. All return to the valley, where Thorn is crowned queen. The Bones return home.

SATRAPI, MARJANE, *THE COMPLETE PERSEPOLIS.*
NEW YORK: PANTHEON, 2007.

Persepolis is Marjane Satrapi's autobiographical account of her childhood in Iran before and during the Iranian revolution and her subsequent flight out of the country. Originally published in 2003 in French in 4 volumes, the complete graphic novel was collected in one volume in 2007, the same year the movie based on the graphic novel was released. Satrapi is heralded as a rebel for telling her story when Iranian women were not supposed to express themselves publically. *Persepolis* has recently been adapted for film, which has earned an Oscar nomination.

Alongside a list of graphic novels that have shaped the medium are books about graphic novels and the study of art form. Many comic book creators have written about how to draw or write comics, but a few have written on the medium itself. Will Eisner wrote *Comics and Sequential Art* (1985), a treatise on the development and evolution of sequential art. Scott McCloud furthered the study of the graphic novel with his series of books starting with *Understanding Comics* (1994).

References

American Library Association. 2009. "Great Graphic Novels for Teens." *American Library Association.* http://www.ala.org/ala/mgrps/divs/yalsa/booklistsawards/greatgraphicnovelsforteens/gn.cfm.

Anderson, P. 2001. "Neil Gaiman: I Enjoy Not Being Famous." *CNN.com.* http://archives.cnn.com/2001/CAREER/jobenvy/07/29/neil.gaiman.focus/.

Comic Art and Graphix Gallery. 1992. "The History of Comics." *Comic Art And Graphix Gallery.* http://www.comic-art.com/history/history3.htm.

C.R. 2007. "Disney Comics Goes to School." *Publishers Weekly,* 254 (19): 15.

Eisner, Will. 1985. *Comics & Sequential Art.* Tamarac, FL: Poorhouse Press.

Ellis, Allen, and Doug Highsmith. 2002. "About Face: Comic Books in Library Literature." *Serials Review,* 26 (2): 21–44.

Jackson, Kathy Merlock, and Mark D. Arnold. 2007. "Baby Boom Children and Harvey Comics After the Code: A Neighborhood of Little Girls and Boys." *ImageText: Interdisciplinary Comics Studies.* Department of English, University of Florida. http://www.english.ufl.edu/imagetext/archives/v3_3/jackson/.

Kinsella, Sharon. 2000. *Adult Manga: Culture and Power in Contemporary Japanese Society.* Honolulu: University of Hawai'i Press.

McCloud, Scott. 1994. *Understanding Comics: The Invisible Art.* New York: HarperCollins.

Texas Library Association. 2009. "YART: Maverick Graphic Novels." *Texas Library Association.* http://www.txla.org/groups/yart/maverickgraphicnovels.html.

2

Manga in Japanese Libraries
A Historical Overview

DAVID HOPKINS

In April 2009, the Japanese government announced that ¥11.7 billion had been allocated for the creation of a new National Center for Media Arts under the aegis of the Agency for Cultural Affairs. The facility was conceived as a museum and research center for manga, anime, games, and other technology-based arts (Corkill, 2009: 7). The timing is significant, as it occurred during the administration of Prime Minister Aso Taro, who is well known as a fan of manga and anime, but struggled with continued low support rates. Clearly, he and his party believed that such a center would be good for their image, especially among young voters.

In fact, the idea for such a center was first proposed at least as early as 1994, but, even though the Cultural Affairs Agency has been sponsoring a Japan Media Arts Festival since 1997, nothing happened. And, even though the "Cool Japan" boom that began in the 1990s continues with little diminution, the national government's recognition of the role of manga, anime and digital games in creating a positive international image for Japan has been slow. Indeed, opposition politicians "pounced on the program in Diet debate, arguing that funds should be more wisely spent on welfare and other purposes" (Ogawa and Ueno, 2009: 1).*

Scholars have felt a need for a research facility dealing with manga, etc. for some time. Meiji University in Tokyo will open its Yoshihiro Yonezawa Memorial Library of Manga and Subcultures in the summer of 2009 (Corkill, 2009: 8). Its beginning collection, some 140,000 items, is made up almost entirely of the Yonezawa (a critic of manga who died in 2003) collection. Also, in Kyoto, as a collaborative project between the city of Kyoto and Kyoto Seika University, an International Manga Museum recently opened to large crowds of tourists and other users. Its large collection is primarily made up of volumes that were owned by a manga lending (for a fee) bookstore. Of course, all publications in Japan are also collected by the National Diet Library, the Japanese equivalent of the Library of Congress, which should therefore, at least in theory, have the largest collection of all.

That in the twenty-first century Japan has recognized one of its great cultural properties is not surprising. The rise of dedicated manga museums and research centers is, however, surprisingly late on the scene, and these museums and centers are still limited to large

---

*All translations are my own and may differ from titles as they are published in English.

cities. This ambivalence of attitude by Japan might shock many non–Japanese whose main interest in Japan is not Noh, or Kabuki literature or ikebana or martial arts, but manga and anime.

This paper, which focuses mainly on library science texts and journals (that is, librarians talking to other librarians), attempts to trace the history of this attitude, by looking at libraries at all levels: school, university, public, dedicated/specialist, and private.

The Library in Japan

Though there were of course book collections in Japan, the concept of "library" first came to Japan as part of the wave of foreign influences that swept the nation in the 1870s. The first library (*toshokan*) in Japan was created in 1872 as a depository for official government records, and in 1880, it became the Imperial Library. It came into existence as a direct result of one of the Iwakura missions to learn from the West, and was an imitation of France's National Library (Kitajima, 1998: 80).

In 1876, a separate Iwakura mission to the United States discovered free public libraries, and in an 1877 report, the Ministry of Education (administrator of the National Library) pushed for public libraries to be widely established as an educational resource (Kitajima, 1998: 84–85). However, there was little actual construction due to lack of funding.

Independently of the government, organizations of teachers and community leaders (the wealthy) set up reading rooms, not lending libraries, again with the aim of improving the level of education in Japan (Kitajima, 1998: 88). In fact, access to the books in these reading rooms was often restricted to teachers, and the content was intended to create teachers, and presumably their students, who were patriotic and committed to the status quo political and economic system.

In contrast to these reading rooms, a separate type of reading room was set up by labor unions and political parties with the expressed intention of raising the political consciousness of workers (Kitajima 1998: 86). With highly politicized holdings, these reading rooms were an easy target for criticism by the authorities. By the end of the nineteenth century, many of these had evolved into more general use, lending libraries that were intended to raise the cultural level of the working class. Called "*tsuzokushosekikan*" ("popular book collections") instead of the more usual "*toshokan*," they had an expressed purpose to "uplift," meaning that the books collected were "wholesome," and intended to keep the working class away from "low behavior" (Iwasaru, 2007: 177–178).

What should be clear here is that all types of libraries heavily censored themselves, by either political or moral standards. This trend became even more serious when Japan began its overseas expansion, at the time of the first Sino-Japanese War and the Russo-Japanese War. School education became more politicized (and almost universal) and libraries in schools, which had become standard by 1908, were increasingly scrutinized as to their support for "patriotism, respect for tradition, and morality" (Kitajima, 1998: 90–92).

Oversight of education became more and more centered in the Ministry of Education and taken away from local school boards. The number of school and public libraries had greatly expanded, but most had small collections and limited access. In 1921, the Ministry established standards of "wholesomeness," which were further strengthened in 1926 as part of a general clampdown on political radicalism. Socialist, farmer-labor alliance, and union reading rooms ceased to exist (Kitajima, 1998: 96).

By 1940, with World War II well under way, the government's official library policy was that "from intellectual books with Marxist content to low level romance and detective fiction, all books not encouraging dedication to the war effort will be banned, and no more will be acquired" (quoted in Kitajima, 1998: 97). At least this proves that, at least to some extent, libraries had continued to collect and offer popular books, despite pressures that had built for years. This is how the first chapter in Japan's library history closed.

The Manga in Japan

The modern history of manga parallels library history quite closely. Most histories of manga begin with a long discussion of the historical roots of manga in traditional Japanese culture that is hundreds of years old. However, that isn't really very important, since most of the population of Japan would not have known of the existence of those works! In fact, outside of the cities, the illustrated popular novels that did have a connection to manga culture, as it developed in the modern age, were not likely to have been common, even among the rich. However, in the modern era, with a rapidly developing urban popular culture, based on modern printing technology, two important root forms of manga became truly popular. Both were intended for adult audiences.

Nishikie Shinbun ("illustrated newspapers") appeared in the late nineteenth century as a popular mass culture reading material. They featured shocking reports of supernatural activity as well as sentimental accounts of filial piety, all illustrated in garish color prints, with plenty of blood and horror. Although this medium had a very short life, it was superseded as newspapers by more standard newspapers, and as sensational stories by cheap novels (with fewer illustrations). The storytelling possibilities, common in popular illustrated stories since the eighteenth century, made a large leap toward a manga style in these papers (see *Taishu Journalism no Kaika*, "The Rise of Mass Journalism," 2006).

Arguably more important and certainly much better known are the satirical and political cartoons that appeared in a variety of magazines beginning in the late nineteenth century. Inspired by overseas models, the cartoons appeared in magazines such as *Tokyo Puck* and *Japan Punch*, and while trouble with the authorities sometimes resulted in the confiscation of printed issues, artists such as Kitazawa Rakuten had no difficulty finding places in which to publish. Newspapers soon began to feature comics, including American-style comic strips, and by the 1910s, manga artists were forming trade associations, often along ideological lines (Shimizu, 2007: 110–111).

The association of newspaper and magazine manga with opposition politics almost certainly guaranteed that when collected editions appeared in book form, libraries would find it difficult to collect them. On the other hand, a new genre (indebted to the illustrated novels of a hundred years before), called *manga shosetsu* (manga novels), was pioneered by Okamoto Ippei, who had begun as a newspaper satirical cartoonist. Okamoto's novels typically had the top half of the page devoted to a cartoon image, with the bottom half typeset text. He was a prolific writer, and his works were very popular. Since their content was not overtly political, these works were perfect for libraries, and the publication of multivolume collected editions of both Kitazawa's and Okamoto's works in the mid–1920s also implies a library audience.

Children's comics also began to appear around this time, again with their start in magazines and newspapers. *The Adventures of Sho-chan*, by Kabashima Katsuichi and Oda Shosei, was the first of these to be published in book form, in 1923 (Shimizu, 2007: 12), while the date, 1921, appears in some other sources. *Sho-chan* is a story manga with repeating characters, a style not previously seen in Japan. With his mischievous pet squirrel creating scrapes that Sho-chan always had to find a way out of, this manga had little to offer to school libraries, whose guidelines were:

1. Provide books for teachers' research.
2. Provide books for students' further study.
3. Provide books for students to read outside of directed study to encourage the habit of reading.
4. Provide books to improve the youth of the community (Kitajima, 1998: 101).

The most popular of all children's manga in the pre-war era was *Norakuro*, the story of a stray dog who joined the army (the dog army, of course). Teachers and censors would have found nothing objectionable in the patriotic and militaristic tone of these stories. Even though he often caused problems by trying to find a lazy way to avoid work, the bad consequences of his laziness were a strong lesson in every episode. Still, this was likely too frivolous for educators in wartime. At any rate, *Norakuro* and all other children's manga ceased publication in 1939, as part of the effort to purify the nation for a total war effort. This led to widespread book banning in libraries.

The Postwar Era

Then, everything changed, except, of course, censorship, which continued under enthusiastic new management. With many adult subjects problematic, the postwar era became a golden age of comics for young people. The history of the manga of this era is probably fairly familiar to students of manga, and is in any case easily studied in books like Frederik L. Schodt's *Manga! Manga!* (1983). After long years of indoctrination, manga must have been quite a relief.

As part of educational reforms enacted by the occupation government, the Civil Information and Education Section of the General Headquarters decreed that public libraries were to "have open, bright atmospheres, with unrestricted access to all books" (Terada, 1999: 170). In other words, Japanese libraries were to become more like the American ideal of a library. There was little money available for this, so instead of bringing the people to this new kind of library, bookmobiles suddenly appeared all over Japan. Collection policies were liberalized, and the concept of the library as an information center began to spread.

Libraries in schools similarly reflected this new image, and in 1962, school libraries were advised by the Ministry of Education to "comprehensively collect, order, and use books *and other materials* as a resource center" (Kitajima, 1998: 124; emphasis mine). By 1968, the Ministry had begun using the term "media center," and specifically recommended an American standard of library collecting and use, including audiovisual and all types of printed matter (Kitajima, 1998: 126).

These changes happened at the same time that manga for adults were returning in a burst of creative activity. Again, this history may be easily studied elsewhere, but in the 1960s, manga as a medium of artistic and literary experimentation made great strides in Japan. Totally freed from overseas models of comics art, the gekiga style, with its free and cinematic use of framing and perspective, allowed the generation raised on the work of Tezuka Osamu and others to continue to read challenging and age-appropriate graphic narratives. These manga were embraced by intellectuals as well as students and workers. In the youth movies of the era, it is very common for characters to be seen holding manga. Oshima Nagisa, known as an experimental film director, filmed Shirato Sanpei's *Ninja Bugeicho* (Record of Ninja Battles) by moving the camera over the pages of the manga, to which voices and music were added. While still long before "Cool Japan," the idea that here was an important and unique new culture was widely recognized and discussed, and so, libraries needed to consider their relationship to manga seriously.

Library Scientists Think About Manga

The professionalization of librarianship was a direct result of American originated reforms of the education system in Japan, and like all reforms imposed from the outside, there was ambivalence about some aspects. Some librarians resisted changes in the paternalistic role assumed by prewar libraries, while others welcomed the idea of media and an information center. The need to deal with a unique (at least at that time) and significant new cultural trend (modern manga culture) brought some of these tensions into the open.

The earliest serious proposal for manga in libraries was published in 1959. It began with a discussion of the important manga of the turn of the century, such as those of Kitazawa Rakuten, and argued that their historical importance outweighed any hesitation by libraries to collect something that is clearly not just a book (Ono, 1959: 96). The author of the study quoted a survey by the Tokyo Prefectural Board of Education, which showed that, at that time, 60 percent of junior high school students were reading manga stories, with works by Tezuka Osamu (many titles) and Hasegawa Machiko (*Sazae-san*) by far the most popular (Ono, 1959: 99–101). The report author argued that, clearly these works would be as important to any future understanding of that era as Rakuten's work was for his era. He also noted the appearance of "science manga," a kind of comics version of school textbooks, which is in a border area between manga and the kind of books libraries have always collected.

The first professional attempt to codify standards for library collection and the use of manga was as follows:

1. no "merely insulting" content (this clearly applies to much humor).
2. no thrilling crimes without a proper moral stance.
3. no unscientific or unrealistic content (the author notes that most children's manga will be rejected by this standard).
4. no "crude" content (perhaps meaning sexual, scatological?).
5. no cheap sentimentalism (many girls' comics are rejected here).
6. no poorly written or slangy content.
7. no low quality artwork (Ono, 1959: 105–107).

Clearly, this was completely subjective, and its basic conservatism is completely in line with paternalistic library administration practices. The recognition that manga would inevitably be collected in libraries is, however, significant and prescient.

As manga culture grew in size, influence, and economic power, libraries in the sixties were faced with difficult problems of image. As Ono had argued in 1959, manga had a place in libraries, but what manga and what place? At its annual meeting in 1970, the Japan Library

Association had a panel discussion on "Public Libraries and Manga" (published in its journal, *Library Magazine* v. 65 n. 3 1971: 150–157). Four professional librarians from Tokyo area public libraries made comments showing the range of issues at the time. The moderator started the discussion by asking each if his or her library had manga:

> YAMAHANA: No. Absolutely not. Even children say that libraries shouldn't lower themselves to the manga level.
>
> KIKUCHI: Yes, we have many kinds of science and history manga, as well as general interest humor manga like *Sazae-san*. We stopped our subscriptions to manga magazines when they changed from monthly to weekly (mainly due to space issues). Kids complained a lot.
>
> ITO: No. There are too many manga that have become problems, with teachers and PTA groups calling for their banning. On the other hand, making them a secret banned "pleasure" may not be a good strategy.
>
> YANO: *Sazae-san* and Tezuka, yes. We also have the recent reissues of *Norakuro*, but recent manga are especially wicked and I for one don't want children to see them.

The chair tried to turn the discussion to manga as a bridge to reading, but the discussion stubbornly stayed on the morality of contemporary manga. Reflecting Ministry of Education directives, Yano said that libraries must be more open to new media, but Ito and Yamahana argued that protecting the image of the library as wholesome and moral must precede all other missions. Clearly, there are echoes of prewar library policy in this way of thinking. While once, children were to read only books that kept their minds on war, now they must learn only peace, democracy and *accepted* morality.

The liberal voice among them, Kikuchi, argued that preserving children's and young people's culture was also an important role of public libraries. In the late 1960s, *Harenchi Gakuen* (Scandalous School) was one manga that drew many attempts at banning and censorship from teachers and PTA groups. The manga mainly featured the lowjinks of some cool students who manage to get the better of their foolish teachers every time the teachers tried to get them to study or obey rules. Kikuchi pointed out that, library users could easily find references to the *Harenchi Gakuen* news incident in normal library materials like books, magazines and newspapers, and that Libraries had a duty to inform; thus they should keep even "wicked" manga in their collections, although they might restrict access in some way. Needless to say, most libraries were and are too conservative to consider this.

By the mid–1980s, manga were firmly established as part of library collections, even in schools, where a 1985 survey by the School Library Association found that 52 percent of elementary, 56 percent of junior high, and 47 percent of high school libraries had manga holdings. The survey said librarians were trying to maintain a standard of "excellent" or "educational" manga (Masuda, 1989: 13).

Librarians called for a national standard to be established, perhaps out of lack of faith in their own judgment, lack of knowledge of manga, or perhaps as a defense in case a particular title came under parental attack as being inappropriate. Accordingly, the School Library Association set up a manga committee, which, at its annual meeting in 1985, announced the following standards for school libraries to follow in selecting manga for their collections:

1. high artistic quality.
2. no bad language.
3. respect for human rights (the vocabulary of this issue had changed).
4. clear plots.
5. no attempt to indecently stimulate the reader.
6. no glorification of wrongdoing.

7. no glorification of war or violence.
8. no prejudice against weaker members of society (very close to no.3).
9. historical accuracy when presenting real incidents.
10. biographical accuracy when presenting real people.
11. age appropriate content.
12. adaptations of literary works must not change the content.
13. paper quality must be good enough for library use.
14. only finished, not continuing, works (Masuda, 1989: 16–18).

Here, there are some significant changes from thirty years before. There is no attempt to weed out fantasy, romance, and crime content, and concern for human rights has become well established as educational policy. Sexual content per se is not banned by item number 5, but pornographic depictions would certainly be. While there clearly remains a great deal of space for subjective judgment, matters of abstract literary or artistic quality are hardly emphasized. Thirty years of experience with manga had shown the librarians that the fears of an earlier generation were largely unfounded.

Although school libraries had accepted manga, university libraries were still far behind. A 1990 study of university manga collections (Yoshida, 1990: 631) found that university libraries were still fighting the same old battle over the appropriateness of collecting manga. While a canon of classic, essential manga was well established by that time, university libraries' holdings of manga were almost exclusively educational titles like *Manga Introduction to Economics* (Yoshida, 1990: 634). This was excused on the grounds that university libraries seldom show interest in current bestsellers of any genre.

In 1994, the Japan Library Association journal, *Libraries Today*, published a special report on libraries and manga. While the report recognized that the old battle over the worthiness of manga as a library material still continued, it made serious suggestions that pushed libraries to go beyond that debate. Most importantly, it recommended that all libraries have a manga reference section, and specifically recommended 17 titles of manga anthologies, histories, or other reference guides. Almost all of the recommended titles were published after 1982, showing that the public and academia, if not all of the libraries, were ready to treat manga and manga history seriously (Shimizu, 1994: 260). (For reference, the list is included an Appendix at the end of this essay.)

More importantly, the *Libraries Today* report recognized that, with the quantity of manga on the market, no library could afford the budget or space to have a comprehensive collection. Therefore, the author called for the National Diet Library to create a manga library. Of course, a librarian talking to other librarians in a library science journal makes few waves, so this proposal languished for a long time. Now that manga libraries exist, and now that the Japanese government supports building an even bigger and better one, the recommendations from 1994 deserve careful consideration (Shimizu, 1994: 259–262).

An ideal Manga Research Library would need five major features or goals, according to the report's author:

First, an historical section dedicated to the roots of manga culture in Japan — particularly *Giga* humorous picture scrolls (and other media) and the social satirists of the Meiji era. These are the closest domestic antecedents of today's manga.

Second, a second historical section on visual arts that contributed to the style now called manga. This should include Western arts as well as Japanese art, so that the Western roots of satirical manga would be clear. Newspaper illustration, in the age of high speed printing technology, should also be a part of this section, and both of these sections could easily be presented in reproductions, so that the cost would not be too great. Both should also include comprehensive reference materials about the art they feature.

Third, the National Diet Library must make every effort to fill in all the blanks in its collection of manga. The report author's own investigation showed that of 66 (essential, according to the author's judgment) titles of manga periodicals searched, 33 were missing in part or entirely. He states, "There are at least 50 more titles the Library needs to have in order to make a collection that represents modern manga culture" (Shimizu, 1994: 262), and says that budgets must be increased for this purpose.

Fourth, the new facility must develop and maintain close relationships with private manga collections, such as the Contemporary Manga Library in Tokyo and Japan Manga Museum in Chiba (early and rather smaller versons of the museums mentioned in the introduction). The former of these collects postwar manga, while the latter focuses on pre-modern roots materials. Relationships with foreign libraries and museums also are essential.

Fifth, librarians must develop a workable system of classification for manga, to make research and access easier for both scholars and the general public. Unfortunately, fifteen years later, this facility is still under consideration.

Manga Collections Today (2009)

Manga are more likely than ever before to be part of public libraries. A report from December 2008 on manga use in Tokyo public libraries showed that manga magazines and collections were widely used by a broad range of customers. Libraries surveyed subscribed to an average of 2.2 weekly manga magazines, and about 5 percent of all book requests were for manga (Takahisa, 2008: 258). The most curious result in the data was that users of all ages were looking at manga that was first published at the time of their youth. They were using the library to revisit manga they remembered nostalgically (Takahisa, 2008: 261). It was also clear that the presence of manga in the library was a motivation for visits. The problem of selection criteria remains, but the connection between libraries and manga seems firmly established.

Meanwhile, the canon of manga continues to firm up. The 15th anniversary special edition of *Da Vinci* ("the new magazine of book and comic information") chose as its cover story "platinum ranking of the top 150 Hall of Fame manga." (This story is available to Japanese-enabled computers at *http://d.hatena.ne.jp/amiyoshida/20090413/1239621005.*) Most of the titles would be familiar to a manga fan in any part of the world today, and more importantly, all of them are still in print. It would seem natural that this type of collection would be the core of any library's manga section, but that is not the case. Many of these are series that run to 50 or more volumes, requiring far too much space for the average public library. The real library for popular and classic manga in Japan is the internet café. In fact, most internet cafes advertise themselves as "internet-manga café." The preservation of manga culture and its history is certainly safe with an active and passionate audience, whether as a public or commercial service.

Appendix: Basic reference titles on manga culture for Japanese public libraries as of 1994

Akiyama, Mitsuru. 1990. *COM no Seishun* [Youth of COM] (a manga magazine edited by Tezuka). Tokyo: Heibonsha.
Erino, Maya. 1990. *Ladies Comic no Joseigaku* [A Feminism of Ladies' Comics]. Tokyo: Seikyusha.
Fukushima, Akira. 1992. *Manga to Nihonjin* [Manga and the Japanese]. Tokyo: Nihon Bungeisha.
Inagaki, Shinichi. 1991. *Kuniyoshi no Kyoga* ["Crazy" Pictures of Kuniyoshi]. Tokyo: Tokyo Shoseki.
Ishigami, Mitoshi. 1977. *Tezuka Osamu no Kimyo na Sekai* [Strange World of Tezuka Osamu]. Tokyo: Kisoten-gaisha.
Ishinomori, Shotaro, *Manga Choshinkaron* [Ultra Evolution of Manga]. Tokyo: Kawade Shobo Shinsha.

Kure, Tomohide. 1986. *Gendai Manga no Zentaizo* [Overview of Contemporary Manga]. Tokyo: Joho Center.

Maeda, Aiya. 1991. *Kindai Manga Zenshu* [Modern Manga Collection 6 vols.]. Tokyo: Tsukuma Shoten.

Matsuyama, Fumio. 1969. *Aka Shiro Kuro* [Red, White, Black]. Tokyo: Zokeisha

Mineshima, Takayuki. 1984. *Kondo Hidezo no Sekai* [World of Konda Hidezo]. Tokyo: Seikabo.

Nagai, Shoichi. 1982. *"Garo" Henshucho* [Editor of "Garo"]. Tokyo: Tsukuma Shobo.

Sekikawa, Natsuo. 1991. *Chishikiteki Taishu Shokun,* Kore *mo Manga Da* [For You Intellectuals, These are Manga, Too]. Tokyo: Bungei Shunju.

Shimizu, Isao. 1989. *Bigot Subyo Collection* [Bigot drawings collection]. Tokyo: Iwanami Shoten.

_____. 1991. *Manga no rekishi* [History of Manga]. Tokyo: Iwanami Shoten.

_____. 1989. *"Manga Shonen" to Akabon Manga* [Manga Shonen and "Red Book" Manga]. Tokyo: Zoonsha.

Yaku, Hiroshi. 1989. *"COMIC baku" to Tsuge Yoshiharu* [COMIC baku (another publication) and Tsuge Yoshiharu]. Tokyo: Fukutake Shoten.

Yomota, Inuhiko. 1994. *Manga Genron* [Basic Theory of Manga]. Tokyo: Tsukuma Shobo.

References

Corkill, Edan. June 2009. "Is a national 'Manga Museum' at last set to get off the ground?" Tokyo, *Japan Times*: 7–8, 14.

"Hall of Fame Platinum Manga Ranking." May 2009. *DaVinci.* 181: 16–31. Tokyo: Media Factory.

Iwasaru, Toshio. 2007. *Nihon Toshokanshi Gaisetsu* [Outline of Japanese Library History]. Tokyo: Nichigai Associates.

Kitajima, Takehiko, editor. 1998. *Tosho Oyobi Toshokanshi* [History of Book Collections and Libraries]. Tokyo: Tokyo Shoseki.

Masuda, Chikafumi. 1989. "Gakko Toshokan to Manga" [School Libraries and Manga]. *Gakko Toshokan* 468: 9–18.

Ogawa, Yuki, and Hajime Ueno. June 2009. "Manga museum draws derision." *Asahi Shinbun* English edition 16: 1. Tokyo

Ono, Noriaki. 1959. "Manga Toshoron" [A Theory of Library Manga Collection]. *Doshisha University Library Science Journal* 2. Kyoto.

"Public Libraries and Manga." 1971. *Toshokan Zasshi* [Library Magazine]. 65 3: 150–157. Tokyo: Japan Library Association.

Schodt, Frederik L. 1983. *Manga! Manga! The World of Japanese Comics.* Tokyo: Kodansha International.

Shimizu, Isao. 1994. "Problems of Manga Materials in Libraries." *Libraries Today* 2, 4: 259–262. Tokyo: Japan Library Association.

_____. 2007. *Nenpyo Nihon Mangashi* [Timeline History of Japanese Manga]. Tokyo: Rinkawa Shoten.

Taishu Journalism — Osaka Nishikie. 2006. *Catalog of exhibition, Itami City Art Museum.*

Takahisa, Shinichi, Mitsuru Shiozaki and Shigeto Hisanaga. 2008. "Shonen, Shojomuke Riyo Sokyo" [General Situation of the Use of Boys' and Girls' Manga Magazines]. *Libraries Today* 46, 4: 257–264. Tokyo: Japan Library Association.

Terada, Mitsutaka, editor. 1999. *Tosho Oyobi Toshokanshi* [History of Book Collections and Libraries]. Tokyo: Jusonbo.

Yoshida, Akira. 1990. "Manga to Daigaku Toshokan" [Manga and University Libraries]. *Toshokan Zasshi* [Library Magazine] 84, 9: 632–635. Tokyo: Japan Library Association.

3

How Librarians Learned to
Love the Graphic Novel

AMY KISTE NYBERG

Librarians discovered comic books in the late 1930s, and what they saw led them to launch a crusade to turn young readers from the lurid "funny" books to more wholesome fare. Sixty years later librarians discovered graphic novels, and what they saw turned them into advocates for a new form of literature. What was it about comics that had librarians up in arms, and why did graphic novels find a place on library shelves? Much of the debate over the place of comics in libraries, then and now, appears in professional journals that serve librarians and teachers. This essay examines that literature, exploring the changing attitude toward comics and identifying factors contributing to that change.

While everyone is familiar with the modern comic book, the definition and history of the graphic novel remains a work in progress. Those who attempt definitions of graphic novels often begin with the caveat that not all graphic novels are fiction. Beyond that, there is some disagreement over whether collected serial comics in trade paperback form constitute a graphic novel, or if that term should be reserved for standalone stories that have not been published previously. Terminology remains problematic — some refer to "graphic novel" as a medium, others as a genre, and still others insist that graphic novel is a term for a format that has nothing to do with content, which can be as varied as the content of any fiction or nonfiction book.

The term graphic novel is most closely linked to Will Eisner, and although it has been established that he is not its originator, many sources still erroneously report he invented the term and that his 1978 graphic novel, *Contract with God*, marks the first appearance of a long-form, standalone comic. Eisner did use the term, however, as a way to avoid the stigma associated with comics in order to attract the interest of mainstream publishers and bookstores (Hatfield, 2005: 29; Krensky, 2008: 76–77). Sabin writes, "On one level, as a piece of marketing hype, the idea of an evolution from 'comics' to 'graphic novels' had a specific purpose — to add prestige to the form and thus to sell more product" (1993, 235).

The mainstream media "discovered" the graphic novel in the mid–1980s with the publication of three major works: *Maus* by Art Spiegelman in 1986, Frank Miller's *The Dark Knight Returns* in 1986, and Alan Moore and Dave Gibbons' *Watchmen* in 1987. Newspapers and magazines trumpeted the fact that comics had grown up. Cord writes that "the stage was set for the new aspect of the comic book as a way of reaching a wider audience" (2006, 546). As Hatfield notes, "Together these three volumes — really not very much alike —

established a beachhead for 'graphic novels' in the book trade and indeed expectations of success that for years went spectacularly unfulfilled" (2005, 30).

While the graphic novels of the mid–1980s did not immediately create a demand for long-form comics on the part of bookstores and the general reading public, the sale of graphic novels grew steadily, and in 2003, sales of graphic novels in bookstores surpassed those in comics specialty stories for the first time (*Comics Shops*, 2003: 22). The next year, sales of graphic novels had topped $200 million. In bookstores, the growth was driven by the popularity of manga, Japanese long-form comics that developed a fan base independent of traditional comics readers (U.S. Graphic Novel, 2005: 15). By 2007, libraries accounted for ten percent of all graphic novel sales, about $30 million annually (Librarians, 2007: 15).

Comics were not always welcome in libraries. In fact, librarians were a significant force in the first wave of criticism directed at comics, and as a result, "their ideas, of course, pervaded future thought on the matter" (Groensteen, 2000: 31). "Comics are seen as intrinsically bad because they tend to take the place of 'real books,' an attitude which crystallizes a double confrontation: between the written word and the world of images, on the one hand; between educational literature and pure entertainment on the other" (Groensteen, 2000: 32).

The Early Debate

Early opposition to comics in the library and classroom needs to be understood in the larger context of the debate over comic books that developed from their introduction in the mid–1930s and culminated in the adoption in 1954 of an industry regulatory code. A detailed history can be found in *Seal of Approval: The History of the Comics Code* (Nyberg, 1998), but a brief recap of that period is in order here. It is significant that almost from their beginnings; comic books were defined as a problematic form of juvenile sub-literature, despite the fact that comic strips were a firmly entrenched part of the American newspaper, enjoyed by child and adult readers alike.

Three distinct groups of critics targeted comic books. First were those educators and librarians, who believed comic books diverted children away from better literature, retarded the development of reading skills, and overexcited young minds with lurid tales of superhero adventure. Civic and religious leaders made up the second group to object to comic books. They feared that the violence and sex in comics were a threat to the morality of young readers, and they patterned their attacks after earlier "decency crusades" aimed at pulp novels. They pressured local retailers who carried comic books to remove selected titles, working from lists of "approved" comics compiled by various organizations.

However, it was the growing concern about media effects that shifted the comics debate from the local to the national stage. Psychiatrist Dr. Fredric Wertham was at the forefront of the third group, which sought to legislate against comic books, arguing that such reading fare did psychological damage to children. This attack culminated in Senate hearings on the comic book industry conducted in New York City in April 1954. While no federal legislation restricting or banning the sale of comic books emerged from this congressional scrutiny (and no doubt would have been ruled unconstitutional if it had), the negative publicity drove most publishers to band together to form a trade association, the Comics Magazine Association of America. The CMAA adopted a strict regulatory code that sanitized crime comics and eliminated the horror comics altogether.

That code remained in effect for 50 years, with modifications in 1971 and again in 1989.

The original code went far beyond addressing the graphic violence and sexual content of some comics to ensure that the moral messages of comics would strive to cultivate respect for authority and obedience to parents' wishes. Initially, publishers submitted comics for pre-publication approval by a group of women overseen by CMAA's regulatory arm, the Comics Code Authority, with Charles F. Murphy serving as administrator. The review process proved to be expensive and unwieldy, and eventually that chore passed to a single individual. Finally, pre-publication review was abandoned, and publishers took it upon themselves to determine which titles should carry the Seal of Approval, with the CMAA stepping in only to deal with complaints.

Changes in comic book distribution from newsstands to comics specialty shops beginning in the 1970s, along with a shifting readership demographic made up primarily of adult males in their 20s and 30s, meant that there was less urgency on the part of the major publishers in monitoring content. In addition, the 1960s rise of independent publishers, who did not subscribe to the code, weakened the hold the CMAA had on regulating comic books, and in recent years the Comics Code has been largely abandoned. Of the two major comics publishers today, Marvel Comics has dropped the code entirely, and DC Comics only retained it for its imprints that are aimed at juvenile readers.

Librarians and teachers were among the first critics of comics because they were on the "front lines" of guiding children's reading. I have argued that along with finding the content and format of comic books objectionable, educators also saw their control of children's reading slipping away. By and large, children's books are purchased by libraries, not by parents and certainly not by young readers themselves. Comic books represented a challenge to the dominance of adults because they were selected and purchased by children, often without any direction from adults. Even those parents who forbade comic book reading could not control the easy access children had to comics through pass-along readership (Nyberg, 2002: 169).

In the 1940s and 1950s, hundreds of articles about comics were published in trade, academic, professional, and popular periodicals. Earlier analyses of this literature (Nyberg, 1998; Nyberg, 2002; Ellis and Highsmith, 2000) found that while comic books had their defenders among teachers and librarians, their predominant view of comics was unfavorable. Articles generally fell into one of three categories. First there were those written by educators who drew on their personal experience, often offering details of activities or experiments in which they used comics as a stepping-stone to introduce children to more desirable reading. A second category was the essay, in which the author presented his or her viewpoint about comics reading, but usually did not support that view with any firsthand experience or research. The final type of article contained reports on academic research conducted on various aspects of comics reading, from analysis of vocabulary to surveys of young readers and their preferences. Such research, published in academic journals in the areas of education and the social sciences, frequently contradicted the widely held beliefs that comics contained simplistic vocabulary and encouraged readers to rely on the pictures rather than the text, but this research made little impact on attitudes of practitioners (Nyberg, 2002: 171).

Early criticism of comics drew on metaphors of disease, noting it was the librarians' responsibility to find the proper "antidote" to the spread of comics. An influential essay by Sterling North, published in 1940, was widely reprinted. His essay concluded that "the antidote to the 'comic' magazine poison can be found in any library or good bookstore." Subsequent articles about comics by educators echoed both his attitude and his language. For example, an article in *Elementary English Review* carried the title "The Plague of the Comics" and asserted that reading comics would leave behind "horrible desolation, grief and putre-faction." The only cure to "comicitis" was to bring children into the public or school library where the proper "treatment" could be administered (Branley, 1942: 181–82).

Those librarians and teachers who moved beyond this hysterical denunciation of comics built a case against them based on the perception that comics retarded development of reading skills. Comics' superficial resemblance to picture books aimed at the youngest readers led practitioners to assume that most readers were following the story by looking at the drawings and skipping the text altogether. When one teacher had his remedial English class read comics aloud, he found the poorest readers simply made up their own stories to accompany the pictures. He concluded, "It appears doubtful that the majority of remedial reading pupils *read* the comics" (Zamchick, 1952: 95–96). The use of poor grammar and slang terms was also a concern, and students' appropriation of the comic book convention of substituting symbols for inappropriate language was troublesome as well: "[They] make use of stars, exclamation points and dashes to express their feelings in the same way that the professional artists circumvent censors," wrote one English teacher (Brumbaugh, 1939: 64).

The major objection to comics however, had to do with their content. Critics argued that the escapist fantasy offered by comics did little to "uplift" students and encourage their interest in literature. Instead, educators feared a steady diet of the one-dimensional char-acters, the simplistic plots, and the emphasis on the action-adventure story would ruin children's taste for other types of reading. An essay in *National Parent-Teacher* asserted, "A child whose reading habits have been conditioned and corrupted by these ungrammatical scraps of narrative and conversation loses the sustained endeavor necessary for reading a full-length novel" (Ronson, 1950: 24).

Early on, librarians recognized their role would be to offer substitutions to comics, and the professional journals were filled with suggestions on how to steer children toward more acceptable reading material. This effort was usually represented as a "challenge" to librarians, or, drawing on a different metaphor, a "battle" or "war" against the comics. The proposed solution to the comic-book problem was two-fold: first, to determine why chil-dren liked comics and then find literature that held the same appeal; and second, to help educate children to be more discriminating in their reading selection (Nyberg, 2002: 175). In many cases, their experiments were a failure. Students happily critiqued comic books— and continued to read them. One high school English teacher wrote that even after study-ing the unit that that she had designed to show students the inferiority of the comics, they still admired Batman and Superman (Lee, 1942: 677–79).

Beyond the debate over comics' literary and educational worth was the simple fact that librarians did not understand the attraction of comics. To them, comics seemed crudely written and drawn, and were, in short, a waste of time. The most extreme expression of this objection came in an essay titled "The Viciousness of the Comic Book." This essay asserted that comic book reading turned children into loafers and day-dreamers, and that this would undermine the American work ethic and would "diminish the power of a great democracy" (Landsdowne, 1944: 14–15).

Even those librarians whose attitudes ran counter to the conventional wisdom of the time stopped short of endorsing comic-book reading. Two librarians who surveyed chil-dren about their reading interests concluded that comics represented "that large mass of literature which, while not harmful, is not particularly distinctive" (Williams and Wilson, 1942: 204–6). Another writer was more succinct: "As literature, I think they are terrible" (Reynolds, 1942: 17).

The advent of educational comics did little to sway most practitioners. *True Comics*, introduced in 1941 by the publishers of *Parents' Magazine*, and *Classic Comics* (retitled *Classics Illustrated* in 1949), which began publishing the same year, were greeted with skepticism by librarians and indifference by the audience they were intended to reach. Witek observed:

> Always queer hybrids of the popular and the highbrow, the *Classics Illustrated* comics seemed at times to be pretentious poor relations in the library and stodgy dowager queens on the newsstands. ... Their goal was to encourage young readers to grow beyond their infatuation with comic books to a love of 'real' literature, to read Shelby Foote rather than Jack Kirby [Witek, 1989: 35].

But educators had trouble seeing beyond the form. An editorial in *Wilson Library Bulletin* titled "Libraries, to Arms" argued that "fighting comics with comics" failed to address the underlying complaint that comics displayed bad taste in color and design (1941: 670).

The Post-Code Years

The furor in the professional journals over comic book reading died down in the 1950s with the implementation of the Comics Code and the introduction of a new medium that would displace comics as primary entertainment for children — television. Efforts to reboot the comic book industry in the 1960s, while heralded as the start of the Silver Age of comics by comic book historians and fans, did not generate much attention from educators (Ellis and Highsmith, 2000: 30–31). But Hatfield suggests that a gradual change in prevailing attitudes toward reading comics took place in the 1970s and 1980s, and he attributes the shift to the growing acceptance of mass culture by academia, the refocusing of media effects research on television, and changes in approaches to reading pedagogy. He concludes: "There remained an underlying consistency between the censorious writings of the forties and fifties and the guarded enthusiasm of the seventies and eighties. This consistency emerges repeatedly in certain rhetorical concessions: comics are designated as strictly utilitarian, and are still regarded as distinctly *other* than 'great literature'" (2005, 35). Groensteen noted, "In time, some child specialists came to rely on comics as the last stand against illiteracy and a teacher's best aid in the teaching of reading (now threatened mainly by television)" (2000, 35).

The 1970s marked the publication of influential articles by creator Will Eisner and noted scholar M. Thomas Inge. These articles strengthened "the prestige of the comic book medium among librarians" (Ellis and Highsmith, 2000: 32), and educators tentatively began to explore the place of comics in the school library and as a supplement to the English and social studies curriculum. Much of this work was collected in a single edited volume by James Thomas, *Cartoons and Comics in the Classroom*, published in 1983. This reference work, which was intended for librarians and teachers, culled 32 articles from the professional literature of the 1970s and was meant to show that educators could benefit from the "motivational factor" by introducing popular comic strips and comic books into lessons (Thomas, 1983: 7). These articles themselves, however, contained misinformation, and according to a review of the book by Inge, revealed that there was still "a general condescension displayed towards comics" (Ellis and Highsmith, 2000: 34). For example, one teacher commented that "comic books should never be expected to serve as art or literature. That is not their purpose, and never has been. In a sense, comic books are still nothing more than entertaining junk ..." (Schoof, 1983: 86).

Two aspects of Thomas' book are noteworthy, however. One is that few of the authors began their articles with a defense of comic books, and it was largely accepted that comic books were not a substitute for traditional textbooks and reading assignments. However, it also was largely accepted that comics had, as Hatfield noted, a certain utility in the classroom. The second was the inclusion of articles from those who taught learning disabled and deaf children. Most professionals still viewed the text of comics as the proper focus on reading. For example, one teacher cautions: "Be careful of one thing: make sure the activities focus on the students' attention on the words, not the pictures. Otherwise, the poorer readers may spend their time on non-reading aspects of the activity" (Swain, 1983: 75). But teachers of children with disabilities were among the first to articulate the idea that "reading" comics might involve complex cognitive skills. One educator observed that dyslexic children had a much easier time mastering the symbolic "code" of imagery (Hallenbeck, 1983: 140). An instructor at the Eastern North Carolina School for the Deaf found that the comic strip character Henry helped students connect their own thoughts with written language through the comics' convention of thought balloons. "Like the majority of the class [Henry] did not speak, but could see, act out, write, and think" (Hoover, 1983: 142).

The mid–1980s is usually identified by comics historians as the period in which graphic novels broke through cultural barriers to erase the stigma associated with reading comics. Ellis and Highsmith argue that this mainstream attention to the rise of the graphic novel marked "the single most important such change insofar as enhancing the status of comic books as appropriate for inclusion in library collections, by making them appear to be more like 'real' books" (2000, 40). However, the professional literature of the decade shows that librarians were slower to embrace the potential of graphic novels than were critics reporting on popular culture in the mainstream press. Coverage of graphic novels in journals read by practitioners did not parallel the enthusiasm of the mainstream press. Some changes specific to the practice of librarianship, however, began to have an impact.

In 1984, Ellis and Highsmith note that Randall W. Scott, who cataloged the comics collection at Michigan State University, identified five factors that "make it worthwhile to re-examine our collection policies." They include:

> (1) a new, much more efficient distribution system for comic books; (2) specialized publications offering "professional or near-professional" reviews and analysis of the medium; (3) a shift in comics' primary target audience from children to young adults; (4) significant comic book collections being housed in a few research libraries; and (5) the appearance of bibliographic records for comic books on OCLC and other bibliographic databases [2000, 34].

Also in the 1980s, a series of articles in the *School Library Journal* dealt with the growing interest in comics on the part of librarians who advocated using them as a way to lure students into the school library (Ellis and Highsmith, 2000: 34). Larry D. Dorrell, at Central Missouri State University, reported in 1987 that his survey at a state librarians' conference found that about 25 percent of schools had comic books in their library collections and 95 percent "indicated a willingness to add comic books." However, nearly 40 percent thought there would be opposition to such a move (1987, 31).

1990–Present

In the past two decades, the library literature has recognized the emergence of the graphic novel. Part of the reason is the increasing acceptance by mainstream publishers and chain bookstores. As Hatfield notes, "graphic novels are surging into bookstores and libraries ... the outlook for long-form comics is considerably healthier than in the past" (2005, 36). As an analysis of nearly 100 articles published in the professional journals shows, with this increasing acceptance across the board, practitioners began to discuss graphics novels as distinct from comic books. The focus, too, has shifted from debates on whether to include graphic novels in the library collection to more nuts-and-bolts discussions of how to select and integrate them. [1]

The first article about graphic novels to appear in the library journals was by *Comics Journal* contributor Keith R.A. DeCandido. His piece in *Library Journal* in 1990 was titled "Picture This: Graphic Novels in Libraries." In this piece, DeCandido notes that "Not many libraries have discovered graphic novels yet" and "many librarians we contacted for this article needed a detailed explanation of what a graphic novel is" (1990, 50–51). The article begins with a brief history of comic books, but moves quickly into giving specific advice about how to select graphic novels and where to buy them. The informal tone and less than respectful terminology he uses when referring to graphic novels serve to detract somewhat from his otherwise positive view of graphic novels in libraries. For example, he invites readers to suggest an alternative for the term graphic novel and comments "you will find an entire medium eternally grateful to you (or at least a few pundits)," and uses headings within the text such as "How does one buy these things?" and "Who reads this stuff?"

Four highly influential books garnered support of librarians for graphic novels. The earliest of these was Will Eisner's *Comics and Sequential Art* (1985), followed by his *Graphic Storytelling* (1995). An articulate advocate of the graphic novel, Eisner was accepted as an expert on the topic by librarians seeking to legitimize the place of comics in libraries. Scott McCloud's *Understanding Comics* (1993) discussed the complex way in which image and text interact and the cognitive processing required to "read" comics. Written in comic book form by a comics creator, this book attracted a readership far beyond the small but growing circle of academics who also were analyzing the way in which comics "texts" functioned. Due to its visibility and accessibility, McCloud's book is often referenced by librarians. Because librarians rely on bibliographic resources in building collections, two early bibliographies were frequently cited by authors writing about graphic novels in the professional journals. D. Aviva Rothschild's *Graphic Novels: A Bibliographic Guide to Book-Length Comics*, which came out in 1995, and Steve Weiner's *100 Graphic Novels for Public Libraries*, published by Kitchen Sink Press in 1996, were hailed as "professional books on graphic novels" (Bruggeman, 1997), and were widely recommended as resources for librarians who found little guidance in the traditional sources they draw on for building library collections.

Another indication of the growing interest of librarians in comics was a series of articles in *Serials Review*. A glossary of comic book terms was compiled by Jane K. Griffin, who noted that in addition to the specialized terms used in comic book publishing, "fandom has its own well-defined culture, making extensive use of slang and shorthand vocabulary" that she did not include in her list (1998, 71). Michael R. Lavin contributed a multipart series, complete with extensive lists, on collecting graphic novels and more broadly on the structure of the comics publishing industry. In "Comic Books and Graphic Novels for Libraries: What to Buy," Lavin begins by defending comics' place in libraries, writing that the "inevitable first question seems to be 'Why comic books?'" (1998, 31). Lavin, however, moves beyond the "begrudging" acceptance of comics by librarians to deal with some of the specific objections they raise, by stating, "... the physical format of comic books is too fragile; comics won't stand up to heavy use; they'll be stolen from the library; the subject matter is inappropriate for younger readers; they're too difficult to acquire and catalog — the list of concerns is quite extensive" (1998). But, Lavin adds, "few of them are especially convincing and none present insurmountable obstacles to establishing a browsing collection."

Also important to note is the increasing awareness that not all comics are suitable for juvenile audiences. Lavin writes, "It is doubtful whether comic books have ever been considered strictly a medium for children," and cites research by DC Comics that showed the average age of comics collectors is 25, (1998). He cautions, "Librarians need to pay attention to the intended audience of a particular comic book because many are designed for mature readers."

One of the more interesting points of view to emerge in the 1990s was the suggestion that bias against comics and graphic novels in the school library is rooted in gender bias. S. Richard Gagnier, a young-adult librarian in Rochester, N.Y., observed that the "tremendous bias" librarians had against graphic novels might be due to the fact that the library profession — particularly in the specialized areas of children's and young-adult literature — is dominated by women, "many of whom were not raised to think of comics as a form of serious literature." He notes that, "The great majority of those who read graphic novels are clearly teenage males," and he argues that graphic novels "offer masculine heroes that teens can identify with, [which] means they have a place in a library" (1997, 143). Five years later, Jim Valentino, publisher of Image Comics, would comment that "librarians seemed to be ahead of the curve" in recognizing the appeal of graphic novels. "We're seeing younger librarians, and comics are part of their vernacular. They're not biased against graphic novels" (McDonald, 2002: 22). The gender bias concerns were echoed in an article in 2006, in which Mary Chelton commented that boys' reluctance to read "has a lot to do with a (dare I say female) bias toward narrative fiction on the part of teachers and librarians" (10).

While the 1990s signaled a shift in attitude toward comics and graphic novels, it has just been in the past decade that this has borne fruit in terms of the widespread discourse on the benefits of graphic novels in libraries in the professional journals. Indeed, the year 2002 might be called "The Year of the Graphic Novel" as far as librarians are concerned. That was when the Young Adult Library Services Association scheduled a preconference session on graphic novels, at the American Library Association national gathering in Atlanta in June, which was attended by 175 people. "Get Graphic @ Your Library" was chosen for that year's theme for Teen Read Week, October 13–19, and was supported with a Web site on the subject of graphic novels (St. Lifer, 2002: 9). This tied in with the industry's first promotional "Free Comic Book Day," which was planned for the Saturday after the opening of the first *Spider-Man* movie. The success of that event ensured that the promotion would continue on an annual basis, and be tied into blockbuster summer movies whenever possible (McDonald, 2002: 22).

My analysis of the professional literature in this decade is divided into two broad categories: first, a discussion of the uses of the graphic novel in the library and classroom; and second, the practical concerns about adding graphic novels to the library collection. As previously noted, the growing acceptance of comics and graphic novels means that articles aimed at librarians spend less and less time on debating whether comics belong in the library and classroom. Ellis and Highsmith found that gradually, over the last thirty years, authors more and more often begin with the premise that comics and graphic novels are a valuable addition to the school, public, and academic library. Increasing emphasis has been placed on "providing practical information that is of use to librarians who are interested in learning more about the comics medium and/or are considering adding such materials to their libraries' collections" (2000, 39).

However, two key themes carry over from earlier debates on comics. The first is that graphic novels have an intrinsic appeal to children and young-adult readers; and second, comics are particularly valuable in targeting the "reluctant reader." The first demonstrates that despite evidence to the contrary, it remains firmly entrenched in the minds of many librarians that children are the primary audience for graphic novels, especially given the dominance of the superhero genre. The second reveals that while librarians may accept graphic novels, even today most feel that eventually young readers will "grow up" in their reading taste and selection. In addition, it perpetuates the idea that reading the comics format is easier because the pictures are secondary and merely illustrate the text, therefore making them an appropriate choice for poor readers.

The primary reason cited in the literature for adding graphic novels to the library collection is to motivate youngsters to visit the library and thereby boost traffic. A byproduct of increased visits is that in addition to checking out comics, these youngsters will also select other kinds of reading material, boosting overall circulation numbers. Representative of this viewpoint is an article by school librarian Maureen Mooney, who wrote, "If you acquire graphic novels, young adults will come," and, "young adults will check out more than just graphic novels in the collection once they realize what is there for them" (2002, 18). Steve Weiner suggests that young-adult librarians in particular, are open to graphic novels because of "the high readability of the books and re-enforced by the high circulation" (2002, 56). Robyn Young, writing in *Library Media Connection*, points out that at her high school, circulation of "graphic books" is consistently high, even though they make up less than two percent of the overall collection (2007, 26).

Once reluctant readers are enticed to try reading graphic novels, the format can serve as a "bridge" or "stepping stone" to other reading. Daniel D. Barron writes that graphic novels are "a bridge to sustained reading," adding that those not ready to read become discouraged in a text-based learning environment, and "(g)rabbing them with comics could help pull them out of the mire" (2002). Kat Kan, who writes regularly about graphic novels, notes the "visual aspect of the form, with its more limited amount of text, does attract readers who may feel intimidated by a regular novel" (2003, 15). A report by a committee of the Association for Library Service to Children cites research showing, "Comic book readers often move on to more serious reading and have positive attitudes toward reading" (ALSC, 2006: 50). One California school librarian boosted circulation 50 percent after the introduction of graphic novels. After "starting" the students on comic books, she directs them to related books in the stacks, and "they become readers without realizing it" ("Adding," 2004: 8). The opinion of one education professor was that graphic novels are motivators for reluctant readers, because if students are reading comics, at least they're reading, and comics can serve as "an introduction" to books. The article's author quotes her as saying, "Start out with what is appealing to them ... but then let them know that there is a library" (Galley, 2004: 6). This is not a uniquely American bias, as one Australian librarian wrote that the comics format was particularly attractive to teenage reluctant readers and the comics' "low readability levels" make it easier "for less proficient readers" (Snowball, 2005: 43).

Those librarians more familiar with the graphic novel, such as Ohio librarian Steve Raiteri, who maintained a Web list of recommended graphic novels, were less likely to automatically assume a link between young readers and the format. He warns against "the assumption that it's a simple equation of GN=YA," pointing out that the 17- and 18-year-olds who are closer to the target demographics for many graphic novels are at the top end of the age range for young-adult literature and "would not want to be caught dead" in that section of the library (2003, 94).

In the last half of the decade, however, practitioners began to recognize that reading comics involved more than deciphering text embedded in word balloons. The burgeoning field of comics scholarship contributed to the understanding of the grammar and language of comics, and expanded "visual literacy" beyond film and television studies to include sequential art.

Two Washington librarians using student testimonials to convey the appeal of graphic novels, concluded by citing Scott McCloud's book, and observed that "the reader must integrate the text and the pictures into an understandable whole" (Dombeck and Gufstason, 2005: 39), while an elementary school librarian argued that graphic novels require more effort to read than conventional books, stating, "That's because as a reader takes in a graphic novel's print and art through a series of panels, word balloons and captions, the reader's brain is bombarded simultaneously with the graphic novels' characters, setting, plot and action" (Luga, 2006: 58). Art librarian Amanda Gluibizzi writes that the art and text in graphic novels are "equivalent, each driving the other, rather than the illustrations supporting or attempting to explain the text. (2007, 28), and she reminds art teachers that graphic novels and comics often serve as students' first art teachers (29). An issue of *Children and Libraries* devoted to graphic novels included interviews with publishers and creators. Mark Siegel, editorial director at First Second, insisted that "the comics format is a unique and distinct reading experience" and reading comics is an acquired skill (Hunt, 2007: 13). A University of Illinois professor writes that reading comics is a "complex task" that "requires more than decoding the words," and that Readers need to understand "the relevant social, linguistic, and cultural conventions if reading is to lead to any meaningful knowledge or action" (Tilley, 2008: 23).

Discussions of graphic novels' popularity and contributions to visual literacy began to give way in the mid–2000s to more practical considerations in the professional library literature. Librarians who were already sold on the idea were searching for assistance in selecting, purchasing, cataloging, shelving and maintaining their graphic novel collections. Initially they found few traditional resources to help them — they were advised to visit the local comics shop and ask the retailer for recommendations, but as sales to libraries increased, library and education journals began to routinely include reviews of graphic novels. Library associations compiled annual lists of the best graphic novels for libraries and schools, and bibliographies were published and updated. Book vendors who catered to libraries began to carry graphic novels, and Web sites that offered a wealth of information about genres, specific titles and creators proliferated. These sites designated graphic novels that were suitable for various age groups and grades to assist librarians and educators in selecting graphic novels.

Steve Weiner wrote, "Finding graphic novels, a difficult task in past years, has gotten easier," and he recommends that librarians visit a local comics shop "in order to learn more and seek the books firsthand" (Weiner, 2002: 56). Similarly, Michelle Gorman advises librarians to establish a working relationship with their local comics retailer to form "a powerful team in recruiting a whole new generation of readers" (2002, 43). By the mid–2000s, resources for librarians had caught up with demand. An article in *Knowledge Quest*, published by the American Library Association, observed, "Here's welcome news: graphic novels now are commonly reviewed in professional library review journals. An increasing number of recommended graphic novel bibliographies have been developed for both school and public libraries" (Rudiger and Schliesman, 2007: 58).

Once libraries decided to add graphic novels, the next challenge was to decide where to put them. Kat Kan noted there were two basic schools of thought regarding shelving graphic novels. One group advocated shelving graphic novels together in a separate area of the library, preferably face-out, to enhance their visibility and accessibility. The second argued for inter-shelving them with the regular collection to encourage readers to browse the library's collection. The Dewey classification system places graphic novels in the 741s, in the nonfiction section with books about cartooning. Kan advocated for the first shelving option, noting that teens seldom browse in the nonfiction section (2003, 15), and Steve Raiteri advised against interfiling graphic novels with other fiction because it made it difficult to browse the collection, saying, "GNs don't need to piggyback on other material to justify their presence — they have their own merits and appeal that justify inclusion all on their own." However, he disagreed with the idea of shelving all graphic novels together, observing that placing material intended for mature readers with preteen graphic novels "could lead to problems that are best avoided" (2005, 52).

Cataloging presented its own challenges, but the intricacies of those decisions were usually left for the academic libraries, which often tackled those problems out of necessity when faced with a donation of comics-related materials. Academic librarians built on the work of pioneers such as Randall Scott at Michigan State University. For example, librarians at Washington State University processed several hundred graphic novels over a period of several weeks, forcing them to "discover patterns and inconsistencies in graphic novels cataloging." Among them was the fact that librarians generally classified graphic novels as "monographic serials" (English, Matthews and Lindsay, 2006). Librarians at Portland State University wrestled with similar issues when, beginning in 2005, the library was given the corpus of Dark Horse published titles, both retrospectively and on a continuing basis. Noting that determining the "chief intellectual content contributor" of a graphic novel was difficult when titles were produced by more than one chief creator, the Portland State Library adopted a system that acknowledged all contributors, while giving the main entry designation to the "primary writer" (Markham, 2009).

Internal concerns about acquisition and shelving were coupled with a growing awareness of the range of content found in graphic novels, which could be problematic for librarians facing questions from patrons, parents, and school and library boards. The library literature noted that complaints about content are easier to deal with if the library has a written policy in place that clearly covers graphic novels. One school librarian noted that the "visual nature" of graphic novels meant that students weren't just reading about violence and sex, "they were actually seeing it," which led to complaints on the part of teachers and parents. She formed a student advisory board to help select books, and decided that graphic novels written for adults would generally be excluded from her high school's collection (Young, 2007). Two New York librarians put the following at the top of a list of tips, "Include graphic novels in your library's collection development policy or statement" (Baird and Jackson, 2007: 6). Another librarian urged colleagues to apply criteria from the selection policy, but not to purchase graphic novels based solely on a review, stating, "Just one gory page could put a graphic novel over the line of what you are comfortable including in the school library." High school librarians who may be buying graphic novels with more mature themes are strongly urged to preview the material prior to circulation (Crawford, 2004).

Public libraries, in particular, began to add adult graphic novel titles, and librarians were strongly advised to make informed decisions about where in the library adult material should be placed. Steve Raiteri noted that graphic novels should be treated like any other material, taking into account content and intended audience. He cautions that "Different libraries make different decisions on what books go where, but those decisions need to be made" (2005, 52). Michelle Gorman warns that while most librarians oppose censorship, "certain genres of graphic novels will be the target of parental or community objections," and "several critically acclaimed graphic novels essential for building a core adult collection" will be inappropriate for children and young-adult readers (2002, 44).

Two cases illustrate the potential problems with adult graphic novels in libraries. In April 2004, the Stockton Public Library pulled *A Child's Life* by Phoebe Glockner after an 11-year-old boy checked out the book. Stockton Mayor Gary Podesto, was quoted as calling the graphic novel "a how-to book for pedophiles." In response, the National Coalition Against Censorship joined with the American Library Association and the Comic Book Legal Defense Fund to create guidelines for librarians on how to handle graphic novels aimed at an adult audience. Svetlana Mintcheva said the policy would protect libraries from attacks, noting, "There's confusion because this kind of genre used to be addressed at younger kids" (Kinsella, 2004: 12). Those guidelines are available at the NCAC Web site as "Graphic Novels: Guidelines for Librarians." In 2006, the Marshall, Missouri library board voted to remove Alison Bechdel's *Fun Home* and Craig Thompson's *Blankets* from the library. The board also agreed to develop a written selection policy. Library director Amy Crump stated, "As a librarian, I'm going to take a stand against censorship, but I do back the board's decision to take a step back and develop a policy" (Oder, 2006: 20). The board did vote in early 2007 to return those graphic novels to the shelf once the policy was in place.

Conclusion

Comics, once the bane of librarians, now populate the shelves of most school and public libraries, primarily in the form of graphic novels. Trade paperback compilations of popular monthly titles, standalone works, and Japanese manga, encompassing a variety of genres and subject matter, circulate among both children and adult readers. This acceptance of the place of comics in libraries is reflected in the discourse found in the professional library literature, which shifted from how to get rid of comics to how to purchase and shelve them.

Researchers have identified a number of factors that contributed to this change, including the restructuring of the comic book publishing industry, the rise of comics specialty stores and changes in distribution, the shifting readership demographics, the success of so-called "comic-book movies," and increasing awareness of the variety of material available in comics. However, my analysis of the library literature of the past two decades suggests that two factors stand out as primary influences in changing librarians' attitudes toward comics. First is the adoption of the book format and the accompanying terminology, "graphic novel." Despite the ongoing debate about definition, "graphic novel" suggested something new, something different — and something that could be considered a book. Once that was established, librarians seemed willing to grant graphic novels a legitimacy that comic books never achieved. Second is the emergence of professional avenues for selection and acquisition. Reviews in the professional library publications, the attention to graphic novels at professional conferences, and the proliferation of bibliographies and Web sites specifically directed to librarians all served to bring the graphic novel under the purview of librarians. The development of these resources is relatively recent, which explains why it has only been in the last ten or fifteen years that articles about graphic novels have proliferated in librarians' professional journals.

Graphic novels in libraries are no longer a novelty, and the professional literature reflects this acceptance. This is a far cry from the "war on comics" launched by librarians encountering Superman and Batman for the first time.

Endnotes

1. For this study, I conducted a textual analysis of nearly 100 articles about graphic novels in libraries drawn from two major databases that catalog journals in education and library science, as well as trade journals such as *Publishers Weekly*. In order to avoid simply duplicating Ellis and Highsmith's excellent analysis of articles indexed in *Library Literature,* I chose to examine articles indexed in the electronic database *Library, Information Science & Technology.* I conducted a search for articles in this database published between 1980 and 2009 using the term "graphic novel," which yielded more than 1,500 entries (the earliest article listed was published in 1990). I eliminated all of the articles that were simply reviews of individual graphic novels or lists without any additional commentary by the author. I also conducted a search of the *ERIC* database from 1980 to the present using the term "graphic novel," which yielded only a handful of publications. Expanding the search to combine the terms "comics" and "library" resulted in a list of thirty entries, although many of these were either book reviews or dealt strictly with monthly comics rather than graphic novels. There was some overlap between the databases, but this search did yield a small number of articles that were not included in the *Library, Information Science & Technology* database.

References

"Adding Comic Books Leads to Super School Library Circulation Gains." September 2004. *Curriculum Review*: 8.

Association for Library Service to Children. 2006. "Graphic Novels for Children: Should They Be Considered Literature?" *Children and Libraries* Winter: 49–51.

Baird, Zahra M., and Tracey Jackson. Spring 2007. "Got Graphic Novels? More Than Just Superheroes in Tights!" *Children and Libraries*: 4–8.

Barron, Daniel D. October 2002. "Sequential Art, the White House Conference, and Library Media Specialists." *School Library Media Activities Monthly*: 48–52. http://search.ebscohost.com/login.aspx?direct=true&db=lih&AN=8584710&site=ehost-live.

Branley, Franklyn M. 1942. "The Plague of the Comics." *Elementary English Review* 19: 181–82.

Bruggeman, Lora. 1997. "Zap! Whoosh! Kerplow! Build High-Quality Graphic Novels Collections with Impact." *School Library Journal* 43/1: 22–27.

Brumbaugh, Florence. 1939. "The Comics and Children's Vocabularies." *Elementary English Review* 16: 63–64.

Chelton, Mary K. Winter 2006. "Perspectives of Practice: Young Adult Collections Are More Than Just Young Adult Literature." *Young Adult Library Services*: 10–11.

"Comics Shops Sell Books, Too." December 22, 2003. *Publishers Weekly*: 22–23.

Cord, Scott. 2006. "The 'Good' Comics: Using Comic Books to Teach History." *International Journal of Comic Art* 8/1: 546–61.

Crawford, Philip. February 2004. "A Novel Approach: Using Graphic Novels to Attract Reluctant Readers." *Library Media Connection*: 26–28.

DeCandido, Keith R.A. March 15, 1990. "Picture This: Graphic Novels in Libraries." *Library Journal*: 50–55.

Dombeck, Peg, and Chris Gustafson. Spring 2005. "Graphic Novels—School Library, Public Library." *Medium*: 13.

Dorrell, Larry D. November 1987. "Why Comic Books?" *School Library Journal*: 30–31.

Eisner, Will. 1985. *Comics and Sequential Art.* Tamarac, FL: Poorhouse Press.

_____. 1995. *Graphic Storytelling.* Tamarac, FL: Poorhouse Press.

Ellis, Allen, and Doug Highsmith. 2000. "About Face: Comic Books in Library Literature." *Serials Review* 26/2: 21–43.

Gagnier, S. Richard. September 1997. "A Hunger for Heroes." *School Library Journal*: 143.

Galley, Michelle. February 18, 2004. "Going Graphic: Educators Tiptoe into the Realm of Comics." *Education Week*: 6.

Gluibizzi, Amanda. 2007. "The Aesthetics and Academics of Graphic Novels and Comics." *Art Documentation* 26/1: 28–30.

Gorman, Michelle. August 2002. "What Teens Want: Thirty Graphic Novels You Can't Live Without." *School Library Journal*: 42–47.

Griffin, Jane K. 1998. "A Brief Glossary of Comic Book Terminology." *Series Review* 24/1: 71–77.

Groensteen, Thierry. 2000. "Why Are Comics Still in Search of Cultural Legitimization?" In *Comics and Culture: Analytical and Theoretical Approaches to Comics*, Anne Magnussen and Hans-Christian Christiansen, eds. Copenhagen: Museum Tesculanumm Press, 29–41.

Hallenbeck, Phyllis N. 1983. "Remediating with Comic Strips." In *Cartoons and Comics in the Classroom: A Reference for Teachers and Librarians*, James L. Thomas, ed. Littleton, CO: Libraries Unlimited Inc., 136–41.

Hatfield, Charles. 2005. *Alternative Comics: An Emerging Literature.* Jackson: University of Mississippi Press.

Hoover, Robinette Curry. 1983. "Language for the Deaf According to *Henry.*" In *Cartoons and Comics in the Classroom: A Reference for Teachers and Librarians*, James L. Thomas, ed. Littleton, CO: Libraries Unlimited Inc., 142–46.

Hunt, Jonathan. Spring 2007. "Taking Comics from Junk Food to Gourmet Meals." *Children and Libraries*: 12–15.

Kan, Kat. April/May 2003. "Getting Graphic at the School Library." *Library Media Connection*: 14–19.

Kinsella, Bridget. November 22, 2004. "Libraries Developing Guidelines for Graphic Novels." *Publishers Weekly*: 12.

Krensky, Stephen. 2008. *Comic Book Century: The History of American Comic Books.* Minneapolis: Twenty-First Century Books.

Landsdowne, James D. 1944. "The Viciousness of the Comic Book." *Journal of Education* 127: 14–15.

Lavin, Michael R. 1998. "Comic Books and Graphic Novels for Libraries: What to Buy." *Serials Review.* 24/2: 31–46. http://search.ebscohost.com/login.aspx?direct=true&db=lih&AN=1876346&site=ehost-live.

_____. 1999. "A Librarian's Guide to Independent Comics: Part One, Publisher Profiles." *Serials Review* 25/1: 29–48. http://search.ebscohost.com/login.aspx?direct=true&db=lih&AN=2674915&site=ehost-live.

Lee, Harriet E. 1942. "Discrimination in Reading." *English Journal* 31: 677–79.

"Librarians out Front at Comic Con." April 1, 2007. *Library Journal*: 15.

"Libraries, to Arms!" *Wilson Library Bulletin* 8: 670.

Luga, Allyson A. W. March 2006. "Graphic Novels for (Really) Young Readers." *School Library Journal*: 56–61.

Markham, Gary W. 2009. "Cataloging the Publications of Dark Horse Comics: One Publisher in an Academic Catalog." *The Journal of Academic Librarianship* 35/2: 162–69.

McCloud, Scott. 1993. *Understanding Comics.* Northampton, MA: Tundra Publishing.

McDonald, Heidi. December 23, 2002. "The Year of the Graphic Novel." *Publishers Weekly*: 21–22, 31.

Mooney, Maureen. November/December 2000. "Graphic Novels: How They Can Work in Libraries." *The Book Report*: 18–19.

North, Sterling. 1940. "A National Disgrace." Reprinted in *Childhood Education* 17: 56.

Nyberg, Amy Kiste. 2002. "Poisoning Children's Culture: Comics and Their Critics." In *Scored Literature: Essays on the History and Criticism of Popular Mass-Produced Fiction in America*, Lydia Cushman Schurman and Deidre Johnson, eds. Westport: Greenwood Press.

_____. 1998. *Seal of Approval: The History of the Comics Code.* Jackson: University of Mississippi Press.

Oder, Norman. 2006. "Graphic Novels Called Porn." *Library Journal* November 15: 19–20.

O'English, Lorena, J. Gregory Matthews and Elizabeth Blakesley Lindsay, 2006. "Graphic Novels in Academic Libraries: From *Maus* to Manga and Beyond." *The Journal of Academic Librarianship*: 32/2: 173–82.

Raiteri, Steve. 2003. "Book Reviews: Graphic Novels." *Library Journal* May 1: 94.

_____. 2005. "Graphic Novels." *Library Journal* September 15: 52.

Reynolds, George R. 1942. "The Child's Slant on the Comics." *School Executive* 62: 17.

Ronson, Roderick. June 1950. "The Comic Corruption." *National Parent-Teacher*: 24.

Rothschild, D. Aviva. 1995. *Graphic Novels: A Bibliographic Guide to Book-Length Comics.* Englewood, CO: Libraries Unlimited.

Rudiger, Hollis Margaret, and Megan Schliesman. November/December 2007. "Graphic Novels and School Libraries." *Knowledge Quest*: 57–58.

Sabin, Roger. 1993. *Adult Comics — An Introduction.* London: Routledge.

St. Lifer, Evan. August 2002. "Graphic Novels, Seriously." *School Library Journal*: 9.

Schoof, Robert N., Jr. 1983. "Four-Color Words: Comic Books in the Classroom." In *Cartoons and Comics in the Classroom: A Reference for Teachers and Librarians*, James L. Thomas, ed. Littleton, CO: Libraries Unlimited Inc., 80–86.

Snowball, Clare. Summer 2005. "Teenage Reluctant Readers and Graphic Novels." *YALS*: 43–45.

Swain, Emma Halstead. 1983. "Using Comic Books to Teach Reading and Language Arts." In *Cartoons and Comics in the Classroom: A Reference for Teachers and Librarians*, James L. Thomas, ed. Littleton, CO: Libraries Unlimited Inc., 72–78.

Thomas, James L., ed., 1983. *Cartoons and Comics in the Classroom: A Reference for Teachers and Librarians.* Littleton, CO: Libraries Unlimited Inc.

Tilley, Carol L. May 2008. "Reading Comics." *School Library Media Activities Monthly*: 23–26.

"U.S. Graphic Novel Markets Hits $200M." March 18, 2005. *Publishers Weekly*: 15.

Weiner, Steve. 2002. "Beyond Superheroes: Comics Get Serious." *Library Journal* February 1: 55–58.

_____. 1996. *100 Graphic Novels for Public Libraries.* Northampton, MA: Kitchen Sink Press.

Williams, Gweneira, and Jane Wilson. 1942. "They Like to Rough: In Defense of Comics." *Library Journal* 67: 204–06.

Witek, Joseph. 1989. *Comic Books as History: The Narrative Art of Jack Jackson, Art Spiegelman and Harvey Pekar.* Jackson, MS: University Press of Mississippi.

Young, Robyn. January 2007. "Graphically Speaking: The Importance of Graphic Books in a School Library Collection." *Library Media Connection*: 26–28.

Zamchick, David. 1952. "Comic Books?" *English Journal* 41: 95–96.

4

The Development of
a School Library
Graphic Novel Collection

HEIDI K. HAMMOND

Pop culture would not be a category in which I would score points in a game of Jeopardy! or Trivial Pursuit. So, it was not surprising that in 2003, the year I accepted a position as a high school media specialist, graphic novels hadn't created a blip on my radar screen. It was at this time, though, that I noticed articles about graphic novels published in the professional literature, and the articles were declaring graphic novels immensely popular. I'd never read a graphic novel, and I wasn't sure I wanted to. With a bit of reluctance, I decided I'd best investigate the "new," or at least new to me, format. Working with teens, I realized I needed to update my pop culture quotient. In the process, I wrote a Ph.D. thesis about graphic novels and developed a respectable graphic novel collection of over 350 volumes in the high school library.

Though graphic novels are presently on a meteoric rise, they've had an erratic history. Evolving from the humble comic book, graphic novels didn't really start gaining public attention until the mid–1980s with the publications of Alan Moore's *Watchmen* (Moore, 1986) and Frank Miller's *The Dark Knight Returns* (Miller, 1986), both of which formed the basis of recent blockbuster movies. Art Spiegelman's *Maus: A Survivor's Tale: My Father Bleeds History* (Spiegelman, 1986), a complicated Holocaust narrative about his parents, was also published with much acclaim in 1986. It was followed by *Maus II: A Survivor's Tale: and Here My Troubles Began* (Spiegelman, 1991), and Spiegelman won the Pulitzer Prize for *Maus* in 1992. While these books elevated comics to a literary form, even the Pulitzer Prize did not help other graphic novels achieve similar literary and commercial success.

Colleges and universities began offering courses on comics as art and literature during the 1990s. However, based on the fact that comics were hybrids mixing images and text, academic prejudice against comics lingered (Christiansen & Magnussen, 2000). In the United States and the United Kingdom, comics had a history of being a despised art form. There was little serious critical study of comics because they were stereotyped as juvenile trash and "viewed with contempt, especially when read by adults" (Versaci, 2007: 2). When measured against traditional novels using criteria derived from evaluating literature, comics were almost always found wanting (Bongco, 2000).

Gradually, comics and graphic novels started shedding the stigma of triviality and began to establish themselves as literature capable of rivaling other narratives (Bongco, 2000). Graphic novelists wrote about serious issues such as incest, homosexuality, cancer, and war. They also won awards competing against traditional books. As mentioned earlier, Spiegelman won the Pulitzer Prize for *Maus*; *Pedro and Me: Friendship, Loss, and What I Learned* (Winick, 2000) which was about the author's relationship with Pedro Zamora, who died of AIDS, won the ALA's Sibert Award for the most distinguished informational books for children; and *American Born Chinese* (Yang, 2006) won the Printz Award. *American Born Chinese*, three interrelated stories based around a theme of self-acceptance, was also nominated for a National Book Award in the Young People's Literature category in 2006.

Approximately fifteen years after the publication of *Maus*, the graphic novel boom took place. The responsibility for its comeback rests largely with the influence of manga, the Internet, and the film industry, followed by the attention given to it by the popular press, librarians, and teachers (Versaci, 2007). In the 2000s, more and more graphic novels are being published, even by non-comics publishers, and many publishers are commissioning their own graphic novels (Serchay, 2008).

Shortly after this time, I began to investigate graphic novels in my role as a new high school librarian. I started with a collection analysis and discovered I had exactly three graphic novels in my collection. There was *Maus* (Spiegelman, 1986; 1991), *The Amazing "True" Story of a Teenage Single Mom* (Arnoldi, 1998), and *Pedro and Me* (Winick, 2000). Using lists in professional journals such as *School Library Journal*'s "Graphic Novel Roundup" section, *Voice of Youth Advocates*' graphic novel column, and *Booklist*'s annual issue devoted to graphic novels, I began to build my collection. I also used lists from books about graphic novels (Lyga & Lyga, 2004; Weiner, 2001). I found books such as *Understanding Comics: The Invisible Art* (McCloud, 1993), *Faster Than a Speeding Bullet: The Rise of the Graphic Novel* (Weiner, 2003), and *Graphic Novels: Everything You Need to Know* (Gravett, 2005) very helpful in my self-study of graphic novels.

Not only did I include graphic novels in my collection development, I also included them in the children's literature and young adult literature courses I taught at a local college. When I read an article in the newspaper about a graphic novelist who lived in our area, I realized he was the brother of a middle school principal in our school district. His name was Sam Hiti and I invited him to visit both the high school and one of my college classes. We read his book *Tiempos Finales* (Hiti, 2004) in preparation for his visit, and when he came, he provided insight about the work of a graphic novelist and shared with us his favorite graphic novels, one of which was *Bone* (Smith, 2004).

At this time, my library's graphic novel collection was heavy on superheroes. I purchased little, if any, manga because I didn't feel I knew enough about Japanese graphic novels. I had the start of a few series. Sam was not impressed with my collection and I renewed my efforts to buy more of the art graphic novels he recommended.

As my collection grew, so did circulation statistics. It was the most popular section of the library. However, I noticed that the most frequently circulated graphic novels were the superhero and manga varieties. The independent or art graphic novels of perhaps more literary quality, based on traditional criteria, were not being checked out by students. I wondered why.

This puzzlement formed the basis of my doctoral research. I knew the responses of the graduate students in my college courses to graphic novels. The younger students embraced the art graphic novels such as *Persepolis* (Satrapi, 2003) and *Blankets* (Thompson, 2003). However, the older students struggled a bit with the format. They tended to read the text quickly and skim over the artwork. They liked the graphic novels once they became accustomed to reading them, but they often had to go back to examine the pictures more carefully in order to understand and appreciate the story because they were not used to reading text and graphics concurrently. Graphic novels are multimodal texts that combine traditional text literacy with visual literacy and require multimodal literacy. "Graphic novels may require more complex cognitive skills than the reading of text alone" (Schwarz, 2002: 263).

I wondered how high school students would respond to an art graphic novel, how they would make meaning in a graphic novel. Did they know comics conventions used in graphic novels, and did this knowledge or lack thereof affect their responses? Would they recognize serious issues when presented in comic book format?

These questions formed the basis of my reader response research. I spent months reading graphic novels looking for one suitable for my study. Adolescent literature is realistic in language and themes, and I hesitated to select one that might be considered too edgy. When *American Born Chinese* (Yang, 2006) won the American Library Association's 2007 Michael L. Printz Award for excellence in young adult literature, I found what I considered a perfect graphic novel for my study (Hammond, 2009).

American Born Chinese has three plot lines that converge at the end of the book. The first story is the Chinese folk tale of the arrogant Monkey King who, unhappy as a monkey, longs to be a god. After a humbling experience, he becomes an emissary of the creator Tze-Yo-Tzuh. The second story is about Jin Wang, an Asian American middle school student trying to fit in with his classmates. He becomes best friends with Wei-Chen Sun, an immigrant from Tai-wan. The third story chronicles the trials of the all–American teenager Danny who is visited annually by his extremely stereotyped Chinese cousin Chin-Kee. Chin-Kee embarrasses Danny so much that he must switch schools every year. At the climax, when the three stories merge, the reader learns that Danny is actually Jin Wang, Wei-Chen is the son of the Monkey King, and Chin-Kee is the Monkey King. The novel includes issues of immigration, culture, racial identity, and stereotyping.

As these issues integrated well with the curriculum of the 12th grade political science class in our high school, that is where I conducted my study. Students read and made oral and written responses to a first reading of *American Born Chinese* (Yang, 2006). This was followed by a lesson I taught about the history of comics and about comics conventions. Then students completed a reading survey about graphic novels and about their reading of *American Born Chinese*. Students read the novel a second time and wrote responses again. Finally, a small group of students participated in a focus group interview, and a few students opted to create their own comics.

I found students responded to an art graphic novel in many of the traditional ways students respond to text novels assigned in the classroom. They responded to literary elements such as plot, theme, and characters, and noted foreshadowing and denouement. They asked questions and made both intertextual and personal connections. This was the way they'd been taught to respond to novels throughout their high school careers. The unique aspect about their responses to graphic novels was their responses to the images. Since images conveyed as much or more of the story than the text, this was a new experience for the students.

Based on what I'd read in the professional literature about the popularity of graphic novels, I was surprised to learn that these students had little experience with them. They were much like I had been a few years previously. Only thirty percent of the class had ever read a graphic novel. During the focus interview, when asked what they knew about graphic novels prior to participating in the study, one girl responded, "Absolutely nothing." Another student thought graphic novels were just about superheroes, while another thought it meant books with graphic violence, language, and sex. These students comprised a fairly representative segment of the average to above average students in a school of approximately 1500 students.

Though most of the students in the study were unfamiliar with graphic novels, they indicated that they enjoyed the book, and they were pleasantly surprised at how much they enjoyed it. Some had to overcome an initial rejection of a book written in comic format and its association with children's literature. They appreciated that serious issues could be presented in comic book form, a form often used for humorous purposes.

The results of this study confirmed that graphic novels were not popular with the general student population; they are popular with only a small percentage of students who check out the books on a regular basis. The students in the study believed they would gain in popularity as students had more exposure to them, and the majority of the study participants indicated they would be interested in reading more graphic novels. One student wrote, "The experience of reading an 'art' graphic novel made me want to read another, my interest is piqued. I don't know if I'll prefer them to traditional novels, but it will certainly be an interesting experience."

Another finding from the study indicated students did not appear to have any difficulty reading a graphic novel. They used a variety of ways of reading, but all their methods included reading both text and images. Most, but not all, students described their reading method as looking at the pictures first, then reading the text, and then looking at the pictures again. No one really knows for sure whether the words are read before or after viewing the pictures (Eisner, 1996). However, Gravett believes that because the words and pictures arrive together and work together, they should be read together. Though there is no one rule, words and pictures are read in tandem and in cross reference, informing each other (Gravett, 2005). While students initially read *American Born Chinese* in their own preferred ways, they noted that on their second reading they gave closer attention to the images and noted more details.

While it was not determined whether students knew comics conventions before they participated in the study, having knowledge of comics conventions or not appeared to have little effect on their comprehension. However, after the discussion and lesson about comics conventions, students acquired terminology and were more aware of comics conventions during the second reading of the novel. They felt they changed their reading method and paid closer attention to the images, noticing more details. For the students who opted to create comics of their own, knowledge of comics conventions appeared to have an effect on the number of conventions used.

From my study, I concluded I needed to expose more students to graphic novels. I moved the graphic novel section of the library close to the checkout desk. I also created graphic novel displays in the display case in the hallway next to the entrance to the library. I'm not certain a broader student population is checking out the graphic novels, but those that do frequently discuss the books with me, and some suggest titles for purchase.

I also found teachers needed exposure to graphic novels. One study found few teachers use them in the classroom (Annett, 2008). Lack of familiarity with the format and with multimodal literacies may prevent some teachers from incorporating them into their curriculums. They may also have a print bias that causes them to reject a book in which images carry much of the narrative.

However, research indicates the educational benefits of comics and graphic novels are many. Probably the most compelling and most frequently mentioned reason for using comics and graphic novels is their ability to motivate students to read. Not only do they motivate reluctant readers to read more, but comics and graphic novel readers do at least as much reading as non-comic book readers. Research shows that comics and graphic novel readers read more overall, read more books, and have more positive attitudes toward reading (Krashen, 2004). Comics and graphic novels challenge and motivate high-level readers as well as struggling readers (Serchay, 2008).

Other benefits of comics and graphic novels include their ability to serve as a conduit to traditional text reading and to bridging a gap that separates reading in school and out of school (Krashen, 2004). They also benefit English language learners as the visuals reduce the amount of written text and provide comprehension clues (Cary, 2004).

Graphic novels provide teachers the opportunity to help students develop multiple literacies. Kress stresses the importance of images and argues that the visual elements of text are becoming more complex (Kress, 2008). He also posits that the screen is replacing the book as the dominant medium of communication and that the dominance of writing has been replaced by the dominance of image. He believes this will eventually change the nature of writing on the page. Writing on the screen, its placement, shape, size, and color, as well as how it relates to the images, is multimodal. One can think of panels in a graphic novel as screens and thus see the value of using graphic novels as a vehicle for teaching visual literacy.

Because graphic novels cover a wide spectrum of topics, it is not difficult to integrate them into the curriculum. Film, drama, and the Internet are widely accepted texts in the classroom and library. Graphic novels, encompassing all types of genres, can be introduced as another form of text, an alternative to traditional textbooks, and can be used in similar ways. Some teachers have successfully integrated them into the classroom for a variety of purposes (Carter, 2007). With my assistance, a social studies teacher and an ELL teacher who team teach a class purchased *Maus II* (Spiegelman, 1991) to teach about the Holocaust. I also loaned my copies of *American Born Chinese* (Yang, 2006) to a special education teacher to use with her students. "The educational potential of comics has yet to be fully realized. While other media such as film, theater, and music have found their place within the American educational establishment, comics has not" (Yang, 2003: 1). Perhaps, if graphic novels are used in the classroom, it will nullify the stigma attached to comics.

I continued to read and learn more about graphic novels. I attended a graphic novel institute at the International Reading Association's Regional Meeting held in Minneapolis in April, 2009, and I enrolled in Robin Brenner's online graphic novel and manga courses through Simmons College. Manga is visually and culturally different from western graphic novels and her book *Understading Manga and Anime* (Brenner, 2007) is very helpful.

My appreciation for graphic novels grows with each one I read. While I tend to favor the art graphic novels over the superhero and manga varieties, I purchase titles to provide balance in my graphic novel collection. More and more books are being written about graphic novels, and the professional literature continues to provide information and reviews. Graphic novels are accepted as a legitimate literary form by scholars and librarians, even though they are firmly entrenched in pop culture and still relatively new to many.

Though librarians have been critical of comics in the past, they are presently champions of graphic novels. I intend to continue to build my collection and to introduce new titles regularly to my students and staff. Graphic novels are not only entertaining, but as multimodal texts they help students develop competencies in multiple literacies necessary to be successful in the workplace and social life. As a librarian and an educator, there is much joy in the task of helping others expand their concept of literacy beyond the printed word.

References

Annett, Douglas. 2008. "Implementing Graphic Texts into the Language Arts Classroom." *Minnesota English Journal* 44: 150–179.

Bongco, Mila. 2000. *Reading Comics: Language, Culture, and the Concept of the Superhero in Comic Books*. New York: Garland Publishing.

Brenner, Robin E. 2007. *Understanding Manga and Anime*. Westport, CT: Libraries Unlimited.

Carter, James Bucky. 2007. "Introduction—Carving a Niche: Graphic Novels in the English Language Arts Classroom." In *Building Literacy Connections with Graphic Novels: Page by Page, Panel by Panel*, J. B. Carter ed. Urbana, IL: NCTE.

Cary, Stephen. 2004. *Going Graphic: Comics at Work in the Multilingual Classroom*. Portsmouth, NH: Heinemann.

Christiansen, Hans-Christian, and Anne Magnussen. 2000. "Introduction." In *Comics and Culture: Analytical and Theoretical Approaches to Comics*, Anne Magnussen and Hans-Christian Christiansen eds. Copenhagen: Museum Tusculanum Press.

Eisner, Will. 1996. *Graphic Storytelling and Visual Narrative*. Tamarac, FL: Poorhouse Press.

Gravett, Paul. 2005. *Graphic Novels: Everything You Need to Know*. New York: HarperCollins.

Hammond, Heidi K. 2009. *Graphic Novels and Multimodal Literacy: A Reader Response Study*. Ph.D. dissertation, University of Minnesota, United States—Minnesota. from Dissertations & Theses @ CIC Institutions database (Publication No. AAT 3344687).

Hiti, Samuel. 2004. *Tiempos Finales*. Minnesota: La Luz Comics.

Krashen, Stephen D. 2004. *The Power of Reading: Insights from the Research*. Portsmouth, NH: Heinemann.

Kress, Gunther. 2008. "'Literacy' in a Multimodal Environment of Communication." In *Handbook on Teaching Literacy Through the Communicative and Visual Arts*, Vol. II, J. Flood, S. B. Heath and D. Lapp, eds. New York: Lawrence Erlbaum Associates.

Lyga, Allyson A. W. and Barry Lyga. 2004. *Graphic Novels in Your Media Center: A Definitive Guide*. Westport, CT: Libraries Unlimited.

Miller, Frank. 1986. *Batman: The Dark Knight Returns*. New York: DC Comics.

Moore, Alan. 1986. *Watchmen*. New York: DC Comics.

Satrapi, Marjane. 2003. *Persepolis: The Story of a Childhood*. New York: Pantheon Books.

Schwarz, Gretchen E. 2002. "Graphic Novels for Multiple Literacies." *Journal of Adolescent & Adult Literacy* 46: 262–265.

Serchay, David S. 2008. *The Librarian's Guide to Graphic Novels for Children and Tweens*. New York: Neal-Schuman.

Smith, Jeff. 2004. *Bone*. Columbus, OH: Cartoon Books.

Spiegelman, Art. 1986. *Maus I: A Survivor's Tale: My Father Bleeds History*. New York: Pantheon.

_____. 1991. *Maus II: A Survivor's Tale: and Here My Troubles Began*. New York: Pantheon.

Thompson, Craig. 2003. *Blankets*. Marietta, GA: Top Shelf Productions.

Versaci, Rocco. 2007. *This Book Contains Graphic Language: Comics as Literature*. New York: Continuum.

Weiner, Stephen. 2003. *Faster than a Speeding Bullet: The Rise of the Graphic Novel*. New York: Nantier, Beal, Minoustchine.

_____. 2001. *The 101 Best Graphic Novels*. New York: Nantier, Beal, Minoustchine.

Winick, Judd. 2000. *Pedro and Me: Friendship, Loss, and What I Learned*. New York: Henry Holt.

Yang, Gene. 2003. "Comics in Education." http://www.humblecomics.com/comicsedu/.

Yang, Gene L. 2006. *American Born Chinese*. New York: First Second.

5

Balancing Popular
High-Circulation Works
with Works of Merit
in Elementary School
Library Collections

DIANA P. MALISZEWSKI

Graphic novels have been an acceptable part of elementary school library collections for some time now. Philip Charles Crawford has noted in his book, *Graphic Novels 101 Selecting and Using Graphic Novels to Promote Literacy for Children and Young Adults*, that graphic novels foster student enthusiasm for reading, and his findings are echoed in other studies (Crawford, 2003). Patrons enjoy graphic novels and have favorite series that they read with gusto. In a past survey conducted at Agnes Macphail Public School in Toronto, the top five titles read by intermediate students were *Beet*, *One Piece*, *Prince of Tennis*, *Ultra Maniac*, and *Naruto* (Maliszewski, 2007). However, school library personnel cannot augment their collections with only the most popular titles available. There are many exceptional, critically acclaimed graphic novels crucial to have in a balanced collection. Award-winning graphic novels such as *Watchmen*, winner of a Hugo Award in 1988, and *American-Born Chinese*, winner of the Michael L. Printz Award in 2007, must have a place on the shelves next to popular titles. To compound this challenge, elementary school library collections must differ from their secondary counterparts. It is the role of the teacher-librarian or other qualified school library staff member to purchase and promote both types of graphic novels, albeit in different ways.

Determining Classic Graphic Novels

Identifying the paragons of the medium is a complex endeavor. In fact, Steve Miller states in his 2005 book *Developing and Promoting Graphic Novel Collections* that the task is "nearly impossible in a field that is still evolving" (Miller, 2005: 3). Michele Gorman supports that opinion in stating "Graphic novels for children, as a category of books, is too new to have any type of canon" (Gorman, 2009). One can consult books, websites, vendors, library associations, professional journals, comic blogs, listservs, and school library staff for assistance in choosing quality material, but some experts are reluctant to compile a permanent "best of" list (Pawuk, 2007). With few exceptions, such as Jeff Smith's *Bone* series, there are not that many common texts on the lists that do exist. Part of the lack of a canon may be due to the sheer number of graphic novels and comics available and the newness of the category. Some may be due to the obscurity in which some comic artists still toil, for many comic luminaries are "well known to fans of the medium but may not be to the average reader" (Pawuk, 2007: xxxi). The lack of consensus may also have contributed to the diverse opinion on what constitutes a children's graphic novel or a great graphic novel. There are several awards distributed to acknowledge what different groups consider the best, such as the Will Eisner Comic Industry Award, the Harvey Kurtzman Award, Ignatz Award, and the Young Adult Library Services Association (YALSA) notable book selection. There are also the Lulu Awards, Reuben Awards, and the Xeric Foundation Comic Book Self-Publishing Grants (Goldsmith 2005). The awards honoring comics specific to elementary aged readers are few and in their infancy. The Joe Shuster Comic for Kids Award was just created in 2004. With this award, the criteria specifically reference the audience. As Chad Solomon explains, "*Adventures of Rabbit and Bear Paws* was chosen based on writing; art; quality as a kids book, including appropriateness, entertainment value, and positive messages; [and] overall impression. Publishers submit their titles to the appropriate award category in the Joe Shuster Awards that were published in the previous year, and a review committee selects what titles reflect the best of all the submitted titles. As a young graphic novel series, only having been in print for the last three years, being nominated for the Joe Shuster will help increase the awareness of the series to the comic book industry and general public" (Solomon, 2009). Other awards do not always take the audience into consideration. As Francisca Goldsmith says, "Developers need to be clear about how relevant particular awarding bodies are to their collection's target audience. ... If the graphic novel collection is intended for a juvenile audience, then awards that do not consider juvenile readership may not be pertinent" (Goldsmith, 2005: 35).

The Elementary Library Conundrum

Although "graphic novels [can] tend to transcend age groupings" (Pawuk, 2007: xxx), not all graphic novels are suitable for all ages and readers. In searching the professional literature, the quantity of "must-have" graphic novels for the youngest reader is relatively few. In Stephen Weiner's book of *101 Best Graphic Novels*, 22 are suitable for under 12 year olds, and 11 of those 22 are of the superhero genre. Miller's list of a beginning core collection has 7 titles for "all ages" out of 17 series titles (Miller, 2005: 104–106). Allyson and Barry Lyga's book suggests 10 all-ages titles, and the appendix lists 16 titles (Lyga, 2004). Philip Crawford describes three types of graphic novels (all ages, mainstream and mature) and points out that mainstream titles "comprise the majority of titles you will find on the newsstands and comic shops ... these titles are suitable for older children and teenagers but may contain violence, strong language, and provocative images of women" (Crawford, 2003: 18). His list of all-ages titles is larger than most, with 36 entries, and his "opening day collection" recommendations for an elementary school library contains 23 titles (Crawford, 2003). Michele Gorman's recent book, *Comics for Kids*, provides a much larger list of possible comics; however, she acknowledges "my goal is to get books in the hands of kids, and not dwell on what's a 'classic' or not. So I believe 'must have' GNs for kids are ones they want to read, gravitate toward, and would hand off to their friends (overtly or covertly depending on how their parents and teachers feel about comics) with a 'you gotta read this' parting message" (Gorman, 2009). She elaborates saying, "the expertise and knowledge of the librarian comes in handy [when determining a classic that should be in an elementary school-age user collection, even if there isn't popular demand for the title]. You keep an eye out for new stuff, ask kids for their opinions, purchase titles and get feedback, keep track of what's being looked at in-house ... and run circulation reports to see what is circulating heavily and what has been 'checked out permanently,' a.k.a. stolen. A decade from now there will be a canon of must have children's GNs, but until then librarians just have to be knowledgeable and open to feedback and suggestions from their young patrons" (Gorman, 2009).

Purchasing and Promoting a Balanced Collection

Once a school library staff member has identified both popular and worthy titles, the next step after purchasing is to encourage both types of materials to circulate. The popular series titles practically market themselves, and word of mouth will soon result in many empty shelves. Others will need a gentle push, a curricular tie-in, or an exciting book talk to find readers. As Miller states, "you may find that manga and superheroes are incredibly popular at your facility. Be sure to acquire more titles in these areas, but do not neglect the other topics necessary to round out a graphic novel collection" (Miller, 2005: 3). Lyga echoes that assertion, saying, "One of the most compelling reasons to include graphic novels in a library collection is that they have so many curricular applications ... students will love to read them (so they will never sit on your shelves), and with the right promotion (from you, the media specialist or librarian) these books can be utilized in the classroom for curricular connections" (Lyga, 2004: 11). Here are four titles that have had critical acclaim but are not immediately sought after by students, and ways librarians can promote them.

Louis Riel by Chester Brown is a powerful comic biography of the famous Metis leader of the Red River Rebellion. The sheer size of the book and the somber, simplified black and white illustrations with the grid-like panel configuration do not attract the same readers who thrill to the energetic lines and irregular panels of their favorite manga. Appreciated by adults but also approachable for middle-school students, the introduction of this title worked best when given to the history teacher. When given the choice of reading a passage from the comic or from their textbook, many students preferred the graphic option.

Alia's Misson by Mark Stamaty is a moving portrayal of the courageous and true story of the chief librarian of the Basra Central Library in Iraq. Alia is a hijab-wearing middle-aged woman, caught in the political upheaval of the time. The content may not necessarily appeal to students at first glance, but with the recent focus on character education and on media studies, this book works perfectly in a language arts classroom. Paired with a picture book account of the same story, *The Librarian of Basra* by Jeanette Winter, it is fascinating to compare and contrast how the same series of events are retold. The story is also a wonderful example of courage. As the anthropomorphized book in the introduction to the graphic novel states, "The story you are about to read tells of a different kind of superhero. It is based on true events in the life of a real person who shows us it's not necessary to see through walls or fly or have any superpowers at all to be a real-life superhero" (Stamaty, 2004).

Imagination Rocket is a compilation of short comics. The science and social studies volume, published in 2002, consists of topics such as adaptation, extinction theories, biotic factors, supply and demand, barter economies, and cultural contrasts. The "mission" of the series is to "provide entertaining and compelling stories featuring comic storytelling with educational relevance" (Clopper, 2002) and with comprehension questions and extension activities following each entry, it is obvious that this is meant for teacher use. "A Mother's Prayer" by Rich Watson is ideal for use during Black History Month, as well as reading lessons on inference, perspective, and mood.

Clan Apis is the story of a bee, told by a neurobiologist who also happens to be a cartoonist. The book works on so many levels, and can make the reader laugh and cry, often within panels of each other. The length and topic may not encourage students to pick it up for recreational reading, but using a passage in a 6th grade science unit on the diversity of living things piqued their interest and led several to request the library copy to "see what happened."

These are just a few of the comics that deserve to be on the shelves but do not necessarily circulate as frequently. This is not meant to be a comprehensive list. Other titles that children may not gravitate to at first glance but are worth promoting include *Korgi*, *Satchel Paige: Striking Out Jim Crow*, *Mouse Guard: Fall 1152*, and *Amelia Rules!* (Gorman, 2009). Allyson Lyga mentions *The Fairy Tales of Oscar Wilde* as another title worthy of recommending to teachers and students (Lyga, 2004: 12). Other strategies for promoting your lesser-used titles include contacting your local press, featuring creator or character displays, providing posters and bookmarks, creating booklists of recommended titles, offering talks on graphic novels to different class audiences, linking to the annual Free Comic Book Day give-away, and starting a comic club or inviting comic book creators to speak (Pawuk, 2007). Either way, the school library is in a unique position when it comes to graphic novels: "unlike comic shops, the library works to balance collections in a variety of formats. Unlike bookstores, we attend both to replacing older works (where interest warrants) and to selecting new materials. Unlike archivists, we work to connect books with readers rather than strive to amass comprehensive collections that include all published examples of a format, regardless of whether the examples speak to our users and would be users" (Goldsmith, 2005: 27).

No Merit-less Graphic Novel?

In investigating how to balance popular, high circulation works with works of merit, an interesting alternative emerged, almost contrary to the idea that comic awards espouse — that there may not be such a thing as a merit-less graphic novel or (conversely) that there may not be such a thing as a graphic novel without a fan base. "Graphic novels, by their very nature, tend to cling to the cutting edge of popular culture" (Lyga 2004: 13). Scott Robins, a blogger for *School Library Journal* on comics for kids, states, "Even the pop graphic novels, you can always find some application, whether it's character education or understanding the graphic novel form" (Robins, 2009). Kent Allin, a secondary school teacher with experience teaching graphic novels, and a fellow panelist with Robins at the Toronto Comic Arts Festival, spun the concept in a different direction. He advised his students to read comics that in their estimation were "poor" (such as mass-market creations from the 1970s), and challenged them to explain exactly why they thought these comics were inferior. He then asked his students to compare them to the comics which they considered exceptional (Allin, 2009). Elitism and post-modern angst over identifying "the best" aside, even if the lines between popular and quality are blurred, there still needs to be a balance in the types of graphic novels in a collection. The Lygas interviewed many school library personnel in their book, and one clarified, "I have four factors: story, art (both good), age appropriateness ... and appeal. Although that doesn't stop me from adding things (like *Barefoot Gen*) which are not going to be wildly popular, but are nevertheless very good" (Lyga, 2004: 85).

Conclusion

Discovering what comics are popular with the clientele of an elementary school library is simple, but determining what titles are indeed works of merit is difficult. The canon has not yet been established, and each school library professional must decide for himself or herself what constitutes a classic graphic novel. The objective criteria for creating a canon specific to a young audience can be similar to those used by award-granting bodies, but it still needs to take into consideration that "every community and every school has individual standards" (Lyga, 2004: 31), and "no two school library collections are alike.... One of the beauties of graphic novels is that the selection is so vast that you have the luxury (and the task) of customizing your collection to fit your tastes, and the tastes of your students, colleagues, and community" (Lyga, 2004: 83). Despite the reassurances of autonomy, what needs to occur in the near future is a concentrated effort by the "experts" in school-age comics, with assistance from others, such as researchers, to put their professional reputations on the line and help establish the canon of all-ages graphic novels.

References

Allin, Kent. 2009. "Will Libraries Save Comics" panel at the Toronto Comic Arts Festival on May 10. http://www.thecomicbooks.com/audio.html.

Brown, Chester. 2003. *Louis Riel*. Toronto: Drawn and Quarterly.

Crawford, Philip Charles. 2003. *Graphic Novels 101: Selecting and Using Graphic Novels to Promote Literacy for Children and Young Adults*. Salt Lake City: Hi Willow Research and Publishing.

Goldsmith, Francisca. 2005. *Graphic Novels Now: Building, Managing and Marketing a Dynamic Collection*. Chicago: American Library Association.

Gorman, Michele. 2008. "Graphic Novels Rule! The Latest and Greatest for Young Kids." *School Library Journal Online*. http://www.schoollibraryjournal.com/article/CA6536654.html.

_____. 2009. Personal interview conducted on July 6.

Hosler, Jay. 2000. *Clan Apis*. Columbus: Active Synapse.

Lyga, Allyson A. W. 2004. *Graphic Novels in Your Media Center: A Definitive Guide*. Westport: Libraries Unlimited.

Miller, Steve. 2005. *Developing and Promoting Graphic Novel Collections*. New York: Neal-Schuman Publishers.

Pawuk, Michael. 2007. *Graphic Novels: A Genre Guide to Comic Books, Manga, and More*. Westport: Libraries Unlimited.

Robins, Scott. 2009. "Will Libraries Save Comics" panel at the Toronto Comic Arts Festival on May 10. http://www.thecomicbooks.com/audio.html.

Solomon, Chad. 2009. Personal interview conducted on July 6.

Stamaty, Mark Alan. 2004. *Alia's Mission: Saving the Books of Iraq*. New York: Random House Inc.

Watson, Rich. 2002. "A Mother's Prayer." In *Imagination Rocket Science and Social Studies Volume*, Brian Clopper ed. Damascus: Behemoth Books.

Weiner, Stephen. 2005. *The 101 Best Graphic Novels*. New York: NBM.

6

Creative Shelving
Placement in Library Collections

AMY HARTMAN

With the advent of graphic novel and comics collections in libraries, librarians have been presented with a Very Special Challenge: where do we put these materials to make best use of traffic flow and space, limited resources and burgeoning demand, and perhaps most importantly of all, to avoid the dreaded Ticked-Off Patron (TOP) encounter? We are a visual culture, and graphically seeing sexuality and/or violence in action tends to far outweigh the outrage in just reading descriptions of it for those in the "I don't like this (and I pay taxes)" category. Even with "clean" content, many people still struggle with seeing graphic novels and comics as legitimately literary enough for a library to purchase (Welch, 2005).

Balancing the demand for these materials with the sensitivity of the public mind continues to challenge us and contort our collections. Regardless of collection size and the relative people-friendliness of the building, library patrons are always struggling to find whatever it is they are looking for, their proverbial needle in a stack of needles. So where do we park graphic novels? In the teen collection? Children's Library? Adult non-fiction graphic arts? Adult fiction?

As with so many policies and procedures, what works well for one library system might not work at all for another, but even when that is the case, sharing ideas and inspiration can contribute to a solution. What follows is the scheme that Ohio's Toledo–Lucas County Public Library (TLCPL) staff have devised to handle this growing piece of their collections, as well as some thoughts on incorporating graphic novels into libraries in general.

Definition(s)

When the term first became popular several years ago, there was a great deal of scuffling over the definition of exactly what constituted a "graphic novel." A lot of readers adamantly insisted that there were tremendous differences between graphic novels and comics, hoping to avoid the stigma of reading something long considered childish and silly. Many non-readers of graphic novels seemed under the impression that calling something a graphic novel was a new term for a *porno*graphic novel, especially when we added the word "adult" to the mix to differentiate between teen and adult materials. That was a major primer for a TOP explosion just waiting to happen, and librarians had to scramble to reassure concerned citizens that their library had not sunk into depravity, not just yet.

Thankfully, the furor didn't last terribly long, the etymological chaos calmed, and we all seem to have survived with our sanity and collections relatively intact. The fierce scrap between the "It's a comic!" and "No, it's a novel!" crowds has given way to a grudging "it's two mints in one" agreement. Indeed, some authors and readers have *always* used the terms "graphic novel" and "comic book" interchangeably. Writer Neil Gaiman, author of the *Sandman* series, responded to someone insisting that the author writes graphic novels, *not* comic books, saying, "...all of a sudden I felt like someone who'd been informed that she wasn't actually a hooker; that in fact she was a lady of the evening" (Bender, 1999: 4).

For others, regardless of terminology, powerful nuances still separate graphic novels from comic books. This sentiment is very aptly described in the "everyone-in-the-pool" definition that has evolved in Wikipedia. The article on the graphic novel defines it as a book that,

> suggests a story that has a beginning, middle and end, as opposed to an ongoing series with continuing characters; one that is outside the genres [which are] commonly associated with comic books, and that deals with more mature themes ... the term is commonly used to disassociate works from the juvenile or humorous connotations of the terms comics and comic book, implying that the work is more serious, mature, or literary than traditional comics ["Graphic Novel," Wikipedia, July 15, 2009].

For the purposes of this chapter, a graphic novel, on the simplest level, is considered to be a bound book, fiction or non-fiction, created in the comic book format and issued an ISBN (Serchay, 2008: 11). Manga, one of the most popular iterations of the graphic novel, has slightly muddied the waters of the concept. It is an enormously popular sequential art style of graphic novel created. It is developed by the Japanese with an extremely distinct appearance and more romantic style of plot. Because manga is a very rapidly growing part of most graphic novel collections, it is mentioned specifically in the shelving plan below.

The TLCPL Graphic Novel Shelving Scheme

The Toledo–Lucas County Public Library is comprised of the Main Library (about 90,000 items circ monthly) and 19 branches (including our Outreach Services/Bookmobile) spread throughout Lucas County in Northwest Ohio. Of the 19 agencies, 6 are large suburban branches (about 50,000–60,000 items circ monthly), 4 are mid-size agencies (about 35,000–45,000 items circ monthly), and 9 are classified as regular sized (about 10,000–20,000 items circ monthly). Most of the large branches are suburban, the regulars are urban or rural, the mid-sized, as their name suggests, lie somewhere in between. The Main Library has a Teen Specialist librarian responsible for overseeing teen programs and collection development. Each branch has a librarian assigned to be a teen liaison, working with the Teen Specialist to make their agency as friendly as possible to patrons in that difficult age range.

Begin at the Beginning: Purchasing

Chicken vs. Egg: Is purchasing based on shelving or vice versa? Conceptually, in many ways, the shelving issue actually begins with the purchase of the item. The TLCPL materials budget has distinct funds for purchasing materials for the Children's Library, the Teen Library, and the Popular Library (among others), all three of which house graphic novels in our system. The Children's and Teen Libraries are fairly self-explanatory, carrying materials intended for their stated audiences. Our Popular Library purchases additional copies of the most in-demand items in our system, keeping titles for about a year and changing out the oldest titles for fresh ones each month. These are stickered "Main Special" and are available for pick-up only at our downtown Main Library as an incentive for our suburban folks to venture past their neighborhood branches. Main Special items do not fill reserves, so often if a hot title has a waiting list, a patron has a good chance of scoring a Popular Library copy.

Initially, the Teen Library purchased and housed all graphic novels. Once the selection of graphic novels expanded into items more appropriate for adults, these titles moved into the Popular Library into their own special collection, as they certainly fit the in-demand part of that department's criteria. However, unlike the rest of the Popular Library's materials, the department's graphic novels were treated like all other library circulating materials, so they could be renewed and could fill reserves. The Popular Library book buyers gradually took on primary responsibility for selecting graphic novels intended for more mature audiences, and the Teen Library selectors retained those more appropriate for their specific age levels. The Popular Library's physical proximity to the Teen Library (they are adjacent to each other) further made this the ideal place for adult graphic novels, as many older teens are interested in these items, and the two collections were within sight of each other.

Our Teen Specialist librarian and the manager of the Popular/Teen Library at Main Library currently order both adult and teen graphic novels, and the 18 branches in our system are tied into those orders according to the needs of each agency. Currently we estimate that about one quarter of the Teen and about 15 percent of the Popular Library book budgets are used to purchase graphic materials at Main Library. Beginning around 2006, graphic novels for children have been ordered through the Children's Library order teams at Main Library, and branches tie into those orders as well. Librarians estimate that about three percent of the Children's Library budget is spent on juvenile graphic materials, which are still a small, but growing part of their collection.

Any librarian (or patron) can suggest a title, but all requests go through either the Teen or Children's Library order teams. If the title is purchased, the team librarians decide were it is to be shelved:

- As "Juvenile Graphic" (intended for children), located in Main Library's second floor Children's Library, or in the children's book area at branches (some of which interfile juvenile graphic materials with the larger children's collection);
- As "Teen Graphic" (intended for teens), located in Main's Teen Library, or the branch teen area;
- Or as "Popular Graphic" (intended for adults), located in an alcove in Main Library's Popular Library area, adjacent to the Teen Library or shelved somewhere separately from the teen area at branches (though usually within sight of the Teen collection).

Every attempt is made at the time an item is ordered to accurately place the item and avoid duplication of effort once the title arrives.

Initially, the higher numbers of duplicate copies for popular titles went out to our biggest branches in the suburban neighborhoods, as we expected the demand would match the large number of people that use those libraries. But, branch staff soon discovered that the demand in the suburbs wasn't nearly as significant as the requirements of the smaller, urban branches, where they were constantly faced with empty shelves. The distribution was adjusted to favor the urban agencies, and now the copies are more accurately distributed to meet the demands of our community.

Judgment Day

As with so many aspects of librarianship, figuring out where it is best to place graphic novels along the child-teen-adult spectrum is far from an exact science, often relying on a "go with your gut" kind of instinct. Because of the separate budgets for the Popular, Teen, and Juvenile collections, shelving is basically determined at the ordering stage, as mentioned previously. Whichever department ordered the title will receive the item once it is processed, but until the materials arrive and we can actually see what they are, appropriate placement cannot be guaranteed. A few titles are moved around once they arrive if the content indicates that locating the item in another area would give us the most circulation bang for our purchasing buck, or the content would be more appropriate for a different age group.

Librarians sometimes have to guess at the intended audience for the title under consideration, unless they are already familiar with an author or series. Just as with children's picture books, there aren't always a lot of professional reviews available in the most common review sources, such as *Booklist*, *Library Journal*, *Voya*, and *School Library Journal*, though the numbers are growing. Many publisher catalogs, such as *Ingram Advance* and *Fantagraphics*, are helpful in introducing new titles, but they don't always indicate the appropriate audience for the material. Even when professional reviews do exist, not all of them are entirely effective in telling us what to expect. Further, some series start as appropriate for children or teens and become progressively more risqué as subsequent volumes are published, causing us to reconsider placement.

The content that requires the most evaluation for teen versus adult status is, of course, the explicitness of nudity and graphic violence or language, but there are more nebulous factors as well. Librarians also consider the thematic or intended audience of a work, i.e., does the work contain humor intended for adults, evoking nostalgia, etc., that teens wouldn't necessarily understand? We've found that the *Little Lulu* series, while content-wise fine for teens, actually gets better use in the adult Popular Graphic area. We suspect this may be due in part to adults who remember reading the series when they were children, or possibly because the style of the work appeals more to an older audience. Some of the newer titles on World War II, such as *Alan's War: The Memories of G.I. Alan Cope*, also fall into this spectrum. And because librarians love making exceptions to their own rules, the grandfather of all graphic novels in the Library, *Maus*, interestingly, lives permanently in with the adult non-fiction Holocaust collection. *Maus* has become an icon of the subject (which lends ammunition to the "format versus genre" brawl discussed later in this chapter). It's not really that these items wouldn't interest teens; it's that they have a clear appeal to adults, who are less likely to peruse the teen shelves than teens would be to look in the Popular Graphic area for items of interest.

Policy-wise, as always, vagueness in official guidelines is helpful. Because our societal norms can change so quickly (and because librarians enjoy having the freedom to control their particular universe wherever possible), TLCPL relies on the judgment of librarians rather than a formal "placement guidelines" statement. So far, this methodology has served us well. The manager of our Teen Library looks at every item that will be shelved "Teen Graphic" upon arrival, so he can defend its placement if necessary. Putting materials in the Teen areas constitutes a recommendation from us to them, and we have a responsibility to present young people with materials librarians can feel solid about. If librarians at a branch disagree with the placement, they have the right to change the shelving designation according to the needs of their agency and the guidelines provided by their managers.

The Teen Library Manager estimates that about ninety percent of the manga purchased by the library goes into Teen collection. The tremendous demand for these materials is such that certain series are almost literally never on the shelf, going from the return carts right back to the check-out desk, with many readers checking out an entire series at a time. The Teen Library shelves manga and graphic novels separately (though adjacent to each other), mainly due to size variances of the books (manga tend to be about mass market paperback height and graphic novels are more likely to be magazine sized), but also to help patrons easily locate manga, which are arranged alphabetically by series title, or by individual titles if they are stand-alone items.

The TLCPL Children's Library shelves all graphic materials together, separated alphabetically by series where applicable, or alphabetically by individual titles for stand-alone volumes; the non-fiction (*Graphic Dinosaurs*, graphic biographies, etc.) has its own shelf as well, organized by call number. Loose comics in magazine formats are shelved by series in pamphlet boxes. Teen and Popular (adult) Graphics are shelved the same way, except the non-fiction titles are shelved in with the stand alone fiction titles, alphabetically by title. With smaller collections, TLCPL branches tend to designate a shelf or shelves for these materials, separating them into juvenile, teen, and adult level collections (thought not every branch chooses to purchase adult graphics).

The teen librarians encourage and receive many suggestions for purchase, and they estimate a high number of readers are girls, especially for manga, which often tends to have more romantic plots. The collection has never really needed a great deal of active marketing. Indeed, many librarians suspect these readers would still be able to find the graphic novels even if we hid the collection under the foundation of the library.

Cataloging: The Great Debate

Once we've decided to purchase the item, the next step in the process of getting it out to the public falls within the ethically well-bloodied arena of the Technical Services department. The never ending showdown between public service staff and technical services staff falls along fairly firm lines from which we hear, "put it where we feel it is most accessible" (from the public service corner) and "put it where the Library of Congress tells us to put it (now go away and leave us alone)" (from the Technical Services corner)

Public service librarians want the flexibility to shape collections to meet the needs of their community, whether or not they align with formal cataloging schemes for certain materials. Technical Services personnel, generally even more understaffed and more overwhelmed by incoming work than public service staff (which in this financial climate is really saying something), tend to focus on reducing the number of changes to a catalog record or pre-processed item. While, each change usually takes only a minute or two, those extra minutes can add up to a great deal of reworking of already technically correct records and processes. Our Technical Services staff also stresses the fact that for every record they have to edit, it will take that much longer for them to catalog and process other new materials. Public Service librarians counter that by saying that by not taking steps to make an item more accessible, we are decimating the almighty circulation count and undermining patron satisfaction with the collection in general.

Cataloging: The Great Debate — By the Numbers

Catalogers have been all over the place in classifying graphic novels. Many focus on the presentation format and frequently give graphic novels a graphic arts call number of some sort, placing fiction in this format with the comics in the Dewey Decimal Classification (DDC) 741 range, though some choose to ignore the imagery and catalog the content, classifying these items as regular fiction. Some movie tie-ins have been assigned DDC entertainment call numbers in the 790s. Non-fiction graphic novels, which are less prevalent than fiction, tend to be more consistently cataloged by content within their subject area, such as a biography (*Persepolis*) or war memoir (*Maus*). As the graphic novel subject spectrum increases, the format seems to be less of an issue than the content, which leads to yet another battleground in the larger war on materials placement and collection development.

Graphic novels are technically a format, which refers to the *physical style* of the book and can cover many genres, or *types of content*. Some argue that these items should legitimately be found within their genres, along with the print materials, rather than in a separate "graphic novels" area (Serchay, 2008: 114). That way, people can see the full spectrum of titles available on any given subject, not just the traditional print materials or just the graphic materials, depending on where the patron happens to be standing at the moment. This shelving system would also introduce many new readers to the pleasures of graphic novels, which would be especially helpful for those who are unaware we own these items, or who have never seen them before. Those who hold these ideals suggest that by segregating materials (and hence, patrons) by format, we are prohibiting opportunities for serendipitous discovery and possible new readers for each format.

Opponents to this view point out that the possibility of crossover appeal might be outweighed by very clear current patron preferences to see all our graphic materials in one area. In our experience, readers would prefer to browse the shelves and see what is new in graphic novels, rather than spend time searching the catalog for items in a graphic format, and then spend additional time hunting and picking them out from the larger collection, which at Main Library numbers about 850,000 items. If these materials are cataloged by subject, rather than grouped by format, many readers would most likely not take the time to hunt down titles buried within the vast general range of books.

The manager of our Teen Library noted that there is tremendous demand for movie tie-in graphic novels, such as *Watchmen, Sin City, The Road to Perdition,* or *Wanted.* While teens almost expect a book to accompany every film, many adults are surprised to learn that a film was based on a graphic novel. Regular graphic novel readers flock in to check out the books after seeing the films. However, the Teen Library manager has not observed a great deal of crossover between graphic novel readers and those who read traditional print materials, with the notable exception of some science fiction/fantasy fans who seem to be able to straddle both worlds. Experiments in publishing graphic novels as prose (i.e. removing pictures) have not been well-received by our patrons (and presumably by most readers) as they were only published for a short time. So it is, in this case quite literally, all about the pictures.

Making people wander all over the library to find their much loved graphic novel format seems like a bad idea to us at this time, though this may change as the format becomes more ubiquitous. At TLCPL, we separate clip-art materials, international business materials, and college and job seeking materials, and some other materials, into smaller, special collections, because patrons here like finding these frequently asked for materials in one area. Graphic novels are just the latest special collection for our system, which at some point could be incorporated into the larger collection if it seems beneficial to do so.

Perhaps a way to validate those who would prefer to interfile graphic novels with the larger collection by subject would be to create "If you Like ..." bookmarks, or electronic lists, to help steer graphic novel readers to print materials and vice versa. This would be a very inexpensive and easy way to tie the collections together, while keeping them shelved in a manner most appealing to the primary readers of graphic materials. Another idea would be to purchase extra copies of the most popular graphic materials and place them in both areas to test the appeal of the inclusionary method. However, this would require an item to be assigned more than one call number/shelving designation, which might be confusing to some patrons and would definitely cause varying levels of despair among catalogers and public service librarians. But, it would certainly be the best way to accurately gauge the effect placement of materials has on circulation of those titles.

Shelving Solutions

At TLCPL, public service librarians tend to prefer the special collection status, as opposed to the integration into the larger collection solution, and each of our three departments (Children, Teen, Popular/Adult) have a separate "Graphic Novels" area in which to house them. Public service staff feel quite strongly that the graphic novel readers differ significantly from the *Peanuts* and *For Better or For Worse* crowd. While readers may certainly appreciate both these styles, many graphic novel readers prefer the longer, more narrative style, and highly stylized artistic layout in graphic novels and narrative comics, as opposed to the daily one-line, cube-style of more traditional comic strips. The differences between the more traditional comics and the newer graphic novels could be compared to the differences between short fiction and print novels. Some readers like the very detailed, fully-explored content of novels; others appreciate the succinct clarity of the short story. Further, the benefit of pulling items from what are increasingly diverse areas of the collection (such as graphic memoirs on people struggling with various diseases, or persons relating specific war stories) makes it easier for these graphic novel readers to appreciate the variety of titles we own.

Even when graphic novels are pulled out into their own collections, the growing numbers of these items can make it difficult to find a specific title within the special collection.

Organizing a graphic novel collection exclusively by author can prove confusing for some patrons. Many series have multiple and varying authors and sometimes even multiple publishers, who may drastically change the appearance of the series cover. Shelving exclusively by title can also be confusing as some books in a series might not display the series title clearly on the cover (like *Degrassi Extra Credit* series). When possible, most of our agencies shelve books alphabetically by series title and then by title for the individually published stand-alone items. Some library systems have developed their own unorthodox classification systems (Weiner, 2008) which seem to work well in combining materials by publisher (DC Comics, Marvel) or by character (*X-Men, Little Lulu*).

Ethics/Complaints

Thankfully, among most librarians in our system, the legitimacy question (i.e., should libraries purchase these materials at all?) is no longer really an issue. Most are willing to concede legitimacy not only due to skyrocketing circulation statistics on these materials, but also due to the rapidly maturing style and content of graphic novels. The rising number of feature films based on these items further instills them with relevance for the formerly skeptical.

Some of our library patrons, however, still take issue with libraries for offering these materials, albeit in an unexpected way. We have had only a few formal objections move up the administrative ladder through Main Library since we've been actively collecting graphic novels (since about 2001). Some of the TLCPL teen librarians have had informal complaints from adults *without* children in tow, who were concerned that children might stumble upon these troubling items and see the gore and/or sex/nudity/language they contain. The "just in case" worries seem to outnumber the occurrences of parents actually upset by something their child has checked out or seen.

So, in our experience, most people who object to a graphic novel's content tend to object to the *placement* of the item on a specific shelf or display, rather than its actual presence in the library. One particularly thoughtful librarian wondered whether adults are far more freaked out by graphic novels than the hypothetical tender teenagers ever will be. In a special situation, our Corrections/Outreach librarians were asked to remove the entire *InuYasha* series from the library at the Juvenile Justice Center, though other similar series continue to be kept there. Librarians were told that there were some behavioral problems among the detainees that occurred due to this series.

Another librarian noted that some of the more explicit Teen designated items can be difficult to hand out to the notoriously mobile tweens (aged 12/13) who eagerly use teen areas. Serious subjects that children sometimes unfortunately have to deal with, like child abuse, rape or drug use, are not sugar-coated just because the story is told in pictures, and librarians need to be prepared to deal with possible objections to these materials. The Popular/Teen Library Manager also noted that a change in the species depicted does not lessen the blow of seeing explicit content. For example, animal characters shown in sexual situations have brought concerns by patrons and librarians alike. "Upskirt" is an interesting new term, most often seen in Japanese manga, where panels can contain titillating peeks up female characters' skirts. How much is revealed (and/or the presence of undergarments, as one librarian reported with a beleaguered sigh) is often an indication of whether these items will be found on the Teen or Adult shelves.

As with most popular collections, theft is a concern, and sometimes effectively shelving these materials is actually less of a problem than keeping them in the system at all. Some libraries have reported an interesting and creative theft-deterrent policy, which involves "... placing a sign warning that not only wouldn't stolen titles be replaced, but future volumes would not be purchased" (Serchay, 2008: 129). While this seems a bit drastic, it has, no doubt, fueled many a librarian's pipe-dream. However, if we were to do that in any other book area, or with the ever-mobile DVD and CD collections, *The Godfather* on DVD, the GED study books, urban fiction, and books on sexuality or raising pit bulls would soon be entirely unrepresented.

Keeping the graphic novel collection in a highly visible area can help with theft prevention, but it is probably more productive to have librarians talk to these readers, finding a way to get them to feel like they already "own" the collection, even though it lives in the library. Encouraging suggestions for purchase, asking their opinions for "year's best" lists, keeping shelves for *their* "readers' advisory" suggestions (as opposed to librarians'), or asking their input in designing signage for the area can all be helpful in this endeavor. It is undoubtedly not the perfect solution to the issue, but it certainly cannot hurt to try this strategy.

Appeal

One final thought regarding graphic novels: The format itself isn't new, possibly dating back to the publication of "The Adventures of Mr. Obadiah Oldbuck," which appeared as a supplement in a New York newspaper *Brother Jonathan Extra* in 1842 (Serchay, 2008: 3). The first use of the term "comic book" was for *The Yellow Kid in McFadden's Flats*, published in 1897 (Serchay, 2008: 3). While the concept isn't particularly new, the presence of graphic novels and comics in most libraries is barely out of its infancy. TLCPL didn't start collecting graphic novels *per se* until about 2000, when we renovated our Main Library facility and created a Teen Library. Before that, we had the aforementioned *Maus* and *The Cartoon History of the Universe* by Larry Gonick but very little else that could seriously be considered a graphic novel.

Because it is a new format, the majority of graphic novel readers tend to be quite young as well. Apparently, graphic novels have yet to overcome the tricky "Newfangled" label most older readers instinctively place upon it. The Popular/Teen Library staff has observed a few people in their 30s and 40s browsing the graphic novel collection, but not anyone much older than that; they estimate the majority of graphic novel readers are under 21 years of age. In discussions with other staff members and a few older library users, they have said that they find it difficult to follow the story line from panel to panel, and they get frustrated with the flow (or perceived lack thereof). For many of us who did not grow up reading comic books, the eye literally needs to be trained to read and understand the format, and most give up in defeat. Perhaps generating programs to help "train" some of those who find it difficult to read graphic novels would be beneficial. It would be a great crossover program for teens and seniors, children and parents, older and younger siblings. We are thinking that as current graphic novel readers age, their preferences will continue with them, and it will be interesting to see how this collection develops as time passes. Someday, it may rival some of our print collections.

Conclusion

Whether it began for us as rapt children, carefully ziplocking doll accessories so as not to lose them, or as teenaged fans, obsessively organizing a comic collection, librarians have been practicing various inspired organizational methods for longer than there have been medications to assist with this obsession. We've weathered microfilm, CD-Rom, filmstrips, cassettes, CD, VHS, DVD, BluRay, and downloadable formats; many of us even have something in the dreaded "kit" format floating around somewhere in a corner (likely with many pieces gone AWOL). Graphic novels are just the latest challenge to test our organizational mettle. They might seem different than the above-mentioned formats, as graphic novels are a variant of our beloved book, but really, they are essentially just another format. Graphic novels have become and will continue to be important parts of our collections and deserve a great deal of thought and care regarding their placement within our hallowed, labyrinthine halls. Librarians have always, used gut feelings and common sense to come up with various effective solutions to the difficulty of figuring out where to place possibly controversial, in-demand items, proving yet again that it's amazing how many problems can be solved by creative shelving.

Many thanks to the TLCPL manager of the Popular/Teen Library, Tony Schafer, the library's Teen Specialist, Mary Plews, and the branch managers and teen librarians in the system who responded to multiple emails and phone calls for details and clarification on the care and feeding of the graphic novel collection, and a heartfelt shout out to our hardworking and infinitely admirable Technical Services staff, especially head cataloger Jeanne Poole.

References

Bender, Hy. 1999. *The Sandman Companion*. New York: Vertigo Books.
Collins, Max Allen. 2002. *The Road to Perdition*. New York: Pocket Books.
Creel, Stacy L. May/June 2007. "Graphic Novels and Manga and Manhwa ... Oh, My!" *Voice of Youth Advocates* 31, no. 3: 197
Dickinson, Gail. May/June 2007. "The Question: Where Should I Shelve Graphic Novels?" *Knowledge Quest* 35, no. 5.
Gonick, Larry, 1997. *The Cartoon History of the Universe*. New York: Doubleday.
Graphic Dinosaurs Series, 2007. New York: PowerKids Press.
"Graphic Novel." 2009. Wikipedia. http://en.wikipedia.org/wiki/Graphic_novels.
Gravett, Paul. 2005. *Graphic Novels: Everything You Need to Know*. New York: Harper Collins.
Guibert, Emmanuel. 2008. *Alan's War: The Memories of G.I. Alan Cope*. Kathryn Pulver, translator. New York: First Second.
Johnston, Lynn. *For Better or For Worse Series*. Kansas City, MO: Andrews McMeel Publishing.
Millar, Mark. 2007. *Wanted Series*. Los Angeles, CA: Top Cow Productions; Berkeley, CA: Image Comics.
Miller, Frank. 2005. *Frank Miller's Sin City*. Milwaukie, OR: Dark Horse Comics.
Moore, Alan. 1987. *Watchmen*. New York: DC Comics.
Ruddy, Albert S. (Producer), and Francis Ford Coppola (Director). 1972. *The Godfather* [Motion picture]. United States: Paramount Home Entertainment.
Satrapi, Marjane. 2003. *Persepolis*. New York: Pantheon Books.
Schulz, Charles. *Peanuts Series*. Various pubs.
Serchay, David. 2008. *The Librarian's Guide to Graphic Novels for Children and Tweens*. New York: Neal-Schuman Publishers.
Spiegelman, Art. 1986. *Maus: A Survivor's Tale*. New York: Pantheon Books.
Stanley, John. *Little Lulu series*. Milwaukie, OR: Dark Horse Books.
Takahashi, Rumiko. *Inu-Yasha Series*. San Francisco, CA: Viz Comics.
Topffer, Rodolphe. 1842. *The Adventures of Mr. Obadiah Oldbuck: Wherein Are Set Forth His Unconquerable Passion for his Lady-love, His Unutterable Despair on Losing Her, His Five Attempts at Suicide and His Surprising Exploits in Search of the Beloved Object. Also His Final Success*. Brother Jonathan — Extra.

Townsend, Edward W., and Richard Felton Outcault. 1897. *The Yellow Kid in McFadden's Flats*. New York: G.W. Dillingham.
Weiner, Robert G. Spring 2008. "Graphic Novels in Libraries: One Library's Solution to the Cataloging Problem." *Texas Library Journal*: 8–16.
Welch, Rollie, and Julianne Brown. 2005. "Y Archive? The Rapid Rise of Graphic Novels and Their Place in the Cleveland Public Library." *Young Adult Library Services* 3, 4 (Summer): 22–24.

7

Graphic Novels
at Los Angeles Public

RACHEL KITZMANN

Graphic novels, as a format, have only recently been introduced into library collections. Graphic novels have to fight for shelf space in institutions that house books, music, DVDs and other visceral materials, as well as staff, furniture and possibly a coffee shop or two. Libraries as institutions are already overcrowded, and adding **another** section, or **another** special collection seems almost irresponsible. The value of graphic novels as a literary format is still being debated, but the arguments in favor of them are gaining ground. Librarians are beginning to recognize the value of graphic literature and the positive impact it can have on patrons of all ages and genders. Studies show that graphic novels are an easy way for reading to become a true pleasure activity, which can lead to other pleasure reading. Graphic novels also increase vocabulary (words like "Nemesis" occur regularly) and stretch understanding of narrative structure (the breadth of the DC universe is astounding, and keeping everything straight is a daunting task even for adults). So, graphic novels seem to have earned a place in libraries. It is now the responsibility of the profession to make sure graphic novels, which librarians advocate for, are able to reach the full potential the medium can achieve.

In 2007, DC Comics announced that it was launching a new imprint (Bakkum, 2007: 12). This imprint was designed to be single issue or small run comics in the manga format (black and white, roughly 9" tall by 5" wide) but written as single-issue books by both established and new authors, and focusing on female identity and coming of age. DC was partnering with Alloy Marketing and Media, the same company that produces the *Gossip Girl* books and produced the *Sisterhood of the Traveling Pants 2* film (Alloy, 2009). The imprint, called *MINX*, was essentially writing YA novels with pictures. Focusing on real world, plausible situations, *MINX* books are an attempt to contract two different formats: the content of YA literature with various types of art. *Kimmie66*, by Aaron Alexovich, which is about a teenage girl in the 23rd Century, still deals with the suicide of a friend, which is not a common trope in traditional graphic literature. The content of *MINX* diverged from the traditional aim as American comic books don't typically put the focus on an internal emotional journey, and even manga aimed at girls (shojo) has an extraordinary element. *MINX* truly focused on the external and internal lives of teenage girls. This was an unprecedented show of interest in a population that traditionally has been alienated by comic books. Contributors to the endeavor include: Mariko Tamaki, the writer of

Emiko Superstar; a noted Toronto playwright and short story author, Cecil Castellucci, who is also an established and known young adult author, whose works include *Boy Proof*; and Brian Wood, an established comic book writer, whose work includes issues 63–75 of *Generation X* and *Counter X*, both spin offs of Marvel's X-Men universe (Wood, 2009). The general reception of the work from reviewers and industry ranged from mediocre to enthusiastic (Karp, 2007: 56; Moon 2008: 53). Yet despite the quality of the work, the partnership with Alloy, and the idea to appeal to a previously ignored population, the endeavor went belly up in little more than a year after it began (Gustines, 2008: E5). The audience was not lacking, as the popularity of shojo (Brenner, 2007: 304) can attest. What was not there was the browsability of the material, either in a bookstore setting or a library setting.

At my library, in my department, we separate our graphic literature into two primary areas: American comics, and manga. Those are the only divisions we have. That means that when works like Castellucci's *Plain Janes* have a specific call number (740.999 C348), they are shelved between multiple volumes of one title and multiple volumes of another title. *Plain Janes* has only a single volume. This type of shelving is not conducive for the *MINX* titles to find the appropriate audience. A graphic novel is not picked up because no one knows about it, and no one knows about it because it is difficult to find. Since it is difficult to find, people don't care to try, which leads to the format stagnating with only a few key publishers/characters that appeal to a devoted few. It is this cycle of exclusion that makes the ending of *MINX* a sad but almost inevitable lesson. Librarians, as a profession, have not realized a way to make sure that works like this can find the right person at the right time. There is a tendency to treat graphic literature as a genre; i.e., all graphic novels are treated as serialized fiction, instead of each title being investigated on a case by case basis, the way fiction is investigated on a case by case basis. If this continues, libraries will continue to fall behind emerging graphic novel publishing trends and good work will continue to go unnoticed, by us and by the public. If the profession persists in seeing graphic novels as a genre, rather than a format, a lot of potential will be lost. Librarians have been at the vanguard of getting graphic novels into libraries, and we have to be at the vanguard to push the format to its logical conclusion. For that to happen, patrons who do not normally read graphic novels have to be able to find them.

DC premiered *MINX* in 2007, and it shut down in 2008 (Gustines, 2008: E2). There have been assurances that the titles that had not yet been published will see the light of day, but to summarily close a line of publishing after only a little over a year was disappointing. Admittedly, the circulation stats for *Plain Janes* at my library is distressingly low (circulating only 11 times since it was bought), particularly for a book written by a popular YA author. Compare that to the second volume of the Japanese manga *Beauty Pop*, by Kiyoko Arai, which has circulated 22 times. *Plain Janes* seems like a natural selection not only for teenage girls that read Cecil Castellucci (given that the book was written by her and thus girls are more likely to seek out her work) but also for readers who are fans of popular authors Meg Cabot or Ally Carter. The problem is that *Plain Janes* is not shelved next to the other Cecil Castellucci books and will thus not be found by her readers, or others who browse the fiction section. These phenomena can be illustrated in another case study, this time focusing on a series of works by Meg Cabot. Meg Cabot wrote a popular book, *Avalon High*. The circulation statistics for *Avalon High*, which came out in 2006, are on a par with Cabot's other work—for the three copies owned by my library, the total circulation statistics come out at 120 times. The sequel to *Avalon High*, *Avon High: Coronation*, which was done in a manga format, has since gone out of print. The readers of *Avalon High* proved unwilling to look for the sequel amidst the already overcrowded shelf; books like *Coronation* and *Plain Janes* are small, in a single volume, and not shelved near their authors. This is not an issue for most manga and American graphic novels because the number of volumes makes them more visible, and thus it is easier to search for a specific author. Readers of Castellucci and Cabot don't typically know how to search a graphic novel shelf. Add to that the smaller size of the two volumes in question, and it becomes clear that the other graphic novels on the shelf will swallow them.

Librarians need to work out a way to get a reader of one to become a reader of another. This crossover promotes reluctant readers to read chapter books, and readers of chapter books to consider the literary value of graphic novels. In my own library (Los Angeles Public Library) it was decided that the best way to deal with graphic novels was to put a call number on them, and shelve them according to the main character or series of characters, using one Cutter number, and then another Cutter number for the primary authors' last name. Thus, *Superman Braniac* has a call number of 741.5 S959Joh-1. "S959" is the number that indicates to the patron that this is a Superman book, and the Joh-1 indicates that the last name of the author is Johns, Geoff. This system works fairly well. It allows for a perusal of graphic novels that are of a particular interest. If a patron wants Superman books, he or she can simply go to 741.5 S959, but a patron who wants to search for a particular author can find that as well. This is great for serialized graphic literature. That's what this system was designed for: serialized literature. American and Asian graphic literature (comic books, manga and manwha) tends to be on-going serialized dramas. The difference between these two is that American graphic literature tends to have many writers writing for a character, or a group of characters, while manga and manwha tend to have a single author for a single series. Hence the primary focus on title and character, rather than specific author.

The flaws in this system, or any system that is predicated on the scope of patrons' character knowledge, become increasingly evident. There is a new breed of graphic novel, both from the U.S. and abroad. With graphic literature gaining more ground in terms of respect and legitimacy, new authors are experimenting in the format, and foreign graphic literature is starting to be published in the U.S. One example is *Second Thoughts*, a graphic novel by the Swede, Niklas Asker, which was published by Top Shelf Production in 2009 (Hudson, 2009). That, however, does not change the fact that graphic novels that are whole and complete works on their own, either fiction or non-fiction, are getting lost on the shelf. The shelf is overwhelmed by an abundance of titles that all have to do with each other. A simple search in the LAPL OPAC yields 86 books related to Superman: 86 books, all on the same shelf or, more accurately, spread out on several shelves. Add other big name superheroes, multi-volume crossover events (*Infinite Crisis*, for example), and manga — which has titles such as *Naruto*, currently at 45 individual volumes with ongoing publication in the U.S. (Viz, 2009) — and that shelf or section is going to be overrun. Something like *The Manga Guide to Statistics*, a non-fiction manga by Shin Takahashi, is unlikely to find its intended audience (people who need help with statistics) on a shelf where people are looking for X-Men. Thus, a patron struggling with the subject, and who would likely benefit from the book, is not going to get it because it is not where he or she expects it to be. It is a grim prospect for graphic nonfiction. As libraries embrace 2.0 technologies, we are not advocating for alternative understanding and literacy. Defining a book by the fact that it has pictures, rather than what the pictures convey, and deciding that the pictures take precedent over the content of the book is not inclusive literacy, it is divisive literacy. A good portion of a librarians' job is anticipation — figuring out trends in writing and publishing, being a step ahead of technology 2.0, and having a working knowledge of our patrons so that we can anticipate their needs. In the case of graphic novels, we have fallen down on the job.

While most libraries don't use call numbers (LAPL created the call number as a means to more closely monitor collection guidelines and what was being collected), separating graphic novels from the rest of the collection is the most common method of shelving. The ease of browsing graphic novels as serials has, until now, outweighed the need to reconfigure a method that would be more successful for multiple types of graphic literature. After all, it is assumed that graphic novels are serials. Since all graphic novels are serials, the best way to organize them is to serialize them by character or team and then by author, creating an easily browsed collection for those with the interest and the understanding. The problem with this model is that graphic novels are not just serials, not anymore. The question of "what is a graphic novel?" has been asked, and the answer has been "anything." Cecil Castellucci has written single issue graphic novels; Harvey Pekar has drawn a graphic history of beat poetry edited by Paul Buhle (2009); and there are manga guides to statistics, electricity, and other science and math subjects. At LAPL, non titles are taken on a case by case basis, with some getting the 740 call number and some getting a call number that goes with the subject of the text. While this is a somewhat workable solution, it does not solve the problem of single issue graphic literature. *Avalon High: Coronation* did not circulate and was thus removed from the collection, despite the popularity of the original work. Traditional graphic novel readers did not want to jump into a world that had already been established, and traditional Cabot readers did not know that *Avalon High: Coronation* was a graphic novel. In this case, the shelving failed the author.

A suggested methodology is that graphic novels should be treated almost as a special library, much in the way a children's or teens' space is a separate library. By doing this, graphic literature can be treated as a subset of the broader literary spectrum, rather than a genre of that spectrum. A library can separate graphic series, graphic fiction and graphic non-fiction. Graphic non-fiction can be shelved in call number order, allowing for topic browsing. The key in this shelving methodology is the separating of series graphic novels and volume graphic novels. It retains the current browsing status, so patrons comfortable with the system don't have to re-learn, but by treating single volume graphic literature as a small fiction collection, patrons who are not familiar with the former status quo will have an easier time finding titles and authors. The reality of the current graphic literature market in the U.S., with its focus on serialized fiction, might make the extent of the divisions appear unwieldy. Devoting so much shelf space to a relatively small number of books would seem to be a poor allocation of valuable library real estate, but libraries need to think in terms of long term gain, and having new literary formats means attracting new populations. This gives a reason to expand service. Where one method is restrictive (the way graphic novels are shelved currently), shelving them as their own small library is expansive. If librarians are going to advocate for graphic literature, action and methodology must mimic argument. The next step is physically manipulating space to make it more accessible to a new audience.

Patrons who are not familiar with graphic literature are going to have a much harder time finding what they want, versus those who have an established knowledge of graphic literature and its standard organizational methodology. Librarians have to orient readers to this particular format, in much the same way we orient new users to the library at large. If we don't make the effort to make graphic novels accessible to all users, *Plain Janes, Avalon High: Coronation* and other books in this style get lost because they are not able to reach the intended audience, and the intended audience is not browsing graphic novels since they do not have the knowledge base to do so. Graphic novel collections in most libraries are not browsing collections for a general audience; they are browsing collections for the initiated few.

In the rush to own graphic novels, the care and promotion of the medium as a whole is lost, resulting in worthy titles not finding the correct hands, or well-researched non-fiction being ghettoized and thought of as "lesser" because it does not have the correct call number. This makes it a struggle to convince a patron, or a teacher, that just because a book has pictures does not mean it should be discounted from being used as a resource. It is a struggle because, while librarians understand and promote serialized and collected serialized graphic fiction, there is little promotion of graphic non-fiction or other graphic formats. If advocacy for literature in any form is to be one of the profession's primary concerns, and if the library profession is arguing that graphic novels are literature, then it is the library profession's duty to understand and promote new types of graphic novels. Library promotion of graphic literature is too new to stagnate. While we promote *Batman* and *Bleach* on lists and in book talks, there should be a conscious effort to make sure the medium is shown to its full advantage, and if that means altering a shelving plan, then that's what should be done.

References

Alloy Media & Marketing-Alloy Entertainment. 2009. http://www.alloymarketing.com/entertainment/index.html.

Bakkum, Beth. March 2007. "New Graphic-Novel Line for Girls Debuts." *The Writer*: 12.

Brenner, Robin E. 2007. *Understanding Manga and Anime.* Westport, CT : Libraries Unlimited.

Buhle, Paul, and Harvey Pekar. 2009. *Beats: A Graphic History.* New York: Hill and Wang.

Gustines, George Gene. October 2, 2008. "Comic Book Imprint for Girls to Fold." *New York Times*: E2.

Hudson, Laura. April 14, 2009. "Top Shelf Gets Sweded." *Publishers Weekly: PW Comics Weekly.* http://www.publishersweekly.com/article/CA6651355.html?nid=2789.

Karp, Jesse. March 15, 2007. "Castellucci, Cecil and Rugg, Jim. The Plain Janes." *Booklist*: 56.

Los Angeles Public Library CARL Solution. 2004. *Circulation Workstation, Version 5.3.0.0.* Institution: Los Angeles Public Library. Branch: Central Library-Teen'Scape.

Moon, Barbara M. November 1, 2008. "Tamaki, Mariko. Emiko Superstar." *School Library Journal*: 153.

Viz Media, 2009. *Shonen Jump, Naruto.* http://www.viz.com/products/products.php?series_id=119.

Wood, Brian. 2009. Books. http://www.brianwood.com/books.html.

8

Teen-Led Revamp

ERICA SEGRAVES

The Mamie Doud Eisenhower Public Library in Broomfield, Colorado, has a graphic novel collection of 1,737 volumes covering Japanese, Korean, and American manga series, American superheroes, single volume graphic novels, and non-fiction graphic novels. In 2008, our graphic novel collection had a total of 10,695 circulated books. The majority of the collection consists of manga series. It is housed in the Young Adult Department which serves grades 6–12 and currently has 5,978 card-holders ages 10–18. The graphic novel collection, however, draws in reading from a larger spectrum with the youngest being around six and the oldest being in their 30's.

The YA Department makes every effort to include its teen population's input in developing the library's Teen Zone and its collection. The Teen Advisory Board, comprised of 20 active members, provides a framework for us as teen librarians to receive and implement creative suggestions and ideas. However, during a redesign of our graphic novel collection in 2007, we decided to survey the readers and pin-point the hardcore fans. After all, the graphic novel collection is their private section of the library and we wished to develop it in a way most pleasing to these readers.

As packed shelves threatened to end further development of this section, we realized that we needed to weed, reorganize, and concentrate our efforts on future development in order to keep the collection updated, relevant, and exciting for the teen patrons. The shelves were loaded with American comics with villain-staunching superheroes, wide-eyed manga cuties, and non-fiction epic tales. The sizes and widths of the volumes were such different sizes that smaller volumes were becoming hidden, squished, or otherwise lost to the passing browser while larger volumes stuck out into the aisle.

Originally, the entire collection was shelved by author and had color-coded overlays on the call numbers to discern the age ranking of the graphic novel. Orange overlays signified the 10+ category, which meant that they were rated All Ages, Everyone, or Youth 10+. Yellow overlays signified the 14+ category and meant the books were rated Teen or 13+ by the publisher. Purple overlays signified the 16+ category and were rated Older Teen or 16+ by the publisher. If the publisher did not rate the graphic novels, we would use professional journals or our own opinion after reading the book. Some non-rated titles were shelved in the age category based on the interest level of the subject at hand. This integrated form of shelving all our graphic novels together by author caused problems not only for the shelvers who had trouble finding space on the packed shelves but it also led to patron problems, especially with the usability and browsability of the collection. What we needed more than anything was the collective teen voice to help us make this section usable and organized.

To achieve reaching this collective, we utilized an informal brief anonymous paper survey including the following questions:

1. Which is more important:
   * Fewer series and more volumes
   * More series and fewer volumes
2. If a manga series has a lot of volumes and we could only have a limited amount here at the library, which volumes would you want?
   * First five volumes
   * First ten volumes
   * First fifteen volumes
   * First twenty volumes
3. What are your five favorite manga series right now?
4. Which manga series do we not have that you wish we did?
5. What are your three least favorite manga series right now?
6. Do you have any more comments or suggestions? Write them in the space below.

We placed the survey on the shelves above our graphic novel collection and at the Teen Zone desk. A sign explained our motives and welcomed teen patrons in grades 6–12 to complete the suvery and drop it in the small box provided. During the three-month survey, a total of 32 patrons voiced their opinions.

Here is the information we received in answer to our survey questions:

1. Which is more important:
   * Fewer series and more volumes—17 votes
   * More series and fewer volumes—15 votes
2. If a manga series has a lot of volumes and we could only have a limited amount here at the library, which volumes would you want?
   * First five volumes— 3 votes
   * First ten volumes— 7 votes
   * First fifteen volumes— 3 votes
   * First twenty volumes—15 votes
3. What are your five favorite manga series right now? A few of the most voted for series included:
   Bleach by Tite Kubo— 7 votes
   Death Note by Tsugumi Oba— 6 votes
   Fruits Basket by Natsuki Takaya— 3 votes
   Full Metal Alchemist by Hiromu Arakawa— 4 votes
   Inu Yasha by Rumiko Takahashi— 7 votes
   Naruto by Masashi Kishimoto— 9
   Ranma ½ by Rumiko Takahashi— 6 votes
   Shaman King by Hiroyuki Takei— 4 votes
   Wallflower by Tomoko Hayakawa— 4 votes
4. Which manga series do we not have that you wish we did? A few of the most voted for series included:
   Chibi Vampire by Yuna Kagesaki—1 vote
   Hana Kimi by Hisaya Nakajo— 2 votes
   Kill Me Kiss Me by Lee Young Yuu—1 vote
   Tsubasa by Clamp—1 vote
5. What are your three least favorite manga series right now? A few of the most voted for series included:

        Astro Boy by Osamu Tezuka — 4 votes
        Dragon Ball Z by Akira Toriyama — 7 votes
        Tenchi Muyo by Hitoshi Okuda — 2 votes
        Yu-Gi-Oh by Kazuki Takahashi — 6 votes

6. Do you have any more comments or suggestions? Write them in the space below. Aditional comments included:

        More *Naruto* Volumes.
        If you put the manga by title or author it wouldn't be so confusing.
        It would be better if the American comics were placed somewhere else.
        Great manga choice and selection so far!
        Please get more anime and manga and *Shojo Beat Magazine*!!
        I think all of the manga should be alphabetized.
        Get more manga faster, you take forever, get more cute books.
        Get more copies of the first book in a series because the first one is always gone.
        Wider expanse of manga. The first volumes are better.
        More Anime.

The results of the survey led to a revamping of our shelves and our catalog. Three core suggestions ultimately led the way to the formation of our future redesign. These suggestions penned by anonymous teens included:

1. "It would be better if the American comics were placed somewhere else."
2. "If you put the manga by title or author it wouldn't be so confusing."
3. "Wider expanse of manga. The first volumes are better."

The result of the first core suggestion was the creation of four broad genres of graphic novels which would become the foundation for the reshelving of this collection: superheroes, stand-alone graphic novels, non-fiction graphic novels, and manga. Our superhero genre is composed mainly of Marvel comics, especially the *X-Men* and *Spider-Man* series. The stand-alone collection includes single issue works or series arranged in an American-style left-to-right reading format like *Bone*, by Jeff Smith. The non-fiction genre includes autobiographies and factual pieces such as Art Spiegelman's *Maus*. The manga genre consists of multivolume works that are in a Japanese or Korean style right-to-left reading format.

Since organizing in this way simultaneously grouped like-sized books together, the reclassifications of these four genres inadvertently led to a solution in shelving space. Therefore, we were able to insert more shelves in the manga section due to their compact size. We were also able to create two large shelves for the superhero, non-fiction, and stand-alone volumes, all of which tended to run larger and had sometimes required the volumes to be placed on their sides.

To address the second core suggestion, we needed to rally the support of our cataloging department. In order to better locate favorite series and volumes, teens suggested that the manga genre of graphic novels be alphabetized by title in a fashion similar to the larger chain book stores. Further reorganization included: shelving the superhero graphic novels by their leading characters such as *X-Men* or *Spider-Man*; shelving the stand-alone graphic novels like *Blankets*, by Craig Thompson, or the *Re-Gifters*, by Mike Carey, by author; and finally, keeping the non-fiction volumes in a separate section utilizing the Dewey Decimal System. Most teens said this organization allowed them to find the books quickly and to notice new books in the collection. One teen even commented that this organization would help those new to graphic novels because it would offer organization based on interest, therefore allow the patron to know where to start browsing.

The final core suggestion concentrated on the quantity issue. The final numbers were so close that no clear cut solution presented itself. Of the 32 teens surveyed, 54 percent voted for fewer series and more volumes, while 46 percent wished for the opposite, liking a wider choice in series with fewer volumes. A total of 53 percent of teens wanted at least the first twenty volumes of each series. Since we could not promise to buy the entirety of the larger sized series, we decided to use the list of teen favorites from the survey to determine the most popular series for which we would definitely reserve shelf space. These series included *Bleach*, by Tite Kubo, *Death Note*, by Tsugumi Oba, *Inu Yasha*, by Rumiko Takahashi, and *Naruto*, by Masashi Kishimoto. We also took the least liked series and used it to help us weed the series that our teens no longer read. These included *Astro Boy*, by Osamu Tezuka, and *Tenchi Muyo*, by Hitoshi Okuda. This made room for the series that teens wished we owned, such as *Chibi Vampire*, by Yuna Kagesaki.

To implement these changes, we also gathered input from the YA Department and the Technical Services Department. We decided the easiest way to recatalog the manga, which was again the majority of our collection, was to do it in small chunks. We used teen volunteers to peel off the overlays, since the catalogers would need to put new call numbers on the manga series in order to switch them for shelving by title. Once they went through processing, the teen volunteers would put the correct overlay back on the book. We also used signs to let teen patrons know which books had been recataloged, which books were currently being processed, and which books were still waiting to be recataloged. Volumes that were checked out were a major problem when trying to reorganize a circulating collection. Therefore, the shelvers, librarians, and teen volunteers did occasional sweeps of the graphic novels to find any volumes that did not get processed. We also utilized a spreadsheet to list all the books in our graphic novel collection, which age ranking they are in, which genre they are considered, and how they should be shelved. This helped the Technical Services Department know which new books would be arriving and how to fit them in the collection.

A minimal level of initial confusion developed after the reorganization. The confusion experienced by the library shelvers was due in large part to the multiple areas for superheroes, stand-alone graphic novels, and manga. Also, there was added uncertainty as to which books were to be shelved by title and which were to be shelved by author. The manager of circulation worked with the Young Adult Department to devise a plan that allowed the shelvers to quickly discern the difference between manga shelved by title and standalone graphic novels shelved by author. Small pink dots placed on the spine of the book above the call number provided the visual clue needed to help the shelvers identify the standalone novels and know where to place them in the collection. Since the utilization of these small dots, further confusion has been avoided.

Our anonymous survey helped us successfully reach out to our teen patrons and include them in an important redesign of the graphic novel collection. The entire reprocessing and reorganization took about five months: three months for the survey, and then two additional months to implement the changes by reshelving and recataloging the books. The fruition of the collected teen suggestions has led to a more aesthetically pleasing shelving arrangement and improved usability and popularity of the collection.

9

Selection and Popular Culture in Large Academic Libraries

Taking the Temperature of Your Research Community

CHARLOTTE CUBBAGE

Scholars love to point to watershed moments, turning points in the reputation of movements, people, and events. Of course once someone establishes a watershed moment other scholars rush in to reference earlier moments, but for academic libraries the year 2005 stands out as an affirmation for book selectors who had incorporated graphic novels into their collections: *Time* magazine named Alan Moore and Dave Gibbon's *Watchmen* one of the "100 Best English Language Novels from 1923 to the Present" (Kelly, 2005:6). At this point, a mere 4 years later, any twentieth, or twenty-first, century research level collection in English (and other) literatures could legitimately contain graphic novels. The *MLA International Bibliography* first assigned "graphic novel" as a subject heading in 1994 and, at this writing, had applied it to 195 articles. The first master's thesis published on graphic novels came out of the University of Georgia in 1989 and concerned *Watchmen* (Hollman, 1989). Twenty-seven dissertations and theses that focus on graphic novels have been published in North America since then, and another eleven include them within broader topics. The format of the graphic novel represents a popular culture phenomenon that illuminates the issues academic librarians face when selecting materials, particularly for creative arts and literatures collections. To serve scholars who focus on contemporary phenomena, librarians should craft methods that will tailor their collecting strategies to fit new formats and genres.

Popular culture has long inhabited a grey area where ephemera may cross an indefinable line into legitimacy, at least from the standpoint of various academic canons. Sometimes what crosses over spins off an entirely new discipline, for example, film studies in the twentieth century. Friction between teaching the establishment and teaching marginalia, teaching the canon and teaching the cutting edge, continues to grow in the current environment. If librarians embrace collection development as a service, we may need new models to grapple with the ways we acquire and curate ever evolving media.

Definition of Terms

Those who write about graphic novels disagree about what terminology to use, as do authors of the format. One school of thought continues to use the term comics, referring to the graphic elements that make up each page: panels, gutters, speech balloons, thought bubbles, etc. Another school would distance graphic novels from comics, for a variety of reasons, using terms like "graphic narrative," "sequential art," and of course "graphic novel." For better or for worse that latter term caught on with publishers, bookstores, and the public, and is a reasonable choice for libraries to use. It also has the political advantage of protecting the selector from allegations of wasting funds on comic books. Academic indexes frequently employ "graphic novels" as a descriptor, although you can find instances, for example in *ARTbibliographies Modern*, where the terms used are "comics" and "narrative art." Because no standardization exists, researchers use both "comics" and "graphic novels" as search terms. A search in *MLA International Bibliography* for Alan Moore with "comic*" yields 7 articles with no mention of graphic novels in the record, and a search for him with "graphic novel*" yields 9 articles with no mention of comics.

Standard dictionary definitions frequently ignore the paradoxical quality of the term: graphic novels, while always containing graphic elements, may not be novels. Art Spiegelman's *Maus: A Survivor's Tale*, perhaps the best known graphic novel in academic circles, is a work of non-fiction (Spiegelman, 1986). *Nevermore: A Graphic Novel Anthology* is a collection of Edgar Allan Poe's short stories (Poe, 2007). The most useful definitions I have found for "graphic novel" from a selector's point of view come, not surprisingly, from library literature. The graphic novel does not constitute a genre, but a format, a design into which a variety of genres may fit. While a graphic novel may be a multi-volume set, it is not a serial publication once complete. Graphic novels include a story arc, with a beginning, middle and end, unlike serialized comic books. Francisca Goldsmith's chapter, "What is the Right Word for a Book that Looks Like This," provides an excellent pathfinder through conflicting terminologies, as well as a good working definitions for libraries (Goldsmith, 2005). Other critical literature is helpful as well. For those interested in a discussion of terminologies, Hillary Chute covers the history of the use of the phrase "graphic novel." It received its impetus as a marketing term, and was partially an attempt to rescue the format from the equally misleading designation of comic book (Chute, 2008). For a succinct history of the rise of the popularity of graphic novels, by any name, see Gene Kannenberg's introduction to *500 Essential Graphic Novels* (Kannenberg, 2008).

Collections and Popular Culture

If your library has not tackled the issue of popular culture collecting in a global way, graphic novels may provide you with a template for other formats. Many of the issues surrounding popular culture materials are the same: how to fund; how to select; how much to collect; where to shelve; how to preserve; how to catalog; and how to decide on circulation policies.

Collecting in a climate of rapid cultural change, and fragmented target markets, comes with its own set of challenges, and may require new methodologies. You need not look far for examples of recent popular culture icons that academia has embraced. Faculty from multiple disciplines are analyzing the magic of Harry Potter. A quick scan of peer reviewed articles in *Academic Search Complete* yields the following subject areas, beyond the obvious, that co-opted Harry Potter in the past two years: addiction research, education, family therapy, gender studies, globalization, and medicine. Television and cinema offer other contemporary examples of popular culture fixtures that became research fodder: *The Sopranos* joins *Buffy the Vampire Slayer* and *The Simpsons* as analytic tools for societal trends. *Star Wars* continues to spin off articles, dissertations, and books. If your institution has a department of popular culture, consider that graphic novels and comics currently provide a test bed for numerous media phenomena; superhero movies continue to break box office records, and comic book writers created NBC's *Heroes* and ABCs *Lost* (Lieberman, 2008: 1b).

What to acquire for academic collections is not a new conversation for librarians. Articles on popular culture collecting for academic libraries date well before the term itself was commonly applied to phenomena. In 1954 one author struggled with classification of dime novels (Durham, 1954). Other materials of concern for librarians through the second half of the twentieth century included pulp science fiction, music and motion pictures (in various formats), serialized comics, magazines, and best-selling novels. What has changed is the overall acceptance within academia of popular culture studies. Where once you found lonely pockets of popular culture collections, you now find major research institutions focusing on, and in some cases digitizing, a variety of genres. Even so, recent articles suggest that libraries, while improving their holdings, are still falling behind in collecting popular culture materials. Robert Holley and John Heinrichs re-examined a 1992 study of 55 magazines which were found in a Kroger grocery store, and point out that there are still some significant gaps in available titles (Holley, 2007). Another article, which addresses the issues of archiving best-selling books, found issues similar to those in the Holley study (Crawford, 2001). Public libraries acquire popular magazines, best-sellers, and other examples of popular culture, but rarely do they have the space or resources to actively archive them. This leaves research libraries with that responsibility.

In a world of finite resources this may mean choosing your popular collection battles with an eye towards supporting, or getting support from, other institutions. You might decide to address graphic novels the way you select contemporary novels, for example, by relying on particular review sources *(The New York Times Book Review, Booklist* etc.), knowing other institutions pursue deeper coverage. If you partner with an institution with complementary needs, cooperative development schemes can reduce the burden of collecting for "just in case" scenarios. However, in order to make informed decisions, it is essential to speak with your constituents, to know the goals and objectives of your institution, and to craft collecting strategies that reflect your environment.

Communication Strategies

How should individual institutions address a format like graphic novels in the current climate? The first step may be to acknowledge that we actually exist in many climates. As with any format, local interest drives many collection decisions. One gold standard of collection management, supporting the research needs of faculty, might be supplemented by analyses of student interests, given that some of today's graduate students will study the popular culture of their youth. It has always made sense to circulate among your institution's faculty, to know their research interests and what they teach. It may also be time to extend your collection related interactions to your student body.

If you haven't interviewed your faculty in the past few years you could incorporate questions about popular culture into an assessment of research and teaching interests. Graphic novels may be of little value to your constituents. You might find that if there is interest in popular culture studies it focuses on anime, computer games, or reality TV shows. Although it requires your time, a face to face interview with as many of your faculty as are willing to meet with you will give you a detailed view of their current interests. Create a questionnaire to ensure a standard approach, but take it to faculty offices and write down responses. If that is not possible, create an online survey that is easy to complete, or send out a brief questionnaire via email.

There is no comprehensive method that will insure finding faculty interested in the graphic novel format. Some titles, like *Maus: A Survivor's Tale* (Spiegelman, 1986) and *Persepolis* (Satrapi, 2003), may be taught in history or gender studies courses. Depending on your institution you may be able to keyword search your course catalog or syllabi for "graphic novels," "sequential art," and "comic books." If not, a scan through your Art, English and Popular Culture Departments' course offerings may reveal faculty who use graphic novels to teach.

There are numerous ways to connect with students. Choose your target market; for example, at the graduate level, seek students in literature or sequential art; at the undergraduate level, identify members of campus groups that require self selection and that indicate student interest in research. Seek out those students who write honors theses in literature, students who are involved in student publications (particularly publications containing sequential art), or students who belong to groups organized around literature, art, anime, or gaming. For other ways to connect with students you may glean ideas from newer library literature on campus outreach and instruction. For example, Scott Walter and Michele Eodice's article on collaboration between academic libraries and campus services focuses on instruction, but their techniques may augment a variety of outreach programs (Walter, 2007). Once you find groups that seem promising, ask if you can meet with them to solicit their input into what students would like the library to collect. Lacking the time or resources for extensive outreach, you can still consult with students. If you conduct instruction sessions, as a warm up exercise, you could include a brief questionnaire on what materials they would like the library to acquire. You could create a survey and link to it from the library's home page, or even print out a short questionnaire that could be distributed and collected in an information commons or other public gathering space. Craft questions that elicit responses on the types of use your constituents believe they will make of a given format, and include a direct question about student interest in graphic novels. Conduct focus groups on libraries of the future, and work to get your colleagues involved.

Usage patterns will drive some of the policies discussed below. Once you collect data you have the material with which to tackle the numerous issues in creating a collection. From both faculty and students interviews the information you glean should provide data that can shape the policies surrounding popular culture collecting decision making (as much as possible within a given institution).

How to Choose Titles

Given the large and growing nature of the graphic novel publishing industry it makes sense to conduct your communications initiatives before you begin all but the most basic of selection processes. A good reason to conduct in-person interviews is the level of specificity they permit in appropriate circumstances. If those interviewed evince interest in graphic novels you then may move on to in-depth questions. What type of graphic novels interest patrons? Do your users primarily want a leisure reading selection, or do their research interests involve particular artists, time periods, geographic areas, targeted age groups or styles? Such information will suggest the amount of collecting in which you should engage, and the types of tools you should use to choose titles. After establishing an initial collection, you can use circulation data to assess the popularity of particular authors or sets. For larger multi volume sets, e.g., *Lone Wolf and Cub* (Koike, 2000) or *Transmetropolitan* (Ellis, 1998), you might order the first 2 or 3 volumes before investing in an entire set, remembering, of course, that titles may go out of print.

If interest comes primarily from a textual/literary standpoint, literary review tools frequently will cover a few graphic novel titles. The *New York Times Book Review* provides an overview of graphic novels in their "Holiday Books: Comics" section in December, and occasionally includes standalone reviews for individual titles, and *Publishers Weekly* regularly reviews graphic novels in its "Comics" section. If, however, the interest at your institution revolves around graphic novels in reading education, your selection tools would focus on the adolescent or elementary school market. A book in the Teens @ the Library series, *Developing and Promoting Graphic Novel Collections*, recommends numerous sources for adolescent collections (Miller, 2005). The *School Library Journal* regularly reviews graphic novels for both children and adolescents. In *Book Links*, Stephanie Zvirin supplies a list of classroom oriented graphic novels (Zvirin, 2008). Those institutions with researchers in graphic arts would apply different criteria. The critical literature in the field of art is less likely to review graphic novels on a regular basis than criticism aimed at literature or education. However, critical articles about comic artists do appear, and can be searched for in *Art Abstracts* and *ArtBibliographies Modern*, which could provide direction for which artists to focus on. Will Eisner, Paul Gravett, and Scott McCloud all provide in depth tool sets for understanding how to evaluate graphic novels.

Institutions with only a minor interest in graphic novels, may find Best-of-the-Year lists offer suggestions for many subcategories, but in depth collecting will require more specialized approaches. Be aware that in this era of narrowly segmented audiences, popular culture items may disappear quickly. Even titles that you will find on every "best" or "classic" graphic novel list may be out of print.

How to Fund

Graphic novel collecting may easily be incorporated into existing budget lines, unless you decide to create a comprehensive or large graphic novel collection. In that case you might want to apply for a grant or request a one-time sum of money to form a core group of titles. Individual titles tend to cost under $20.00 apiece (multivolume sets usually run under $20.00 per volume), and have achieved a high enough profile in academia to justify as literature, for adult, children's, or educational book collections. They fit well into leisure reading collections, and you may find they take the lead in circulation statistics. If your library is faced with dwindling circulation or entry statistics, high use can provide a compelling funding argument. If you face arguments about the format, point to the number of peer reviewed articles being written about graphic novels.

Unfortunately, if your patrons are more interested in graphic novels as graphic art, or if you wish to purchase better quality editions for preservation reasons, the prices increase. In recent years publishers have brought out art book quality editions of *Watchmen* ($75.00), *Sandman* ($99.00/volume as a 4 volume set) and *Dark Knight* ($99.00). Occasionally, books like the seventh in the series, *Kramers Ergot*, a compilation of new graphic works by well known authors, will receive a high quality edition and a $125.00 price tag. Use faculty support, as you would for other new areas of research, to solicit a small fund increase to cover the deluxe editions.

Classification and Location Issues

If you have the luxury of choice at your library, patron needs can help drive classification issues. There may be distinct collections that seem most appropriate for the use your constituencies envision in, for example, Literature, Education or Art libraries. Choice of collection may drive choice of classification schemes. If you want to keep the graphic novels shelved together, short of creating a specific location or a distinct collection of graphic novels, non-fiction art classification numbers may work. For example, the Dewey 741s or Library of Congress NCs could be used. If you have a leisure reading or education collection this approach works well, as there will probably be very few other art books located in those areas, and the graphic novels will stand out. If the primary interest at your institution revolves around the graphic art aspect of the collection, it definitely makes sense to apply art classification schemes to graphic novels.

However, if interest is more about textual content, and your institution houses separate art collections, or even just a large section of art books, you will run the risk of burying the collection by applying art classifications. Patrons will have to use the catalog to find the graphic novels, and may even be put off if they do not recognize the classification number or location. Another option for Library of Congress classification users is to employ the LC scheme for comics: PN 6700–6790. Otherwise, graphic novels mostly will be in fiction, but separated by author, country of origin etc., and some will end up shelved in history or other non-fiction collections. While there is no correct answer, patrons will benefit from a consistent approach. If organizational rules, research interest or other considerations prevent you from using a single classification scheme, consider asking cataloging to assign a 655 genre heading of "graphic novel." A consistently applied genre heading will allow you to create a list of your graphic novels regardless of their location.

To truly collect for the ages, you may want to establish a non-circulating collection. It could be housed and cataloged in an art library, a rare books, or another non-circulating collection that seems appropriate, according to local practices.

Do the cataloging department a favor, and make as many decisions as possible before you begin a major acquisitions project for graphic novels. You also may want to insure that the cataloging staff understands the numerous classification issues, that they feel a part of the conversation, and that you work together to create workflows and standards that support your collecting strategies.

If, during your communication stage, you discover a fair amount of student interest in graphic novels, consider creating a visible, separate collection, or, again, incorporating them into a browsable leisure collection. Although we tend to not think along the lines of display in research libraries, particularly not display of contemporary popular culture, graphic novels lend themselves to exposure. They sport eye catching covers, and they frequently come in oversized or abnormally shaped editions. Their art work, media tie-ins and contemporaneity may boost your library's image in the mind of undergraduates. There are precedents for shelving items by format, e.g., DVDs and microfilm. Easy availability of graphic novels could communicate a user friendly attitude with a fairly small commitment of time, effort and money.

Circulation Issues

One positive side effect of creating a graphic novel collection may be raised library visibility and circulation statistics. Circulating graphic novels as part of the main collection makes sense from a public relations point of view. However, depending on the type of use your patrons envision, you may want to establish special circulation policies and locations for second copies. If graphic novels are important research tools at your institution, consider the heavy use circulating collections may receive. The format is not hardy, particularly for heavy library use, and is at risk for theft. If you wait for circulating copies to fall apart, to be lost or stolen before you replace them, you may find titles have become out of print.

Preservation Issues

Generally, cheap construction, coupled with potentially heavy use, leads to familiar dilemmas for popular culture collecting: how much do you collect for the ages and preserve for future scholars, and how much do you purchase for current use? Depending on the type of collection you create, you might try a two pronged approach. First, collect certain titles, books that pop up on the graphic novel best seller list, according to leisure reader desires. *The New York Times* now has a Graphic Books Best Seller list that includes hardback, paperback and manga titles (<*http://artsbeat.blogs.nytimes.com/tag/graphic-books-best-seller-lists/*>). Second, apply no preservation techniques, and let circulation handle these titles as they do any other piece of the circulating collection.

For those titles and authors receiving critical accolades, you may want to adopt preservation measures to help insure longevity. When possible, purchase a hardback edition. As graphic novels move into libraries some vendors supply reinforced bindings. Brodart and Ingram have large lists of graphic novel titles, and provide library binding. If your institution contracts with a binder, or has an in-house bindery operation, be sure that the original covers remain visible. Nothing will kill a graphic novel's circulation faster than a standard, opaque periodical binding. However, if you wish to build an ongoing, research level collection, the best preservation measure would be, as suggested in the "Classification and Location" section above, to purchase a second, non-circulating copy.

Censorship Issues

Sex, violence, sexuality issues, drug use, and other commonplace taboos for children's collections, exist and are explored, researched and exploited in numerous materials you will find in research libraries. In fact you may find more resistance in an academic setting to the "comic book" quality of graphic novels than in their content. Fortunately you can point to a variety of academic research on the format, and justify it as you would a popular film, novel or music collection. If your institution is uninterested in popular culture, graphic novel collecting makes little sense. Similarly, if your institution frowns on collecting materials that do not actively support the curriculum, and no one teaches or researches in the area of graphic novels, there is little point in interviewing students about their current reading interests. However, if you face internal resistance from colleagues, but have found support from campus constituencies, try starting with a small, core collection. Local usage statistics will provide you with data to make an informed argument as to possible next steps.

Conclusion

For large academic libraries graphic novels represent the evolution of a popular culture phenomenon in ways that mirror other formats. The issues surrounding collection development in an era of ever changing media markets and demands for consumer entertainment will not disappear. Selectors do not have the resources to collect exhaustively, and yet they must address evolving research needs. Collaborative efforts could help archive multiple types of materials, lessening the burden on individual selectors and collections, but they cannot be used to support active local needs. A good communications program is essential for selectors who wish to grow their collections in new ways that reflect their campus culture and requirements.

If graphic novels fit the profile of research materials necessary to your institution it is important to craft a plan to classify and shelve them. Should interviews or questionnaires suggest that graphic novels would be popular for leisure reading, and your institution supports non-academic selection, visually promoting a collection may yield public relations benefits, raise circulation statistics, and bring more undergraduates into the library. Lacking campus support to collect graphic novels, it still makes sense for a large academic contemporary literature collection to add a few critically acclaimed titles. Most literary selection tools review at least a few graphic novels, and books now exist with lists of those titles deemed most important to collect. Graphic novels have moved into the academic canon, becoming yet another format for selectors to evaluate for inclusion within their collections.

References

Chute, Hillary. 2008. "Comics as Literature? Reading Graphic Narrative." *PMLA: Publications of the Modern Language Association of America* 123: 452–465.

Crawford, Gregory Alan, and Matthew Harris. 2001. "Best-sellers in Academic Libraries." *College & Research Libraries* 62: 216–25.

Durham, Philip. 1954. "A General Classification of 1,531 Dime Novels." *Huntington Library Quarterly* 17: 287–91.

Eisner, Will. 2008. *Comics and Sequential Art: Principles and Practices from the Legendary Cartoonist.* New York: W.W. Norton.

Ellis, Warren, Darick Robertson. 1998. *Transmetropolitan.* New York: DC Comics.

Gaiman, Neil, Sam Keith. 2006. *The Absolute Sandman.* New York: DC Comics.

Goldsmith, Francisca. 2005. *Graphic Novels Now: Building, Managing, and Marketing a Dynamic Collection.* Chicago: American Library Association.

Gravett, Paul. 2005. *Graphic Novels: Everything You Need to Know.* New York: Collins Design.

Harkham, Sammy. 2008. *Kramers Ergot 7*. Oakland: Buenaventura Press.

Holman, Curtis Lehner. 1989. *Reinventing the Wheel: A Multi-Perspective Analysis of Alan Moore and Dave Gibbons' Graphic Novel "Watchmen."* M.A., University of Georgia.

Kannenberg, Gene. 2008. *500 Essential Graphic Novels: The Ultimate Guide*. New York: Collins Design.

Kelly, James. 2005. "Time's 100 Best Novels." *Time* 166: 6.

Koike, Kazuo, Kojima Goseki, and Lewis Dana. 2000. *Lone Wolf and Cub*. Milwaukie, OR: Dark Horse Comics.

Lieberman, David. August 25, 2008. "Comic Boom." *U.S.A. Today*: 01b.

McCloud, Scott. 1994. *Understanding Comics: The Invisible Art*. New York: HarperPerennial.

Miller, Frank, Klaus Janson, Lynn Varley, et al. 2006. *Absolute Dark Knight*. New York: DC Comics.

Miller, Steve. 2005. *Developing and Promoting Graphic Novel Collections*. New York: Neal-Schuman Publishers.

Moore, Alan, and Dave Gibbons. 1987. *Watchmen*. New York: DC Comics.

_____. 2005. *Absolute Watchmen*. New York: DC Comics.

Poe, Edgar Allan. 2007. *Nevermore: A Graphic Novel Anthology of Edgar Allan Poe's Short Stories*. London: Self Made Hero.

Satrapi, Marjane. 2003. *Persepolis*. New York: Pantheon Books.

Spiegelman, Art. 1986. *Maus: A Survivor's Tale*. New York: Pantheon Books.

Walter, Scott, and Michele Eodice. 2005. "Meeting the Student Learning Imperative: Supporting and Sustaining Collaboration Between Academic Libraries and Student Services Programs." *Research Strategies* 20: 219–25.

Zvirin, Stephanie. 2008. "More on the Graphic Format." *Book Links* 17: 12–13.

10

Maus Goes to College

Graphic Novels on Reserve at an Academic Library

Anne-Marie Davis

Graphic novels are currently one of the most popular formats in libraries, and many articles have been written about the value of including graphic novels in public libraries and K–12 school libraries. A search in the LISA database turns up dozens of articles on how to entice reluctant young readers with the hottest new graphic novel. However, there are far fewer articles on incorporating graphic novels into the university curriculum. Why have academic libraries been slow to support the inclusion of graphic novels in their collections, lagging far behind public and school libraries? Is there still a perception that comics and graphic novels are too "juvenile" to be the subject of serious academic study? Some have argued that graphic novels are important in supporting the recreational reading mission of academic libraries (O'English, 2006: 175), but are they actually supporting the curriculum as well?

To find out if graphic novels are being used in academic instruction at the University of Washington, a list of all books that were cataloged with the genre "Graphic Novel" and were put on reserve for a course at any of the three University of Washington campuses was created. The results indicated that graphic novels and comics are indeed being used as texts in academic courses at the UW and their use has been increasing, especially since 2006. While a couple of the courses were specifically about graphic novels, most courses used only one or two graphic novels as a supplement to other materials. They were largely used as textbooks in a wide variety of academic disciplines, including Art, Anthropology, English, History and Comparative History of Ideas. This increase in the use of graphic novels as texts implies that scholarly interest in graphic novels and comics has been growing, and that college and university instructors are beginning to see the value of comics both as icons of popular culture and as important additions to the established curriculum. Subsequent interviews with instructors who use graphic novels as texts revealed that graphic novels were employed in a variety of ways, including as examples of art, as examples of racist imagery, as examples of portrayals of women, as a way to expose students to different literary genres and as historical documents.

The titles put on reserve most often were Art Spiegelman's *Maus*, Marjane Satrapi's *Persepolis*, Daniel Clowes' *Ghost World* by and Warren Ellis' *Transmetropolitan*. Remarkably, *Maus* was put on reserve for ten different courses in multiple subject areas, including Art, English, History, Comparative History of Ideas and Interdisciplinary Studies. The bulk of the titles put on reserve were popular works that should be a part of any academic library's core graphic novel collection, but some were less well-known titles, such as *Corridor,* by Sarnath Banerjee. While it was no surprise that the Pulitzer Prize winning *Maus* and the critically acclaimed *Persepolis* were used often, it was eye-opening and useful for collection development purposes to see the variety of other texts that instructors were using. For example, in examining the reserve records it was discovered that at least one instructor in the Japanese department was using manga titles in their instruction, and as a result of this discovery more manga titles were ordered for the UW Libraries collection.

Once the list of graphic novels that had been put on reserve was created, the instructors of the courses that used them were contacted via email and asked the following questions:

1. Which graphic novels did you use in your class?
2. Did you call them graphic novels or use another term?
3. How were they used in your class?
4. Why did you decide to use graphic novels and what benefits do you think they to bring to learning?
5. What was the students' reaction to them? Did they engage with the books?
6. What were your colleagues' reactions? Did you ever have to defend your use of graphic novels as texts?
7. Do you plan to use graphic novels in your courses in the future? Which titles and courses? (if you know)
8. Are there graphic novels the UW doesn't own that you would like us to buy? Do you have any suggestions for how the libraries can better support the use of graphic novels at the university?

The faculty who responded did so either via email or in a personal interview.

Responses to the question of what term instructors used when referring to the books were fairly consistent. They overwhelming used the term "graphic novel," although a few used terms such as "graphic journal," "comic" or "manga." The term "graphic novel" has been used for decades as a way to legitimize the genre and to distinguish more "serious" graphic materials ever since. Will Eisner debatably coined the term in the 1970's "as a marketing technique to increase the chances that his illustrated series of interlinked short stories about working class Jewish families during the Great Depression might be published" (O'English, 2006: 173). One instructor who referred to the books she used as "comics" did so because she had found in her research that many authors preferred the term and felt that the term graphic novel was an unnecessary effort to assign academic value to the text she was using.

Student's reactions to graphic novels in academic courses were somewhat mixed, though usually positive. Instructors found that some students came in thinking that comics didn't have academic merit and had preconceived ideas about what role comics fill in society, but that they often (but not always) changed their minds by the end of the course. One student complained about the use of manga in a Japanese Literature course because, she said "I can read that ON MY OWN." Her assumption was that a manga, unlike a novel, isn't so challenging and doesn't require an instructor to help her appreciate it (Holt, 2009). Students also struggled with some of the content. For example, a same-sex relationship depicted in a manga title "well, wasn't everyone's cup of tea" (Holt, 2009). A few students reported finding Maus "depressing" (Bernard, 2009).

Most of the instructors reported very favorable experiences using graphic novels as texts. Several instructors said that students who had not spoken in class before would suddenly contribute to class discussions when the graphic novels were under discussion. Instructors also mentioned that students were usually pleasantly surprised by how much they enjoyed reading graphic novels, and reluctant readers were often drawn in for the first time. Students were less intimidated by graphic novels than other texts, and the graphic novel or comic would provide a relief from the heavy reading load during the rest of the quarter. One instructor who used several of Joe Sacco's works in a Visual Anthropology course reported that "the students definitely responded well; it brought out discussion from students who were less inclined to engage purely written texts.... The main benefit was that it allowed for a whole different kind of discussion about how one documents events—through narrative, through visuals. In another class it created a discussion around stereotypes and visual cues about race and ethnicity — how does one draw race, what physical stereotypes does one rely on to convey ethnic difference" (Hoffman, 2009). An instructor in the Comparative History of Ideas department reported, "*Maus* was really useful because it's a deceptively simple text, one that is easy to read critically, yet when students really do read it critically, it's just so very rich, and poses such interesting and challenging questions. It's 'fun' not because there are pictures, but because if you push it just a little bit, it pushes you back and raises such intriguing challenges. Reading *Maus* was one of the first truly rich and intellectual experiences that many of my students had had in their education. Several of my students produced much more sophisticated work after reading and working through *Maus* than they had earlier in the quarter" (Magi, 2009). Another instructor who used *Maus* in a History class commented that she liked how it juxtaposed the past and present, which made a more emotionally complex point. The focus of *Maus* is not just World War II, but how World War II is remembered by Americans (Bailkin, 2009). "Unlike Literature, comics are able, quite literally, to 'put a human face' on a given subject" (Versaci, 2007: 13).

The only instructor who reported a negative experience using a graphic novel in a course admitted to being unfamiliar with the genre. She only used Alan Moore's *V for Vendetta* because a colleague had recommended it, and because she hadn't read it before the class, she failed to allot enough class time to fully discuss it. Another instructor mentioned that she would never use violent or misogynistic graphic novels such as *Watchmen* and *Preacher*, not because she felt that the students would be offended, but because she personally was uncomfortable with the content. Familiarity with the genre and personal enjoyment of the text seem key to successful use of a graphic novel in instruction.

Two instructors had suggestions for titles they wished the UW Libraries would purchase. One requested that the library keep on top of serially published titles, as it is frustrating when the entire series has not been collected. Another asked if the UW Libraries could provide a quick guide to critically reading graphic novels and noted that many students lack the analytic skills to read them closely. Most instructors were delighted to talk about graphic novels, and they were pleasantly surprised that a librarian was interested in discussing their curriculum and willing to buy materials needed to support their instruction.

Colleagues of instructors who used graphic novels as texts were almost universally supportive, indicating that many in the academic community are already invested in the educational value of graphic novels. *Maus* in particular was highly regarded by the History department. Only one instructor, who was using manga in a Japanese Literature course, reported any negative feedback from his colleagues, who were slightly shocked at first (Holt,

2009). Graphic novels are still not completely accepted by the academic community, although the use of such materials in a growing number of academic courses points to increasing acceptance. "Many faculty members retain antiquated notions of graphic novels based on their own past exposure to comic books in their youth, or are unaware of them at all, resulting in what one European scholar calls a 'deeply rooted suspicion towards the medium in [the] American academy'" (O'English, 2006: 178).

If graphic novels and comics are going to be fully accepted as valid capital-L Literature or capital-A Art, and thus texts worthy of academic study, academic libraries need not only to collect them, but also to promote them to instructors. In 2004, a collection development librarian, when describing comic book scholars, wrote, "One or two of the 'radical' instructors surely reside on every college campus, and allied with the power of critical thinking practiced by development librarians, academic collections can be on the brink of a remarkable transformation" (Matz, 2004: 79). Five years later, in examining books on reserve for university courses, it is clear that there are now more than one or two "radical" instructors on campus who are using graphic novels and comics as textbooks in their courses. And academic libraries should be collecting the texts instructors need to support the academic curriculum.

Table 10.1 Graphic Novels and Comics on Reserve at the University of Washington, 2006–2009.

Mirror, Window (An Artbabe Collection) by Jessica Abel. Art 120–Influences in Contemporary Art.

Just Who the Hell Is She, Anyway? by Marisa Acocella. Bothell Interdisciplinary Studies 219–The Politics of Sex Education.

King, by Ho Che Anderson. English 407–Special Topics in Cultural Studies.

The Tale of the Genji: Stars and *The Tale of the Genji: Flowers,* translated by Stuart Atkins and Yokko Toyozaki. Japanese 321–Japanese Literature I.

Epileptic, by David B. English 207–Introduction to Cultural Studies.

Corridor by Sarnath Banerjee. Art 120–Influences in Contemporary Art.

One Hundred Demons by Lynda Barry. English 497–Honors Senior Seminar.

Dykes and Sundry Other Carbon Based Life Forms to Watch out For by Alison Bechdel. Bothell Interdisciplinary Studies 219–The Politics of Sex Education.

Fun Home: A Family Tragicomic by Alison Bechdel. English 200–Reading Literature.

Our Cancer Year by Joyce Brabner and Harvey Pekar. English 207–Introduction to Cultural Studies.

I Never Liked You: A Comic Strip Narrative by Chester Brown. Art 120–Influences in Contemporary Art; Bothell Interdisciplinary Studies 219–The Politics of Sex Education.

Ghost World by Daniel Clowes. English 497–Honors Senior Seminar; Comparative Literature 352–Themes in World Literature: Death and Transfiguration; Comparative Literature 350–Themes in World Literature: Parents and Children.

Like a Velvet Glove Cast in Iron by Daniel Clowes. Art 120–Influences in Contemporary Art.

The Contract with God Trilogy: Life on Dropsie Avenue by Will Eisner. English 207–Introduction to Cultural Studies.

A Life Force: A Graphic Novel Will Eisner. English 207–Introduction to Cultural Studies

Transmetropolitan by Warren Ellis. English 407–Special Topics in Cultural Studies; English 541–Contemporary Literature; English 302–Critical Practice.

A Child's Life and Other Stories by Phoebe Gloeckner. Art 120–Influences in Contemporary Art.

Life's a Bitch by Roberta Gregory. English 407–Special Topics in Cultural Studies.

Adventures of Tintin by Herge. General Studies 197–Freshman Seminar (The Pulp Romanticism: Comics as Literature).

Luba in America by Gilbert Hernandez. Bothell Interdisciplinary Studies 219–The Politics of Sex Education.

Luba: The Book of Ofelia by Gilbert Hernandez. Bothell Interdisciplinary Studies 219–The Politics of Sex Education.

Luba: Three Daughters by Gilbert Hernandez. Bothell Interdisciplinary Studies 219–The Politics of Sex Education.

The Girl from H.O.P.P.E.R.S. by Jaime Hernandez. Bothell Interdisciplinary Studies 219–The Politics of Sex Education.

Ghost of Hoppers by Jaime Hernandez. Bothell Interdisciplinary Studies 219–The Politics of Sex Education.

Locas in Love by Jaime Hernandez. Bothell Interdisciplinary Studies 219–The Politics of Sex Education.

Locas: The Maggie and Hopey Stories by Jaime Hernandez. Bothell Interdisciplinary Studies 219–The Politics of Sex Education.

Night Fisher by R. Kikuo Johnson. Bothell Interdisciplinary Studies 219–The Politics of Sex Education.

Mail Order Bride: A Graphic Novel by Mark Kalesniko. Art 120–Influences in Contemporary Art.

Lone Wolf and Cub by Kazuo Koike. Japanese 323–Japanese Literature III.

Shutterbug Follies by Jason Little. English 207–Introduction to Cultural Studies.

The League of Extraordinary Gentleman by Alan Moore. General Studies 197–Freshman Seminar (The Pulp Romanticism: Comics as Literature).

Saga of the Swamp Thing by Alan Moore. English 407–Special Topics in Cultural Studies; English 541–Contemporary Literature.

V for Vendetta by Alan Moore. Comparative Literature 240–writing in Comparative Literature.

Watchmen by Alan Moore. Bothell Interdisciplinary Studies 384–Literary and Popular Genres.

Cinema Panopticum by Thomas Ott. English 497–Honors Senior Seminar.

Blue Pills: A Positive Love Story by Frederik Peeters. Bothell Interdisciplinary Studies 219–The Politics of Sex Education.

Postcards: True Stories That Never Happened edited by Jason Rodriguez. English 207–Introduction to Cultural Studies.

Palestine by Joe Sacco. Bothell Interdisciplinary Studies 364–Public Memory and Dissent in American Culture; English 207–Introduction to Cultural Studies; Anthropology 536–Seminar in Visual Anthropology.

The Fixer: A Story from Sarajevo by Joe Sacco. Anthropology 536–Seminar in Visual Anthropology.

Neon Genesis Evangelion by Yoshiyuki Sadamoto. Japanese 323–Japanese Literature III.

Persepolis by Marjane Satrapi. English 131–Composition: Exposition; English 207–Introduction to Cultural Studies; General Studies 197–Freshman Seminar (The Pulp Romanticism: Comics as Literature); Bothell Interdisciplinary Studies 384–Literary and Popular Genres; Bothell University Programs and Studies 104–Discovery Core I: The Arts.

Maus I: A Survivor's Tale: My Father Bleeds History or *Maus II: A Survivor's Tale: And Here My Troubles Began* by Art Spiegelman. Art 120–Influences in Contemporary Art; English 207–Introduction to Cultural Studies; English 498–Senior Seminar; History 269–The Holocaust: History and Memory; Modern European History 290–Topics in European History; Modern European History 274–Twentieth Century Europe; Modern European History 303–Contemporary European History Since 1815; Comparative History of Ideas 498–Special Colloquia (Historical Experience Beyond the Academy); General Studies 197–Freshman Seminar (The Pulp Romanticism: Comics as Literature); Bothell Interdisciplinary Studies 364–Public Memory and Dissent in American Culture; Bothell University Programs and Studies 190–Contemporary Literature.

Deogratias, a Tale of Rwanda by J.P. Stassen. English 131–Composition: Exposition.

The Tale of One Bad Rat by Bryan Talbot. Bothell Interdisciplinary Studies 219–The Politics of Sex Education.

Rent Girl by Michelle Tea. Bothell Interdisciplinary Studies 219–The Politics of Sex Education.

Adolf by Osamu Tezuka. English 207–Introduction to Cultural Studies.

Blankets: An Illustrated Novel by Craig Thompson. Bothell Interdisciplinary Studies 219–The Politics of Sex Education.

Cat Eyed Boy by Kazuo Umezu. Japanese 323–Japanese Literature III.

Y: The Last Man: Unmanned by Brian K. Vaughan. Comparative History of Ideas 250–Special Topics (Biofutures).

Jimmy Corrigan: The Smartest Kid on Earth by Chris Ware. Art 120–Influences in Contemporary Art.

Girl Stories by Lauren Weinstein. Bothell Interdisciplinary Studies 219–The Politics of Sex Education.

References

Bailkin, Jordanna. 2009. Personal interview conducted on May 7.

Bernard, Noell. 2009. Personal interview conducted on May 7.

Hoffman, Daniel. 2009. Personal email sent on May 4.

Holt, Jon. 2009. Personal email sent on June 12.

Magi, Heidi. 2009. Personal email sent on June 23.

O'English, Lorena, J. Gregory Matthews, and Elizabeth Blakesley Lindsay. 2006. "Graphic Novels in Academic Libraries: From Maus to Manga and Beyond." *Journal of Academic Librarianship* 32: 173–182.

Versaci, Rocco. 2007. *This Book Contains Graphic Language: Comics as Literature*. New York: Continuum.

11

The Library After Dark

The Promotion of Collections and Services

GWEN EVANS

Graphic novels that are rich and multilayered are one means to help students appreciate the complexity of history.

— Cromer and Clark, 2007: 583

Replace the word "history" in the quote above with "libraries," and you have the premise of the graphic novel project at Bowling Green State University (BGSU) Libraries. Visually oriented students find the dense blocks of text with which librarians typically try to inform or attract them less than compelling. Why not create a graphic story about the library told from students' perspectives, relying on the genre's blend of text, graphics, and storytelling? We devised a project with student artists who created an imaginative story meant to evoke the traditions of the genre, while offering information about the library in an entertaining but informative way.

The genesis of the project was a throwaway line during a brainstorming session of the librarians responsible for instruction and collection development for the arts on campus. We were discussing how studio and other art majors used the library, and how daunting, unfriendly, and boring text-based handouts, brochures, and guides could be, especially for first-year students who are not yet writing research papers. We discussed audiovisual methods to supplement or replace our textual guides—YouTube videos, screencasts, more virtual tours and games, and other visually centered aids. Nancy Down, Head of the Popular Culture Library, remarked, "Why do we always have to do text? Why can't we make a comic book?" It seemed an entirely felicitous convergence of medium and message — use a highly attractive genre to point to the many resources available in that genre.

Other librarians have had similar ideas about using comics for student outreach — O'English *et al.* suggest "recruiting a student or student library employee to write and draw a regular library strip highlighting library staff, issues, resources, and the student research process" (2006, 9). I took a different approach with the development of this project, privileging the students' experience of the library rather than that of the librarians, and using the novel as an object of analysis in itself. The format works extremely well as an educational and promotional tool for libraries— not only for visually oriented and graphically sophisticated fine arts majors, but also for library systems like the BGSU University Libraries that have visually intensive special collections (e.g., the Browne Popular Culture Library, the Music Library and Sound Recordings Archives, and the Curriculum Resource Center). As the project developed, we as librarians learned to think about the library in a visual way that was unfamiliar to us, and we learned or confirmed some things about the way students viewed the library in general.

Developing the Project

Recruiting interested students to work on the project was easier than expected, and gave some indication of the probable success of the finished project; when I asked Charles Kanwischer, a professor of drawing, which of his students were interested in comics, he replied, "All of them." Then with the help of Anthony Fontana, faculty advisor to the BGSU Comics and Cartooning club, I emailed students who might be willing to work on such a project. Eventually I ended up with six students who were art majors and Comic Club members: Geneva Hodgson, Carly Trowbridge, Eric Kubli, Kelli Fisher, Jory Griffis, and Jessi Zabarsky. They had a strong interest in working as a group, which presented some logistical and artistic challenges, but these were offset by some intriguing advantages. They served as an informal focus group both to test the attractiveness and viability of the idea, and to explore art students' perceptions and experiences of the library and special collections. They were so enthusiastic about the project that they were willing to work for free, donating a significant amount of their time over the course of a semester, although we did hire them later to create some subsidiary materials. We successfully applied for two on-campus grants, one to support undergraduate research and scholarship, and one to support instructional improvement, but almost the entire funding went to pay for the production and printing costs of the graphic novel.

Our initial discussions centered on genre, content, and length. We decided we needed an overarching narrative to contain and structure the work of six different artists. While I initially proposed a 10–12 page comic (one or two pages per person), the artists successfully argued that it would be difficult to create a visually interesting story line in only twelve pages, especially while integrating six styles. While no undergraduate (or graduate student, or faculty member) would willingly read a 60-page text on library services and resources, the graphic novel format is simultaneously expansive and compact in its ability to convey information in multiple modes. What sounded shockingly long as a book turned out to be a rather short graphic novel.[1]

Given the nature of genre fiction and collection organization in the Popular Culture Library, we discussed whether this should be a genre novel — horror, romance, superhero, or adventure. While the artists didn't settle on a particular genre and follow that convention, the spooky aspects of the library after closing and the nature of the evocative historical material in the closed archives influenced their choice of "The Library After Dark"— the tale of a group of students who fall asleep while studying, get locked in after closing, and discover the resources of the library (complete with ghosts).

Because the University Libraries Jerome Library is a tower building, with the general collection and services on the first floor, and each ascending floor contains a special collection, each artist chose a "story," with one artist tying all the narratives together in the first and final chapters. As research, the artists took behind-the-scenes tours of each floor, which included: the Curriculum Resource Center (Children's books, picture files, puppets, and other teaching aids for the K–12 education programs); The Music Library and Sound Recordings Archives (notable for its extensive collection of popular music, especially vinyl, and related paraphernalia like zines, teen periodicals, and marketing materials); The Ray and Pat Browne Popular Culture Library (including non-traditional library resources such as dime novels, story papers and nickel weeklies, pulp magazines, fanzines and other amateur publications, comic books, graphic novels, posters, postcards, greeting cards, and mail-order catalogs); and the Center for Archival Collections (archival materials on the history of Northwest Ohio and the University). Individually they went back and took photographs and notes, made sketches, and picked up what brochures and handouts already existed.

Plot lines grew out of the discussions between us about library services, librarian subculture, and how students, especially first-year art students, use the library and what they think of it. For instance, the Minotaur in the section of the novel devoted to the first floor arose out of a conversation in which I learned that the first floor architecture baffled students because a rather convoluted suite of rooms, including the rooms used for scheduled library instruction, blocked east-west passage at the back of the building. The students referred to the first floor as "the labyrinth." We as librarians were so used to the layout that we didn't think about the navigational difficulties of students trying to get from the main stacks to the periodicals area, or entering on the "wrong" side of the main floor and trying to get to their library instruction session. We realized that some simple maps and directions at the dead ends would help students trying to get from one side of the building to the other.

As the project developed, it became clear that it would be difficult to pack much specific, directional, instructional material into the narrative. The five separate floor adventures could give an overview of resources of specific interest to art majors and first-year students, but there was no easy place to insert the type of explicit information typically issued in library orientation handouts: "You need your student ID to check out books," or "You can make individual research appointments with a librarian to get started on your research topic or assignment." We decided to incorporate some of that information in advertisements styled after the comics ads of the past: powerful bibliographies "pumped up" with OhioLINK consortial library resources took the place of the Charles Atlas Muscle Man;[2] and a "psychic" research consultation with Bill Schurk, sound archivist, proclaimed "Disco is not Dead! Bill Schurk can help it speak to you through our mystical musical confabulation!" This idea proved wildly popular with both library staff and student employees, and we sent out a call for submissions and suggestions. More people than one would think have fond and vivid memories of poring over ads in comic books. In addition, the library hired the art students to do some short, one page comics meant as handouts, flyers, and web comics embedded in the library catalog or in online research guides.

As project manager, I tried to give the

The Paper That Made a MAN Out of "Mac": part of an ad for OhioLINK consortial borrowing (Eric Kubli, 2009, Creative Commons license).

I Can Deliver YOUR Books, Too — in Only a Few Days!

HAVE YOU ever needed source material like Mac — absolutely fed up with other fellows having bigger, huskier "research papers"? If you have, just give me a few days ! I'll PROVE you can have a research paper you can be proud of, packed with red-blooded vitality!

OhioLink.™ That's the secret ! That's how I changed myself from a C-average nogoodnik to winner of the title "World's Most Perfect Research Paper Writer."

The Paper That Made a MAN Out of "Mac": part of an ad for OhioLINK consortial borrowing in *The Library After Dark* (Eric Kubli, 2009, Creative Commons license).

artists as much authorial latitude as possible, while retaining final editorial control over content that would be regarded as controversial in the library context. For example, theft or destruction of materials is a serious professional concern. At one point in the development process, I vetoed a part of the story line that had the trapped students actively trying to dismantle the security alarms. Instead, the plot was changed so that a character suggests disabling the security system only to have this course of action emphatically rejected by the group.

Some changes were requested because the artists inadvertently called into question the professionalism of library staff. The Center for Archival Collections narrative features a persnickety 19th century ghost who shows the lost students around, while admonishing them for touching things and making noise. We let stand his finicky and stereotypical librarian behavior because, after all, he is dead — a ghost who simultaneously represents the past entombed in the archives and a certain kind of attitude displayed by librarians and archivists of the past. The narrative reconciles the desire of the students to read and engage with the archival materials with the need of the archives/ghost to protect them by having the ghost show the procedures for requesting materials. However, in establishing the contrast between the ghostly forbidding attitudes of the past and the "live flesh" helpfulness and friendliness of the current archival staff, the artist inadvertently impugned the practices of the current archivists. The text was changed to "It's such an unending task to keep this in order, I fear. Red Rot everywhere, books are easy to misplace, tsk, tsk. The work of an archivist is never done, not even after we're dead."

As a library, we had a strong preference for a Creative Commons license for the final work. The students and I settled on a Creative Commons Attribution-Noncommercial-No Derivative Works 3.0 license. We had a separate agreement granting the library a non-exclusive license to make derivative works for the purposes of instruction, promotion, marketing, and other non-commercial activities connected with the University Libraries and Bowling Green State University.[3] While technically this was a work for hire, and we could have requested more liberal permissions, we chose to treat it more as a collaborative artistic venture, and acquiesced to their desire for restrictions on the ability to modify and adapt their work.

The novel itself was published using lulu.com, an Internet self-publishing company used by many comics and graphic novelists. The initial print run was 150 copies of a 66 page black and white novel, letter size, with saddle stitch binding, at a production cost of $4.95 apiece for a total of $742.00. All but one of the artists normally worked in ink, so keeping the costs low by printing in black and white wasn't a design compromise. We are also publishing the novel as a web comic.

In a first draft of **The Library After Dark**, the ghost in the archives asserts his displeasure with the current archival administration (Carly Trowbridge, 2009, reproduced by permission under a Creative Commons license).

It would be hard to put an exact monetary figure on the artistic time and talent, since the artists worked for free, as part of a semester-long grant project from the BGSU Center for Undergraduate Research and Scholarship. All of the grant money went to pay for initial supplies, printing costs, and a small honorarium for each artist. One of the challenges of having six artists was that any grant money didn't go very far split amongst them. However, they were so thrilled that someone was taking their comics work seriously that they didn't care that they were working pro bono. This was an interesting commentary on the passion of graphic novel aficionados and the problematic status of comics and graphic narratives in the academy (even at BGSU with its degree programs in Popular Culture and American Culture Studies). We did hire some of the students for a month to create the short comics and finish up the scanning, formatting, and publication of the novel.

The novels will be distributed in the fall of 2009 to classes in the campus Arts Village, a residential learning community for arts majors. There will be assessment instruments designed to investigate whether graphic narratives and comics do increase retention of library information (especially over time) versus purely textual information — and whether students who read the graphic novel are more likely to visit the libraries during their first year. The original artwork, plus the finished published novel, will be cataloged in the Browne Popular Culture Library as archival material.

The Library After Dark: A Close Reading

Art professors with whom I discussed the project were unanimous that art students would respond better to a graphic novel than to standard text guides. "Pictures work better" was the simple statement of one instructor.[4] While this contention will be tested in our assessment activities, the scholarly literature on comics and graphic narrative supports the use of graphic narrative as a particularly apt tool for portraying the library.

Visual artists are more dependent on browsing and visual exploration of the physical library than other researchers and scholars. Due to the structure and indexing of many classification and search systems, searching the catalog is often unproductive for visual artists—most catalogs do not support limiting by illustrated items, for example. Hemmig, in the review of the literature on studio artists in the library, cites a number of authors who describe art students as "compulsive browsers" with a "natural antipathy toward scholarly research, and who will, whenever possible, avoid card catalogs and bibliographic indexes in favor of browsing the stacks" (Hemmig 2008, 345). Gluibizzi (2007, 29) emphasizes that bibliographic instruction (especially with graphic novels) is most effective if items are pulled out and displayed during the session so that students can see the results of catalog searching and drive home the point that not all books of interest will be found by browsing. Hemmig's literature also underscores that the entire library is an object of visual attention and interest — including the books themselves as designed objects, the arrangement of the library, the serried ranks of the stacks, etc. The overview makes several interesting suggestions and analyses based on the consistency of results reported over time and with a variety of methods. Browsing is central (but often seen by the artists themselves as a serendipitous, passive, anxiety-provoking activity rather than active information seeking); artists prefer human help to self-help using catalogs and indexes; and library services in general have ignored the particular needs of visual artists, including art students and faculty (Hemmig 2008).

Scholarly and philosophical analyses of graphic novels and narratives confirm that the structure and semiotics of comics and sequential art are peculiarly apt for addressing the behavior and preferences of visual artists in libraries as described above. A number of scholarly articles, both those dealing with the more literary graphic novels—*Maus: A Survivor's Tale* (Spiegelman 1986), *Persepolis* (Satrapi 2003), *Fun Home: A Family Tragicomic* (Bechdel 2006), and *Jimmy Corrigan: The Smartest Kid on Earth* (Ware 2000)—and those addressing more fantasy-based or escapist graphic narratives and comics, extensively analyze the interdependence of text and image.

> Highly textured in its narrative scaffolding, comics doesn't [sic] blend the visual and the verbal—or use one simply to illustrate the other—but is rather prone to present the two nonsynchronously; a reader of comics not only fills in the gaps between panels but also works with the often disjunctive back-and-forth of reading and looking for meaning [Chute, 2008: 452].

Word and text may amplify or subtly undermine each other, by their proximity creating "implicit antagonism" as Saklofske describes in the analysis of "Wordsworth" by writer Neil Gaiman and artist Dave McKean (2008, sec. 11). Rocco Versaci (2007, 13) goes further in pointing out that "comic narration blends and modifies features shared by other art forms—especially literature, painting, photography and film." I would argue that these characteristics of graphic or comic narration make the form more suitable for visual arts students than text alone or even video or other visually enhanced instructional and orientation material. The nature of the genre itself encapsulates and recapitulates in some sense all the things that the library contains— not just text, but photographs, multimedia, and digital resources. Graphic narrative even resembles hypertext, since reading comics often breaks the conventional left-right, top-bottom directional flow (Cromer and Clark, 2007: 578). The graphic novel is a complex portrayal of space, time, and content — apropos for the complexity of libraries and archives, which are full of more than just text, and which have complex relationships with the past and its spatial organization.

Using images and text as an instructional and promotional tool demonstrates to artists and other readers that the library is full of images and that images are as pertinent to portraying the library as words. Graphic novels "lead us back to an appreciation of the image as a positive and integral part of our use of written language; they reconnect us with the world of the picture and the icon ..." (Cromer and Clark, 2007: 581). I would suggest that for student artists, it is the word with which students reconnect by using graphic narratives, whether novels or comics, to portray the library and its resources.

Indifference to, anxiety towards, or antagonism to text as well as to the library on the part of the artist-student is illustrated in *The Library After Dark*'s content and in interviews with the artists. "Pretty much when books stopped having pictures in them, that's when I stopped reading," said Eric Kubli in a group discussion we were having about their pleasure reading habits.[5] This resistance to what I'll call the textual library is displayed in the novel in various ways. The characters fall asleep on the study floor, surrounded by books with titles like *Really Old Art Stuff, Bleh,* and *Snore.* Shane, exploring the first floor main stacks, is hit on the head by a hefty volume falling out of the shelves. He has a series of encounters with a (female) Minotaur, Athena, Jane Austen, Kali the Hindu Goddess, and Mildred from *Of Human Bondage,* and has to be repeatedly hit on the head with another book by his friend Lisa to snap out of it. It's easy to see it as a playful rendition of the reaction of the stunned and overwhelmed first year student faced with a large university library.

On the archival floor, the students give the cold shoulder to the ghost's personal favorite, a book entitled *Tax Revenues of Paulding County*, in favor of the graphic resources—maps, posters, photographs, and the calligraphy of diaries from the civil war. Some of this emphasis on the chosen resources was by design. One of the explicit param-

Shane envisions several literary characters after being hit on the head with a book — Lisa must keep hitting him with another book to get him back to normal (Kelli Fisher, 2009, reproduced by permission under a Creative Commons license).

eters of the project was to showcase the many visual or multimedia resources of the libraries and special collections, so that incoming freshman would know that the library wasn't just books. However, the exact ways that the artists chose to do that are revealing.

Initial resistance to the library on the part of the student protagonists and overcoming that resistance appear in other story lines and vignettes. For example, the staff of the Curriculum Resource Center (CRC) loved the portrayal of the relationship between Mike, the recalcitrant student, and Lionel, the insanely enthusiastic puppet — a relationship that invokes Krazy Kat and his/her unrequited love for Ignatz. Lionel chases Mike all over the CRC, describing its abundant resources in awful doggerel, provoking Mike into putting him into the Ellison die cut machine. A last minute rescue is performed by some more worldly puppets, who chastise Mike thus: "What's your problem? He was giving you a tour! Just because he's a little musical ... doesn't mean you can turn him into sailboats! Cutting up a library puppet! You make me sick, kid!" The head of the CRC told the artist, Geneva Hodgson, that the story captured how staff felt when giving tours or orientations to freshman — wild enthusiasm and love on one side, and ennui and resistance on the other. Geneva said that she wasn't thinking specifically of Krazy Kat, but that she did want to capture the "kid versus the library" feeling that many students feel, especially as first year students.[6]

Two other recurrent themes in the novel are those of restriction and invisibility. This is understandable in a narrative that deals with a number of collections that are closed archives, but given the nature of the Bowling Green State University Libraries, it was instructive for us as librarians to see just how prominently those restrictions and the resulting invisibility of our resources define the whole of the library.

Students (the non-fictional, live flesh ones) are constantly frustrated by the inability to physically browse or borrow from the sound recordings and popular culture collections. All of the artists, as a narrative necessity, chose to penetrate in normally disallowed ways into the closed collections to show hidden resources. The novel deals with the tension between the restrictions and the desire to reveal these areas of the library in various ways. The character in the Popular Culture Library attempts to gather an armload of materials to show his

Lionel the lion puppet chases Mike through the Curriculum Resource Center while reciting the different kinds of teaching aids available (Geneva Hodgson, 2009, reproduced by permission under a Creative Commons license).

friends, and is sucked back into the closed stacks by the tentacles of an ancient creature that feeds on pop culture. In the Music Library, one of the characters reminds the other that while listening to the music in the music library may be a bit burdensome, peer-to-peer music downloading on campus is blocked. The ghost in the Archives chastises the over-enthusiastic students, but shows them how easy it is to fill out a request form to have the materials pulled.

Jory Griffis in particular engages both the restricted nature of the Popular Culture Library and the debate about the value of collecting popular culture materials at all. His student confronts the Popular Culture monster, which quotes various tough-guy movies, appears as both Yoda and Tom Hanks, and defends the decision to include the movie *Splash* in the collection. Nancy Down, the Head of the Popular Culture Library, was struck by how concisely the few words and pictures in a scene invoked a whole scholarly debate about collecting and protecting such ephemeral popular culture artifacts.

While most librarians and archivists are well aware that students are often frustrated by library policies and restrictions, especially in contrast to the seeming freedom of the internet, one of the more interesting developments was the extent to which the invisibility of our archival resources was a marketing and instructional problem. Since visual browse is the primary discovery strategy for artists, closed collections present a particularly over-looked feature of the library.[7] Academic collections focused on other disciplines, such as BGSU's Music Library and Sound Recordings Archives, are often missed by artists—even though the album cover art of the extensive vinyl collection is of great interest to graphic designers. Since artists often don't know what they are looking for until they see it, searching the catalog or even working with special collections staff is a frustrating exercise, both

for artists and for library staff (Hemmig 2008). Eric Kubli, Jessi Zabarsky, and Nancy Down (Head of the Popular Culture Library), and I had a conversation in June 2009 about the development of the story and the problems of presenting access to the closed collections. Both Eric and Jessi were aware of the comics in the Popular Culture library because of a Comics Club tour they had taken—one in which the staff brought out the materials to show them. When they took their "insider's tour" into the stacks, they were struck by the wealth of visually compelling resources—everything from comics to posters to realia. Eric said that while he was on the initial project tour of the library (before they got the behind the scenes tour), "I sort of was thinking it would be so *boring* drawing a comic of just, y'know ... being on a tour ... other than getting on the computer and looking it up, that's the only other way that you can actually get back there."[8] These conversations and the prominent place that the restric-

A student debates collection development with the Popular Culture Library monster (Jory Griffis, 2009, reproduced by permission under a Creative Commons license).

tions play in the navigation and narration of *The Library After Dark* have sparked a series of conversations among the librarians about possible alternative ways to enable access and discovery in the closed collections, including ideas such as "supervised exploration" in the closed stacks.

This emphasis on the visible is also apparent in the short comics that the students prepared for more specific information and instruction. In a comic about the characteristics of scholarly journals, it was striking that the librarian in the comic leaves out what many of us think of as the salient feature of scholarly literature—the fact that it's peer-reviewed. Jessi Zabarsky, the artist, was working from one of the standard library guides, and she explained that she had concentrated on the elements that someone could *see* in an article. It was a deliberate focus on details that were immediately accessible to those whose dominant mode is visual. The language the student uses in the comic is also indicative of an orientation towards a visual learning style.

While library instructional and promotional materials can and do incorporate non-drawn visual media such as photographs and video to show the resources of closed collections, there are reasons that the graphic narrative genre is more effective. The classic *Understanding Comics: The Invisible Art*, points out that increased graphic abstraction in the portrayal of characters increases the ability of the reader to enter the narrative. "Thus, when you look at a realistic drawing of a face ... you see it as the face of another. But when you enter the world of the cartoon—you see yourself" (McCloud, 1994: 36). The active participation of the reader is involved in performing closure between every panel; the gutter is the space into which the viewing subject can insert her/himself (1994, 69). Comics Journalism, the term used to refer to works like Joe Sacco's books on Palestine, Sue Coe's

work, or Ted Rall's *To Afghanistan and Back,* relies on a deliberate invoking of the artist/author's subjectivity in the center of the action, and a concomitant shift in the perspective of the reader (Versaci 2007; Williams 2005). Graphic narrative thus has the effect of embedding the reader into the story in particularly vivid ways. Bob Thompson (*Washington Post*, August 24, 2008) describes comics' journalism as opposed to first-person non-fiction prose: "What seems different is the literal immediacy of the graphic versions. Within seconds, they can pull you into strange worlds." Johanna Drucker, on the visual presentation of graphic novels, asserts that,

The effect of immersion and absorption this creates for a reader goes beyond the account of a verbal or literary "story." I

In one of the shorter comics, a student talks with a librarian about navigating the research databases (Jessi Zabarsky, 2009, reproduced by permission under a Creative Commons license).

would argue that the graphic-ness of these works results in the production of that rich domain the Russian formalists referred to as the fabula, or life-world imagined as the scene of the tale [2008b, 40].

For the graphic artists on the project, this immersive identification with graphic narrative is so pronounced that it influences all their reading. Jory Griffis and Jessi Zabarsky, both of whom described themselves as liking to read traditional textual works, described a process of slowing down, caused by the inability to read faster than "hearing" it out loud — essentially they narrated the text to themselves. They thought that it was the influence of comics whereby they were accustomed to silently narrating the different characters in graphic narratives with different voices and personalities.[9]

Since the primary problem with first year art students is enticing them into the library and getting them comfortable with it, the effect of identification and immersion is a key component in this graphic novel approach to library orientation. The graphic novel works to engage the reader personally with the action and locale in a way that can influence or guide them when they later come to the library. "We don't just observe the cartoon, we become it" (McCloud, 1994: 36).

Comics or graphic novels can enhance this effect of vicariously traveling through the library in a way that film or photography can't.[10] One of the specific advantages in the labyrinthine library environment is the ability to show layouts and angles that it would be difficult or impossible to achieve with photographs or video. The artists played extensively with the angles of the book stacks and the characters' navigation between and around them to give a vivid sense of the 3D environment.

Many standard library orientation brochures or virtual tours have head height photographs of interiors that are overwhelmed with detail, since libraries are extremely complex visual environments. By contrast, drawings can selectively display salient features, even in a panoramic view — like the "free items" giveaway shelf in the Curriculum Resource Center — that can get lost in a photograph. All of the separate narratives pay particular attention to movement and space — the protagonists' travels up the elevators and stairs, their peeking around corners and through the book stacks, and in particular the delineation of accessible and restricted space in the closed, archival collections.

Students walk through the Center for Archival Collections stacks (Carly Trowbridge, 2009, reproduced by permission under a Creative Commons license).

The Library After Dark foregrounds the library's spatial arrangement and narrates navigation through the physical library in a way that academic libraries often background, given a

Top: Drew searches for Jen in the Music Library and Sound Recordings Archives. The small labels on the shelves contain a series of music jokes and references. One of the ranges has labels that successively read "ABC ... Easy As ... 123 ... Simple As ... Do Re Mi." Another range reads "M-Y...LP Records ... And ... They're All ... Scratched" (Eric Kubli, 2009, reproduced by permission under a Creative Commons license). *Above:* Lionel the puppet tangles with Mike at a Curriculum Resource Center computer workstation (Geneva Hodgson, 2009, reproduced by permission under a Creative Commons license).

growing library and instructional emphasis on digital resources and virtual, not physical, access. But browsing through the physical library is likely to remain an important part of visual artists' mode of discovery for some time. Since research and anecdotal evidence indicate that they have a vexed and anxious relationship with the academic library to begin with, using graphic narration as a way to help student artists visualize their way around the library would seem to be an effective strategy for orientation and instruction. Using student characters drawn in a fairly abstract, iconic style allows the readers to participate in the narrative more effectively than does the impersonal prose of textual guides. It is also much easier and cheaper to draw imaginative but instructive situations or stories than it is to film or videotape them.

While creating an entire graphic novel may not be feasible for all libraries or collections, creating shorter comics, especially on the web, could be. Some of our shorter comics are meant to replace the banner in the library OPAC at periodic intervals so that information about library services is delivered while users are engaged in related activities. Clicking on the banner leads the reader to a single page comic with a few links to more information. A teaser for a comic has information about the consortial library system and how easy it is to order books from another library.

Other possible activities to generate the same sorts of anthropological information about how students see the library include: comics contests, or activities where users are asked to "draw the place of the library in your life"— similar to what the technology writer, Kevin Kelly, does with the Internet Mapping Project (*http://www.kk.org/internet-mapping/*), or what the Undergraduate Research Project at the University of Rochester has done with photo essays and mapping diaries (Foster and Gibbons 2007).

One of our aims in the project was a true collaboration with the student artists, since they represented our target audience. We wanted to avoid the pathos of librarians trying to be cool and failing. We were fearful of producing an overly safe, bland, or corporate ersatz comic — fearing that such a publication would undercut the power of the genre and its associations with popular culture, the underground, and humor. Further, we wanted the finished product to have the kind of appeal that would generate discussion and sharing amongst the students. We hope to see the unlikely sight of students poring over a library orientation text, re-reading it, and passing it along to friends. We are interested in whether this approach actually increases retention of specific information, or whether it is more suitable as marketing and orientation material — a replacement for the standard brochure or tour. Graphic narratives also introduce a certain amount of pleasure to instructional reading about library services, and as O'English *et al.* (2006) point out, pleasure reading is an important component to academic library use, and is one of the arguments for collecting graphic novels in academic libraries at all.

Undergraduates, especially fine arts majors, already have an interest in and familiarity with graphic novels and comics from their own reading habits. As Gluibizzi asserts, "I only see the popularity of comics and graphic novels growing. They are the reasons that many of our students came to art school, and for many students they served as their first art teachers" (2007, 29). Bookstores, education experts, and librarians have introduced K–12 students to graphic novels and comics as both pleasure reading and serious objects of study, and graphic novel/publishing industry sales to schools and libraries have increased from $1 million to $30 million in six short years (Hudson 2008). It's time to think of expanded ways of using this genre for library information, marketing, and instruction — especially for academic libraries with substantial collections of popular culture materials or visual resources.

Teaser comic for the library OPAC banner, featuring a common student dilemma (Jessi Zabarsky, 2009, reproduced by permission under a Creative Commons license).

Endnotes

1. I am aware of the differences of and debates about terminology—comics versus graphic novel versus graphic narrative. I will continue to refer to the project as the graphic novel, as this is what the students (who are also aware of the terminology debate) used in reference to their own work. For more concerning terminology and distinctions, see Chute 2008; Cromer and Clark 2007; McCloud 1994.

2. You can see the original Charles Atlas ads at *www.charlesatlas.com.*

3. See http://creativecommons.org/licenses/by-nc-nd/3.0/

4. Ricardo Quinonez, drawing instructor, in discussion with the author, March 2009.

5. Eric Kubli, artist, in discussion with the author, June 2009.

6. Geneva Hodgson, artist, in discussion with the author, June 2009. All of the students were aware of several foundational graphic artists in the field, especially George Herriman, the creator of Krazy Kat (1999); Winsor McCay, creator of Little Nemo (1997), and Art Spiegelman, creator of Maus (1986). For Krazy Kat's gender, see Crocker 1994.

7. While writing this article it was instructive to be reminded how visual the language of seeking, discovery and exploration is; language that reinforces the utility of graphic novels, comics, and other visual media in attracting students to the library.

8. Eric Kubli, artist, in discussion with the author, taped interview June 2009.

9. Jory Griffis and Jessi Zabarsky, artists, in discussion with the author, June 2009.

10. For a discussion of navigation devices and the difference between film, graphic narrative, Second Life, and other graphically navigated interfaces, including books, see Drucker 2008a.

References

Bechdel, Alison. 2006. *Fun Home: A Family Tragicomic.* Boston: Houghton Mifflin.

Chute, Hillary L. 2008. "Comics as Literature? Reading Graphic Narrative." *PMLA: Publications of the Modern Language Association of America* 123 (2): 452–465.

_____. 2007. "Decoding comics." *MFS Modern Fiction Studies* 52 (4): 1014–27.

Crocker, Elisabeth. 1994. "'To he, I am for evva true': Krazy Kat's Indeterminate Gender." *Postmodern Culture* 4 (2). http://0-muse.jhu.edu.maurice.bgsu.edu/journals/postmodern_culture/v004/4.2crocker.html.

Cromer, Michael, and Penney Clark. 2007. "Getting Graphic with the Past: Graphic Novels and the Teaching of History." *Theory and Research in Social Education* 35 (4): 574–91.

Drucker, Johanna. 2008a. "Graphic Devices: Narration and Navigation." *Narrative* 16 (2): 121–39. http://muse.jhu.edu/.

_____. 2008b. "What Is Graphic about Graphic Novels?" *English Language Notes* 46 (2): 39–55.

Foster, Nancy Fried, and Susan Gibbons, eds. 2007. "Studying Students: The Undergraduate Research Project at the University of Rochester." Chicago: *Association of College and Research Libraries.* http://docushare.lib.rochester.edu/docushare/dsweb/View/Collection-4436.

Gluibizzi, Amanda. 2007. "The Aesthetics and Academics of Graphic Novels and Comics." *Art Documentation: Bulletin of the Art Libraries Society of North America* 26 (1): 28–30.

Hemmig, William S. 2008. "The Information-Seeking Behavior of Visual Artists: A Literature Review." *Journal of Documentation* 64 (3): 343–62.

Herriman, George. 1986. *Krazy Kat: The Comic Art of George Herriman.* Ed. Patrick McDonnell, Karen O'Connell and Georgia Riley de Havenon. New York: H. N. Abrams.

Hudson, Laura. December 22, 2008. "Comics in the classroom." *Publishers Weekly.* http://www.publishersweekly.com/article/CA6624192.html.

McCay, Winsor. 1997. *The Best of Little Nemo in Slumberland.* Ed. Richard Marschall. New York: Stewart, Tabori, & Chang.

McCloud, Scott. 1994. *Understanding Comics: The Invisible Art.* New York: HarperPerennial.

O'English, Lorena, J. Gregory Matthews, and Elizabeth Blakesley Lindsay. 2006. "Graphic Novels in Academic Libraries: From Maus to Manga and beyond." *Journal of Academic Librarianship* 32 (2): 173–82.

Rall, Ted. 2002. *To Afghanistan and Back: A Graphic Travelogue.* New York: Nantier, Beall, Minoustchine.

Saklofske, Jon. 2008. "Tales Worked in Blood and Bone: Words and Images as Scalpel and Suture in Graphic Narratives." *ImageTexT: Interdisciplinary Comics Studies* 4 (1). http://www.english.ufl.edu/imagetext/archives/v4_1/saklofske/.

Satrapi, Marjane. 2003. *Persepolis.* New York: Pantheon Books.

Spiegelman, Art. 1986. *Maus: A Survivor's Tale.* New York: Pantheon Books.

Versaci, Rocco. 2007. *This Book Contains Graphic Language: Comics as Literature.* New York: Continuum.

Ware, Chris. 2000. *Jimmy Corrigan: The Smartest Kid on Earth.* New York: Pantheon Books.

Williams, Kristian. March/April 2005. "The case for comics journalism." *Columbia Journalism Review* 2. http://www.cjr.org/.

So Many Options, So Little Money

Building a Selective Collection for the Academic Library

LIORAH ANNE GOLOMB

My library's collection of sequential narrative, graphic novels, book-length comics—call them what you will—exists, as I suspect do most collections of the kind, because of one librarian's personal passion. In my mid-sized academic library, I am that person. The passion was awakened by Bazooka Joe gum wrappers, *Mad* magazine, Archie and friends, Little Lulu, Spider-Man, and the Incredible Hulk. Those were gateway comics, as Art Spiegelman has called them (Spiegelman, 2009). From these the passion brought me to the Funny Pages section of *National Lampoon*, R. Crumb's *Zap*, and other titles I found in funny little shops in Greenwich Village. It lay dormant for a good long while until it was reawakened by Spiegelman's *Maus: A Survivor's Tale*, the book largely credited with spawning the current wave of interest in the particular form of storytelling that I will call, for the sake of convenience, the graphic novel.

Passion alone should never be the basis of collection building, and that is all the more true during bleak economic times. My personal tastes in literature are irrelevant when it comes to spending my library budget. What matters in any academic library is that the collection supports the educational needs of the faculty and students. A subject librarian, however, can influence teaching faculty by introducing them to material they did not even know existed, or by demonstrating the usefulness of material they might not have recognized as appropriate for their courses. As the Humanities Librarian, I had to demonstrate that a collection of graphic novels would be used not just for entertainment but for actual educational purposes.

Graphic novels carry one unfortunate bit of baggage that makes them a hard sell to many university faculty: they are, essentially, long comic books. While their value in courses on popular culture or graphic design may be evident, it is unclear to most instructors why they should include graphic novels on their syllabi. For example, responses to a query sent to faculty in my university's School of Education elicited a few negative responses. One professor of Curriculum and Instruction looked up "graphic novel" on Wikipedia and then replied that she does not use comic books in class.

This professor may find herself somewhat behind the curve: K–12 educators and public and school librarians have become increasingly more receptive to collecting and using comics and graphic novels. A survey of library literature on the subject through the 1990s, done by Allen Ellis and Doug Highsmith, shows how thinking towards the form has changed over the decades (Ellis and Highsmith, 2000). More recently, Steve Miller's book *Developing and Promoting Graphic Novel Collections* provides an excellent guide for middle and high school librarians seeking to collect graphic novels and convince teachers of their usefulness. Terry Thompson has written about using comics and graphic novels to teach reading comprehension to grades two through six (Thompson, 2008).

Far less attention has been paid to graphic novel collections in university libraries. Williams and Peterson (Williams and Peterson, 2009) explored graphic novel holdings in universities with teacher education and librarianship programs, but did not address university librarian holdings for undergraduate or graduate classroom use. A valuable overview on the subject of graphic novels in academic libraries was published by three librarians at Washington State University (O'English, Matthews, and Lindsay, 2006). The authors provide background about graphic novels, their value as leisure reading, and the challenges of cataloging them. They also supply several good ideas on promoting graphic novels to faculty and staff.

In 2007 Annette Haines published an article in comics form on developing a graphic novel or comic book collection at the University of Michigan (Haines, 2007). While Haines offers an interesting bullet-point outline in a fun-to-read format, she does not delve deeply into the subject.

This chapter builds on the research discussed above, particularly that done at Washington State University, and addresses the challenge of collecting in a strained economic environment in which each title purchased for a collection may be subject to scrutiny, and the value of literature in the form of comics is doubted by some faculty members.

Know the Product

The first step in establishing a graphic novel collection is to read them — lots of them. Become familiar enough with the material to be able to speak enthusiastically on the subject of graphic novels. Borrow some from the public library; take advantage of interlibrary loans; spend some time in the chain bookstores; or re-channel your book buying addiction.

As in any collecting area, reviews can be valuable tools. A fine starting point is *500 Essential Graphic Novels: The Ultimate Guide* (Kannenberg, 2008). Kannenberg divides graphic novels into ten categories: adventure, non-fiction, crime and mystery, fantasy, general fiction, horror, humor, science fiction, superheroes, and war. Each title is presented with its cover art, a plot summary, a brief review, and suggestions for further reading and related titles. Kannenberg is loose with his genre distinctions, in part no doubt to fit the "500 Essential" structure, but his titles overall are well chosen.

There are numerous blogs and websites that a librarian can use to evaluate and select titles. A few that update fairly regularly include: Diamond Comic Distributor's Bookshelf (*http://bookshelf.diamondcomics.com*), which is geared to librarians and breaks its reviews into age groups; the Daily Crosshatch (*http://thedailycrosshatch.com*), which focuses more on the independent comics realm; Comics Worth Reading (*http://comicsworthreading.com*), of note because it gives a woman's point of view; Thought Balloonists (*http://www.thought-balloonists.com*), written by academics; the Comics Reporter (*http://www.comicsreporter.com*); 1Journalista! (*http://www.tcj.com/journalista*), daily blog of the periodical *The Comics Journal*; and Read About Comics (*http://www.readaboutcomics.com*).

By now it will be apparent that graphic novels are a format, not a genre. Indeed, not all graphic novels are novels, and by at least one definition, none are. The *Oxford Dictionary of Literary Terms* begins its definition of "novel" with "Nearly always an extended fictional prose narrative" (Baldick, 2008). Miller identified biography, history, science, and art among nonfiction topics covered in graphic novels, and superhero, fantasy, science fiction, drama/real life, horror, and classics as subgenres of fiction (Miller, 2005). Other broad genres of the graphic "novel" include short stories, journalism, politics, philosophy, and memoir.

Some graphic novels were originally published as comic books, which adds to the number of book-length comics to consider. Whereas it is tricky to catalog and provide access to comic strips and comic books, many have been collected into a much more durable bound format and they too can now be considered for the shelves of academic libraries. For example, the *Sandman* series, written by Neil Gaiman and illustrated by a variety of artists, was created in a 75-issue series of 32-page comic books (Sanders, 2002). The format alone might preclude a library from adding *Sandman* to its collection. But the publisher, Vertigo (a DC imprint), reissued the series in ten trade paperback volumes and then again in a four volume hardcover set, so that format is no longer a barrier. It is likely that this trend will continue, as most recently evidenced by Vertical's current project of releasing an English translation of Osamu Tezuka's *Black Jack* stories in 17 book-length volumes.

Many comic strips that originally appeared in daily and Sunday newspapers have also been gathered into books, among them Charles Shulz's *Peanuts*, George Herriman's *Krazy Cat*, Hal Foster's *Prince Valiant*, Garry Trudeau's *Doonesbury*, Scott Adam's *Dilbert*, and Bill Watterson's *Calvin and Hobbes*, to name only a very few. These are by no stretch of the definition "graphic novels," though a solid argument could be made for including them in an academic library on the grounds of their valuable insight into the culture. Indeed, a look at the ComicsResearch.org website (*http://www.comicsresearch.org/ComicsDissertations.html*) reveals quite a number of doctoral disserations and masters theses on sequential narrative of all kinds, including newspaper strips. In a different economic climate I would be thrilled to add some of this work to my library's collection.

However, the current climate requires us to make choices. There are various ways to parcel out the world of graphic novels that a librarian could use in determining how to get started building a collection. Here are some possible limiters:

Works that were created by a single person. It has been suggested that "the more 'pure' graphic novels are those with art and text by the same person" (Lanham, 2004). There are dozens of writer-artist creators including Art Spiegelman, Chris Ware, Charles Burns, Megan Kelso, Marjane Satrapi, R. Crumb, Will Eisner, Jessica Abel, Gilberto Hernandez, Jaime Hernandez, Adrian Tomine, Craig Thompson, Eddie Campbell, Yoshihiro Tatsumi, Gabrielle Bell, and many, many others. However, some of the most notable graphic novel creators would be excluded in this strategy, including Alan Moore, Neil Gaiman, and Harvey Pekar.

Time period. You may want to forgo some of the "classics" in favor of building a collection that goes back only a few years but keeps current.

Nationality, gender, or ethnicity of creator(s). Most graphic novels are written by white men, so this can be very limiting if you're looking to represent a different population. However, a little digging will yield some fine results, including work by Jaime and Gilbert Hernandez, Adrian Tomine, Gene Luen Yang, Jessica Abel, Rutu Modan, Toufic el Rassi, Yoshihiro Tatsumi, and Marjane Satrapi. An excellent collection of reviews of graphic novels by women has been assembled by Johanna Draper Carlson and can be found at *http://comicsworthreading.com/comics-by-women*.

Discipline. Gear your collection towards areas such as gender and sexuality studies, health, or history. Alison Bechdel's *Fun Home* (2006) and Howard Cruse's *Stuck Rubber Baby* (1995) are two excellent works on homosexuality. The graphic novel format has been used effectively to discuss epilepsy (*Epileptic* by David B, 2006), spina bifida (*The Spiral Cage* by Al Davison, 2003), and cancer (*Our Cancer Year* by Harvey Pekar, Joyce Brabant, and Frank Stack, 1994; *Mom's Cancer* by Brian Fies, 2006; *Cancer Made Me a Shallower Person* by Miriam Engelberg, 2006; and Marisa Acocella Marchetto's *Cancer Vixen*, 2006). And a number of titles treat historical subjects, including the multi-volume *Charley's War* by Pat Mills and Joe Colquhoun (2005–07) and *Laika* by Nick Abadzis (2007).

Realistic and mostly realistic fiction with something to say about society, culture, or the human condition. I comfortably place Charles Burns's *Black Hole* (2005) into this category in spite of characters who sprout tails or shed their skins because it captures the essence of the high school experience with amazing accuracy. I would also include Alan Moore and Dave Gibbons's *Watchmen* (1986), Chris Ware's *Jimmy Corrigan: The Smartest Kid on Earth* (2000), Daniel Clowes's *Ghost World* (1998), and Kim Deitch's *The Boulevard of Broken Dreams* (2002), for example.

Journalism and documentary. The most prominent creator of this type of graphic novel is Joe Sacco, winner of the 1996 American Book Award for *Palestine* (2001). Peter Kuper's travelogue, *Comics Trips* (1992), provides another example.

Autobiography and memoir. The essentials, it almost need not be said, are the two volumes of Art Spiegelman's *Maus* (1986, 1991) and the two volumes of Marjane Satrapi's *Perspepolis* (2003, 2004). Craig Thompson's *Blankets* (2005), slightly less well-known, also fits nicely in this category.

Biography. Among those notables whose lives have received the graphic novel treatment are Martin Luther King, Jr. (Ho Che Anderson, 2005), Malcolm X (Andrew J. Helfer and Randy DuBurke, 2006), Che Guevara (Spain Rodriguez, 2008), Isadora Duncan (Sabrina Jones, 2008), and J. Edgar Hoover (Rick Geary, 2008).

Stories of childhood. There is overlap between this category and several of the preceding ones, but it's worth including because there are so many fine titles that fit this description one could make it a focus of its own. Among the best of those not mentioned above: *Skyscrapers of the Midwest* by Joshua W. Cotter (2008), *The Tragical Comedy or Comical Tragedy of Mr. Punch* by Neil Gaiman and Dave McKean (1995), and *A Child's Life and Other Stories* by Phoebe Gloeckner (rev. ed. 2000).

Adaptations. It might be particularly difficult to justify purchasing adaptations because faculty would generally, and understandably, prefer their students read Stevenson's *Dr. Jekyll and Mr. Hyde* or Shakepeare's *King Lear*, say, than the comic book versions. However, some adaptations present material in a way that enhances information as well as making it more accessible. *The 9/11 Report: A Graphic Adaptation* by Sid Jacobson and Ernie Colón (2006) is one such example. The visual format allows for a parallel timeline that helps the reader understand the events of that September morning.

Fantasy, horror, science fiction. This category runs the gamut from Jeff Smith's *Bone* books to Joss Whedon's continuation of the television series *Buffy the Vampire Slayer* and includes, of course, all the favorite superheroes and villains.

My Experience

I confess I began with a definite idea of what I wanted to collect: a category I refer to as "personal history." By my definition, these included memoirs of "ordinary" people and might be the creator's own story (as is the case in *Persepolis*) or a story related to the creator (as in the first volume of *Maus*). But I also include in this category stories that I've classed above as realistic and mostly realistic fiction. My sense is that these types of graphic novel would have the greatest appeal to faculty in the Humanities; if my institution had strong programs in graphic design or popular culture, I might have focused on a different genre.

The graphic novels I select for my library typically fit within certain parameters. They are drawn and written by the same person — though some "must-haves" such as the above-mentioned *American Splendor* and *The Tragical Comedy or Comical Tragedy of Mr. Punch* are too exquisite, important, or popular to be ignored. I tend to like stories that tell of a culture outside the mainstream, and that's a pretty roomy area for a mid-sized university library located in the center of the United States. Conversely, I also purchase stories that reflect middle–American experience, such as *Ghost World* and *Skyscrapers of the Midwest*. Coming of age stories, especially those dealing with sexuality, are another favorite genre, as are Joe Sacco's war correspondences.

Having determined what I wanted to collect, I set about getting support from the faculty. I began by looking at recent course descriptions and identifying instructors who seemed likely to either use or be amenable to using graphic novels in the classroom. I looked for courses in popular history, seminars on the novel, creative writing classes, special topics, and faculty who tend to include "outsider" writings on their syllabi. I found candidates in departments such as English, History, Political Science, and Women's Studies. I then contacted those instructors by phone or email and asked them whether they had ever used graphic novels in their classes. Some had; others were open to the idea. One member of the English Department told me that she uses both volumes of *Persepolis* in her multicultural studies class and another has used Alan Moore and Kevin O'Neill's *The Black Dossier* (2008), part of the *League of Extraordinary Gentlemen* series, in two separate courses. A history professor emailed that he discusses the "Marvel/DC variety" of comic books in his popular culture class, but felt it would be useful to branch out.

For further support, I contacted the collection development administrator of my city's public library (since part of my university's mission is service to the community). She was enthusiastic about having a collection of personal history graphic novels available locally, especially since she could not collect such books with her own budget.

I also looked at the circulation of the few graphic novels that we already had in our collection, and saw that they had circulated and been loaned to other libraries. This helped to confirm that there was interest in the format, though admittedly, it does not demonstrate usage for academic purposes.

I wanted to build a collection that was not duplicated by libraries all over the state, and to that end, I used WorldCat to check the holdings of other libraries in the region. Two other universities in the state have sizeable graphic novel collections, but I was still able to identify about 60 titles that I wanted to purchase. Some were not owned by any other library in the region. In other cases, only one or two copies were owned, or the title was so important that I felt we ought to have our own copy.

In 2007, armed with the evidence I'd collected, I applied for a grant. But that year the granting body changed its distribution policy and I did not receive the grant. However, my proposal convinced the head of collection development at my library that my desire to build the graphic novel was well-founded, and she gave me the funding I'd requested. Table 12.1 shows my October 2007 initial purchase of 48 titles along with their checkout rates as of June 8, 2009. These titles were all purchased on Amazon.com and came to roughly $600.00.

Table 12.1: Forty-eight titles purchased with June 8, 2009, checkouts

Title	Checkouts	Title	Checkouts
B, David. *Epileptic*. Pantheon, 2006.	3	Larcenet, Manu. *Ordinary Victories.* ComicsLit, 2005.	1
Blanchet, Pascal. *White Rapids*. Drawn and Quarterly, 2007.	1	Lemelman, Martin. *Mendel's Daughter: A Memoir*. Free Press, 2006.	0
Briggs, Raymond. *Ethel & Ernest: A True Story*. Pantheon, 2001.	1	Max. *Bardin the Superrealist*. Fantagraphics, 2006.	2
_____. *When the Wind Blows*. New Ed. Penguin, 1988.	0	Mccloud, Scott. *Understanding Comics: The Invisible Art*. Harper Paperbacks, 1994.	3
_____. *Alec: The King Canute Crowd*. 1st ed. Top Shelf Productions, 2000.	1	Modan, Rutu. *Exit Wounds*. Drawn and Quarterly, 2007.	5
_____. *Alec: Three Piece Suit*. Top Shelf Productions, 2001.	1	Moon, Fabio, and Gabriel Ba. *De: Tales*. Dark Horse, 2006.	2
_____. *The Black Diamond Detective Agency*. First Second, 2007.	2	*Mr. Punch : The Tragical Comedy or Comical Tragedy*. Vertigo/DC Comics, 1994.	2
_____. *The Fate of the Artist*. First Second, 2006.	1	Nakazawa, Keiji. *Barefoot Gen Volume One: A Cartoon Story of Hiroshima*. Last Gasp, 2004.	2
Campbell, Eddie, and Eddie Campbell. *Alec: After the Snooter*. Top Shelf Productions, 2002.	0	_____. *Barefoot Gen Volume Two: The Day After*. Last Gasp, 2004.	2
Crumb, Aline Kominsky. *Need More Love: A Graphic Memoir*. M Q Publications, 2007.	2	Nakazawa, Keiji, and Art Spiegelman. *Barefoot Gen Volume Three: Life After the Bomb*. Last Gasp, 2005.	3
Deitch, Kim. *Alias the Cat*. Pantheon, 2007.	1	_____. *Barefoot Gen Volume Four: Out of the Ashes*. Last Gasp, 2005.	2
_____. *The Boulevard of Broken Dreams*. Pantheon, 2002.	1	Pekar, Harvey. *The Quitter*. Vertigo, 2006.	1
Delisle, Guy. *Pyongyang: A Journey in North Korea*. Drawn and Quarterly, 2005.	2	Rassi, Toufic El. *Arab in America: A True Story of Growing Up in America*. Last Gasp, 2007.	3
Eisenstein, Bernice. *I Was a Child of Holocaust Survivors*. Riverhead Books, 2006.	0	Sacco, Joe. *Palestine*. Jonathan Cape, 2003.	2
Eisner, Will. *Last Day in Vietnam: A Memory*. Milwaukie, Or: Dark Horse Comics, 2000.	4	_____. *The Fixer*. Jonathan Cape, 2004.	0
Engelberg, Miriam. *Cancer Made Me a Shallower Person: A Memoir in Comics*. Harper, 2006.	0		

Title	Checkouts	Title	Checkouts
Gloeckner, Phoebe. *Child's Life and Other Stories*. Revised. Frog, Ltd., 2000.	1	_____. *War's End: Profiles from Bosnia 1995–1996*. Drawn and Quarterly, 2005.	1
Huizenga, Kevin. *Curses*. Drawn and Quarterly, 2006.	3	Sacco, Joe. *Safe Area Gorazde: The War in Eastern Bosnia 1992–1995*. Fantagraphics Books, 2002.	2
Katchor, Ben. *Julius Knipl, Real Estate Photographer: The Beauty Supply District*. Pantheon, 2003.	0	Satrapi, Marjane. *Chicken with Plums*. Pantheon, 2006.	1
_____. *The Jew of New York*. Pantheon, 2000.	0	_____. *Embroideries*. Pantheon, 2006.	2
Katchor, Ben, and Michael Chabon. *Julius Knipl, Real Estate Photographer: Stories*. Little, Brown and Company, 1996.	1	Spiegelman, Art. *Maus II: A Survivor's Tale: And Here My Troubles Began*. Pantheon, 1992.	2
Kelso, Megan. *The Squirrel Mother*. Fantagraphics, 2006.	3	Tatsumi, Yoshihiro. *Abandon the Old in Tokyo*. Drawn and Quarterly, 2006.	2
Kuper, Peter. *Comics Trips*. Nantier Beall Minoustchine Publishing, 1992.	1	_____. *The Push Man and Other Stories*. Drawn and Quarterly, 2005.	2
_____. *Stop Forgetting to Remember: The Autobiography of Walter Kurtz*. Crown, 2007.	0	Tomine, Adrian. *Shortcomings*. Drawn and Quarterly, 2007.	4

The first volume of *Maus* and the two volumes of *Persepolis* were already in the library's collection. *Maus: My Father Bleeds History* has circulated 14 times as of this writing, and the two volumes of *Persepolis* have each circulated 11 times.

Faculty Use and Experience: Two Cases and an Assignment

I communicated at some length with two professors from my university's English Department regarding their use of graphic novels in their classes. Even though one response refers to a class taught several years ago, it is interesting to note that in both cases, then and now, there was resistance to the assigned works, but classroom discussion was lively.

Back in 2003, Kerry Jones used the first volume of *Maus: A Survivor's Tale* in a 300-level course on American Multicultural Literature, and she is interested in teaching it again now that the graphic novel format is more widely accepted. I asked her why she chose the material, what her teaching objectives were and whether she felt he achieved them, and how the students reacted to being assigned a "comic book." Her response was:

> The class was primarily discussion-based, and then students had the opportunity to explore their thoughts further on their take-home exams. I remember being surprised because I expected more students to enjoy it than they actually did. Many students felt a lot of distance between the story itself and the way Spiegelman tells it (one student told me she hated it, another couldn't wait to go out and buy *Maus II*). Strangely, it seems more of the males enjoyed it than the females. But this was six years ago, so it would be interesting to teach it again and see what the reaction would be. ... Spiegelman chose such an intriguing way to tell his father's story, as well as the relationship he had with his father. It was something different, and it gave us the opportunity to discuss the blurring of different artistic genres. ... I wanted them to see and read something most of them hadn't encountered before. That was accomplished, and whether they enjoyed the format or not, the class discussions went very well.

More students were resistant to reading a comic book than I expected. Those who disliked it from the beginning didn't really change their views—maybe one or two, but that's not many, and I recall that I tried very hard. The common argument was that *Maus* wasn't literature. What to do with *Maus* and similar works was something we came back to again and again [Jones, 2009].

Dr. Darren DeFrain has used both volumes of *Maus* in a class on War Literature; more recently, he used Moore and O'Neill's *The Black Dossier* in a 500-level Contemporary Literature course and is planning to use it again in a course on Narrative. I asked him the same questions that I asked Professor Jones. His response is regarding the *The Black Dossier*.

It is absolutely nuts. [The objective was] to discuss visual narrative and rhetoric and the rise in their influence on the novel. Also, to consider the newer form as literature.... We had great discussions of the work. This book is a bit pornographic in places, but even my evangelical students came around to appreciating it by the end of the semester. It is a real tour de force and a good introduction for more advanced students to the concepts and conceits of literary fiction and pretty much any literary theory of the last 100 years you'd care to throw at it [DeFrain, 2009].

A third professor from the English Department, Dr. Kimberly Engber, shared with me an assignment she gave to a class in Exploring Literature. The assignment is in two parts. First, the students participated in a library scavenger hunt revolving around the first volume of *Persepolis* (both volumes were used in the class). Among the tasks were to find a scholarly article on Marjane Satrapi or *Persepolis*, find a definition for "graphic novel," and compare images from another graphic novel to certain of those in *Persepolis*, with an eye to panel composition, drawing style, and the emotional impact of the drawings. The second part of the assignment takes a more traditional approach to the work as literature, asking students to briefly respond to questions about a chapter in *Persepolis*.

There are other instructors at my university who teach with graphic novels, but more might do so with a little persuading. How to increase faculty use of graphic novels?

Provide Useful Information

Instructors who continue to associate graphic novels with children's comic books might be interested to learn that professors of History, English, Area Studies, Womens Studies, and Communications are teaching graphic novels at such revered institutions as Columbia, Yale, New York University, Stanford, and Penn State. Often, their syllabi and course descriptions are available on the web. Articles in peer-reviewed journals and chapters in scholarly books further raise the respectability factor of graphic novels. An entire issue of *Modern Fiction Studies* was devoted to sequential narrative in 2006. Articles also have appeared in *PMLA*, *Women's Studies Quarterly*, *The Missouri Review*, *The Harvard Review*, *Twentieth-Century Literature*, and *The English Journal*.

I wanted faculty at my institution to know about these classes, and to know that our library has the resources they would need to incorporate graphic novels into their teaching, too. To that end, I prepared a small packet of information to distribute to selected faculty members. It is important to keep the packet small and focused; no one has the time to sift through lengthy articles. Included in the packet are a brief cover letter (2 pages); a bibliography of titles owned by the library, including call numbers and arranged by theme (4 pages); a separate bibliography of recommended reading from scholarly journals (1 page);

course descriptions in various areas found on the web (10 pages); and my business card. The cover letter describes the history of the collection at my institution, the difference between a graphic novel and a comic book, themes in graphic novels, and a few sentences on their value in the classroom. I have received positive feedback from faculty, but more time is needed to gauge the effectiveness of the packet.

Conclusion

Librarians are partners with teaching faculty in the education of our students. One of our most important roles in this partnership is the selection of quality resources with enduring value. The growth in popularity of the sequential narrative format means that more graphic novels are being published, but they are not all worth adding to your library's collection. As librarians, we can find and promote quality work for the benefit of our liaison faculty and students, and even if we cannot purchase every graphic novel we would like, they are relatively inexpensive. Start small, get feedback, and grow the collection as your budget permits.

You will not be able to convince everyone to consider using graphic novels in their classes. To put things in perspective: the modern novel is only 400 years old, and there was a time not long ago when novels were not considered a form worthy of academic attention. Television and movies are studied in universities everywhere, and it is only a matter of time before the graphic novel gains the same degree of acceptance.

References

Abadzis, Nick. 2007. *Laika*. New York: First Second.

Anderson, Ho. 2005. *King: A Comic Book Biography*. Seattle WA: Fantagraphics.

Baldick, Chris. 2008. *The Oxford Dictionary of Literary Terms*. Oxford Reference Online. Oxford University Press. *http://www.oxfordreference.com/views/ENTRY.html?subview=Main&entry=t56.e788* .

B[eauchard], David. 2006. *Epileptic*. New York: Pantheon.

Bechdel, Alison. 2007. *Fun Home: A Family Tragicomic*. Boston: Mariner Books.

Burns, Charles. 2005. *Black Hole*. New York: Pantheon Books.

Clowes, Daniel. 1998. *Ghost World*. Seattle, WA: Fantagraphics Books.

Cotter, Joshua. 2008. *Skyscrapers of the Midwest*. Richmond, VA: Adhouse Books.

Cruse, Howard. 1995. *Stuck Rubber Baby*. New York: Paradox Press.

Davison, Al. 2003. *The Spiral Cage*. Los Angeles: Active Images.

DeFrain, Darren. 2009. E-mail of April 13.

Deitch, Kim. 2002. *The Boulevard of Broken Dreams*. New York: Pantheon.

Drechsler, Debbie. 1996. *Daddy's Girl: Comics*. Seattle, WA: Fantagraphics Books.

Eisner, Will. 1985. *Comics and Sequential Art*. Expanded Edition. Tamarac, FL: Poorhouse Press.

Ellis, Allen, and Doug Highsmith. 2000. "About Face: Comic Books in Library Literature." *Serials Review* 26, no. 2: 21–42.

Engelberg, Miriam. 2006. *Cancer Made Me a Shallower Person: A Memoir in Comics*. New York: Harper Paperbacks.

Fies, Brian. 2006. *Mom's Cancer*. New York: Abrams ComicArts.

Gaiman, Neil. 2006–08. *The Absolute Sandman*, Vols. 1–4. New York: Vertigo.

_____. 1995. *The Tragical Comedy or Comical Tragedy of Mr. Punch : A Romance*. New York: Vertigo.

Geary, Rick. 2008. *J. Edgar Hoover: A Graphic Biography*. New York: Hill and Wang.

Gloeckner, Phoebe. 2000. *A Child's Life and Other Stories*. Revised. Berkeley: Frog, Ltd.

Haines, Annette. Spring 2007. "Strategies for Developing a Graphic Novel/Comic Book Collection." *Art Documentation* 26, no. 1: 31–36.

Helfer, Andrew. 2006. *Malcolm X: A Graphic Biography*. New York: Hill and Wang.

Jacobson, Sidney and National Commission on Terrorist Attacks upon the United States. 2006. *The 9/11 Report: A Graphic Adaptation*. New York: Hill and Wang.

Jones, Kerry. 2009. E-mail of April 14.

Jones, Sabrina. 2008. *Isadora Duncan: A Graphic Biography*. New York: Hill and Wang.

Kannenberg, Gene. 2008. *500 Essential Graphic Novels: The Ultimate Guide*. New York: Collins Design.

Kuper, Peter. 1992. *Comics Trips*. Northampton, MA: Nantier Beall Minoustchine Publishing.

Lanham, Fritz. August 29, 2004. From Pulp to Pulitzer: How the Underground Comic Found Its Way to the Mainstream. *The Houston Chronicle*.

Marchetto, Marisa Acocella. 2006. *Cancer Vixen: A True Story*. New York: Knopf.

McCloud, Scott. 1994. *Understanding Comics: The Invisible Art*. New York: HarperPerennial.

Miller, Steve. 2005. *Developing and Promoting Graphic Novel Collections. Teens @ the Library*. New York: Neal-Schuman Publishers.

Mills, Pat. 2005a. *Charley's War: 2 June–1 August 1916*. London: Titan Books.

_____. 2005b. *Charley's War: 1 August–17 October 1916*. London: Titan Books.

_____. 2006. *Charley's War: 17 October 1916–21 February 1917*. London: Titan Books.

_____. 2007. *Charley's War: Blue's Story*. London: Titan Books.

_____. 2008. *Charley's War: Return to the Front*. London: Titan Books.

Moore, Alan. 2008. *The League of Extraordinary Gentlemen: Black Dossier*. La Jolla CA: America's Best Comics.

_____. 1987. *Watchmen*. New York: DC Comics Inc.

O'English, Lorena, J. Gregory Matthews, and Elizabeth Blakesley Lindsay. 2006. "Graphic Novels in Academic Libraries: From Maus to Manga and Beyond." *The Journal of Academic Librarianship* 32, no. 2: 173–82.

Pekar, Harvey. 2003. *American Splendor and More American Splendor*. New York: Ballantine Books.

Pekar, Harvey, and Joyce Brabner. 1994. *Our Cancer Year*. New York: Four Walls Eight Windows.

Rodriguez, Spain. 2008. *Che: A Graphic Biography*. London and New York: Verso.

Sacco, Joe. 2001. *Palestine*. Seattle, WA: Fantagraphic Books.

Sanders, Joe. 2002. "Neil Gaiman." In *British Fantasy and Science-Fiction Writers Since 1960*. Darren Harris-Fain, ed. *Dictionary of Literary Biography* Vol. 261. Detroit: Gale Group.

Satrapi, Marjane. 2003. *Persepolis*. New York: Pantheon Books.

_____. 2004. *Persepolis 2: The Story of a Return*. New York: Pantheon Books.

Spiegelman, Art. 2009. "History of Comix 101." Presented at the American Library Association Midwinter Meeting, January 25, Denver, CO.

_____. 1986. *Maus I: A Survivor's Tale: My Father Bleeds History*. New York: Pantheon Books.

_____. 1991. *Maus II: A Survivor's Tale: And Here My Troubles Began*. New York: Pantheon Books.

Tezuka, Osamu. 2008–09. *Black Jack*, Vols. 1–5. New York: Vertical.

Thompson, Craig. 2003. *Blankets: an Illustrated Novel*. Marietta, GA: Top Shelf.

Thompson, Terry. 2008. *Adventures in Graphica: Using Comics and Graphic Novels to Teach Comprehension, 2–6*. Portland, ME: Stenhouse Publishers.

Ware, Chris. 2000. *Jimmy Corrigan: The Smartest Kid on Earth*. New York: Pantheon Books.

Williams, Virginia Kay, and Damen V. Peterson. July 2009. "Graphic Novels in Libraries Supporting Teacher Education and Librarianship Programs." *Library Resources & Technical Services* 53, no. 3: 169–176.

13

The Spinner Rack in the Big Red and Ivory Tower

Establishing a Comics and Graphic Novels Collection at the University of Nebraska–Lincoln

RICHARD GRAHAM

Summary

The rising prominence of multi-disciplinary academic fields and interest in alternative texts within traditional areas has turned serious critical attention and scholarship toward comics and graphic novels. Many research libraries have only just begun to collect these materials not only to support these growing research interests, but also as a means of appealing to more patrons as they rethink the concept of elitist culture.

This article discusses the potential impediments to growing a graphic novel/comics collection specific to the academic environment, and the strategies and resources adopted at the University of Nebraska–Lincoln (UN-L) to establish a successful and popular collection. Other academic libraries and librarians have blazed a trail in this area, and their diverse holdings and accomplishments are noted throughout.

In describing the process of building such a collection and listing collection development resources, it is hoped other academic libraries will also be successful in implementing an appropriate representation of the comics medium within their own collections. An annotated core list of titles with circulation statistics is provided as a suggested starting list for beginning acquisitions.

In 2005, Doug Highsmith delivered a paper, titled "Comic Books Built to Last: A Survey of Academic Library Holdings of Graphic Novels and Hardcover Comic Book Collections, A Preliminary Report" at the Popular Culture Association conference, in San Diego. It described his hunt through OCLC's WorldCat database to identify widely held graphic novels and compare the holdings of selected titles. His aim was to measure the graphic novels' presence in academic library collections, determine the interest level for supporting such a collection, and question which titles should be "deemed worth adding" (Highsmith, 2005: 4).

In comparing the University of Nebraska–Lincoln Libraries holdings to those listed titles, only four matched: Art Spiegelman's holocaust memoirs *Maus I* and *Maus II*, Chris Ware's *Jimmy Corrigan's the Smartest Kid on Earth*, and Joe Sacco's *Palestine*. An additional search in the Libraries catalog for materials listed under the LC subject heading *Comic books, strips, etc.* yielded a Spanish-language version of a Peanuts digest and an audio record (LP) from 1955 that included a social critique of comics by John Mason Brown and a rebuttal by cartoonist Al Capp. It became apparent that UN-L Libraries did not include graphic novels or other versions of the comics medium as a substantial part of its collection.

A question that immediately emerged was, "*Should* there be a greater presence of comics and graphic novels at the University of Nebraska?" To someone who is well-versed in the genres of graphic novels and comics, the benefits from an increased presence seem clear: increased circulation, as was discovered in Lubbock, Texas (Weiner, 2001); encouragement of verbal literacy and visual literacy which earlier librarians had pointed out (Scott, 1990); and a greater appeal to patrons who are visual learners (Simmons, 2003). By actively collecting the comics medium, the library could also progress towards settling what Barbara Moran described as the "long and uneasy relationship between popular culture and libraries" (Moran, 1992: 3). Bridging this gap would also serve to recognize previously excluded authors and artists who have strong connections to the University itself.

Though it was quickly concluded that there should indeed be a larger selection of comics and graphic novels, it was imperative to discover what was preventing UN-L (and other academic libraries) from collecting these types of materials. Are decisions based on format and possible technical issues that arise from describing or cataloging items? Dismissive attitudes regarding content (controversial subject matter or low-brow popular culture)? Or a lack of curricular justification? Exploring these issues and following the path already established by other libraries and librarians provided a framework to implement a growing and successful comics collection that serves the academic needs of the University of Nebraska and participates in forming the emerging canon of graphic novels.

There certainly are technical challenges in acquiring comics and graphic novels. Gary Markham discovered these challenges when Portland State alumnus Mike Richardson, founder and president of Dark Horse Comics, donated copies of all past and future publications generated by Dark Horse (Markham, 2009). These publications include individual comic books, reprints, and anthologies. Lorena O'English and her colleagues discuss at great length the difficulties of classifying and cataloging these types of items. They point out numerous examples of inconsistencies found in the various volumes and editions of graphic novels that can affect shelf placement and call number assignments (O'English, Mathews, Blakesly, 2006). Part of this problem resides in the very definition of the term "graphic novel."

Will Eisner described graphic novels as complete narratives told in the comics format, published as a book with generally between 50 and 200 pages (Eisner, 1994). Eisner coined the term "graphic novel" in an attempt to differentiate the artistic seriousness found in his publication, *A Contract with God, and Other Tenement Stories,* published in 1978, with the "pulp" or low-brow stories found in daily strips or comic books. Today, however, the term graphic novel is used much more loosely. Some may be collections of comic books published serially, but containing just one story arc, while others are sequential novels, à la Charles Dickens. Graphic novels may also be anthologies. Generally, the term graphic novel can cover all these variations, and this complexity adds to the classification and cataloging process. Format may be the most complex issue because of these anthologies, monographs, folios, DVD-ROMs (e.g., the GIT Corp's .pdf collections of the Fantastic Four, X-Men, Avengers, and Spider-Man) and even microfiche (e.g., the Golden Age titles put out by Micro-Color International)!

Despite the many problems these materials may pose, the librarians at Washington State University have found a coping strategy worth remembering: "Consistency. Although many graphic novels are issued in series consisting of uniquely titled volumes, the cataloging staff has identified very little cataloging copy that includes series notes which allow users to conduct title searches at the series level. Adding, say, a 440 field would make these records more useable and make indexing throughout the catalog more consistent" (O'English, Mathews, and Blakesly, 2006 : 177).

Another obstacle for academic libraries may be attitudes toward the readers and content traditionally associated with comics. Despite increased sales among increasingly diverse demographics (Brown, 1997), academic librarians may be unwilling to accept the idea that comics can transcend juvenile interests and have an appeal beyond an audience of young adults. Academic libraries may be concerned that a collection of comics would appeal only to high school boys and lead to a host problem associated with such a patron-type (e.g., an increase in vandalism, book theft, disruption). An amusing parallel is that more than one hundred years ago, Henry James, in his book *Art of Fiction,* was forced to defend the Victorian novel as a legitimate form of artistic expression because it, too, was judged solely by its primary audience (James, 1884).

Librarians may hesitate to include graphic novels because they believe their addition will invite more challenges and controversy to the library, including the demand to know why student fees or tax dollars were spent on such "trash." We have early comics-critics, including Frederic Wertham and acolytes such as John Mason Brown, to thank for the pervasive attitude that comics corrupt our young. In a speech in 1948, Brown proclaimed, "The comic book is the marijuana of the nursery, the bane of the bassinet, the horror of the home, the curse of the kids and a threat to the future" (Brown, 1955), and that idea still lingers on. David Hajdu's book *The Ten-Cent Plague* is an excellent retelling of the comics inquisition in the United States during the 1950s which was brought about out of the concern for their content. This movement had the lasting effect of decimating the comics industry, and led to the installation of the Comics Code Authority (Hajdu, 2008). Amy Nyberg described the Comics Code as an attempt at self-censorship by the industry that ultimately reduced the medium, primarily, to heroic adventure stories aimed at adolescent boys (Nyberg, 1998). The narrowing and culling of genres that followed the code's enforcement only perpetuated the common misconception that comics were (and are) merely simple-minded superhero stories. This resulted in comics "being greeted with disdain and outright hostility by many of the (largely self-appointed) arbiters of American cultural tastes and values. Numbered among these anti-comic book cultural elitists were many members of the library community" (Ellis and Highsmith, 2000; 39).

Later critics, including Alan Bloom, have condemned comic books as a popular-culture phenomenon without any legitimate history or established canon. In this argument, a supposed lack of authoritative presence renders comics insignificant. This stems from the impression that comics are formulaic and disposable for having been written by anonymous writers (Brown, 1997). It may have been hoped that these misconceptions were shattered (as James Sturm pointed out in the *Chronicle of Higher Education*) with the publication of *Maus I* in 1986, and thoroughly demolished when *Maus II* won the Pulitzer in 1992.

Unfortunately, many academic libraries have viewed *Maus* as an exception, and not an example of how the medium had grown (Sturm, 2002: B14).

Conversely, the cultural and critical history of comics and the industry features several well-known thinkers and scholars who have argued for the medium's validity, including Leslie Fiedler, Umberto Eco, and Marshall McLuhan, who all rejected the "elitist" dismissal of comics. Their essays challenged moralists and cultural decliners who feared popular culture, or saw nothing meaningful in it, and thereby laid the groundwork for contemporary cultural studies. (Heer and Worcester, 2004). In *Arguing Comics: Literary Masters on a Popular Medium*, edited by Jeet Heer and Kent Worcester, the traditional superhero is championed through the collected essays that describe superhero tales as allegories to modern life that provide a means of escape for readers. Others believe that superheroes can be compared to archetypal figures found in mythology and other narratives (Heer and Worcester, 2004).

To understand and advocate the role comics and graphic novels can play in academic libraries, librarians will need to become acquainted with how diverse and complex the medium can be. An important book for librarians considering the challenges and presence of comics in libraries is Randall Scott's *Comics Librarianship: a Handbook* (1990). Though nearly two decades old, many subjects covered in this book are pertinent, especially in the chapter entitled "Being the Comics Expert." Scott describes a librarian's need for responsibility in properly discussing, educating, and articulating the reasons and benefits for building and maintaining a comic book collection.

By being aware of the historical and possible cultural bias against comics, a librarian is better able to fend off questions of their value or placement in academic libraries. Promoting or recommending complex works to colleagues can help dispel many of these notions. Titles such as Joe Sacco's *Palestine* (a work of nonfiction about the Israeli occupation) with an introduction by Marjane Satrapi (author of *Persepolis*, which shows how an intensely personal comic-memoir can illuminate a history of a nation) or Edward Said (a leading intellectual on the Middle East crisis) demonstrate firsthand how comics can be understood as not merely pulp entertainment but as appropriate materials deserving.

If it seems clear that graphic novels should be welcomed because of their long-term neglect and unfair characterizations by libraries, suspicion and misapprehensions may still need to be dispelled. Allen Ellis' and Doug Highsmith's survey of professional library literature shows an interesting history of the resistance to legitimizing comics within libraries as an attempt to define and protect elitist culture (Ellis and Highsmith, 2000).

Perhaps the strongest justification an academic librarian can make for including certain materials is by proclaiming that material's support of the curriculum. Early on, librarians were accomplices in vilifying comics by proclaiming them a distraction from better reading, which helped drive them out of education as an enemy of literacy. It was not until the 1970s and 1980s that comics were brought back into the classroom, in efforts such as Richard W. Campbell's fourth-grade reading program and Robert Schoof's language-arts class (Koenke, 1981). Those using comics in their curriculum probably breathed a sigh of relief when Art Spiegelman's *Maus* won the Pulitzer Prize in 1992, because it was a very public example of how sophisticated the medium had become.

Slowly over the next decade, comics began gaining ground in the world of higher education as well, despite the continued rejection by school and academic libraries. Leslie Bussert writes, "Many in the fields of history, sociology, and arts and literature realize the unique and valuable insight inherent in studying comic books and graphic novels" (Bussert,

2005: 103). Comics and graphic novels have found their way into classes through educators such as University of Minnesota physics professor James Kakalios. Dr. Kakalios has received national media attention for his popular introductory physics course "Science in Comic Books," in which he uses excerpts and panels from comics and graphic novels that depict or discuss science concepts (Kakalios, 2002).

Scott McCloud's *Understanding Comics* is a popular graphic novel that is taught in Meghan Dougherty's Basic Concepts of New Media course at the University of Washington, and is a principal text in both the New School's Foundations of Media Design class and Douglas Rushkoff's Post Linear Narrative Lab at NYU.

At the University of Nebraska–Lincoln, Professor Rose Holz uses *Stuck Rubber Baby*, a graphic novel set in the South in the early 1960s, with themes of homophobia, racism, and gay subculture, in her History of Sexuality class. She also includes the documentary *Crumb*, Terry Zwigoff's 1994 film about the noted underground artist, to compare the different attitudes each artist holds. Several English courses at UN-L use graphic novels as "literature" texts as well. Alan Moore's masterful deconstructionist/revisionist superhero tale *Watchmen* is popular in introductory classes, as is Daniel Clowes' *David Boring*, a symbol-laced, semi-autobiographical metatext, and Marjane Satrapi's *Persepolis*, with its themes of identity and history. Art classes, such as Bill Schaffer's Seminar in Illustration, examine the influence of comics on graphic design, with many reserve readings of Chris Ware's *Jimmy Corrigan*, and Will Eisner's *Comics and Sequential Art*.

While many colleges and universities may not have specific comics courses, perusing the local campus bookstore shelves that contain the text book requirements of other offered courses may turn up various graphic-novel titles. However, limiting one's searches for course requirements may miss an important aspect of the use of comics within academia: faculty research. Through a chance encounter at the Inter Library Loan office, it was discovered many UN-L faculty were using comic books as primary texts for their own academic pursuits (e.g., the professor in art history who needed the complete series of *X-Men* to trace the evolution and codification of comic art, or the advertising instructor interested in the history of marketing who found individual comic books an invaluable source). From these instances, determining the potential for academic support by a comics or graphic novel collection should also include consideration of faculty research.

Engaging in background research within one's own institution regarding internal attitudes and community or students needs, and anticipating possible resistance towards comics, informs the later processes of acquiring and maintaining an appropriate and well-used collection. Uncovering which graphic novels and comic books are being used in academia, and how they contribute to the curriculum, also creates a perfect starting point for deciding which titles to collect.

Randall Scott, the comics librarian at Michigan State, advocates for an expert to handle the acquisitions of comics (Scott, 1990), but there also needs to be an expert to communicate the implementation of such a collection with administrative chairs or deans. Kat Kan, a public librarian at Fort Wayne, Indiana, outlined three rules to assist any librarian in the beginning stages of collection. In one of her series of monthly articles for *Voice of Youth Advocates,* she presents some good advice for those re-introducing others to comics, starting with getting the support of your supervisors (Kan, 1999). Being an expert can help overcome possible objections by those in doubt, as can having a plan and being aware of cataloging and circulation issues. Deciding what to add is the last step (Kan, 1999).

There are a number of ways to identify a core collection of essential graphic novels.

As mentioned earlier, Doug Highsmith constructed and justified a list of important titles he felt were under represented but deserving of inclusion (Highsmith, 2005). Steve Weiner's *100 Graphic Novels for Public Libraries* (2001) and Randall Scott's earlier publication, *Comic Books and Strips: An Information Sourcebook* (1988), are useful and still relevant references for the task of identifying initial titles. Despite their age, these books remain a valuable starting point.

Several excellent articles deal with collection development, many of which discuss tools and tactics worth considering. As Doug Highsmith points out, "Unless a library wants to compete directly with the likes of Bowling Green State University, Michigan State University, or Ohio State University, it is better advised to acquire books— both those currently being published and "back issues"— which meet more narrowly focused selection criteria" (Highsmith, 1992: 61). Because of the plethora of comic book and graphic novel titles available, many libraries shouldn't necessarily consider comprehensive collections. Rather, Highsmith emphasizes limiting a collection to a specific time period, artist, or theme (Highsmith, 1992).

Michael Lavin, while lamenting the slow acceptance of comics within North American libraries, notes the many genres and essential titles associated with them in his article, "Comic Books and Graphic Novels for Libraries: What to Buy in *Serials Review*" (1998). Robert Weiner (2001), in discussing the popularity and success of a comics and graphic novels collection in the Lubbock, Texas, library system, offers additional titles worth considering. Many of the titles on these lists overlap, and help form an initial canon worth considering for an academic library interested in representing major general works. Eric Werthmann discovered that many of these share common characteristics, such as those from "more serious" genres, including memoirs, history, and "literary fiction" (Werthmann, 2008: 27). He concocted his own list of those that have won either of the two major awards in the comics field: the Eisner Awards and the Harvey Awards (Werthmann, 2008).

If the goal is to have a small and contemporary collection, one can consider purchasing the titles discussed in reviews in mainstream publications like the *New York Times Magazine* or *Newsweek*. These titles appear sporadically in introductory English composition courses and will certainly be checked out from the library. *Booklist* also publishes a section called "Graphic Novel Showcase," and alternative periodicals that regularly review comics include *Giant Robot*, *Bust*, and the *Utne Reader*.

Leslie Bussert's article in the February 2005 *College and Research Libraries News* is also a thorough guide to available resources for librarians delving into comics. It includes numerous online resources that include ideas for building a collection. The listserv "Graphic Novels in Libraries" (www.topica.com/lists/GNLIB-L) helps librarians to learn more about graphic novels and communicate their experiences of collecting comics with each other. It also offers assistance in dealing with challenges, and recommends new titles and reviews. One aso can find practical advice, ranging from cataloging issues to content complaints.

Libraries such as Columbia University's have materials available online that can act as a guideline for developing a comics-specific collection policy and invite comparison (see http://www.columbia.edu/cu/lweb/services/colldev/graphic_novels.html). Michael Lavin also has an in-depth guide for librarians crafting collection development policies with links to reviews, examples and several related topics at his University of Buffalo Libraries site. (see http://library.buffalo.edu/libraries/asl/guides/graphicnovels/). Defining terms (graphic novels or comics?), describing the scope (grad student/faculty research/undergraduate/ leisure?) and outlining specific delimitations (monographs only?) in a collection development statement helps narrow down the many titles for consideration.

Ultimately, the UN-L libraries' guidelines for collecting comics and graphic novels emerged after consulting in-house collection development policies and the above literature and resources. Previously existing mission statements were broad enough to include the comics format without needing to draft an explicit policy. A main point that was highlighted included the directive that materials must be primary texts or potentially merit secondary support of the curriculum. Ample evidence already existed to begin collecting materials that fit this description. For a sample list of works that complemented, enhanced or supported existing strengths or research interests and formed the initial acquisition, see Appendix A.

The UN-L overarching mission to have representative works by Nebraska authors, artists, and scholars in the entire collection invited Special Collections considerations. Notorious 1960s comic book illustrator S. Clay Wilson is a graduate of UN-L, making the collection of his work a relevant addition to our holdings. In 2008, the Archives received several pieces donated by Wilson, which prompted several further donations by other alumni who were creators, collectors, or scholars of comic books and graphic novels. One of these donations contained materials by a local artist, Scott Stewart, including his 1974 "Comix Trip" comic book, which featured a single-panel cartoon that mocks the University of Nebraska's sports culture by (eventual) Pulitzer Prize–winning poet (and UN-L faculty member) Ted Kooser.

Michigan State University has the largest academic collection of comics and comics-related materials in the country. Their collection includes more than 120,000 comic books, graphic novels, and fotonovelas, including foreign titles and Golden Age comics on microfilm and microfiche. Additionally, books, fanzines, and periodicals about comics and animation make up a sizable supplemental collection (Scott, 1990).

The largest collection of original editorial cartoons and comic strips is located at the Ohio State University's Cartoon Research Library. From Milton Caniff's initial donation of proofs and clippings to the San Francisco Academy of Art's contribution of comic strips, the Cartoon Research Library boasts some of the most extensive holdings of newspaper comics. Ohio State also hosts a Triennial Festival of Cartoon Art that attracts a large number of practitioners and academics to celebrate and discuss comic art (Scott, 1990). One of the original journals dedicated to the scholarly writing of comics and cartoons, *INKS: Cartoon and Comic Art Studies*, was edited by Lucy Caswell, the head librarian and archivist of the Cartoon Research Library.

In addition to the well-known and comprehensive collections held at Michigan State University, and the Ohio State Cartoon Research Library, many other academic libraries have established important and ambitious projects. The Lynn R. Hansen Underground Comics Collection at Washington State University is the accumulation of comic books published between 1963 and 1994 by an active critic and reviewer. The comic arts collection in the James Branch Cabell Library at Virginia Commonwealth University boasts nearly 25,000 comic books dating from the 1960s through today.

As academic libraries have come to see comics as a valuable addition to their collections, many academic librarians have become active in their creation and research. Jim Ottaviani, a librarian at the University of Michigan, and former writer for *Comics Journal*, publishes and writes comic books about the history of science. A popular work, *Two-Fisted Science: Stories about Scientists* is a collection of biographical stories featuring Galileo, Isaac Newton, Niels Bohr, and other scientists (Ottaviani, 2001). Comic Book Markup Language (CBML), designed to accommodate the XML encoding of comics and graphic novels, was designed by John Walsh, an assistant professor at the School of Library and Information Science at Indiana University (Walsh 2006). Allen Ellis, an associate professor of library services at Northern Kentucky University, has addressed the growing rate of scholarly analysis of comics and graphic novels by developing a citation guide. These librarians have found a niche in the scholarship, preservation, and production of comics and graphic novels.

While many libraries cannot afford an exhaustive collection, and cannot mirror the accomplishments of established comics librarians, all libraries can learn from the pioneering efforts of those who came before us by studying their policies, investigating their holdings, reading their scholarship, and seeking their advice.

Comics and graphic novels may not fit easily into the traditional scope of library collections, which makes their acquisition and access a challenge. Christopher Matz succinctly articulates the benefits from confronting such a challenge when he said,

> In an academic or school setting, comics can be used to support teaching and research across a variety of fields, by enhancing the current curriculum or inspiring new avenues of scholarship. Libraries can lead the way to an advanced consideration of comic books as more than mere pop culture artifacts, as a form of literature and art inherently worthy of study. At the same time, librarians can challenge the historical absence of popular culture within academic library by promoting the unrealized potential of comic books, and extending the concept of "library" for their patrons [Matz, 2003: 4].

At a time when most academic libraries are busy responding to the electronic research needs of their patrons, comics and graphic novels are a resilient reminder of print culture. These materials can present opportunities to highlight a library's collection. National Library Week and Free Comic Book Day can be invitations to patrons to be re-introduced to the library and can contribute to attendance and circulation statistics.

Randall Scott has long advocated building comics and graphic novel collections in academic libraries. He views librarians as both scholars and leaders, believing that the "library profession is in a unique position to contribute to the future of scholarship" (Scott, 1993 : 84). By investigating factors that impeded a comics collection and following the advice and strategies of the many public, school, and academic librarians who have helped build a foundation for other research institutions to follow, the University of Nebraska continues to build its circulating comics collection and to reach out to local comics creators and artists for additions to our archives. UN-L has taken advantage of the many opportunities graphic novels and comics have presented to promote the humanistic ideal and the aspect of its mission that says that reading should educate and delight as well as search the research and academic needs of our patrons.

Appendix A

SELECTION OF CORE TITLES WITH LOCAL USE DATA

In addition to the titles already mentioned above, the books included in this appendix are intended to support academic collections. Some titles included are controversial and have been challenged in public libraries. Titles listed include their circulation and renewal totals as of March 1, 2009, and include the date the item was entered into the catalog. *denotes an item has been replaced. Arrangement is by genre.

Autobiography/Fictional Memoir

The illustrated memoir, both real and fictionalized, is an increasingly popular genre within graphic novels. Some titles appropriate for an academic library include:

Title	Author(s)	Year Entered Catalog	Circulation History
Stuck Rubber Baby	Howard Cruse	2005	8 total checkouts, 1 renewal
Persepolis	Marjane Satrapi	2005	23 total checkouts, 18 renewals*
Cruddy	Linda Barry	2005	5 total checkouts, 3 renewals
A Child's Life	Phoebe Gloeckner	2005	12 total checkouts, 1 renewal*

Superheroes

Superhero comics, early and postmodern, offer a variety of interesting avenues of scholarship to consider, and are always popular reading.

Title	Author(s)	Year Entered Catalog	Circulation History
Wonder Woman Archives, Vol. 1.	D.C. Archive Editions	2006	5 total checkouts
44 Years of the Fantastic Four	GIT Corp.	2005	5 total checkouts, 3 renewals
Watchmen	Alan Moore, Dave Gibbons	2005	9 total checkouts, 4 renewals*
Marvels	Kurt Busiek	2005	17 total checkouts, 2 renewals
Dark Knight Returns	Frank Miller	2005	27 total checkouts, 7 renewals*
Kingdom Come	Mark Waid, Alex Ross	2005	23 total checkouts, 1 renewals*

Early Comics/Newspaper Strips

Journalism students may be interested in delving into the historical relationship between comic strips and newspapers.

Title	Author(s)	Year Entered Catalog	Circulation History
Little Nemo in Slumberland: So Many Splendid Sundays!	Winsor McCay	2006	3 total checkouts, 1 renewal
Krazy & Ignatz 1925–1926	George Herriman, Bill Blackbeard	2005	5 total checkouts, 1 renewal
Sydney Smith's the Gumps	Herb Galewits, Sydney Smith	2005	5 total checkouts, 1 renewal
Walt and Skeezix, Vol.1	Frank O. King	2005	4 total checkouts, 1 renewal

"Literary" Fiction

Many of the titles below have additional volumes to consider or are representative of authors who have more works to consider.

Title	Author(s)	Year Entered Catalog	Circulation History
Bone, One Volume Edition	Jeff Smith	2005	15 total checkouts, 8 renewals
Blankets	Craig Thompson	2006	24 total checkouts, 3 renewals
Age of Bronze, Volume 1: A Thousand Ships	Eric Shanower	2005	4 total checkouts, 1 renewal

Title	Author(s)	Year Entered Catalog	Circulation History
Summer Blonde: Four Stories	Adrian Tomine	2005	10 total checkouts
LOCAS: A Love and Rockets Book	Jaime Hernandez	2005	9 total checkouts, 2 renewals
Palomar: The Heartbreak Soup Stories	Gilbert Hernandez	2006	6 total checkouts, 4 renewals

International and Foreign Languages and Culture

South American countries like Argentina and Chile, as well as European countries such as France and Belgium, have a long connection with comics and should also be considered for the collection. Comics published in foreign countries and in foreign languages may be used as tools for enhancing learning language skills and gaining insight into other cultures.

Title	Author(s)	Year Entered Catalog	Circulation History
Masters of the Ninth Art: Bandes Dessinees and Franco-Belgian Identity.	Matthew Screech	2006	2 total checkouts
The Francophone Bande Dessinee	Charles Forsdick, Laurence Grove and Libbie McQuillan	2006	1 total checkouts, 8 renewals
Cartooning in Latin America	John Lent	2006	2 total checkouts
Adventures of TinTin: TinTin in America	Herge	2007	16 total checkouts, 17 renewals

Comic Criticism and History

As mentioned earlier, Randall Scott's *Comic Books and Strips: An Information Sourcebook* exhaustively lists titles that are appropriate for any scholarship or research in the medium (1988). The University Press of Mississippi is also a reliable publisher of numerous excellent and essential tomes of comics scholarship.

Title	Author(s)	Year Entered Catalog	Circulation History
The Many Lives of the Batman: Critical Approaches to a Superhero and His Media	Roberta E. Pearson and William Uricchio	2006	3 total checkouts, 2 renewals
From Girls to Grrlz: A History of Women's Comics from Teens to Zines	Trina Robbins	2005	3 total checkouts, 2 renewals
Rebel Visions, the Underground Comix Revolution 1963–75	Patrick Rosenkranz	2005	6 total checkouts
Black Images in the Comics: A Visual History	Fredrik Stromberg and Charles Johnson	2005	2 total checkouts

Manga

One of the major difficulties in collecting manga is its immense scope. There are multiple genres to consider, and many titles seem to never end, making collecting them a hardship. There are many excellent titles academic libraries immediately should consider, however, including:

Title	Author(s)	Year Entered Catalog	Circulation History
Barefoot Gen Volume One: A Cartoon Story of Hiroshima	Keiji Nakazawa	2005	10 total checkouts, 2 renewals
Even a Monkey Can Draw Manga Volume One	Koji Aihara and Kentaro Takekuma	2007	3 total checkouts, 2 renewals
Manga: Sixty Years of Japanese Comics	Paul Gravett	2006	6 total checkouts, 4 renewals

Title	Author(s)	Year Entered Catalog	Circulation History
Akira, Volume One	Katsuhiro Otomo	2006	14 total checkouts, 2 renewals*
Dreamland Japan: Writings of Modern Manga	Frederic L. Schodt	2006	2 total checkouts, 2 renewals
Kapilavastu: Buddha Volume One	Osamu Tesuka	2006	6 total checkouts

Comics Journalism

In the early '90s, University of Oregon journalism graduate Joe Sacco spent two months observing Palestinians living in the West Bank and Gaza Strip and articulately documented his first- and second-hand accounts. This book helped coin the term "comics journalism" as a genre.

Title	Author(s)	Year Entered Catalog	Circulation History
Palestine	Joe Sacco	2004	11 total checkouts, 5 renewals
Safe Area Gorazde: The War in Eastern Bosnia 1992–1995	Joe Sacco	2004	3 total checkouts, 4 renewals
Fax From Sarajevo	Joe Kubert	2005	1 total checkout

References

Brown, Jeffrey A. 1997. "Comic Book Fandom and Cultural Capital." *Journal of Popular Culture* 30 (4): 13–31.
Brown, John Mason. 1955. "What's Wrong with the Comics" *Town Meeting: A Twenty-Year Cavalcade with Narration by John Daly*. New York: Heritage.
Bussert, Leslie. 2005. "Comic Books and Graphic Novels: Digital Resources for an Evolving Form of Art and Literature." *C&RL News* 66 (2): 103.
Columbia University Libraries. 2006. Collection Development of Graphic Novels. http://www.columbia.edu/cu/lweb/services/colldev/graphic_novels.html.
Dorrell, Larry, Dan Curtis, and Kuldip Rampal. 1995. "Book Worms Without Books? Students Reading Comic Books in the School House." *Journal of Popular Culture* 29: 223–234.
Eisner, Will. 1994. *Comics and Sequential Art*. New York: Poorhouse Press.
Ellis, Allen and Doug Highsmith. 2000. "About Face: Comic Books in Library Literature." *Serials Review* 26 (2): 21–44.
Heer, Jeet, and Kent Worcester, eds. 2004. *Arguing Comics: Literary Masters on a Popular Medium*. Jackson: University Press of Mississippi.
Highsmith, Doug. 2005. "Comic Books Built to Last: A Survey of Academic Library Holdings of Graphic Novels and Hardcover Comic Book Collections–a Preliminary Report." Paper presented at the annual international meeting of the Popular Culture Society. San Diego, California.
_____. 1992. "Developing a 'Focused' Comic Book Collection in an Academic Library." In *Popular Culture and Acquisitions*, Allen Ellis, ed. Haworth: The Haworth Press, Inc.
Kakalios, James. October 2002. "Adding Pow! to Your Physics Class with Comic-Book Lessons." *Curriculum Review*: 14–15.
Kan, Katherine. October 1999. "Comics and Graphic Novels in the Library." *VOYA*: 252–253.
Koenke, Karl. 1981. "The Careful Use of Comic Books." *Reading Teacher* 34: 592–595.
Lavin, Michael R. 1998. "Comic Books and Graphic Novels for Libraries: What to Buy." *Serials Review* 24 (2): 31–45.
Markham, Gary W. 2009. "Cataloging the Publications of Dark Horse Comics: One Publisher in an Academic Catalog." *Journal of Academic Librarianship* 35 (2): 162–169.
Matz, Christopher. July/August 2003. "Hot and Now! Comic Books for Grown Ups II." *The Memphis University Libraries Newsletter*: 4.
McCloud, Scott. 1993. *Understanding Comics: The Invisible Art*. Northampton: Kitchen Sink Press.
Moran, Barbara. 1992. "Going Against the Grain: A Rationale for the Collection of Popular Materials in Academic Libraries." In *Popular Culture and Acquisitions*, Allen Ellis, ed. Haworth: The Haworth Press, Inc.
Nyberg, Amy Kiste. 1998. *Seal of Approval: The History of the Comics Code*. Jackson: University Press of Mississippi.

O'English, Lorena, J. Gregory Mathews, and Elizabeth Blakesley Lindsay. 2006. "Graphic Novels in Academic Libraries: From *Maus* to Manga and Beyond." *Journal of Academic Librarianship* 32 (4): 173–182.

Ottaviani, Jim, Mark Badger, Donna Barr, and Sean Bieri. 2001. *Two-Fisted Science: Stories About Scientists.* Ann Arbor: G.T. Labs.

Scott, Randall W. 1988. *Comic Books and Strips: An Information Sourcebook.* Phoenix: Oryx Press.

_____. 1993. "Comics and Libraries and the Scholarly World." *Popular Culture in Libraries* 1 (1): 81–84.

_____. 1990. *Comics Librarianship: A Handbook.* Jefferson, NC: McFarland.

Simmons, Tabitha. 2003. "Comic Books in My Library?" *PNLA Quarterly* 67 (3): 12, 20.

Stewart, Scott. 1974. *Comix Trip.* Lincoln: Corn Belt Comix.

Sturm, James. April 5, 2002. "Comics in the Classroom." *The Chronicle of Higher Education*: B14–5.

Walsh, John A., and Michell Dalmua. 2006. "CBML: Comic Book Markup Language." Paper presented at the Digital Resource for the Humanities and Arts Conference. Dartington, England, UK.

Weiner, Robert G. 2001. "Graphic Novels in Libraries." *Texas Library Journal* 77 (4): 130–135.

Weiner, Stephen. 2001. *101 Best Graphic Novels.* New York: NBM.

Weiner, Steven. 1996. *100 Graphic Novels for Public Libraries.* Northampton: Kitchen Sink Press.

Werthmann, Eric J. 2008. *Graphic Novel Holdings in Academic Libraries: An Analysis of the Collections of Association of Research Libraries Members.* A Master's Paper for the M.S. in L.S. degree. Chapel Hill.

14

Comic Art Collection at the Michigan State University Libraries[1]

RANDALL W. SCOTT

My name is Randy Scott, and I am the Comic Art Bibliographer at the Michigan State University Libraries. I started working on the comics collection there in the Summer of 1974, when there were only 6,000 comic books and they were just barely in alphabetical order. I soon decided that a career of sorts was to be made in nurturing this collection. If I had written out a one-paragraph goal, thirty years ago, for the kind of collection I was hoping to develop, it would have been a lot less ambitious-sounding than the following collection description paragraph sounds now.

The Comic Art Collection at Michigan State University is a special library/archive of about 240,000 items, all comics or related to comics. The collection is fully cataloged and is available for public use 44 hours per week. The cataloging and much of the indexing of the collection is useable on the internet as the Reading Room Index. If you visit us, we can bring to your reading table, on demand, any of about two-thirds of all American comic books, one-third of all American newspaper comic strips, and just about any book, magazine or fanzine written about American comics. We also have the largest collections of French, German, Dutch, Italian, Spanish and Mexican comics to be found in North America.

Although our collecting scope is very broad, there are a few philosophical restrictions. Libraries are designed to collect books, and we collect comics as books, not as curiosities or as objects of art. We are not an archive or a gallery or a museum. We do not have unique archival materials. We do not have original art for comics. We do not have cool exhibits to bring your grandchildren to. We concentrate on collecting published books and magazines to be read and consulted. Our business is to be a library, and we want to be the best library of comic books. That means we want to be the biggest and the most organized library of comics, and the one most likely to have everything that a comics scholar might want to read.

Here is another philosophical statement: We collect comic books for their content, and not primarily for their published format. Thus a comic book in "good" condition is probably better for us than one in "mint" condition, because we are going to let people touch it and read it — hopefully a lot of people. We also welcome comic books in microfilm

123

and digital forms. We will cooperate with reprint and digitization projects even if they might damage our originals a little. The prime directive is to get the material into the hands of the reader, but of course this is balanced against our responsibility to preserve and protect the materials. Our readers and library workers are supervised and taught careful handling of comic books; we use acid-free enclosures and we do deacidification projects. Our materials do not circulate, meaning they do not leave our reading room. InterLibrary Loan is done by scanning, when it is safe. Our collection includes all ages and genres of comics, from the works of the Swiss artist Rodolphe Töpffer (1799–1846), who is called the originator of comics by most European scholars, to the most recent 24-hour comics produced at local comic book stores. We collect golden age superheroes and new wave minicomix with equal intensity, and we have dozens of Tijuana Bibles as well as Christian religious comics. We collect books of 19th century caricature and we have Tarzan comic books in both Icelandic and Arabic.

Cataloging

The key to the growth and usefulness of our collection is cataloging. The cataloging of our collection of comic books started in 1975, and before that there were no professionally cataloged collections of comic books. The national academic library scene consisted of about 40,000 comic books at the Library of Congress, and smaller numbers at Michigan State and Bowling Green State. The comics at the Library of Congress were not being respected at that time, and there was even a written rule that comic books were not to be cataloged. The coming of OCLC and on-line cataloging was what made it possible for a few dedicated people in Michigan and Ohio to start documenting libraries of comics. Why is cataloging so important? Because cataloging is the first order of research after accumulating; cataloging begins to make sense of piles of stuff. And if you can't say what you have, why would scholars visit, or why would donors donate?

Cataloging comics was something of an uphill battle at first, back in the 1970s, but the current situation is much better. Dozens of academic libraries have reasonably well-managed comics collections, and the Library of Congress even cataloged its comic books, starting in the 1990s. The temptation is to say, let's get together on this and have a national policy and make sure everythings's covered. Let's cooperate.

Cooperative Acquisitions and the National Scene

I visited the Library of Congress, summer before last, with cooperation in mind. The main possibility on my agenda was trading extras. We typically have 30,000 extra comic books looking for a good library home, and the Library of Congress is supposed to get two copies of everything by copyright deposit. I'd be glad to check their holdings and send them anything they missed, if they'd return the favor. I was ready to negotiate extremely favorable terms. We really need to get rid of those 30,000 comic books! But here's what I discovered:

First, the Library of Congress doesn't know which issues of a given comic book periodical it owns. Cataloging was done without holdings records. The comic books have been deacidified, but as of 2006 they were still tied up in the boxes that the deacidifier put them in, so it takes days to find the right box, open it, and figure out what issues of a comic book are held. For this reason they require three days' notice from prospective comics researchers.

Second, the Library of Congress operates under a regulation that says they can't give copyright deposit copies to other libraries, even extra copies. They're hoping to change that, but I don't think they're moving in that direction. So much for cooperation with the Library of Congress. They don't know what they have, and they can't trade extras.

In a more global sense, meaningful cooperation in collection policy seems hard to imagine. What would be the point of choosing only five or six libraries to collect American literature, or books about chemistry? Every library needs to maintain resources appropriate for its own users, and that means comics collections of reasonable size are needed wherever people study comics. Two libraries (outside Michigan and Ohio) have made serious beginnings— the University of California at Riverside, and Virginia Commonwealth University are collecting and cataloging. Several other libraries have started general collections of American comic books. Duke University, Brown University, University of Minnesota, University of Florida, and the New York Public Library are the best examples. But they have not committed to cataloging their materials. Several smaller libraries have accepted a few thousand of our duplicates, but it seems that when they realize how large and bibliographically complex the field is, they get cold feet. To further complicate matters, some libraries are collecting what they call "graphic novels," but won't accept comic books." The University of Michigan and Columbia University in New York are examples of this. It comes down to this— the library profession has still not recovered from the 1950s anti-comics campaigns. Digitization is probably the only way we as a profession will ever catch up. Some projects are underway, and we will always support them both by allowing our comics to be scanned, and by maintaining our "real" collection as backup.

In Michigan and Ohio, meaningful cooperation is already happening. OSU and BGSU are consistently cataloging their comic book collections, and so we are sharing cataloging information. The two Ohio collections and MSU's collection duplicate each other quite a bit, but that's because local users in each place need significant collections. We have divided the territory somewhat. Ohio State is the go-to resource for newspaper comics, original art, and papers of cartoonists and cartoon-related institutions. In comic books, OSU has chosen to collect Japanese comics at the most complete level. Michigan State tries to collect all of American comic books, and foreign comic books in general, but with slightly less intensity. This cooperation is formalized in meetings of a group called the Consortium of Popular Culture Collections in the Midwest, but it isn't rigid, or binding, or inhibiting in any way. Again, each library's first responsibility is to its own patrons.

What Will the Future Be?

Changes in comics and their production are underway. Digitization of retrospective collections and digital production of new comics are upon us. Newspapers are shrinking and the number of strips in each seems to be gradually diminishing. But most of all, the American comic book, as a mass phenomenon, seems to be disappearing. Sales of newsstand comic books are way down. Works of single authorship and small press publications, though, are more and more visible in bookstores and Internet sales venues like Amazon.com.

Many current comics or "graphic novels" don't seem to be popular culture in the sense that we understood comics to be when we first got into collecting them. If it weren't for manga and superhero movies, most of current comics wouldn't be popular culture.

That's okay with us. It's comics as a literary form that we're collecting, and like any other literary form, comics includes examples that are both popular and elite, exotic and erotic, comedic and tragic, amateur and professional, and good and bad. Comics is, in other words, a very healthy literary form overall.

I look forward to the day when comics are mainstreamed in libraries. That will mean separate special collections won't be needed, except for things that are truly rare. That will mean that bibliographers and other scholars of comics won't be pigeonholed as *otaku*, and that will be when the current young generation of graduate students and new faculty are chairing departments, and near retirement age. That gives us about thirty more years to rejoice in our sense of innovation and difference, and to stimulate among ourselves as much thoughtful collecting and scholarship as we can. By then, *Action Comics* No. 1 will be 100 years old, and comics might just be said to have arrived.

Endnotes

1. Originally presented at the Libraries and Galleries panel at the Comic Books in Popular Culture Conference, Bowling Green State University, October 24–25, 2008.

15

Interview with
Randall W. Scott

Nicholas Yanes and Robert G. Weiner

Yanes and Weiner: *Most comic book academics have a childhood attachment to the medium. When did you start reading comic books? And who were some of your favorite characters?*

Randall W. Scott: I started reading comics when I was six years old, I suppose, which is when I started reading. My Uncle Eddie was a Great Lakes sailor, and he'd go away for a couple weeks and come back with a bag of comics for my cousin Jimmy. I remember reading all kinds of mid–50s stuff, Dells, EC's, DC science fiction titles, etc. But my favorites were (2) Batman, (3) Superman, and (1) *World's Finest*, where you got both Batman and Superman in the same story.

You received your B.A. in humanities from Michigan State University in 1972 and your M.S. in library service from Columbia University in '77. When did you realize that you could use the library system to preserve comic books and raise awareness about the value to academic research?

The idea that libraries are the appropriate technology for housing, organizing, and understanding comics came gradually into my consciousness over the weekend of July 4, 1974. I was already working as a typist at the MSU Library, and I started a card file. I typed about twenty cards, which look pretty much exactly like some of the entries in the online Reading Room Index <comics.lib.msu.edu/rri/index.htm> today. The whole concept suddenly seemed exciting. Then I put them away and went camping in Canada for a long weekend, with the understanding that if it still seemed exciting when I got back I'd work on it for a few years. Well, it still seemed like the right thing to do. Before long I was in library school, and the card file had grown to 74,000 cards when I quit typing them in 1978.

What are some of the challenges you've come across in building a library's comic book collection? Do you have any advice for other librarians who want to establish a comic book collection?

The administration of the Library was not universally in favor of having the world's biggest comic book collection, so I didn't tell them. Since I worked in cataloging, I just started cataloging. Soon scholars were noticing our holdings, and newspapers were doing articles on the collection. The time arrived when it seemed like the administration was seeing the collection as a positive thing. That's when I donated my own collection so I wouldn't have to organize two collections. The challenge was to foster an environment in which comics were integral to the collection. It was almost 20 years before I actually had a budget. My advice is to be patient and work hard.

The book that you've most recently written is European Comics in English Translation: A Descriptive Sourcebook. *It has been my experience that comic book studies have usually been limited to the Americanist sections of English, history, and interdisciplinary departments. How do you think the rise of European and Asian comic book industries are going to change how graphic literature is cataloged and studied? Will Americanists have to begin caring about other nations?*

The European comics tradition "rose" before the American one, and started getting academic attention in Europe long before we were studying comics here. The provincial nature of American consciousness about comics has been a real motivator to me since 1973 when I first discovered European comics. The world of comics is just so much bigger than what I got from Uncle Eddie. I still see American scholars spending all their time on superheroes, and I just don't get it. The only thing I know to do about it, though, is to present a collection that integrates all the world's comics traditions and makes it hard to ignore the wealth of world comics. It doesn't involve any change in library practice. Real research libraries have always collected internationally. I do think "Americanists" should study the enormous outpouring of European comics about America (westerns, etc.), but it's probably the scholars in French departments and German departments that should begin to notice where the literature in their respective languages is going.

Your resume says you indexed Frederic Wertham's Seduction of the Innocent. *What was it like working on a book that most comic book historians view as the greatest threat to the medium? Where you at all worried that while working* Seduction of the Innocent *you would suddenly agree with Wertham's comic book stance and start burning your collection?*

Seduction of the Innocent was fun to index, because [there] are lots of little absurdities to point out alphabetically. Wertham isn't that convincing of a writer ... but everybody interested in comic books should read the book, really. It's the first book about comic books!

How did you "fight" the negative stereotypes associated with comics and collecting in a library/archive? (That must have been difficult.)

My fighting has mostly been cataloging. Once an item is formally cataloged in a research library, most of the threat is gone. Newspaper publicity is one place that struggle goes on. That battle happened a long time ago here locally, but my advice is to always be polite and formal with reporters, and always stress research value. And never mention collector's prices or the words "Bam, Zip, Powee!" People are going to add that to their stories anyhow, and that's where the negative stereotypes reside.

I read once that you really don't like the term "graphic novel"?

"Graphic novel" is the new pretentious word for "comic book." Most aren't even novels. If you start telling people you collect graphic novels for research, and then they realize it's just comic books, what good have you done? Might as well start out honest.

You wrote Comics Librarianship: A Handbook. *What was the response to that? Have your views changed in the last 20 years since the book's release?*

Comics Librarianship is still being used, at least some chapters. I get letters. Quite a few things have changed. I looked it over with the idea of doing a second edition a few years back, and it would need to be completely rewritten. The basic ideas are still sound (whatever they were ... it's been two decades!)

Your Comic Books and Strips: An Information Sourcebook *is an early classic in the field. I've used it extensively. Any comments about that project?*

Comic Books and Strips was my first book-length project, and it was fun. In retrospect, I don't think there was enough stuff to fill a book at that time. The publisher required that it list only separately published items, and not articles, so I was stuffing all kinds of fanzines into it. Not wrong, really, but the MSU Library is the only place that has them. A couple of really thick bibliographies would be needed to cover the territory now (books about comics, and edited volumes of comics reprints). Somebody should do that.

Talk about your indexing project "A Librarian's Perspective." Do you think the same techniques still apply in today's digital world? Where does Metadata fit into Comics cataloging?

"Indexing the Comics: A Librarian's Perspective" was a paper I delivered at a conference in 1978. As I remember, the bold, original thrust of the paper was to say that comics need to be indexed. I don't think the question of indexing techniques came up. And metadata? The online Reading Room Index <comics.lib.msu.edu/rri/index.htm> has a metafile governing all [of] its links. It's called an Authority File.—Absolutely essential for coordinating a hypertext document that big.

Please talk a little about these projects you did: Blank in the Comics; The Harry "Λ" Chesler Collection of Illustration and Comic Art at Fairleigh Dickinson University: a booklist; Tijuana Bibles; The Comics Alphabetizer; Incredible Hulk #1–6, 102–200; Citation Index to Marvel Comics, 1961–1980 — The Avengers #1–100; Index to Wonder Woman, *a Ms. book published by Holt, Rinehart and Winston and Warner Books, New York, Chicago, San Francisco in 1972;* An index to Comic Book Rebels, *a book edited by Stanley Wiater and Stephern R. Bissette, and published without an index by Donald I. Fine, New York, 1993.*

Blank in the Comics started as an apazine in Capa-Alpha. Each month I'd pick a topic and then reprint as many strips as I could find about that topic. Like "Eyecharts in the Comics" or "Lasagna in the Comics." The project now is part of the Reading Room Index <comics.lib.msu.edu/rri/index.htm> online, with about 15,000 topics listed. I'm still clipping the strips from at least 5 newspapers per day, and arranging them by topic. For the most part patrons will need to visit the library and look in the envelopes. This started in 1983.

I have indexed several books that were published without indexes, and the indexes are also included in the Reading Room Index <comics.lib.msu.edu/rri/index.htm>. Lately I've done a few European books to help realign our research priorities: G. Blanchard's *Histoire de la bande dessinée* (1974); A.C. Baumgärtner's *Die Welt der Comics* (1972), and H. Morgan's *Principes des littératures dessinées* (2003). It's something to do on long plane rides to Europe.—Which the library sends me on, in order to buy comics.

Some of the other indexes you list were done for APA-I, the Amateur Press Alliance for Indexing, of which I'm a former member.

You also did some other work related to Courts, Radical Newspapers, Sing Out. *Would you care to comment on some of your non-comics work?*

Naw.

The boom in libraries collecting comics/graphic novels is now huge. What do you think about all of it today?

Is it huge? I'm still doing a lot of original cataloging, which means that however big the boom, the library establishment as a whole isn't covering the territory. It's great that there are so many libraries collecting, of course, but I guess I just can't expect most of them to have the breadth of appetite our library is able to have. We get both manga and mini-comics. We get Mexican pornographic comics and Bible stories from religious publishers. We get the latest from France and Argentina. We get both *Blue Beetle* and *Blue Corn* comics. Unfortunately, though we try to represent everything, we don't get all of anything. I'd say the number and variety of comics available is what's really huge.

16

The Perils of Doctor Strange

Preserving Pennsylvania-Centered Comics at the State Library of Pennsylvania

WILLIAM T. FEE

The State Library of Pennsylvania's graphical materials collection, unlike many comic book research libraries, has grown more out of a need to preserve the materials than to serve a patron base. While the collection does indeed serve the needs of the comic book scholar or student of popular culture by appointment, this is second to the safeguarding of a valuable and oft overlooked form of popular culture. Much like the collection of the State Historical Society of Wisconsin, which collects Kitchen Sink Press and Krupp Comix Works publications in the interest of preserving the heritage of the state of Wisconsin (Scott, 2007), the State Library strives for both depth of collection and preservation of more unusual titles. Unless an item is donated, the number of libraries owning an item on WorldCat drives collection development.

Approximately five years ago, the State Library of Pennsylvania underwent a mission restructure, from a more general collection serving state agencies to a research collection, "For, by and about Pennsylvania." While, as a chartered mission, the needs of state agencies are still a foremost task, this focus allows for a greater depth of coverage in newspaper and periodical formats, as well as a more defined set of collection needs. It was during this period that I, as a bit of a comic book geek, realized that the narrowness of mission actually broadened the number of formats we could collect. While we still do not collect video or the traditional trade paperback novel or short story collection (unless that is the only format a needed item is published in), pulps and comic books became a possibility, especially as money that would have been spent on topics, creators and publishers other than those concerned with Pennsylvania became available. Since there happens to be a number of comics either published in Pennsylvania or by creators born and raised in Pennsylvania, it just became a matter of convincing the State Library that the preservation of these items was a need we should fill.

Due to the less-than-positive attitude of librarians in general toward the floppy comic book, the planning of this change in collection development would have to be both extensive and complete. While there is much material written within library science volumes about collecting graphic novels (one of the better volumes has come out of ALA Press—see *Graphic Novels Now: Building, Managing, and Marketing a Dynamic Collection*) (Goldsmith, 2005), there was little written in the field on the cataloging of these items save for a few paragraphs here and there in the more general collection development books. Much of this material referred specifically to the classification of the items. There was nothing on the cataloging of the actual floppy monthly comic since Randall Scott's *Comics Librarianship* (Scott, 1990), published in 1990. This format is what the State Library needed to preserve, with trade paperbacks (in this case a collection of issues originally released in floppy format) or graphic novels for patron use.

Goal in hand, it was time to write policy, as this is the first step in getting a new format or subject accepted for addition to the State Library of Pennsylvania's collection development policy (with at least a vague idea of specific procedures waiting in the wings for back up). Needing an example to template said policy, at this point it was time to turn to Randall Scott's list of comics research libraries (last updated in February, 2009 and available online at *http://www.lib.msu.edu/comics/director/comres.htm*). Since this was the type of collection I was looking to add to the State Library's collections, I began to look at their websites. Few actually had a development policy specific to graphical materials available online, and not surprisingly, since Michigan State has the oldest and largest comic book collection in the country outside of the Library of Congress, it had the best.

As the adaptation began, it was found, as per the norm, that there were a few sections that could be changed to fit the State Library's collections, but many more that were so specific to the Michigan State University collections and their donation policies that they were unusable even in adaptation. In policy writing, however, this is about normal. What these parts can do is start one thinking about what items and policies specific to one's own library need to be included. For example, the history of comic books in the MSU policy suits their policy of collecting most comics, both national and international, but was too general for Pennsylvania's use. To make a section like it work in the State Library of Pennsylvania's collection development plan, it had to be scratch-built and based on a history of comic books in Pennsylvania, with only enough more general comics history details to place this Pennsylvania production in the context of the publication of the American art form.

It was at this point that I got very lucky finding like-minded staff. Not only was my digital technician, Jesse Noonan, even more knowledgeable on the subject of comic books than I was, but our Pennsylvania Documents Cataloger, Mary Spila, while not as well-informed on the topic, had more than a slight interest in adding the format to our collections. She was my back-up in the librarians' meetings, where such decisions are debated, as Jesse was my database and sounding board on comic book information. When one ventures into a policy-level change of this nature, it is always important to have more than one staff member on one's side.

So, policy in hand and basic procedures set down, it was time to enter the lion's den (the librarians' meeting) having argued the agenda item onto the schedule all the way through my supervisor, my Assistant Director, and on to the chair of the meeting. Surprising is a good way to describe the meeting into which so much preparation for debate was placed — there was little debate, and much of it related to the funding that would be pulled from other collection priorities. This recommendation coincided with the beginning of the tightening of the State Library's funding, which had been announced just before I introduced the idea of graphical formats collection. This became the primary point of debate, save for a half-hearted argument from a few of the more traditional thinking librarians who felt, as many do, that the library is no place for comic books. The [growing] collection of graphic novels and trade paperback collections in public and academic libraries has weakened this attitude, but it is still there. By setting a rather low budget of $1,000 a year (mainly depending on donations), taking on the policy and procedure writing myself, and promising to put candidates through the literature subject specialist committee, the acquiescence of the librarians was almost anti-climactic.

As has been said before, the State Library of Pennsylvania is a very specialized library. Unlike most comic research libraries, the focus of the collection is on preservation first and foremost, with access a secondary matter. Thus, while a public library must argue the addition based on an increase in circulation and patron base, the argument here was for the place of comic books in both the literary "canon" and its importance to Pennsylvania's history. Procedure and placement of the collection were as important as access policy, and donation policy was a foremost concern, not an afterthought.

The one major similarity between the types of collection, however, is the idea of challenges to the collection. As many comic books from the 1970s forward have had an adult audience in mind, many of these items must be carefully watched for appropriateness to the age of the patron. This problem was solved at the State Library of Pennsylvania in several ways. The first was the application of the "Challenges to the collection" policy, standard to all gifts, to the graphical materials section of the collection development policy, and to the stand-alone graphical materials policy. This Challenges policy gives procedures for challenges, and possible outcomes. The second method comes simply from the location of the materials. As pulp periodicals and books, these items are stored in the Workroom location of the State Library of Pennsylvania's state of the art Rare Books Room. This means that patrons must make an appointment to see the materials, allowing the Rare Books Librarian to turn down requests for materials outside the age range of the patron requesting them. Lastly, and this is part of the procedures which I wrote for the cataloging of graphical materials, all cataloged items contain a 521, or "Target Audience Note." This gives, in the record and in the OPAC display, an age level to which the material is appropriate and a double check before an appointment is scheduled or materials are retrieved. So, for example, if an item is tagged teen +, as many of Steve Ditko's self-published or Robin Snyder-published materials are, due to the philosophies and violence portrayed, it would not be given to a child.

First hurdle accomplished without a spill, it was time to identify needed procedures, in more depth than already had been accomplished prior to policy and proposal, and to actually write them. As mentioned earlier in this article, there was no real firm set of procedures for cataloging floppy monthly comic books, outside of those given in Randall Scott's book. Eighteen years old at the start of policy writing, *Comics Librarianship* could only be used as a rough guide. For instance, while giving a rather in-depth classification scheme (which was adapted for the subject-based classification scheme at the State Library of Pennsylvania), the volume did not deeply cover MARC fields and adaptations to them, other than a recommendation to use the LCRI for "most stable source of title" (12.0B1- Continuing Resources, Basis for Description, under Printed Serials: Retrospective Cataloging (Cataloger's Desktop, 2004)).

As a matter of fact, the cataloging procedures I wrote were expanded to article length, and can be found in *Serials Review* (Fee, 2008). While in this case mainly dealing with the FRBR record set and its implications for the comic book form, many of the MARC field specific guidelines in the article apply to any MARC comic book record, and those which do not are clearly marked (along with information on the application of those that are applicable to a flat record). Admittedly, the comic book cataloger at the State Library of Pennsylvania (myself) has much more time to devote to individual items and records, but the utilization of even a few of the MARC fields and the variations thereupon will greatly enrich comic book records for everyone's use. Thus I became Graphical Materials Librarian, as well as Digital Collections Librarian. This extra time is a result of the combination of three variables. The first is that the collection was established from the beginning as the collection of a comic research library. Secondly, it is a special collection, to be housed in a state of the art Rare Books room, to which a great deal of the Administration's attention has been directed. Lastly, the same person who wrote the rules is actually doing the cataloging. Since I am not applying someone else's cataloging rules to a special format (save, of course, for MARC and AACR2/RDA), I can very quickly employ sections that come up in most every record, spend more time on the differences, and adapt the rules on the fly, as I intimately know the way they were intended to be used. This is not the situation in most libraries, where understaffed cataloging departments struggle to even get the items into the system, in the midst of the other backlogged records.

In the midst of this, it rapidly became apparent that a definitive list of Pennsylvania-based comic book creators, publishers and subjects was needed. This would drive a number of field choices and usages within the MARC record, as the goal was to bring out the "Pennsylvania-ness" of the material. It also drove both acquisition and classification of the material, such as what writers and artists to write to request information and material, and what the scheme within PN672x would look like. Thanks to the Internet, including that hated "rival" of libraries, Wikipedia (actually rather trustworthy on many comics issues), this was soon accomplished in at least a higher level form, although it is, of course, an ever-growing list. Probably the best step we took was to write a short blurb on the library's website about comic books in Pennsylvania and post the master list, with a request that members of the public feel free to send us names that we missed (Fee, 2009). Combined with a month-long lobby display on the topic, this has resulted in the addition to the list of a number of new creators, as well as a relationship with the ToonSeum in Pittsburgh,[1] whose existence had not been suspected by the Graphical Materials Librarian before this contact.

MARC fields set and list completed, the next step was to decide where and how to store them. Although the where was generally set as the Rare Books Room, this location actually consists of two vaults and a work room, all climate-controlled at differing temperatures and humidities based on the material contained within them. The first vault, known simply as the Rare Books Vault, is intended for rag-based materials, and has a differing filtration system, although the same target range of approximately 50–55 degrees and 40–50 percent humidity as the Work Room. Due to the material intended to be stored here, it is also to be used mainly for materials published prior to 1870, which comic books were not. This left either the Newspaper Repository or the Work Room as a potential location. The Newspaper Repository, while seemingly a logical choice, is designed for post–1870 pulp newsprint, and is kept at approximately 45–50 degrees, with a humidity of 15–20 percent. These are not the best conditions for comic books, which would become brittle and fall apart with the humidity this low. The materials are also designed to lie flat, consisting as they do of bound and flat-wrapped newspapers, which would make locating a particular issue of a comic problematic, to say the least. Thus the Rare Books Work Room was designated the location for the materials, and it became a matter of how best to store them.

It is at this point that it was necessary to turn outside the library world, and into that of the comic book collector, as Randall Scott advised in *Comics Librarianship*. Collectors have been storing comics for years, and, as for many it is an investment as much as reading material, have a vested interest in keeping them from falling to pieces or becoming otherwise damaged. They also have a rather unique cataloging and retrieval system, as detailed in David Serchay's "Comic book collectors: The serials librarians of the home" (Serchay, 1998). So we set about acquiring short drawer boxes, a variant of the comic book short box, which holds about 200 comic books (as opposed to the long box, which holds 300), bags and boards. The archival bags used in comic book storage not only accomplish preservation, but allow one a place to stick a call number label without damaging the volume. The boards, also acid-free, stiffen both bag and comic, allowing them to stand upright, where they can be easily scanned for the title and call number label at the top of the book/bag. The drawer boxes are also the perfect height to fit on most library shelves, though at 26 inches deep are too long for any shelves that are not backed with another, such as in a two-sided shelf range without a divider. This setup was perfect for the State Library of Pennsylvania, and by buying all three from comic book supplies manufacturers and distributors, rather than their equivalents from an archival library supplier, we approximately halved the cost.

Having cataloging procedures, a place to put the comic books, and a way to store them, the next step was classification. The State Library's collection of graphical literary formats revolves, as does the whole collection, around the "Pennsylanianess" of the material. Therefore, the call number needed to reflect this. This was accomplished by adapting the Michigan State classification scheme, and changing the first cutter to reflect the Pennsylvania connection of the item. In cuttering the call number, Pennsylvania creator is preferred over Pennsylvania publisher, and Pennsylvania publisher over Pennsylvania subject.

Standard cataloging procedure (MSU) would be a two-cutter system based on author (6727), title (6728), or publisher (also 6728), with a numeral after the classification number based on the decade in which the item was published. A subject-based system, in this case Pennsylvania-based, uses 3 cutter numbers, with the first based around the Pennsylvania connection of the item. The second cutter is publisher (or, in the case of a Pennsylvania published title with no Pennsylvania creator, artist), and the third cutter is title, which allows one to distinguish multiple titles created for the same publisher by a creator. In a perfect world, it would also use a numeral after classification number to indicate decade of publication, like the Michigan State University scheme. The reality is that the collection at the State Library of Pennsylvania has not yet grown that large. Due to the location in the Rare Books Work Room, we accomplish the same thing by following the location's standard procedure of using the year at the end of the call number. We also add (after the call number, but before the year, an issue number), either a volume and number or simply a number, to keep runs straight. It's easier than attempting to see a possibly non-existent issue number on the front of the item itself while it is encased in its Mylar bag. However, it does require one to make a call when cataloging the first issue as to whether to use volume/number or sequential number (v.3:no.12 vs. no.246, for example) in cases where there are both. Our tendency is to use just number in most cases, as long as they are sequential over the run. The whole process results in a number such as: PN 6729.2 .O759 .W577 .F747 no.102 1962 (*Forbidden Worlds 102*, 1962). The construction of this number will be discussed later in this essay.

One major break with code that is required in a subject-based collection centering around a geographic location or ethnic background (such as Wisconsin born artists or Irish-American comic book creators) is that creator **must** be preferred. Standard Library of Congress and CONSER practice is that, due to the multiple creators of most comic books, they must be cataloged and classified under title. When one is trying to bring out a particular connection, such as the fact that the artist was born and raised in Johnstown, PA, this does not work. Thus Steve Ditko's works are given his name in the 100 field (or 700 for those which he did not himself script), and classified with a first cutter of .D1. As the most prolific and famous of the Pennsylvania creators, we made a command decision to give him a special cutter. These works fall under PN6727, though in Dewey they would fall under the 800s, such as American comic books under either 810 or 818 (depending on whether one considers them "miscellaneous literature"). Dewey would also require some manipulation of decimal coding to adapt a system designed to run from the beginning of American literature to one which runs from 1934 to the present, unless one chose to merely wholesale steal MSU's LC Age/Decade decimals and substitute them for the standard Dewey decimal scheme.

PN6728 and PN6729 are where the Dewey numbers truly break down. Although this was not a problem at the State Library of Pennsylvania, where graphical materials fall into the Library of Congress collection, it is impossible to obtain the same differentiation in Dewey (by author, by title, by publisher, by subject) simply from the classification number. This one has to rely on the cutter, although this will cluster author-cuttered numbers with publisher-cuttered, and so on. As many academic libraries (the normal home for comic research libraries) are LC-classified, this should not cause great problems, but the warning is indeed necessary. From here we will proceed with the LC-based scheme, as this shows both the power and the problems of a subject-based classification scheme.

PN 6728 is where works by Pennsylvania publishers fall, as well as works in which the title is the important feature. Until the 1990s, comic book producers in Pennsylvania (such as Fox Feature Syndicate in Wilkes-Barre or Home Comics in Philadelphia) were often imprints of larger, non–Pennsylvanian companies, or like Apple Press, publishers of reprints. This is one of those rare cases where the imprint is more important than its mother company, and the cutter should reflect this. In cases such as Cat Wild or Red Rose Studio (Pennsylvania publishers producing original work) this cutter becomes even more important, as the actual creators can be from and/or located in a wide variety of places. Some can be across the country or even in different countries. Titles, also placed in PN6728, are a trickier topic, as it is often hard to decide whether one has a Pennsylvania title, like *The Pitt*, where the Pennsylvania location or character's Pennsylvania connection is an integral part of the work, or like Rob Liefeld's 1997 run on Captain America, which could have taken place anywhere. However, Philadelphia was chosen as the home base of the villains (Liefeld, 1996). While standardization of procedure is a wonderful thing, this is a case where the decision comes down to cataloger intuition and the question of, "Can the patron find it?"

PN6729 covers individual comic strips or comic books of Pennsylvania, by subject, A-Z. It also is unused in LC Classification, so I stole it for this particular classification, although it is unlikely to already be in use for anything else at other libraries. Before we cover subject cuttering, it should be stated that, in the State Library of Pennsylvania's case, putting a subject cutter in a graphical literary format call number in addition to its placement in a MARC subject field should be a last resort. However, that said, in a subject-based scheme not based on Pennsylvania (or another locale), this might actually be the preferred cutter. For us the main times this might occur would be either gift comic books, where only the main story in an anthology title is actually set in Pennsylvania, or gift artwork for a particular story, where the same holds true.

This is also where we place character-cuttered works, a situation that occurs more often than one might think. A number of important characters were written as born and raised in Pennsylvania, such as Dr. Strange (Doctor Stephen Strange, Philadelphia, PA) and Sgt. Rock (assumed to be born and raised in or near Pittsburgh, PA, and who was actually given a street address there by his latest scripter/penciller, William [Billy] Tucci). Other characters, while not born and raised in Pennsylvania, have an important connection to the state that fundamentally shapes their character, such as the 1940s Liberty Belle (AKA Liberty Belle I), whose powers are activated by her sidekick's ringing of the Liberty Bell in Philadelphia. All of these characters, while not created by Pennsylvanians (save Dr. Strange, who was created and drawn by Steve Ditko until he left Marvel), would be cuttered by subject. Though Liberty Belle would seem to fit into a title cutter, her character, at least the first Liberty Belle, was actually one story in an anthology comic, and none of the other titles were Pennsylvania-based. Hence, she was paced in PN6729. For a number of reasons, in cases where a character's secret identity (real name) is known, we also cutter items by that name. First, it solves the problem of multiple incarnations, only one of which is Pennsylvania based, such as Deathlok (only the Michael Brant incarnation is a Pennsylvanian). Secondly, since we are a research, not access, collection, there is a good chance that the patron will know that name as well. And lastly, it allows for standard cataloging inversion, without ending up with a heading like the infamous America, Captain. Although this relies on the MARC record to make the link clear, if proper comic book cataloging procedures are followed this should not be a problem.

There are some additional points to our PN6729 usage — it is not as much of a free-for-all dumping ground as it sounds. In the case of a Pennsylvania-based team, the team name should be used as the cutter, like the Liberteens. However, Pennsylvania born/linked members of the team also have cutters generated and added to the list of potential cutters, in case of a spin-off book involving just these members. In a geographic sense, a town name would only be used in a case where the town itself becomes a character in the story (e.g. the aforementioned Captain America, in which the Sons of the Serpent are based in Philadelphia, PA). Another example in which the location of the action is significant is in *Forbidden Worlds 102*, where the feature story's action takes place in a haunted house in Orrsville, Pa., but the publisher is not in Pennsylvania, and the author cannot be proven to be. To reiterate an earlier statement, a town name would only be used in cases where the location is integral to the story.

At this point, it may help to see the process in action, using subject-based cuttering, as this may be the most difficult to imagine. In hand is *Forbidden Worlds 102* (1962), which, since it has been accepted by the State Library as a gift, we know to be a Pennsylvania-related title. In checking the Grand Comics Database, we find no identifiably Pennsylvania creator. Frankly, no one knows much about Ogden Whitney (the penciller), so he may be a Pennsylvanian, but since there is no proof we can not cutter by him. If one had time, one could run Internet checks to see if any of the people involved are from the state, assuming that the Bails Project[2] has already been consulted, and has failed to identify a place of birth or residence for them. If one decides to check, I would actually, in this case, recommend starting with Wikipedia. Although not a standard or perfect source by any means, on the topic of comic books their information tends to be fairly accurate. If information is not found there, it falls to a web search, or a database like *Contemporary Artists* or *Con-*

temporary Authors. As this is extremely time intensive, I cannot see too many catalogers being able to go this far.

So, there is no Pennsylvania creator connection, and the company which published this item, American Comics Group, was located in New York. This means it has to be a subject cutter, but what is the connection? It falls to that old standby, the item scan, to identify what one needs to cutter by, adding to the PN6729 call number gained because the item is being classified by subject. To make identifying the cutter easier, one should base the subject decision on the feature story, usually the longest, or first long, story in the issue. The cover sometimes also helps, since, if there is an octopus attacking a man, and there is a story inside where a man is attacked by a giant octopus, then this is the cover, or feature, story. The Grand Comics Database can also help; in most cases, the feature story will be identified as such when the issue details are searched out here. If neither of those work, in many Golden Age comics, the cover artist is also the artist on the feature story. If all these methods fail, it falls to cataloger intuition, though it may be that the feature story is not about a Pennsylvania topic, or by a Pennsylvania creator, but that later stories are. If one finds a story later in the issue, other than the feature, which is about Pennsylvania or by a Pennsylvania artist or writer, then this should be used as the basis for the call number, and it should be ensured that this tie is brought out in the bibliographic record.

In scanning the first page of the feature story in *Forbidden Worlds 102*, one finds that the hero has been asked to investigate a case of haunting, in Orrsville, Pennsylvania. As Pennsylvania is added to the town name in letting him know the location of his next case, it is likely that the hero is coming from outside the state, and that both he and his employers are non–Pennsylvanians. Thus there is no Pennsylvania main character, meaning it is not a character subject cutter. We do not cutter by a secondary character (in this case, the owner of the home, who merely provides a place for the action). Since we have neither a Pennsylvania character nor a Pennsylvania team, it must be classified by location, and by scanning the story, we find that the house is a character in its own right, confirming the decision.

Thus, the call number for *Forbidden Worlds 102* is PN 6729.2 .O759 .W577 .F747 no.102 1962. I added the decade decimal, although we do not use them at the State Library of Pennsylvania, as this is merely a local peculiarity. The addition of the decimal 2 means Fifties comics, which is when this particular title began, although this issue was published in the Silver Age, which would normally mean a 3. There are indeed times when one gives an item a decimal extension for when an issue was published, such as Marvel post–Spider-Man, to reflect the tone. This issue, however, has kept the 1950s vibe, though with a Post Comics Code Authority downplaying of the horror, so there is no reason to change the decimal here. The call number assigned breaks down thus:

> PN 6729.2 for its 1950s title start date (and tone)
> .O759 for Orrsville
> .W577 for the artist on the feature story, Ogden Whitney (You could use .A5 for ACG, from the MSU scheme. Whitney is a personal choice, but this choice should be consistent across titles)
> .F747 for the title (*Forbidden Worlds*). Issue number to distinguish it from other *Forbidden Worlds* cuttered by Whitney or ACG
> Year because of local practice

What has been presented here is, of course, only one subject-based classification scheme, and one based on a limited, and geographic, subject, although it could be adapted for use with other subjects, and in other collections, or used wholesale, with subject-based changes. It could even be re-adapted to stop the catalogers from shuddering at the collocation quirks, since subject-based collocation breaks title collocation, and vice versa. What one needs to remember, however, is that this scheme is based on the MSU classification scheme, as outlined in *Comics Librarianship: A Handbook*, which is out of print, but well worth finding a copy of—it will be a comics cataloger's best friend, and should be consulted for second and third cutters, past the subject based first.

Cataloging and classification out of the way, let us look at the funding issue mentioned earlier, as the State Library of Pennsylvania is a perfect example of how the best laid plans can go awry. During the process of writing procedures and policy, a short list of authors to buy first was drafted, with seminal works that, even with two copies (one preservation copy, one circulating), priced out under the $1000.00 limit. In an effort to stimulate a relationship, the local comic shop was contacted and informed of our interest in buying these titles through them. While this seems like a simple procedure, as a state government institution, the State Library of Pennsylvania has a certain process for confirming vendors for invoicing. After spending a couple of months convincing the shop to undertake the process so that we could pay them, they finally filled out the online form, which went into the queue, with an agency outside the Pennsylvania Department of Education. It was held up here for several months, with the State Library unable to order from a non-approved vendor, and the comic shop unable to supply us, since we could not pay them. Before they could get the vendor number and vetting we required, disaster struck—the budget was exhausted much sooner than anyone expected. Therefore, the library was left without the graphical materials we wished them to supply, and the comic shop was left disappointed in what they thought would be an ongoing relationship and a thousand dollar sale. Although we were later able to order some of the materials from other, vetted sources, the needed relationship with the local comic dealer was left unconsummated for an indefinite period of time.

This is also where donations came into play, and in a big way. I had written to a major Pennsylvania-born creator, well-known but unnamed here due to a promise of anonymity, asking for a list of his seminal works, and suggesting that we would be glad to preserve any of his works that he wished to donate. He was a test-run for me, as I figured if I could get him to respond, I could get almost anyone to do so. Respond he did, well beyond any expectations. For a period of three months, the State Library of Pennsylvania received a package a week, ranging from reprint editions (some of which had only been released a week or two before) to production proofs, original artwork, and odd and unique items like sticker sets. All of us eagerly waited for the day each week when we knew a package might come in. Although he has since run out of items to send us, the library ended up with thousands of dollars in material, all for the cost of postage on the initial letter and follow up Thank Yous. Cataloging these materials was also a great deal of fun—I could write an entire article just on the challenges of the cataloging of production proofs and original artwork, with and without the lettering. There are, of course, plans to contact other creators, as even a list of works they consider their best work, most deserving of preservation, would save the library much money from unneeded, or not needed yet, volumes.

The current future of the graphical materials program, like many programs such as digitization, is in some doubt, due to a 50 percent reduction in budgeting across the board. Combined with a reduction in staff, this means fewer materials coming in (save, hopefully, donations) and less time to catalog them properly once they are here. While items that are already at the library and cataloged will be preserved for the rest of eternity (or as close as we can get), the program will likely be taking a break for the next several years. This is a shame, but, as at many libraries across the nation, budget cutbacks close less essential programs. It will be nice to see what we can do if the money starts to flow again, but until then I share our experience for those who may be able to use it. We can no longer look down our noses at the "not-so funny books."

Endnotes

1. Toonseum. Located in the Children's Museum of Pittsburgh at 10 Children's Way, Pittsburgh, PA 15212. http://www.toonseum.org/.
2. Bails, Jerry G. 2006. Who's who of American comics, 1928–1999 (AKA The Bails Project). http://www.bailsprojects.com/.

References

Fee, William T. September 2008. "Do You Have Any Ditko? Comic Books, MARC, FRBR and Findability." *Serials Review* 34, no. 3: 175–189. http://www.sciencedirect.com/science/article/B6W63–4T2RYVT-1/2/d8 47af0269ebc7427a9a9539a1a7ba2b.
_____. 2009. "Pennsylvania in the Comics Trade." http://www.statelibrary.state.pa.us/libraries/cwp/view.asp? a=254&Q=147836&PM=1.
Goldsmith, Francisca. 2005. *Graphic Novels Now: Building, Managing, and Marketing a Dynamic Collection.* Chicago: American Library Association.
Library of Congress. 2004. *Cataloger's Desktop.* Washington, DC: Cataloging Distribution Service, Library of Congress.
Liefeld, Rob, scripter. 1996. *Captain America* (1996 series). New York: Marvel Comics.
Scott, Randall. *Comics Librarianship: A Handbook.* Jefferson, NC: McFarland, 1990.
_____. 2009. "Comics Research Libraries." Michigan State University Special Collections. http://www.lib.msu. edu/comics/director/comres.htm.
Scott, Randall. 2007. E-mail to author on the subject of the Jerry Bails microfilm library of comic art.
Serchay, David S. 1998. "Comic book collectors: The serials librarians of the home." *Serials Review.* 24, no. 1: 57–70. http://www.sciencedirect.com/science/article/B6W63–3YCMD93-B/2/5dff9fd4cb30b577f070d34 43e092f39.

17

Graphic Novels and the Untapped Audience

RUTH BOYER

Many librarians today embrace graphic novels as an effective way to attract reluctant readers and students into their libraries. Educators are incorporating graphic novels into their curricula. Libraries see their circulation numbers increase when they build their graphic novel collections and movies, toys, and media recognition all attest to the popularity and accessibility of the format. However, despite the ever-growing acceptance of graphic novels, their true potential is yet to be fully realized. This is the challenge for libraries and librarians.

Librarians and libraries have a mission to provide resources that inspire and enrich the lives of their communities. Librarians must also be willing to promote these resources to the best of their capabilities. They are not performing their duties if they continue to take a passive approach to the status of graphic novels in their collections. Graphic novels are there not only to reflect the needs of a ready audience, but also to inspire creativity, introduce art and literature in a new format, and connect generations in the timeless art of storytelling.

Yet, because graphic novels attract an already established audience, librarians often do not seek out the untapped audience. These are persons who disregard graphic novels as a legitimate format and have no desire to sample this section of the library's collection. It is important for librarians to take responsibility and identify this untapped audience and their beliefs regarding graphic novels. Librarians must understand the common misconceptions and views concerning the format, and why this often deters many people from accepting and appreciating graphic novels.

By identifying this untapped audience, librarians can implement strategies for reaching out to this group. Graphic novels are not only a tool to attract reluctant readers and teens. They are also a very powerful form of storytelling. However, this medium can only reach its full potential if librarians are proactive in advocating their graphic novel collections to both their traditional supporters and the untapped audience.

For many people, graphic novels are a new genre that libraries are introducing to the teens and children in their communities. Yet, librarians know that this is a misnomer. Graphic novels are not part of any written genre. As Steve Miller describes it, "graphic novels are stories told in a comics format that express a continuous tale. The art is what brings dimension and flavor to the story, bringing the dialogue and narrative to life" (Miller, 2004:

2). This format justifies its own place within the library. However, even more important than a physical place within a library is the intellectual and emotional place that graphic novels have yet to conquer.

Graphic novels admittedly have popular value and help increase circulation numbers for many library collections. However, they are also a unique form of storytelling in which art and literature meet. As Scott McCloud describes it:

> In comics at its best, words and pictures are like partners in a dance and each one takes turns leading. When both partners try to lead, the competition can subvert the overall goals ... though a little playful competition can sometimes produce enjoyable results. But when these partners each know their roles and support each other's strengths, comics can match any of the art forms it draws so much of its strength from" [McCloud, 1994:156].

This marriage of art and literature is one of the most effective ways of communicating ideas and sharing dreams. It is up to librarians to harness this power within their libraries and their communities.

As librarians, we develop our collections not only to meet readership needs, but we also seek to introduce diversity and new ideas to the community. Graphic novels, as a format, produce some of the most thoughtful and beautiful stories in the history of humanity. Yet, misunderstandings and stereotypes continue to hinder its potential. In 2001, McCloud stated that "comics is a powerful idea, but an idea that's been squandered, ignored and misunderstood for generations. Today, for all the hopes of those who value it, this form seems increasingly obscure, isolated and obsolete" (McCloud, 2001: 238). This statement is equally true today. Despite all the discussions surrounding graphic novels as a format, much of the dialogue revolves around its popularity and marketability.

The history of graphic novels often dwells on its pop culture status, media acceptance, and its attraction to reluctant readers. This discussion can provide the new librarian with valuable context and an introduction to graphic novels, if the newcomer was not previously exposed. However, it does not pass on the true beauty of the format. Librarians who work with graphic novel collections and understand the philosophical underpinning of the format have a responsibility to share their knowledge with staff as well as their communities. The place of graphic novels in a library is not only defined by their shelf space. It needs to also occupy the hearts and minds of those who walk into the library.

Graphic novels already have strong proponents in many communities due to their popularity among children and teens. However, if librarians truly wish to utilize the full potential of the format, they must seek out the untapped audience, while maintaining the loyalty of the current patron-base. What groups are included in this untapped audience? The groups may vary depending on the community, but the attitude is recognizable in its many forms.

The main attitude for a member of the untapped audience is one where they feel graphic novels have nothing to offer them. To this group, graphic novels are part of pop culture and only appealing for the children and teens in their community. The most dangerous part of this attitude is the belief that graphic novels are fun, and only fun for kids and teens. This is a dangerous stereotype because it limits the actual potential of the entire format. Those who hold this belief never feel the desire to explore or discover anything about graphic novels. Patrons that may represent this way of thinking vary. Examples include members of the senior population who might feel a generational gap with current graphic novels, parents who refuses to allow their children to read graphic novels, or even teens who stereotype graphic novels based on certain series or their peers who read them. All these people may believe that graphic novels have nothing to offer them. It is this challenge that librarians must face.

The untapped audience includes another group that often escapes the librarian's notice when discussing graphic novels. This group is library staff itself. It is as important, if not more important, to advocate this exciting format to our co-workers as it is to our patrons and community. However, by talking with internal staff, a librarian can often identify the similar belief found in many patrons that graphic novels are a popular genre suitable only for teens and children. Reader's advisory is as important between co-workers as it is with our patrons.

The promotion of graphic novels often revolves around displays, events, and recommendation booklists. However, these marketing tools are often geared towards those who already read graphic novels. Reader's advisory continues to be one of the most powerful tools librarians have when advocating a new library resource. In terms of graphic novels, librarians can integrate traditional reader's advisory skills alongside newfound understanding of the format to introduce a tentative newcomer to graphic novels.

There is no magic bullet in doing the perfect reader's advisory, even less so when dealing with graphic novels. The librarian's toolkit still includes an abundance of active listening, patience, and reading the body language for clues, while recommending items that might interest the patron. The person's reading habits and favorite genres are important clues to their interests. As a librarian trying to promote graphic novels, know your collection in terms of genres and the audience they might appeal to. Whether it is romance, fantasy, history, drama, or mystery; graphic novels have something for everyone. It is the job of the librarian to connect those interests to the resources available. When retrieving that new mystery book for your patron, consider grabbing a mystery graphic novel on the way back to booktalk. If they are looking for personal stories of the Holocaust, consider *Maus* along with Anne Frank's *Diary of a Young Girl.* When doing reader's advisory to a member of the untapped audience, the patron will not request items from the graphic novel collection, so it is up to the librarian to advocate this resource.

Along with active advocacy, it also important to know the boundaries of reader's advisory, especially when trying to introduce the patron to a new format. The untapped audience may already have preconceived ideas about the graphic novel, and these ideas often may not be discarded after one venture into the format. They may hold onto their beliefs for the rest of their lives, And that is ok too. Remember to "always respect a person's reading tastes" (Alesi, 2009). As librarians, it is not our job to convert our patrons to what we might consider the best parts of our collection. However, it is the foundation of our profession that we connect our communities to the best resources we have to offer. Whether they ultimately utilize those resources is still their choice.

It is important that librarians do not become discouraged when trying to outreach to the untapped audience. No matter what the response, planting seeds of ideas is part of librarianship. While it is true that a large part of the appeal of graphic novels is the fun or entertainment value, it is also an effective way of communicating ideas and thoughts in an easily accessible form. As librarians, we must truly believe this as we redefine the format to a reluctant listener. Each person has their own strengths. Just remember that you can "become a fanatic, or softly speak your feelings as a lone voice in the wilderness — use whichever method fits your style of promoting the collection, but promote, promote, promote" (Miller, 2005: 12). We must remember that "a proper definition, if we could find one, might give lie to the stereotypes and show that the potential of comics is limitless and exciting" (McCloud, 1994: 3). A librarian who personally believes in graphic novels as an exciting form of storytelling can also communicate their enthusiasm to their audience. Oftentimes, keeping faith may be the first step.

Graphic novels continue to be a growing part of a library's collection. However, the misconception that it is a popular genre for teens and children prohibit it from reaching its potential. Librarians themselves must believe in the legitimacy of this format in order to better advocate it to their peers and their communities. By identifying the untapped audience and utilizing basic librarian tools like reader's advisory, librarians can meet this challenge head on. It is important to remember that "if your library's mission includes taking responsibility for exposing your community to ideas and providing ideas that inform, educate, or entertain, there is a place for graphic novels in both the collections and the services you offer" (Goldsmith, 2005: 90). The fight for graphic novels is not over. As Goldsmith so eloquently puts it, "when it comes to best practices for graphic novels in libraries, we are, indeed, in a neonatal phase. We have begun. And it is no time for complacency" (Goldsmith, 2005: 92). The call to action is out there, and it is up to each librarian to decide whether they will rise up to meet the challenge.

References

Alesi, Stacy. 2009. "Reader's Advisory Advice." *BookBitch*. http://www.bookbitch.com/READERS%20 ADVISORY.htm.

Frank, Anne. 1977. *The Diary of a Young Girl*. Mattituck, NY: American Reprint Co.

Goldsmith, Francisca. 2005. *Graphic Novels Now*. Chicago: American Library Association.

McCloud, Scott. 2001. *Reinventing Comics: How Imagination and Technology are Revolutionizing an Art Form*. New York: Perennial.

_____. 1994. *Understanding Comics*. New York: Perennial.

Miller, Steve. 2004. *Developing and Promoting Graphic Novel Collections*. New York: Neal-Schuman.

Spiegelman, Art. 1997. *Maus: A Survivor's Tale*. New York: Pantheon Books.

18

Comic Relief in Libraries
Motivating Male Adolescent Readers

Karen Gavigan

And then the whining schoolboy
With his satchel and a shiny morning face
Creeping like a snail
Unwillingly to school.
(From *As You Like It* by William Shakespeare)

Holy cow, Batman, how can librarians get male adolescents to read? Robin has never spoken these words in the popular Batman comic book or television series; however, he might do so today if he read the latest literacy statistics. Reports on reading achievement scores in the United States consistently indicate that male adolescents are being outperformed by female adolescents (Booth, 2002; Gurian, 2001; Smith & Wilhelm, 2002). The 2005 *Nation's Report Card* reveals that female students scored higher on average in reading than male students in both grades 8 and 12. And 12th grade females score 13 points higher on average in reading than male students (Perie, Grigg, & Donahue, 2005). Regrettably, by the time males enter high school, over half identify themselves as non-readers (Smith & Wilhelm, 2002).

Furthermore, there is a growing body of research to indicate that boys read less than girls (Baker & Wigfield, 1999; Educational Alliance, 2007). For example, a study of *Contemporary Juvenile Reading Habits* showed that only 16.78 percent of boys in all age groups would prefer to read a book, whereas 42.44 percent of girls would prefer to read a book rather than watch television (Booth, 2002).

Understandably, many librarians, educators, and researchers from developed countries around the world agree that there is a current "boy crisis" in male adolescent literacy. Brozo (2002) writes, "It is perhaps this long well-documented history of male underachievement that has helped contribute to an entrenched popular perception, and indeed an expectation that many boys simply will not become thoughtful, accomplished readers" (306). As Shelley Peterson stated in her article, "Supporting Boys' and Girls' Literacy Learning," "We should always be concerned when one group of students consistently performs less successfully than another group, particularly in an area such as literacy that is so important in defining who we are as contributing members of society" (Peterson, 2000: 33).

Consequently, a burning question for librarians is "*How can we motivate reluctant male adolescents to enter into the world of reading?*" Graphic novels are a promising, increasingly popular avenue for motivating adolescent males to read. Many libraries and media centers recognize the growing popularity of graphic novels and are increasing the sizes of their graphic novel collections. At the same time, librarians are looking for strategies to use graphic novels to motivate reluctant male readers.

This chapter presents the case that graphic novels can serve as an effective literary format for engaging male adolescent readers. An overview of the growing popularity of graphic novels is presented, as well as suggestions for using them in libraries and media centers. For the purpose of this paper, the term *librarian* refers to both public librarians and media specialists.

Gaining Popularity: "Faster Than a Speeding Bullet"

The author David Eggers writes that, "[T]he graphic novel is not literary fiction's half-wit cousin, but, more accurately, the mutant sister who can often do everything fiction can, and just as often, more" (Gravett, 2005). There is a growing belief among librarians and other literacy educators that graphic novels can help reluctant readers achieve reading enjoyment and success (Bruggerman, 1997; Cary, 2004, Crawford, 2004; Gorman, 2003; Krashen, 2005; Lyga & Lyga, 2004; Schwarz, 2002). They can serve as visually engaging and satisfying forms of comic relief from more daunting, less appealing literature for reluctant male readers. Graphic novels are skewed towards boys' interests and naturally grab the attention of many male readers (Thompson, 2008). Middle-school media specialist Karen Perry agrees. "Boys eat them up! If you want to get middle school males excited about coming to the library then put graphic novels on your shelves" (personal interview, May 19, 2009). When she started her graphic novel collection at her middle school in 2006, only thirty-two titles accounted for 14 percent of the media center's circulation for the academic year.

Graphic novels have received increasing coverage in the media spotlight in recent years. Once viewed as a form of sub-literature, they are now being recognized as "hip, hot, and smart" (Myers, 2006). For example, the U.S. Military Academy at West Point requires cadets to read the graphic novel *Persepolis* before they graduate (Foroohar, 2005).

Graphic novels are also gaining increased recognition in the literary world. Recently, respected journals and newspapers such as *School Library Journal, Publisher's Weekly, The New York Times, English Journal*, and *Education Week* have published articles about graphic novels as well as graphic novel reviews. Additionally, the International Reading Association has its own special interest group, *Science Fiction, Fantasy, and Graphic Novels*. One of the goals of the group is to implement best teaching and research practices in the classroom of science fiction, fantasy, and graphic novels.

Furthermore, the four major comic book publishers have all reported sales increases with Marvel Comics experiencing a 400 percent increase from 1999 to 2002 (MacDonald, 2008), and a 208 percent increase in 2001 alone (Flores as cited in Foster, 2004: 31). The overall estimated sales of graphic novels in 2006 were $330 million, with Scholastic Book Fairs reporting that they have sold 4 million graphic novels since 2004 (Reed Business Information, 2007). In 2007 graphic novel sales in the U.S. and Canada were $375 million, a 12 percent rise from 2006 and quintuple the sales number from 2001 (MacDonald, 2008).

Moving Beyond Superheroes

Although many adolescent males enjoy the fictional exploits of Spider-Man and Superman, others are reading graphic novels dealing with a variety of genres, subjects, and social issues. Robin Brenner, author of *Understanding Manga and Anime* (2007), writes, "... [S]uperheroes are still the bread and butter of the big companies, but genre diversity is increasing every day with more and more independent companies publishing a range of genres, from memoir to fantasy to historical fiction" (Brenner, 2006).

Graphic novel guru Michele Gorman states, "[R]esearch done by professionals in the field and real-life experiences of librarians have shown that there is one format that covers a variety of genres, addresses current and relatives issues for teens, stimulates the young people's imagination, and engages reluctant readers: graphic novels" (Gorman, 2003: xi). Recently, Gene Yang's graphic novel, *American Born Chinese* (recipient of the 2007 Michael Printz Award and a National Book Award Finalist) deals with immigration issues in describing a lonely Asian-American middle school male who yearns to fit in with his classmates (Yang, 2006). Calvin Reid, editor for comic coverage in *Publisher's Weekly*, says, "What we're seeing is some sort of tipping point that has been a long process in coming. Really, for the first time ... more people are seeing there is more variety than superhero comics" (Myers, 2006).

Graphic Novels — Dynamic Forces in Reading Motivation

As additional genres of graphic novels become available, many librarians are recognizing the role that graphic novels can play in helping to motivate reluctant male adolescent readers. As Andera states, "[G]raphic novels, with their visual appeal, may be just what the library collection needs to assist the development of students to be life-long readers" (Andera, 2007: 5).

Overall, there are three key reasons that graphic novels may significantly impact the reading motivation of male adolescents: variety and choice, visual appeal, and a conduit to other reading materials. They are listed below.

1. Variety and Choice

When students were asked what advice they would give future English teachers, Aaron said, "Choice would be a big part of it" [Smith & Wilhelm, 2002: 110].

Research indicates that choice in reading is an effective tool to motivate readers (Baker, Afflerback, & Reinking, 1966; Guthrie & Humenick, 2004). Librarians need to ensure that their collections have a variety of resources, such as graphic novels, that meet the literacy needs of male adolescents. Additional studies show that when given the opportunity to select reading materials, boys often choose graphic novels (Cary, 2004; Krashen, 2004). The non-traditional, visual format of graphic novels typically appeals to male readers. They consistently engage readers through humor, heroes, artwork and more (Cary, 2004). Furthermore, graphic novels offer fast-paced action and conflict making them an ideal choice for hooking unmotivated readers (Gorman, 2003). In the words of the author, Robert Lipsyte, "So, you say, we have to change society first, and then boys will read good books. This is true. But if we can get just a few boys to read a few good books, we will have started the change. Cajole, coerce, do whatever needs to be done to get one book into one boy's hands or back pocket ..." (as cited in Brozo, 2002:. 23).

2. *Visual Appeal*

"I enjoy reading graphic novels such as *Maus* because it is direct and you can see it" [Yuri, a middle school male, as cited in Smith & Wilhelm, 2002: 152].

The rising popularity of graphic novels may be the result of an increasingly visual culture on today's youth. The non-threatening visual format of graphic novels appeals to male adolescents better than text alone, and can foster an enthusiasm towards books and reading. Research indicates that males respond positively to images because they are more oriented to visual/spatial learning (Ministry of Education of Ontario, 2004).

In graphic novels, illustrations blend with text, often attracting males whose reading motivation tends to wane during adolescence. They offer a stimulating means by which to develop the visual literacy of students (Carter, 2007). Gene Yang, author of *American Born Chinese* (2006) writes, "The comic's medium by its very nature is a multimedia medium. It is a single unified medium made up of two distinct media: text and still imagery. By teaching your students to read and create comic books, you are teaching them to analyze the very nature of information, a 21st century skill" (Yang, 2008). Fernando Garcia, a freshman in Santa Rosa, California, agrees: "I like comic books because they are interesting, funny, easy to read, short, and they have pictures to help you understand" (as cited in Cary, 2004: 65).

3. *Serve as a conduit to other reading materials*

...you have done a great deal when you have brought a boy to have entertainment from a book. He'll get better books afterwards" [Samuel Johnson as cited in Brozo, 2002: 77].

Graphic novels can be the perfect entry point for motivating male adolescents to read more challenging materials. Brenner writes,

Even if a guy is a natural reader, as guys pass into their teen years, reading becomes a far less 'cool' thing to be doing. Comics represent a widespread and still 'cool' way to read that will keep the spark of enjoying reading alive. When they're ready, they'll remember that reading can be fun, and will gradually branch out into other formats, from traditional prose to poetry [personal communication, August 28, 2007].

Case studies support the view that reading light materials, such as comic books, is the way many students develop a taste for reading (Krashen, 2004). Krashen and others believe that when male readers select graphic novels, it can help them find their reading voices by choosing to read rather than choosing not to read at all. They can also serve as bridges to traditional texts. For example, the results of a study of seventh grade boys showed that reading comics did not inhibit other kinds of reading. Rather, the study was consistent with the hypothesis that comic book reading facilitates heavier reading (Ujiie & Krashen, 1996).

Circulation data from school and public libraries further support the theory that graphic novels can fuel the desire for additional reading materials. Some libraries have reported 25 percent increases in overall circulation after adding graphic novels to their collections (Miller, 2005). Allison Steinberg, a media specialist in California, increased her library circulation by 50 percent after purchasing $1,000 worth of graphic novels. Her approach is to start students out with graphic novels and then direct them to related books in the same genre (Curriculum Reviews, 2004). Additionally, a librarian in a Catholic school system in South Dakota found that overall circulation increased when she added graphic novels to her collection (Andera, 2007). Significantly, she found that there was an increase in the number of books that third through sixth grade boys were checking out.

Many librarians believe that there are additional ways in which graphic novels can positively influence the literacy lives of male adolescents. Several have touted the educational benefits of using graphic novels with students. Gorman (2008) writes that graphic novels address relevant social issues for young readers such as bullying and divorce. Schwarz (2002) states that an important benefit of using graphic novels is that they present alternative views of culture, history and human life. Schwarz and others also believe that graphic novels can be used effectively to teach multiple literacies (Schwarz, 2002; Carter, 2007; Frey & Fisher, 2008; Thompson, 2008). Along with these authors, Miller (2005, pp. 90–91) asserts that the following are some of the advantages of using graphic novels in libraries and other educational settings:

1. Graphic novels can help students develop literacy and language skills by reinforcing vocabulary
2. Graphic novels offer students a chance to explore visual literacy and develop critical thinking skills
3. Graphic novels can present information about literature, history, and social issues in ways that appeal to reluctant readers
4. Graphic novels provide stepping stones to full-text classics and spring boards to extra learning activities
5. Graphic novels can inspire challenged students who lack reading confidence, reading ability, or motivation for self-guided reading

Using Graphic Novels in Public Libraries and Media Centers

With the explosive popularity of graphic novels, and their sometimes controversial content, how does a librarian know where to begin? Fortunately, since 2003, a variety of books have been published that deal with graphic novels and their use with children and adolescents in libraries and classrooms. These books can guide interested librarians through the process of developing quality graphic novel collections. Many of them also provide information regarding literacy strategies and graphic novel programming for libraries.

Table 18.1: Getting Started with Graphic Novels—Print Resources

Brenner, Robin. 2007. *Understanding Manga and Anime.* Westport, CT: Libraries Unlimited.

Carter, James Bucky. 2007. *Building Literacy Connections with Graphic Novels: Page by Page, Panel by Panel.* Urbana, IL: National Council of Teachers of English.

Cary, Stephen. 2004. *Going Graphic: Comics at Work in the Multilingual Classroom.* Portsmouth, NH: Heinemann.

Frey, Nancy, and Douglas Fisher. 2008. *Teaching Visual Literacy: Using Comic Books, Graphic Novels, Anime, Cartoons, and More to Develop Comprehension and Thinking Skills.* Thousand Oaks, CA: Corwin Press.

Goldsmith, Francisca. 2005. *Graphic Novels Now: Building, Managing, and Marketing a Dynamic Collection.* Chicago, IL: American Library Association.

Gorman, Michele. 2003. *Getting Graphic! Using Graphic Novels to Promote Literacy with Pre–teens and Teens.* Worthington, OH: Linworth Publishing, Inc.

Gorman, Michele. 2008. *Getting Graphic! Comics for Kids: A Comprehensive Resource for Selecting Comic Books and Graphic Novels for Kids at the Elementary Level.* Worthington, OH: Linworth Publishing, Inc.

Lyga, Allyson W., and Barry Lyga. 2004. *Graphic Novels in Your Media Center: A Definitive Guide.* Westport, CT: Libraries Unlimited.

Miller, Steve. 2005. *Developing and Promoting Graphic Novel Collections.* New York: Neal-Schuman Publishers, Inc.

Pawuk, Michael. 2007. *Graphic Novels: A Genre Guide to Comic Books, Manga, and More.* Westport, CT: Libraries Unlimited.

Serchay, David S. 2008. *The Librarian's Guide to Graphic Novels for Children and Tweens.* New York: Neal-Schuman Publishers, Inc.

Thompson, Terry. 2008. *Adventures in Graphic: Using Comics and Graphic Novels to Teach Comprehension, Grades 2–6.* Portland, ME: Stenhouse Publishers.

Weiner, Stephen. 2006. *101 Best Graphic Novels.* New York: NBM Publishing.

Regular reviews of graphic novels can be located in the following periodicals:

- *Booklist*
- *Horn Book*
- *ICv2 (http://icv2.com)*
- *Library Journal*
- *Library Media Connection*
- *Publishers' Weekly*
- *School Library Journal*
- *VOYA (Voice of Youth Advocates)*

These, and other literacy periodicals, can be an excellent source for helping librarians select appropriate graphic novel titles for their collections.

In addition to books and magazines, there are a number of helpful websites with lists and strategies for using graphic novels with students.

Table 18.2: Getting Started with Graphic Novels: Web Resources

Comics in Education by Gene Yang
   http://www.humblecomics.com/comicsedu/index.html
Comics in the Classroom
   http://comicsintheclassroom.net/index.htm
Good Comics for Kids
   http://www.schoollibraryjournal.com/blog/540000654/post/1020042902.html
Graphic Classroom
   http://graphicclassroom.blogspot.com
Great Graphic Novels for Teens— YALSA
   http://www.ala.org/ala/yalsa/booklistsawards/greatgraphicnovelsforteens/gn.htm
Graphic Novels: Resources for Teachers and Librarians
   http://library.buffalo.edu/libraries/asl/guides/graphicnovels
Kids Love Comics!
   http://www.kidslovecomics.com/index.html
Librarian's Guide to Anime and Manga
   http://www.koyagi.com/Libguide.html
No Flying! No Tights!
   http://www.noflyingnotights.com/index2.html

The following is a selective list of suggestions for using graphic novels with male adolescents in libraries and media centers:

- The classics can be brought to life for male readers through graphic novel adaptations such as *Frankenstein* (Reed, 2005) and *The Red Badge of Courage* (Vansant, 2005). Short stories such as *Graphic Classics: O. Henry* and *Sherlock Holmes, Plus*

Great Tales of Ghost, Pirates & Mystery are also available for library collections (Geary et al., 2005).

- Male adolescents can become engaged in history by reading titles such as *The 9/11 Report: A Graphic Adaptation* (Jacobson & Colon, 2006), and the *Graphic History* line of books by Capstone Press, which includes *The Battle of the Alamo, The Boston Tea Party, and The Sinking of the Titanic* (Doeden, 2005). Other possibilities are Rosen's *Graphic Battles of World War II Series* which features *The Battle of Guadalcanal* and *The Battle of Iwo Jima* (Hama, 2007).

- Graphic novel biographies are an important part of a library's graphic novel collection. Titles of interest for male adolescent readers include *King, A Comic Biography of Martin Luther King* (Anderson, 2005), *Houdini, The Handcuff King* (Lutes & Bertozzi, 2007), *Blackbeard's Sword* (O'Donnell, 2007), and *Pedro and Me* (Winnick, 2000). An extremely popular sports biography series for adolescent males is the *Greatest Stars of the NBA* by Tokyopop. The Shaquille O'Neal title features a foldout with the actual size (22) of the basketball star's foot (Finkel, 2004).

- Librarians can introduce mythology to patrons and students through series such as *Graphic Mythology* (2006) by Rosen Publishing, which includes Greek, Roman, African and Chinese myths that should interest male adolescent readers.

- Engaging graphic novel titles such as *Two-Fisted Science: Stories about Scientists* (Ottaviani, 2001) can inspire future scientists. The popular Max Axiom series by Capstone Press includes *A Crash Course in Forces and Motion with Max Axiom, Super Scientist* (Sohn, 2007). Rosen Central's series on Graphic Novel Disasters includes *Hurricanes* (Jeffrey, 2007) and six other titles dealing with disasters such as tsunamis and earthquakes.

- Another series by Rosen Central is Graphic Careers, a set of seven career titles. *Astronauts* (West, 2008) and others in the series, such as *Fighter Pilots* and *Race Car Drivers*, offer an opportunity for teenage males to read about seven action-packed careers.

In order to promote these titles, librarians can book talk and/or display them in creative ways throughout their libraries. They may consider using these and other titles with male adolescents in graphic novel book clubs. Many librarians and teachers have discovered that boys-only book clubs are a way to engage males in positive reading experiences by providing them with a sense of identity and ownership, and helping them to develop into lifelong readers (Brozo, 2007; Sullivan, 2003 & 2009; Taylor, 2005). Librarians can also offer graphic novel programming as another way to help male adolescents discover the joy of reading.

Is Relief in Sight?

"It may be that how we accompany children into the print world will determine their future as literate being" [Booth, 2002:.9].

Today's librarians are struggling with how to attend to the current "boy crisis" in literacy education. "Reversing the stereotypes of boys as weak readers and addressing the complex problems facing those who have been turned off by reading is perhaps our biggest challenge" (Brozo, 2007: 7). Given that the gap between male and female reading achievement increases over time (Tyre, 2005), librarians need to look for new and innovative ways to help male adolescents become readers. Graphic novels can provide comic relief to struggling male adolescent readers by allowing them to choose visually appealing, high-interest literature that captures their imaginations. When librarians use graphic novels to bring about positive changes in the literacy lives of male adolescents, the results can be "more powerful than a locomotive" (May, 2006).

References

"Adding comic books leads to circulation gains." 2004. *Curriculum Review* 44 (1): 1–3.
Andera, Sandy. 2007. "Graphic Novels in the School Library Help Promote Literacy for Boys." *PNLA Quarterly*, 71 (4): 5–8. Pacific Northwest Library Association.
Anderson, Ho Che. 2005. *King: A Comics Biography of Martin Luther King.* Seattle, WA: Fantagraphics Books.
Baker, Linda, and Allan Wigfield. 1999. "Dimensions of Children's Motivation for Reading and Their Relations to Reading Activity and Reading Achievement." *Reading Research Quarterly*, 34 (4): 452–477.
Baker, Linda, Peter Afflerback, and David Reinking. 1996. *Developing Engaged Readers in Homes and Communities.* Mahwah, NJ: Lawrence Erlbaum Associates, Inc., Publishers.
Booth, David. 2002. *Even Hockey Players Read: Boys, Literacy and Learning.* Markham, ON: Pembroke Publishers.
Brenner, Robin. March/April 2006. *Graphic Novels 101: FAQ.* New York: Horn Book Inc. http://www.hbook.com/magazine/articles/2006/mar06_brenner.asp.
Brenner, Robin. 2007. *Understanding Manga and Anime.* Westport, CT: Libraries Unlimited.
Brozo, William G. 2002. *To Be a Boy to Be a Reader: Engaging Teen and Preteen Boys in Active Literacy.* Newark, DE: International Reading Association.
Bruggerman, Lora. January 1997. "Zap! Whoosh! Kerplow! Build High-quality Graphic Novel Collections with Impact." *School Library Journal*: 22–27.
Carter, James Bucky. 2007. *Building Literacy Connections with Graphic Novels: Page by Page, Panel by Panel.* Urbana, IL: National Council of Teachers of English.
Cary, Stephen. 2004. *Going Graphic: Comics at Work in the Multilingual Classroom.* Portsmouth, NH: Heinemann.
Crawford, Philip C. February 2004. "A Novel Approach: Using Graphic Novels to Attract Reluctant Readers." *Library Media Connection*, 26–28.
Doeden, Matt. 2005. *The Battle of the Alamo.* Mankato, MN: Capstone Press.
_____. 2005. *The Boston Tea Party.* Mankato, MN: Capstone Press.
_____. 2005. *The Sinking of the Titanic.* Mankato, MN: Capstone Press.
Educational Alliance. Winter 2007. "Gender Differences in Reading Achievement: Policy Implications and Best Practices." www.educationalliance.org/teaadmin/attachments/GenderDifferences.pdf.
Finkel, Jon. 2004. *Greatest Stars of the NBA: Shaquille O'Neal.* Los Angeles: Tokyopop.
Foroohar, Rana. August 22, 2005. "Literature: Graphic Novels as Serious Art." Newsweek International on MSNBC.com. http://www.msnbc.msn.com/id/8941787/site/newsweek/print/1/displaymode/1098.
Foster, Katy. February 2004. "Graphic Novels in Libraries: An Expert's Opinion." *Library Media Connection*, 30–32.
Frey, Nancy, and Douglas Fisher. 2008. *Teaching Visual Literacy: Using Comic Books, Graphic Novels, Anime, Cartoons, and More to Develop Comprehension and Thinking Skills.* Thousand Oaks, CA: Corwin Press.
Geary, Rick, et al. 2005. *Graphic Classics, Volume Two: Arthur Conan Doyle.* Mount Horeb, WI: Eureka Publications.
_____. 2005. *Graphic Classics, Volume Eleven: O'Henry.* Mount Horeb, WI: Eureka Publications.
Goldsmith, Francisca. 2005. *Graphic Novels Now: Building, Managing, and Marketing a Dynamic Collection.* Chicago, IL: American Library Association.
Gorman, Michele. 2008. *Getting Graphic! Comics for Kids: A Comprehensive Resource for Selecting Comic Books and Graphic Novels for Kids at the Elementary Level.* Worthington, OH: Linworth Publishing, Inc.
_____. 2003. *Getting Graphic! Using Graphic Novels to Promote Literacy with Pre–Teens and Teens.* Worthington, OH: Linworth Publishing, Inc.
Gravett, Paul. 2005. *Graphic Novels: Everything You Need to Know.* New York: Collins Design.
Gurian, Michael, and Patricia Henley. 2001. *Boys and Girls Learn Differently: A Guide for Teachers and Parents.* San Francisco, CA: Jossey-Bass.
Guthrie, John T., and Nicole Humenick. 2004. "Motivating Students to Read: Evidence for Classroom Practices that Increase Motivation and Achievement." In *The Voice of Evidence in Reading Research,* P. McArdle & V. Chhabra. eds., 329–354. Baltimore, MD: Paul H. Brookes.
Hama, Larry. 2007. *Battle of Guadalcanal: Land and Sea Warfare in the South Pacific.* New York: Rosen Publishing Group.

_____. 2007. *Battle of Iwo Jima: Guerilla Warfare in the Pacific*. New York: Rosen Publishing Group.

Jacobson, Sid, and Ernie Colon. 2006. *The 9/11 Report: A Graphic Adaptation*. New York: Hill & Wang.

Jeffrey, Gary. 2007. *Graphic Novel Disasters: Hurricanes*. New York: Rosen Publishing.

Krashen, Stephen. 2004. *The Power of Reading: Insights from the Research*. Second Edition. Portsmouth, NH: Libraries Unlimited.

Lutes, Jason, and Nick Bertozzi. 2007. *The Center for Cartoon Studies Presents Houdini: The Handcuff King*. New York: Hyperion.

Lyga, Allison W., and Barry Lyga. 2004. *Graphic Novels in Your Media Center: A Definitive Guide*. Westport, CT: Libraries Unlimited.

May, Ross. 2006. *The Super Guide to the Fleischer Superman Cartoons*. www.supermanhomepage.com/movies/movies.php?topic=m-fleis2.

McDonald, Heidi. 2008. "ICv2 Confab Reports 2007 Graphic Novel Sales Rise 12%." *Publishers Weekly*. http://www.publishersweekly.com/article/CA6552534.html.

Miller, Steve. 2005. *Developing and Promoting Graphic Novel Collections*. New York: Neal-Schuman Publishers, Inc.

Ministry of Education of Ontario. 2004. *Me Read, No Way: A Practical Guide to Improving Boys' Literacy Skills*. http://www.edu.gov.on.ca/eng/document/brochure/meread/meread.pdf.

Myers, Randy. April 4, 2006. "Graphic Novels: Evolution of a Genre." *Greensboro News & Record*: D1, D3.

Neilson, W.A., and C.J. Hill. 1970. *The Complete Plays and Poems of William Shakespeare*. New York: Houghton Mifflin Company.

O'Donnell, Liam. 2007. *Blackbeard's Sword: The Pirate King of the Carolinas*. Mankato, MN: Stone Arch Books.

Ottaviani, Jim. 2001. *Two-Fisted Science: Stories about Scientists*. Ann Arbor, MI: G.T. Labs.

Pawuk, Michael. 2007. *Graphic Novels: A Genre Guide to Comic Books, Manga, and More*. Westport, CT: Libraries Unlimited.

Perie, Marianne, Wendy Grigg, and Patricia Donahue. 2005. *The Nation's Report Card: Reading 2005*. (NCES 2006–451). U.S. Department of Education, National Center for Education Statistics, Washington, DC: U.S. Government Printing Office

Peterson, Shelley. 2000. "Supporting Boys' and Girls' Literacy Learning." *Orbit Magazine: OISE / UT's Magazine for Schools*. http://www.oise.utoronto.ca/orbit/girls_boys_sample.html.

Reed, Gary. 2005. *Mary Shelley's Frankenstein, the Graphic Novel*. New York: Puffin Books.

Reed Business Information. March 5, 2007. "Graphic Novels by the Numbers." New York: *Publishers Weekly*. http://www.publishersweekly.com/article/CA6421266.html?q=Graphic+Novels+by+the+Numbers.

Rothschild, D. Aviva. 1995. *Graphic Novels: A Bibliographic Guide to Book-Length Comics*. Englewood, CO: Libraries Unlimited.

Schwarz, Gretchen E. 2002. "Graphic Novels for Multiple Literacies." *Journal of Adolescent & Adult Literacy*, 46, 3:262–265.

Serchay, David S. (2008). *The Librarian's Guide to Graphic Novels for Children and Tweens*. New York: Neal-Schuman Publishers, Inc.

Smith, Michael W., and Jeffrey D. Wilhelm. 2002. *"Reading Don't Fix No Chevy's": Literacy in the Lives of Young Men*. Portsmouth, NH: Heinemann.

Sohn, Emily. 2007. *A Crash Course in Forces and Motion with Max Axiom, Super Scientist*. Mankato, MN: Capstone Press.

Spiegelman, Art. 1992. *Maus: A Survivor's Tale*. New York: Pantheon Books.

Sullivan, M. 2003. *Connecting Boys with Books*. Chicago: American Library Association.

Taylor, D. December 2004. "Not Just Boring Stories: Reconsidering the Gender Gap for Boys." *Journal of Adolescent & Adult Literacy* 48(4): 290–298.

Thompson, Terry. 2008. *Adventures in Graphic: Using Comics and Graphic Novels to Teach Comprehension, Grades 2–6*. Portland, ME: Stenhouse Publishers.

Tyre, P. January 30, 2006. "The Trouble with Boys." *Newsweek*, 5, 44–52.

Ujiie, Joanne, and Steven Krashen. Spring 1996. "Comic Book Reading, Reading Enjoyment, and Pleasure Reading among Middle Class and Chapter 1 Middle School Students." *Reading Improvement* 33: 41–54.

Vansant, Wayne. 2005. *Stephen Crane's The Red Badge of Courage, The Graphic Novel*. New York: Puffin Books.

Weiner, Stephen. 2006. *101 Best Graphic Novels*. New York: NBM Publishers.

West, David. 2008. *Graphic Careers: Astronauts*. New York: Rosen Publishing.

_____. 2008. *Graphic Careers: Fighter Pilots*. New York: Rosen Publishing.

_____. 2008. *Graphic Careers: Race Car Drivers*. New York: Rosen Publishing.

Winnick, Judd. 2000. *Pedro and Me: Friendship, Loss and What I Learned*. New York: Henry, Holt and Company.

Yang, Gene. 2006. *American Born Chinese*. New York: Roaring Brook Press.

Yang, Gene Lang. 2008. "Gene Yang on Comics and Education." *Asian American Comics*. http://www.asianamericancomics.com/2008/02/gene-yang-on-comics-and-educat.shtml.

19

"Forty-one-year-old female academics aren't supposed to like comics!"

The Value of Comic Books to Adult Readers

SARAH ZIOLKOWSKA AND VIVIAN HOWARD

"A taste for comics is excusable only by extreme youth because it involves acquiescence in hideous draughtsmanship and a scarcely human coarseness and flatness of narration."
— C.S. Lewis, 1961

"I love to read, I love art, and I love fiction. Comics are just one more medium in which I can enjoy all that."
— Hermione, interview participant

The twenty-first century is experiencing a comic book renaissance: film adaptations of *The Dark Knight, 300* and *Sin City* have been huge box office successes; Japanese "manga" comics are stocked in most libraries and bookstores; and Free Comic Book Day is celebrated on the first Saturday of May throughout North America. However, not much is known about comic book fans, outside of the stereotyped (and frequently stigmatized) images of "fanboy" or "fangirl" (Lopes, 2006). Within public libraries, comic book circulation comprises an important percentage of the total figures, yet librarians remain largely uninformed about who is actually using the comic collections (McPherson, 2006; Nichols, 2004). While the reading patterns and behaviors of various populations of readers have been investigated by previous researchers (Bender, 1944; Bergin, 2005; Fry, 1985; Krashen, 1993; Smith and Wilhelm, 2002; Snowball, 2005; Worthy, Moorman, and Turner, 1999), adult comic book readers have been overlooked. This paper addresses this gap in the research literature by investigating why adult comic book readers choose to read comics.

Literature Review

Comic book scholarship can be analyzed into three main categories: efforts to stigmatize the content and medium of comics; efforts to counteract the stigmatization and legitimate the medium; and efforts to identify the benefits resulting from reading comics.

STIGMATIZATION

In 1953, Frederic Wertham published his now infamous book *The Seduction of the Innocent.* Effectively, this work demonized comic books, painting them as largely responsible for the moral decay and educational ruin of children. This publication, as well as others, set off a whirlwind of moral outrage, resulting in the establishment of the Comic Book Code in 1954 (Lopes, 2006; 547). Lopes notes that comic books continue to be stigmatized, and are considered by many to be juvenile and unworthy of adult readership. Ironically, Stephen Krashen's *The Power of Reading*, which analyzed the literary benefits of pleasure reading, sought to remove the harmful stigma that had plagued comic readership by promoting comics as "easy reading" and a "gateway for reluctant readers" (Krashen, 1993). However, instead of removing stigma, classifying comics as "easy" promoted the idea that they were not "real reading," and further reinforced their lowbrow status.

LEGITIMATION

The second major theme found within the literature is the attempt to establish the legitimacy of the comic book format as an art form and medium. This approach is exemplified by Will Eisner's 1985 publication, *Comics and Sequential Art*, which was one of the primary catalysts for legitimizing comics and cartoons. One year later, Art Spiegelman published his graphic novel, *Maus: A Survivor's Tale*, which went on to win, among many other awards, the Pulitzer Prize in 1992. Eisner and Spiegelman effectively changed the scholarly discourse on comics.

Similarly, Scott McCloud's work, *Understanding Comics* (1993), is now one of the quintessential resources for comic scholarship. McCloud sought to prove that, contrary to being "easy reads," comics are actually complex and challenging, and as a "cool" medium (McLuhan, 1964; McLuhan and Fiore, 1967), requiring a high level of participation from the reader. While McCloud's ideas are not entirely original, drawing largely on his predecessors Eisner and McLuhan, he synthesized and expanded their ideas, making it possible for serious academic comic book scholarship to come into being.

BENEFITS

In the late twentieth century, the development of the New Literacy approach to reading, which maintains that the meaning of "literacy" is constantly being negotiated and renegotiated, also encouraged serious academic consideration of comic books as well as other forms of popular media (Dombeck and Gustafson, 2005; Gravett, 2005; McCloud, 2006; McPherson, 2006; Mulholland, 2004; Nichols, 2004; Schodt, 1996; Schwarz, 2002; Yannicopoulou, 2004). New Literacy theorists called for an expansion of the concept of literacy as single faceted and text-based literacy into a more inclusive and multi-faceted definition. Known variously as visual literacy, multimodal literacy, and multiliteracy, this expansion takes into account the various types of media and media-related skills needed for the successful negotiation of the current environment (Cope, Kalantzis, and New London Group, 2000). Comics, which by their very nature boast a combination of two types of media (text and image, were seen as contributing to the multi-modal skills of their readers. New Literacy theorists argued that comics, which require a level of proficiency in both textual and visual literacy, are an effective teaching tool for multi-modal skills. Francesca Goldsmith's *Graphic Novels Now* (2005), for example, explores the cognitive appeal of graphic novel reading: how the interplay of word and image on the page replicates the way our brain incorporates the two forms of information. Nevertheless, while several recent publications have focused on the benefits of comic books to teen readers (Dombeck and Gustafson, 2005; Leckbee, 2005; Snowball, 2005; Welch and Brown, 2005), and despite Charbonneau's findings that a large proportion of adult library patrons are comic book readers (Charbonneau, 2005), the benefits of comic book reading for adult readers have not been investigated.

Other Relevant Literature

More broadly, several researchers have investigated how people become readers, and the value that reading has in their lives. Examples of such qualitative research include *Reading Don't Fix No Chevys* by Michael Smith and Jeffrey Wilhelm. In their study, the authors examined the reading habits of forty-nine boys, from a variety of ethnic backgrounds, and socio-economic levels, enrolled in the seventh grade through twelfth grade, from urban, suburban and rural schools, in private and public educational settings. They found that the approach commonly taken in the teaching of reading and literature is completely out of step with how these young men make meaning of communication in all of its forms. Ultimately, Smith and Wilhelm (2002: 42) conclude: "None of the boys in the study rejected literacy; what they did ... reject was 'school literacy.'" The boys in their study had rich, literate lives outside of school, but were not intrinsically motivated to read by their educational experiences.

The psychologist Csikszentmihalyi uses the concept of "flow" to explain why some activities are so enjoyable and absorbing, offering the following definition of "flow" in his seminal work, *Flow: The Psychology of Optimal Experience* (1990: 50):

> At the core of the flow experience is enjoyment. For an activity to be truly enjoyable, it must have clear goals, permit immediate feedback, require effortless involvement, and have a clear chance of completion. A truly enjoyable experience leads to an altered sense of time duration, a sense of control over one's own action, and the emergence of a stronger sense of self.

"Flow" is an optimal psychological state that occurs when individuals are so engrossed in an activity that nothing else matters. In a state of flow, individuals find great satisfaction in an activity regardless of their external circumstances. According to Csikszentmihalyi, reading for pleasure is the most frequently reported flow active, and any type of reading material can result in a flow experience.

Lastly, two studies of role-playing games (Carter and Lester 1998, Waskul and Dennis 2004) provide insight into the previously unexplored relationship between playing fantasy games and reading comics.

Study Aims and Objectives

This exploratory study examines what adult readers enjoy about comic books. By examining the reasons that adult readers are attracted to comics, and why they choose to read them, we sought to identify the core reasons why some readers become comic book fans. Furthermore, we explored whether readers are aware of any benefits from their comic book reading, as well as how they feel about their identity as comic book readers. Lastly, we hoped to discover if comic book readers share any common characteristics.

Methodology

This qualitative study was conducted through semi-structured face-to-face interviews with voluntary adult participants. The interview instrument (See Appendix) was formulated based on themes found through a literature review incorporating reading theory, psychology, sociology, and art theory. In total, five participants were recruited through posters advertising the study which were posted in local comic book shops, libraries, and universities. Snowball sampling was used to identify four further participants; participants who responded to the advertising poster were asked whether they knew of any other adult comic book readers who might be willing to participate. Six local participants gave face to face interviews, in which the audio was digitally recorded and later transcribed. Participants who were unable to attend the interview in person completed an email interview, wherein the interview instrument was sent to them and they completed it and then sent it back. In all cases, the confidentiality of participants was assured, and the names of individuals were not identified on the transcripts. The real names of participants were replaced by pseudonyms, but their language is reproduced without any grammatical corrections. All interviews were analyzed and coded using Nudist 4 QSR software. Use of a standardized interview schedule facilitated the comparison of responses from different individuals.

Description of Participants

All nine of the participants were over 18 and had finished high school. Of the nine, only three were female. Two of the participants were professionally involved in the comic book industry; one owned a comic book shop in Halifax, Nova Scotia, while the other managed a different comic book store in Moncton, New Brunswick. Five out of the nine were either in the process of completing, or had already completed, graduate level studies of some kind. All participants were employed at the time of their interviews. Below is a short summary of the participants, including pseudonyms, occupations, approximate age at which they began reading comics, and favorite comic book genres.

Table 19.1: Overview of Participants

Name	Occupation	Approximate Age They Started Reading Comics	Preferred comic book genre
Beverly	Graduate student	11	Manga—*Shoju* (geared towards girls)
Clarence	Copywriter and filmmaker	7	No favorite genre given
Elliot	Owner of a comic book store	4	No favorite genre given
Hermione	Professor and author	13	Manga—*Yaoi* (boy to boy romances geared toward girls)
Janet	Librarian	6	Manga—*Shojo* and *Shonen* (geared towards boys)
Jason	Clerk	15	Romance

Name	Occupation	Approximate Age They Started Reading Comics	Preferred comic book genre
Louis	Manager of a comic book store	4	Superhero
Paul	Law student	7	Superhero
Ruben	Law student	10	Superhero

Why Do They Read Comics?

All nine adult participants were asked: "Why do you read comics?" Their reasons for reading comics were analyzed in terms of Csikszentmihalyi's four defining principles of the "flow" state: control, challenge, feedback and focus. While each participant had a unique perspective or story that brought him or her to comics, clear patterns of similarities were also apparent. First, all of the participants were avid readers, who had found in comics a format that they thoroughly enjoyed. Second, all participants were aware that comic books are socially stigmatized, and this awareness influenced their self-perceptions as readers.

Control

Csikszentmihalyi explains control as "a sense of control and competence" (Csikszentmihalyi, 1990). All participants in this study articulated a distinct understanding of the different experience achieved when reading a comic versus reading solely text-based material, and deliberately chose the appropriate format according to their desired state. Therefore, a sense of control and competence was inherent in both their decision to read comics and their experience in doing so. Their answers showed that their knowledge both about the length of comics and the overall different experience of reading text-based materials compared to comics informed them when and why they chose to read comics. Elliot explicitly describes how this sense of control makes comic book reading enjoyable:

> ELLIOT: I've always just enjoyed the stories that comics tell. I find that it gives the reader a lot of control. Because when you get to a good part of a story, you can slow it down. You can read fast, you can come back to it at any time you want.

The sense of control and competence also applies to the type of content chosen. Although some participants were flexible regarding genre or topic, the majority of participants had a favorite genre, and they reported a feeling of competence and authority when doing so because of their familiarity with the genre and its conventions. Successfully following and understanding story and character developments gives the reader a sense of authority and control, as expectations are never threatened. Louis, for example, explains how reading within his favorite superhero genre is easier and less risky than reading other genres.

> LOUIS: I guess it's easy. 'Cause there is so much history to them. And you always know what to expect. 'Cause when you go into an indie comic ... there is some which are probably much better than the superhero ones that I am reading, or that I would probably like more, but you are taking a chance ... and three quarters of the time, it's just crap. Whereas the superhero book, you go in knowing what to expect ... even when it's bad it's still fun.

This aspect of control also affects particular works which must be made within specific limitations and constraints. For instance, countless artists, writers, inkers and storyboarders have created Superman's adventures over the years, but their work is constrained by the way in which Superman's character has been established over the comics' seventy year history. These constraints add to Clarence's appreciation of the stories within a genre. The limitations on what the characters can do test the imaginations of the writers, challenging them to find a new way to tell an old story. Successfully working within the limitations is what makes the story-telling exciting. Clarence believes that it takes a superior writing talent to achieve this:

> CLARENCE: I get more from a really good writer in a comic book than I get from a novel sometimes. They've got these constraints they have to work in, like these years of continuity. You can't have like, Superman, punch a guy in the face and kill him because that's not Superman. Everyone's got pre-determined characteristics and pasts that you can't expand out of.

One surprising element that emerged through the interviews was a relationship between role-playing activities and comic books. Five out of the nine participants mentioned that they had once engaged, at varying levels of intensity, in role-playing games. The most popular of these was Dungeons and Dragons. In their qualitative investigation into the personalities and behaviors of role players, Waskul and Dennis (2004) found that many players enjoyed the activity specifically because of the sense of control and competence they achieved through playing. The relationship between comics and role playing games is twofold. The first connection is that a significant number of participants were introduced to comics through their role playing activities. Introductions to comics through role playing games happened in two ways: at role playing tournaments, which take place at comic book fairs or conventions, and by individual members of the role-playing group suggesting or lending comic book titles.

The second connection is the similar storytelling structures in comics (especially in serials) and role playing (Carter and Lester, 1998): both are forms of story-telling that take place in fantasy worlds built within strict boundaries (Waskul and Dennis, 2004). While the storytelling in role playing is participatory, the stories in both must be consistent with their predecessors. These magical and fantastical worlds exist within specific controls of precedents and rules. Similarly, comic book readers can gain expertise within a favorite genre; by reading one genre for a significant period of time, readers become experts, able to catch subtle references and understand the significance of events in terms of the greater story.

Challenge

The second principle of achieving "flow" relates to the experience of partaking in a challenging activity requiring an appropriate level of skill. After analyzing the responses of the participants, it was clear that the second component of Csikszentmihalyi's "flow" state was apparent in their answers. Participants displayed an understanding that they had gained the skills necessary in order to appreciate comics, and because of these skills, found an ease and enjoyment in reading the medium. Skills required in order to achieve a feeling of competency include a proficiency in visual literacy, such as an ability to decode representations of the human figure and body language. Also required is a comprehension of the unique metalanguage of comics, such as dialogue bubbles, panels, and reading directions. Recently, these multi-modal skills have been the subject of academic scrutiny, and numerous researchers have espoused the benefits of becoming multi-literate (Dombeck and Gustafson, 2005; Eisner, 1985; Goldsmith, 2005; Gravett, 2005; McCloud, 1993; McCloud, 2006; McPherson, 2006; Mulholland, 2004; Nichols, 2004; Schodt, 1996; Schwarz, 2002; Yannicopoulou, 2004).

All participants were asked if they believed that reading comics was easier than reading text-based material, and almost all agreed that it was, with the caveat that this did not necessarily make comic books any less demanding on the reader. Elliot explains:

> ELLIOT: While I would agree that it's easier, I don't agree that it is any less challenging, as far as a story. Certainly, the picture is worth a thousand words, so every panel gives you that much more description.

Elliot's comments highlight the fact that comic books are often densely packed with information presented in both visual and textual forms, and this dense information needs to be navigated in a manner unique to the format of comic books. Accordingly, theorists like Scott McCloud contend that comic book reading requires the acquisition of entirely new and challenging skills (McCloud, 1993, 2006). Beverly's response supports this view:

> BEVERLY: I think there are a lot of sophisticated things going on in comic books. Sure you don't have to *read* [in words] what the character is doing, but you have to be aware of what's going on in the panel. Sometimes panels can get tricky, and following them can be confusing.

Will Eisner's analysis detailed the skill sets required to appreciate comics fully, including the skills necessary to understand the human figure's expressions of affect (the less detailed the figure, the more difficult the interpretation) (Eisner, 1985) and the ability to "bridge the gap" between the panels within a comic. Connecting the panels requires a high level of participation on behalf of the reader; these gaps can only be filled by the reader's imagination (Eisner, 1985). Achieving mastery of these skills makes comic book reading a challenge.

Many participants were consciously aware of their "comic book learning curve," especially if they started reading comics at an older age. Hermione explains how she learned to read Manga, but still finds it challenging:

> HERMIONE: I had to re-learn how to read in order to read manga, and while I'm accustomed enough to it now to have opened a borrowed copy of Moore's *The Swamp Thing* from the back when I first picked it up — duh! — I still tend to read it a bit more slowly than I read pure text because I find it more difficult to figure out which dialogue boxes belong to which characters.

Clearly, reading comic books can be challenging, and depends on various multi-modal skills. Thus, comic book reading achieves the second principle of "flow": "a challenge that requires an appropriate level of skill" (Csikszentmihalyi, 1990). Skills that are required to read comics successfully include knowledge about how to read body language and expression, and a command of the unique language of comics.

Feedback

According to Csikszentmihalyi, the third element needed to achieve "flow" is the establishment of clear goals, accompanied by feedback when those goals have been attained (Csikszentmihalyi, 1990). In this study, comic book readers identified both clear attainable goals and feedback as intrinsic elements in their enjoyment of reading comics.

Although none of the readers participating in this study were themselves "reluctant readers," they all shared a strong belief that reading comics would be a rewarding experience even for unenthusiastic readers. In one example of this, Beverly lamented that comics were not used as a reading intervention for her brother.

> BEVERLY: I think they [comics] are very good for literacy. [I] kind of wish my brother would have been more into comics, because he would have bought comics, and he probably would have read more in high school. It wasn't until university that he discovered that he liked reading. But now he's a chiropractor and can only read medical books.

Participants explained that one of the reasons comics are rewarding is their length: serials are short, and can easily be finished in 15 or 20 minutes, depending on how long the reader chooses to linger over the art. This short reading time gives the reader a sense of satisfaction at finishing something whole, which cannot be replicated by reading a single chapter of a book or an article in a magazine (Krashen, 1993). Even a longer bound "graphic novel" or a trade collection of serials is much faster to read than the average solely text-based novel (Schodt, 1996). Many of the participants in this study stated that the short time it takes to finish a comic book was a huge benefit for them, and that the act of finishing a comic book was, in itself, very gratifying.

> CLARENCE: I think one of the big things for me in comics is a tactile thing. It's looking at the covers, and one of my favourite things is getting a whole stack of comics and watching it go down from ones I've read to ones I haven't read, until eventually it's gone.
>
> LOUIS: With a comic book, it's like 15 minutes, and then you are finished and you can go do something else ... there is something that you can take away with a short investment.

Clarence and Louis make it clear that they read comics not just for the pleasure of reading them, but also for the pleasure of *finishing* them. For Clarence, reading comics has clear goals (finishing as many as possible) and constant feedback (seeing the "read" stack getting noticeably taller). These observations strongly support Krashen's hypothesis that comics provide positive feedback to readers (1993). Clarence's enjoyment of his tangible signs of achievement confirms that readers can gain satisfaction from the number of pages they have read.

The participants also pointed out other avenues of feedback that become available through comic book reading, such as social networks and friendships. Smith and Wilhelm (2002) point out that for some, reading can provide feedback by way of friendship. Dombeck and Gustafson (2005) observed that students reading graphic novels in the school library often read in a group, while avidly discussing their reading. Many of the readers interviewed in this study shared anecdotal evidence of social networking through comics in their own lives. Some had met friends, roommates or online pen pals through comics. Bonding over comics sometimes cemented friendships more firmly, or provided a loosely structured routine for social engagement. Elliot stated that he met people through comics more times than he could recall.

> ELLIOT: Oh yeah, sitting around reading a comic, and someone will come up, [and ask] "what are you reading?" "Superman." "Oh, I like Batman." And you just start a conversation. I've had so many conversations like that.

Jason mentioned that he too met a lot of people through comics, in a variety of ways:

> JASON: I've met lots of online friends, and I've met a couple of people in real life because of *Loveless* [a Manga title]. I was walking around school, reading the comics and lending them to random students who were interested.

Comic book readership can also provide opportunities for ritualized low-stakes socializing with people with similar tastes. Much like a book club, comic book fans informally gather at comic books stores on the days when new items are delivered(usually Wednes-days) to discuss the new acquisitions as well as old favorites. Louis, a manager of a store in New Brunswick, talks about what happens on a typical Wednesday at his store.

> LOUIS: It's like a ritual for a lot of people. And there are some people who will stay and talk the whole night, and go and talk to other people in the store.

From the responses of the interview participants, it is clear that they read comic books for the enjoyment obtained from setting and attaining clear goals as well as receiving feed-back. Readers mentioned two types of feedback: the tangible feedback from the finished comic book as well as the less tangible feedback derived from social opportunities devel-oped through comic book reading.

Focus

Csikszentmihalyi's concept of the experience of "flow" consists of one final element: focus (Csikszentmihalyi, 1990). To achieve focus, one must be absorbed in the immediate experience, without distraction from the outside environment. For the interview subjects, all avid comic book readers, comic books are an intensely engaging form of entertainment. From the readers' responses it can be concluded that, despite any difficulty that arises from reading comics, the high level of reader engagement makes the acquisition and deployment of these skills seem effortless.

An ability to focus, or tune out all other distractions in order to tune completely on to one, especially one pursued for entertainment purposes, can be considered escapism (Lewis 1961). Most of the participants relished the thrill of escapism found through comic book reading. Beverly explains why escapism is so attractive.

> BEVERLY: [Reading comics is] an escape from your own life. I've heard a lot of people say that everything is just so boring in this world, and in fantasy things happen that you don't expect. It's nice to imagine yourself as a pirate on the seven seas, you know, swashbuckling, and get-ting booty. It's fun to imagine these things, and it's fun to see what other people imagine.

While the format of comics makes it easier for readers to "escape," the subject matter may also encourage escapism. Narrations that span many issues conjure up elaborate, but famil-iar, worlds. For instance, Louis, a fan of the superhero genre, describes the primary reason he reads comics:

> LOUIS: I guess it is just for escape; I know all these characters, and I know all their histories and I want to find out what happens next.

The combination of highly engaging stories and an evocative format absorbs the reader's attention, leading to an intense focus, and with this, an absorbed escape. Thus, the enjoyment of comic book reading demonstrates the final element of "flow": a focus on the immediate experience (Csikszentmihalyi, 1990).

The Social Stigma of Being a Comic Book Fan

Many psychologists and psychiatrists in the 1950's wrote about the damaging effects of comic books upon young minds. Publications lambasting comic books' use of pictures, content, and even their very ubiquitousness were rampant in both the mainstream media and in academic journals (Beaty, 2001; Lewin, 1953; Mosse and Daniels, 1959; Wertham, 1953, 1954). According to these writers, comic book reading could at the very least, make children become poor readers and at the very worst, could encourage children to kill without remorse (Mosse and Daniels, 1959; Wertham, 1954)

Mainstream publishers have continued to be reluctant to publish comic books, relegating both comics and their fans to a subculture (Lopes, 2006). Despite recent mainstream acceptance of comic books as a legitimate literary and artistic form, Lopes (2006) points out that the stigma on comic book fans has not lessened. In fact, the social identify of either "fanboy" or "fangirl" continues to be delegitimized: avid comic book fans are stereotyped as lacking both social status and social competence (Lopes, 2006). This unfortunate stereotype has penetrated the self-image of the participants in this study; they are keenly aware of the social stigma associated with their reading preferences. For example, Hermione, a published author and tenured professor, confesses to feeling conflicted about telling her peers about her hobby and research subject.

> HERMIONE: It's interesting that even though I personally enjoy comics/graphic novels/manga, research it, and read other scholarly studies about it, I still feel embarrassed to admit my enthusiasm to my peers. Forty-one-year-old female academics aren't supposed to like comics! In the U.S., comics are still "kid's stuff," and adults who read comics are expected to look like the comic guy on *The Simpsons*—male nerds.

Interestingly, participants in this study did not view the social stigma experienced by comic book readers as static and fixed; rather they described a spectrum of stigma. Similar to Lopes' 2006 findings, participants in this study rarely believed that they were justifiably stigmatized for their literary tastes and practices, but often disdained others who displayed their fandom in different ways. Participants who only read within one genre were often disdainful of readers of other genres. Furthermore, participants who only read comics but did not engage in fan culture believed that such engagement was outside "normal" behavior. Finally, participants who attended comic book fairs often looked down upon participants who wrote fanfiction[1] or participated in cosplay.[2] Hills, in his research on comic book fan culture, found similar competing theories of value within the fans themselves (2002).

To illustrate this finding, during his interview, Clarence (who has a tattoo of the superhero Green Lantern on his upper left arm) was asked if he ever wrote fanfiction. He responded with surprise and dismissively retorted "No!" Then, after a pause he added, "I have a friend whose girlfriend used to write Sailor Moon fanfiction. It's weird. Fanfiction and cosplay I don't get it. It's pretty wacky." Clarence, whose pride over his own comic book reader identity has manifested itself in permanent body art, did not appreciate different demonstrations of fandom. These divisions of acceptance within the fan community highlight the heterogeneity of comic book fans.

Conclusions

This exploratory study investigated the reading habits and attitudes of adult comic book readers in an effort to understand the reasons for the appeal of this format from the point of view of comic book readers themselves. While the number of interview subjects was fairly small, this study was successful in identifying some key commonalities which are useful in explaining the appeal of this format to adult readers.

In particular, this study determined that adult comic book readers find comic books enjoyable because, when reading, they achieve a state of "flow" characterised by control, challenge, feedback, and focus. The sense of control over the reading experience results from the readers' deep knowledge of the conventions of comic book genres and their familiarity with the specific constraints of particular storylines. Comic books provide readers with a dense and multimodal reading experience and challenge readers by demanding both textual and visual literacy and an ability to decode the meta-language of the comic book format. The relatively short length of comics provides readers with tangible feedback; the completion of a comic book, or a series of comic books, gives readers immediate satisfaction and positive feedback. Furthermore, readers' ability to expand their social networks through comic books provides further positive feedback for their reading preference. Finally, readers report that comic books are very absorbing, both in their format and subject matter, and they encourage readers to escape into fantasy worlds.

Despite these avid comic book readers' articulate descriptions of the perceived benefits of reading in this format, however, the comic book readers interviewed for this study expressed a clear awareness that their reading preferences were socially stigmatized and internalized this stigma through a reluctance to share their interest in comic books with others who might not share an appreciation for the form.

Appendix: Interview Schedule

Before the interview begins read aloud the following short script:

Although you just read and signed the consent forms, I'm just going to repeat a few key things about the interview before we start. First, the purpose of the interview is to learn about how you feel about reading graphic novels and comic books. Second, this research is going to be used only for academic purposes, and your participation is completely voluntary. That means that you have the right to not answer any questions that you do not want to answer. It also means that you are totally free to stop the interview at any time you want, for whatever reason you want. Do you have any questions?

Answer any questions that the participant has, and then continue with the script.

Do you still want to participate in the interview?

If the participant says yes, continue with the script.

1. Describe your first reading experience.
2. Describe your first experience with comics or graphic novels.
3. What genre of comics or graphic novels do you like the most?
4. Do you consider yourself to be a serious comic book fan? Why or why not?
5. Do you only read exclusively within your favorite genre or do you read other genres as well?
6. What is the title of your favorite comic or graphic novel and why do you like it so much?
7. What do you find different between reading graphic novels or comics and reading regular books?
8. What do you think appeals to you the most about graphic novels or comics?
9. Some people say that reading graphic novels or comic books is easier than reading books that only have text. Do you agree with them? Why or why not?
10. Who is your favorite character in a comic book or graphic novel? How do you feel you compare to him/her/it?
11. What is the connection between personal fantasy and comics for you?
12. What do you think is the primary reason that you read comics is?
13. What would you do instead of reading comics?
14. Who in your family reads a lot? What kind of things do they like to read?
15. Do your family or friends encourage you or discourage you to read graphic novels or comics?
16. Do your teachers or librarians encourage you or discourage you to read graphic novels or comics?
17. How do you obtain the comic books or graphic novels that you read?
18. Do you ever use the library's comic book collection?
19. Do you think the library should collect more comics?
20. Who in your life was your biggest influence when it comes to reading?
21. Do you make comics yourself?
22. Do you have friends who make comics?

23. Do you follow any webcomics? Which ones?
24. How do you think reading comics online is different from reading comics in a book or novel form? Which one do you prefer?
25. Have you met any friends through comic books or graphic novels? How did that happen?
26. How is your friendship or networking with others facilitated by comic books or graphic novels?
27. Do you go to comic book conferences or fairs?
28. Do you go online to talk about comic books or graphic novels?
29. Do you ever write fanfiction based on favorite comics or graphic novels?
30. Do you ever post your fanfiction for others to see?
31. Do you ever use video sharing sites like YouTube as a way to communicate with us about comic books or graphic novels?
32. Is there anything else about reading comic books or graphic novels that you would like to add?

Endnotes

1. Fiction written by the fans of various stories already produced in popular culture whereby the characters and/or settings are "borrowed" for use in new stories of the fans making (Schodt, 1996).
2. Short for costume-play, cosplay is the practice of dressing up and perhaps even performing as an imaginary character, particularly popular with fans of Japanese anime (Schodt, 1996).

References

Beaty, Bart H. 2001. "All Our Innocences: Fredric Wertham, Mass Culture and the Rise of the Media Effects Paradigm, 1940–1972." *Dissertation Abstracts International Section A: Humanities and Social Science* 61 (12): 4597–4597.

Bender, Lauretta. 1944. "The Psychology of Children's Reading and the Comics." *Journal of Educational Sociology* 18: 223–231.

Bergin, Melissa. 2005. "Who Is Reading Manga?" *Young Adult Library Services* 3 (4): 25–26.

Carter, Robert, and David Lester. 1998. "Personalities of Players of Dungeons and Dragons." *Psychological Report* 82 (1): 182–182.

Charbonneau, Olivier. 2005. "Adult Graphic Novel Readers." *Young Adult Library Services* 3 (4): 39–42.

Cope, Bill, Mary Kalantzis, and New London Group. 2000. *Multiliteracies: Literacy learning and the Design of Social Futures.* London; New York: Routledge.

Csikszentmihalyi, Mihaly. 1990. *Flow: The Psychology of Optimal Experience.* New York: HarperCollins.

Dombeck, Peg, and Chris Gustafson. 2005. "Graphic Novels—School Library, Public Library." *Medium* 29 (3): 13–39.

Eisner, Will. 1985. *Comics & Sequential Art.* Tamarac, FL; Guerneville, CA: Poorhouse Press.

Fry, Donald. 1985. *Children Talk about Books: Seeing Themselves as Readers.* Milton Keynes, Buckinghamshire, Philadelphia: Open University Press.

Glaser, Barney G., and Anselm L. Strauss. 1967. *The Discovery of Grounded Theory: Strategies for Qualitative Research.* Chicago: Aldine.

Goldsmith, Francesca. 2005. *Graphic Novels Now: Building, Managing, and Marketing a Dynamic Collection.* Chicago: American Library Association.

Gravett, Paul. 2005. *Graphic Novels: Everything You Need to Know.* New York: Collins Design.

Krashen, Stephen D. 1993. *The Power of Reading: Insights from the Research.* Englewood, CO: Libraries Unlimited.

Leckbee, Jodi. 2005. "I Got Graphic!" *Young Adult Library Services* 3 (4): 30–31.

Lewin, Herbert S. 1953. "Facts and Fears about the Comics." *Nation's Schools* 52: 46–48.

Lewis, C. S. 1961. *Experiment in Criticism.* Cambridge: University Press.

Lopes, Paul. 2006. "Culture and Stigma: Popular Culture and the Case of comic books." *Sociological Forum* 21 (3): 387–414.

McCloud, Scott. 2006. *Making Comics: Storytelling Secrets of Comics, Manga and Graphic Novels.* New York: Harper.

McCloud, Scott. 1993. *Understanding Comics.* New York: Paradox Press.

McLuhan, Marshall. 1964. *Understanding Media: The Extensions of Man.* New York: McGraw-Hill.

McLuhan, Marshall, and Quentin Fiore. 1967. *The Medium Is the Message.* New York: Random House; Toronto: Random House of Canada.

McPherson, Keith. 2006. "Graphic Literacy." *Teacher Librarian,* 33 (4): 67.

Mosse, Hilde L., and Clesbie R. Daniels. 1959. "Linear Dyslexia: A New Form of Reading Disorder." *American Journal of Psychotherapy* 13: 826–841.

Mulholland, Matthew J. 2004. "Comics as Art Therapy." *Art Therapy* 21 (1): 42–43.

Nichols, C. Allen. 2004. *Thinking Outside the Book: Alternatives for Today's Teen Library Collections*. Westport, CT: Libraries Unlimited.

Patton, Michael. 1990. *Qualitative Evaluation and Research Methods*. 2nd ed. Newbury Park, CA, London: Sage.

Ross, Catherine Sheldrick, Lynne McKechnie, and Paulette M. Rothbauer. 2006. *Reading Matters: What the Research Reveals about Reading, Libraries, and Community*. Westport, CT: Libraries Unlimited.

Schodt, Frederik L. 1996. *Dreamland Japan: Writings on Modern Manga*. Berkeley, CA: Stone Bridge Press.

Schwarz, Gretchen E. 2002. "Graphic Novels for Multiple Literacies." *Journal of Adolescent & Adult Literacy* 46 (3): 262.

Smith, Michael W., and Jeffrey D. Wilhelm. 2002. *Reading Don't Fix No Chevys: Literacy in the Lives of Young Men*. Portsmouth, NH: Heinemann.

Snowball, Clare. 2005. "Teenage Reluctant Readers and Graphic Novels." *Young Adult Library Services* 3 (4): 43–45.

Waskul, Dennis, and Matt Lust. 2004. "Role-Playing and Playing Roles: The Person, Player, and Persona in Fantasy Role-Playing." *Symbolic Interaction* 27 (3): 333–356.

Welch, Rollie, and Julianne Brown. 2005. "Y archive?" *Young Adult Library Services* 3 (4): 22–26.

Wertham, Fredric. 1954. "The Curse of Comic Books: The Value Patterns and Effects of Comic Books." *Religious Education* 49 : 394–406.

_____. 1953. *Seduction of the Innocent*. New York: Rinehart.

Worthy, Jo, Megan Moorman and Margo Turner. 1999. "What Johnny Likes to Read Is Hard to Find in School." *Reading Research Quarterly* 34 (1): 12–27.

Yannicopoulou, Angela. 2004. "Visual Aspects of Written Texts: Preschoolers View Comics." *L1— Educational Studies in Language and Literature* 4 (169): 181.

20

Graphics Let Teens OWN the Library

CHRISTIAN ZABRISKIE

This essay examines the phenomenon of ownership and explores how a dynamic graphic collection, as well as the programming created around it, makes teens feel as if it is "their" collection. A vibrant graphics collection promotes Young Adult ownership of the traditional brick and mortar library in surprising and successful ways. In turn this leads to regular and casual use of the library, increased circulation, and more sophisticated use of library resources. Circulation statistics will show the extremely high turnover of graphic materials as well as prove the cost-effectiveness of these items in a YA space. Interviews augment these statistics by looking into this concept of ownership and examine how a love of comics has lead to a love of the library. The data for this study has been drawn from an urban library whose teen population is comprised almost entirely of minority teens. Since most of the study participants are minorities the article includes a short discussion of race and identity in graphic narratives. While graphics may not be perceived as "traditional" library materials, they are incredibly effective as a way to instill traditional library behaviors (circulating materials, program participation, engaged reading), in today's Young Adults.

Graphics bring young people into the library, motivate them to use the library, and keep them in the institution in both dynamic and very traditional ways. Investing time and resources into these materials, and fostering a reading culture around them, yields results in a teen library community, results which in turn invest themselves back into the library. This cycle of activity engenders a proprietary sense in YA patrons as more of "their" stuff is showing up in what is demarcated as "their" library space. Once they have possession teens, although not often seen as "traditional" patrons, engage in very traditional library behaviors.

The purpose of this study is to explore these concepts of ownership and traditional library usage as motivated by graphic novels in a large, dedicated young adult collection. Arguments and ideas herein are based on a combination of qualitative observation and quantitative data. It is a given that all observations are based on a small dataset from this limited one room example. The article is based on the collection and patrons of the Young Adult Room of the Central Library of Queens Library in Queens, New York, which is a borough of New York City. Queens County is often cited as the most diverse county in the United States and may be one of the most eclectic places in the world. A short list of demographic facts prepared by the Queens Library New American Program, and taken from the 2007 American Community Survey (ACS), shows that 49 percent of the population is foreign born, 56 percent speak a language in addition to English at home, and students in the public schools in Queens have a staggering 140 languages among them. The Central Library is in the heart of a working class, inner city neighborhood which has been transitioning from what was, a decade or so ago, considered a rough area.

The patrons of the Central Library YA room are an incredibly diverse cross section of urban teenagers. A large percentage of patrons are African-American and most of the remaining patrons are immigrants from Haiti, the Indian subcontinent, Central Africa, Central America, and China. There are users who are part of the Orthodox Jewish community and many Sikhs and devout Muslims from both the Middle East and the Philippines. This YA community consists almost entirely of minorities. Many families in the area struggle with financial difficulties as the 2000 census suggests that approximately 38 percent of the local population has an annual household income of less than $30,000. This situation is, of course, exacerbated by the high cost of living endemic to residence in New York City.

Central Library, like many of the 62 branches of Queens Library, has a dedicated YA space and collection. This is the largest YA space in the system and it has three full time YA staff as well as children's librarians who cover desk shifts in the YA room. The room is open seven days a week, 10:00–9:00 Mon–Fri, 10:00–5:30 Sat, and 12:00–5:00 Sun. There is a large collection of over 91,000 volumes (per 2008–2009 materials holdings report) with both fiction and a full Dewey range of age appropriate non–fiction. In the calendar year 2008–2009 the YA collection circulated 149,670 items (per internal circulation reports). Typically there is regular programming three days a week during the school year with special programs (consisting of movie screenings, concerts, and author/artist visits) every other month or so.

The graphics collection is shelved in its own area of the YA room. All books are given a 741.5 Dewey number and are then shelved within the graphics area by type. Superhero books are broken out by publisher; "art" and underground books have their own area; and manga (the largest part of the collection), is shelved alphabetically by title. Due to the high turnover of books and the relative frequency with which they go missing, it has been difficult to keep track of the true size of the collection. Best estimates place it as hovering between 1800 and 2000 volumes. The manga collection alone has at least some representation in over 140 series with multiple volumes in each, and often multiple copies of individual volumes. In an attempt to minimize constantly replacing gaps in the series, typically two copies of each graphic are initially purchased although this practice is flexible depending on the title. Maintaining the collection is a constant labor. Typically, returned graphics materials needing to be shelved typically fill a book truck every day and hours of work by paraprofessionals and librarians goes into keeping them tidy and up to date.

This initial description does nothing to convey the dynamism of these books. Reader engagement with this collection is visible and palpable. This is literature which they are excited about, which they discuss with friends and seek out in the library. It is amazing to watch teens group around a book truck full of returns and pick away a good part of it before the pages even begin shelving. These young people are very regular and casual in their library habits incorporating the latest graphics into their time in the library along with homework and the internet. Of course these patrons may just be those self–motivated teens who would use the library anyway but the books that come off the shelves are often graphics and lots of them at that. They engage teens in dynamic reading, keep them engaged in library activities, and motivate them to both circulate materials and spend time within the library itself. Graphics are an effective means by which librarians can make personal connections with teens, and they provide a unique toehold of ownership for teens in a large urban setting.

In an attempt to capture qualitative input interviews were conducted with ten YAs, five who were over the age of 18 and five who were 17 or younger. Half of the participants were African American, and the other half were either Latin or East Asian. For purposes of this study the 17 and unders act as informative indicators, but are taken as a whole and are not directly quoted here. All quotations herein are taken from those over 18, who consented to be interviewed for the purposes of the study. Study participants were established graphics users who interviewed with a librarian with whom they had pre–existing relations around graphics in the library setting. Their responses establish them as sophisticated library users and as individuals who felt that this collection was uniquely "their" collection.

When asked how often they checked graphics out of the library most indicated weekly or biweekly. One participant replied "more than I check out any other kind of book." With a three week loan period this represents steady and regular use of the library's main resource, its circulating collection. When asked how many they usually borrowed at a time, most estimated about five, although some power users definitely borrowed more (up to 20–30 at a time). One young woman explained, "If there are a lot in a row I will just grab them." Most participants indicated that they got about half of the graphics that they read from the library, other sources being friends, bookstores, and personal collections. It is interesting that for all their adolescent independence they are still relying on the library for materials which they look forward to reading.

The teens had entirely mixed responses when asked if the library responded to their needs. All wanted more, but freely conceded effort on the part of the library. The same young woman observed, "You can find things when you aren't looking, but if you *need* a book, forget it." The freedom to criticize and offer suggestions could indicate a feeling of teen ownership over an institution as they are seeing it as something in which they are stakeholders, and can move to change. If so, then these teens clearly own their library. When asked how responsive the library was to what they wanted in the collection, patrons felt that the library tried to be responsive, but that it needed to get newer books and have fewer gaps in the series that were already on the shelves. They felt that it was very important for the library to have the latest materials.

All of the participants were long-term library users and long-term users of the graphics collection in particular. One young man indicated that he had been checking graphics out of the library "since I found out there was a library." Again there are indicators that if graphics are not the sole draw to the library, they are at least a strong one. Many of these young people indicated that they had been using the graphics collection since they were children. They discussed library usage through their tween and early teen years casually, and saw these books as touchstones for their changing tastes in reading.

The patrons interviewed for the study felt that their library was superior to others when it came to graphics, and their sense of ownership was evident as they indicated civic pride in the size and range of the collection at Central. Although there were graphics in many places in their lives, this one had the most, the best selection, and was most accessible. One young man pointed out that graphics collections in Queens are often in other languages (Korean, Japanese, Chinese, French, and Spanish, all of which have traditions of graphic publishing), which he found problematic, but which is expressive of the breadth of collection development required by today's libraries. Everyone felt that they would use the library even if it didn't have graphics, though many indicated that they felt that their usage would decline. One young man pointed out that because "the internet's here," he would continue to come to the library, though perhaps with less of a community investment in it. Others stated that they would continue to use the library for school, to read other stuff, and to participate in programming. The vast majority indicated that graphics had, indeed, lead them to other kinds of books in the collection with sci-fi, fantasy, mystery, and drawing books being their favorites. Almost all of them had tried to make their own comics and many considered it as a possible career path. There is a kind of ownership in creation and it is exciting to see young people giving serious thought to careers in the arts. Everyone in this sample read comics, mostly manga, online, often at the library but also at home, school, and wherever they could get access to the internet.

A working library card is very important to these regular patrons, and they have sophisticated skills in maintaining their borrowing privileges. They renew materials online and through self–check machines at the library, and they monitor their accounts online from home and school. Queens Library has an excellent program whereby those under 18 can read down their fines. Every half hour spent reading in the library earns them a "library buck," which can be used against fees on their account. Graphics are a popular way of earning these bucks, and those who are able to read down fines do so when they incur them. Of the five participants who were too old to read down their fines two of them were quite vocal in wanting the program extended to older patrons. Taken all together these are regular, sophisticated, and motivated library patrons who have full possession of their library accounts, and are well aware of what their library has available to them. Perhaps these teens would still use the library without graphics, but it is doubtful, based on their own responses, that they would be as excited about the library as an institution.

In order to quantify some of this anecdotal observation, an attempt was made to gather hard data regarding the turnover of this collection. Circulation figures can offer a sense of library ownership as they represent those materials in the collection that are in the patrons' actual possession. When they take the books out, patrons essentially own a small part of the library in their personal and home lives. One of the measures considered here was the percentage of items that were actually out in circulation at a given time. It proved to be impossible to capture the entire collection so a small subset was chosen.

Twenty-five manga titles were selected at random and tracked over fifteen weeks, a period which would represent five of the library's standard three week loan periods.[1] Each week the number of books in a series which the library owned was compared with the number of those books which were checked out in order to determine the percentage of books in that series then in circulation. These averages were, in turn, averaged to determine what percent of the books were checked out, and finally an average over the fifteen weeks was determined. Typically, 52 percent of the manga were out at any given time, showing a very high rate of turnover. Of course each week showed a wide range of circulation rates, but books typically fell between 30 percent and 70 percent, with outliers to either side. As rough as the math is on this study, it is still exciting to see any collection have such steady activity, and clearly graphics are popular materials that are circulating regularly and in volume.

The regular use and ownership of the collection necessitates regular weeding and replacement due to wear and tear. In capturing ISBNs, cost, and circulation figures in order to facilitate replacement and evaluate which titles were popular an interesting data set presented itself. This data may offer insight into the impact of graphics on the larger collection and substantiate their value as purchases. Simply put, graphics provide a great deal of bang for the buck. In reviewing data from 395 records, some trends become readily apparent. These books moved a great deal, circulating 39 times on average, and they were relatively inexpensive with an average cost of $11.10. Looking at a comparison of the cost of the book divided by the number of times it has circulated (before being removed from the collection) provides interesting insights regarding the value of these materials in the collection. This ratio, taken at the point of withdrawal, can give a rough gauge as to the popularity of the work and the value of the collection monies spent on it. In this group, the average cost to circ ratio (based on individual books) was a low 0.38.

These figures at withdrawal led to a further and potentially much more interesting study. Any attempt at generalizing relative popularity or value from materials which are being removed from the collection, due to condition brought on by frequent use, is defeated by the very nature of the materials themselves. Of course these books would have a low cost to circ ratio; their turnover was ultimately what was getting them removed from circulation to begin with. In an attempt to gauge the popularity and value of the graphics in comparison to the rest of the collection, data was captured regarding the cost and circulation of materials currently in circulation. Three categories were considered: a baseline group, consisting of randomly selected materials from the YA room; a random group of graphics made up of items from the entire range of the graphics collection; and a high performance group of deliberately selected high-interest, high-circulation materials (including multiple copies of the *Twilight* and *Harry Potter* books and testing materials and other books which consistently fly off the shelf). Data was collected on 108 books in the baseline and high-interest groups and 104 books in the random graphics sample. Cost and circulation numbers for each were recorded and used to determine cost/circ comparisons. Each of these categories was then averaged to produce overall indicators.

The baseline average cost of an item in the YA collection was $17.15 and it had circulated 12 times from its date of addition to the collection to the date of recording. This set produced an average cost/circ ratio of 3.76. On average, the high performance group cost less at $12.14, had a much higher circ average of 23, and produced a much lower average cost/circ ratio of 1.02. Surprisingly, the random graphics group cost still less, $11.40 on average, circulated the most with an average of 26 circs at time of record, and had far and away the lowest cost to circ ratio of any of the sets at 0.81 (less than a fourth of the baseline group).

Although other indicators supported the idea that these are very popular materials, it is startling to see that, within the very limited parameters of this study, graphics are tracking on par or even better than the most popular materials in the room. What's more, they seem to be giving good value for the investment, costing less to add to the collection and to circulate. One factor which was not considered here is the relative loss rate of graphics versus other materials in the collection. This cost of replacement may erode some of the cost savings at purchase, but with such a low cost to circulation ratio the books are certainly working for their hire. A much larger dataset, ideally from multiple collections, would be necessary to explore these issues with any true reliability. These numbers do however give some preliminary statistical merit to the observation that these are incredibly popular materials which will circulate as well or better than the best in a collection.

It is axiomatic that in publishing and filmmaking a few blockbusters pay for all the award winners. Likewise, in library environments, dominated by the need to show relevance through circulation figures, the graphics could potentially buoy a classics and non–fiction collection, which typically require a higher initial investment and circulate less. If it is taken as a given that bestsellers bring in patrons and garner community support, then these materials have a comparable relevancy in YA collections.

When looking at patron behaviors, one form of engagement is in table reading, which teens will engage in for hours at a time. Those patrons who have issues with their cards continue to use the library, without borrowing materials, by being physically present in the space and doing their reading there. Patrons often read down their fines, and graphics are a favorite means of doing so. Telling young people that, while they are reading, they can read whatever they want often elicits an excited response from patrons who then sit down for marathon manga sessions of often up to 2 or 3 hours at a stretch. It is not uncommon to observe table readers with six or more books stacked up and ready to go. A very informal survey of pages and librarians pegged graphics as the materials most collected off of tables to be reshelved, with some rough estimates suggesting as much as 50 percent.

As library behavior, this is time spent in the institution, engaged in active reading, albeit of a somewhat unconventional sort and, in the case of manga, backwards. This contributes to the sense of owning the space, a real physical possession of their library area as a comfortable and casual meeting ground. While reading down fines, chatting with friends is discouraged, but it is perfectly acceptable in the YA room in general. Patrons often engage in active discussions concerning narrative, character, and plot. This is unelicited, free discussion among minority teens regarding books, while ensconced in the municipal public library. Graphic literature is a common element across race, age, gender, and nation of origin for these young people. This behavior of informal book discussion groups and literary communities has a long tradition with romance and classics groups also sharing a love of a form and the esoteric knowledge and codes that only enthusiasts can participate in. Instead of seniors bandying romance novels or the staid members of the Mystery Society, it is African-American, East Asian, and Latin teens hanging out and discussing *Death Note* and *Naruto*.

Formalized book discussion and outreach are provided through the Manga/Anime Club, a YA group that off and on has been in existence for almost three years as of this writing. At its height, (when the group was meeting every Tuesday in a spacious and separate programming area, without noise concerns) it averaged 15 to 20 teens per week. This group alternates between screening anime and literary and cultural discussions, collection development meetings, and crafts. This is a club which they saw as the sole proviso of teens who share a common interest, and their ownership of it was quite palpable. Programming was fairly easy, and successful activities could be recycled to further acclaim. Collection development advice was actively sought out, and patrons made suggestions as to which series should be continued and which should go. There are always series which need to be filled in, and often the teens notice those needs first when they seek out elusive volumes which have gone MIA. Suggestions for new titles are elicited and (when possible) acted upon. It is, of course, impossible for any budget to please absolutely everyone, but this process often brought on lively discussions among reading teens who are actively engaged in the shape of their library's collection, a collection which they see themselves as having had a hand in creating. Patrons often requested volumes or series at the desk outside of these meetings making further connections with their library and librarians. These kinds of discussions are common among buffs of every genre, but with these teens it was overwhelmingly dominated by discussions of graphics. It forms an easy point of contact with teens by librarians and can lead to discussions of other literature, school, life, or other graphics that the teen or librarian absolutely must read.

Crafts for the Manga/Anime club were fairly rudimentary, but overall surprisingly well received. Origami is an obvious option; the J (children's) collection contains a number of books with multi–cultural crafts; and Japan is well represented both in monographs and anthologized texts. Drawing sessions were popular and mainly consisted of passing out paper, pencils, and drawing books. The librarian who lead these sessions cannot draw, but he worked his way through exercises in a how to draw manga text, and while working on his drawings he encouraged teens. In turn, they cheered him on, and got into the spirit of it. Coloring pages were surprisingly well received, despite fears that they would be perceived as too babyish for our cosmopolitan young people. This program was particularly easy to pull off on short notice. When given images taken from the web, en masse, along with plenty of markers, crayons, and colored pencils, over a dozen teens can be easily entertained for an hour. New manga were often (though not exclusively), premiered at Manga/Anime meetings, and getting first shot at the new books was a point of pride among readers.

A side-benefit of the Manga/Anime Club was that it also seeded other programs. Attendance at a Teen Gaming program on Wednesdays was comprised of many of, though not exclusively, the same faces. Budding artists were recruited for the Teen Zine on Thursdays. Indeed, much of the motivation for starting the zine came as a result of observing so many teens drawing in the library. The collection contains many technique books in a range of levels and subject. Books that focus on graphic illustration, comic books, and particularly manga are the most popular. Teens go from the original graphics as well, copying favorite characters for themselves. There is always a box of scrap paper at the YA desk as well as however many golf pencils a patron wants. The first issue of the zine saw numerous submissions consisting of single-page sequential narrative art.

Since graphics are a visual medium, some aspects of character are more rigidly defined by their creators than in other literary forms. The depiction of race is one such rigid constraint, characters are locked into what they are drawn as. Manga offers some flexibility on this account due to its black and white palette, but they are for the most part so racially uniform that books have little if any diversity in them. The relationship of minorities to comics is, in many ways, a complicated and problematic one. Marc Singer's excellent article, "Black Skins and White Masks: Comic Books and the Secret of Race," is utterly unflinching in its assessment. Singer hammers at the issue when he comments, "comic books, and particularly the dominant genre of superhero comic books, have proven fertile ground for stereotyped depictions of race" (Singer, 2002:107). These questions are increasingly the focus of academic study though principally as textual interpretations and analysis rather than examinations of social impact. As Scott McCloud points out in his book, *Reinventing Comics*, even when black superheroes were present "their white creative teams often seemed unsure how to present positive role models without draining their subjects of their humanity" (McCloud, 2000: 107). Singer raises similar questions about the creators when he states that the "system of visual typography combines with the superhero genre's long history of excluding, trivializing, or 'tokenizing' minorities to create numerous minority superheroes who are marked purely for their race: 'Black Lightning,' 'Black Panther,' and so forth" (Singer, 2002: 107). These issues persist in very real ways for the patrons in this study, yet their natural teenage resiliency allows them to appropriate characters for their own identification regardless of race. Their reading, popular culture, creative life, and even fashion sense takes characters and images from these works and owns them in very practical ways.

When asked directly if they recognized any characters who "look like you" in graphics, most of the interview subjects replied negatively. One young man laughed as he replied. Another young African-American man launched into a discussion about the Marvel Comics teen super group, The Runaways. "There is Alex from The Runaways" he pointed out, and this character is indeed a middle class African American teen. "'Course he's also a traitor, figures the black guy is the bad guy right?," which is also true. Alex does try to sell out his friends and teammates, and he ultimately dies in the attempt. The interviewer pointed out the character of Xavin on the same team. Xavin came onto the team as the transgender love interest of the team's lesbian, alien energy wielder. This seemingly convoluted love story actually works quite well, and has a Capulet/Montague feel as their races have traditionally been at war with one another. As a Skrull, Xavin is a member of a race of shape-shifting aliens and he/she typically manifests as either a young black man or young black woman. This argument of inclusion was quickly shot down by the young man in the interview who pointed out, "Xavin's green. He/She is green with an ugly chin." Skrull are naturally green with protruding wrinkled chins. For this young man, whatever blackness Xavin had was a mask at best. Returning to Singer it is clear that to some degree "comics still perpetuate stereotypes either through token characters who exist purely to signify racial clichés or through a far more subtle system of absences and erasure that serves to obscure minority groups, even as writers pay lip service to diversity" (McCloud, 2000:106).

This kind of textual bias can only be truly be addressed by greater minority representation in the creative work of the comics industry. Robert Morales and Kyle Baker, both of whom are black, created *Captain America: The Truth*, which tells the story of a group of African-American soldiers, reminiscent of the Tuskegee Airmen, who are subjected to medical experiments in order to perfect the super soldier serum, which turned Steve Rogers into Captain America. Originally created as an alternative timeline story, it has been brought into the official Marvel Universe and carried on in the character of Patriot, grandson of the black Captain America, member of the teen super group the Young Avengers, and eventually a super soldier in his own right. This book has proven to be extremely popular. The idea of a black Captain America particularly resonated with some young men as does the figure of Patriot, a black teen from the Bronx. Exploring their stories lead readers on to other titles such as *The Avengers* and the large body of work featuring the original *Captain America*.

Many of the young people who are reading graphics today aspire to be creators someday. True diversity and representation will only be possible when minorities are present in writing and illustrating graphic novels. To go back to McCloud, "it is reasonable to say that when writing about a social or physical condition which only a minority experience, members of that minority will have an advantage in portraying it. Nearly everyone else is just guessing" (106). Most of the young people interviewed for this study had attempted to create some comics, and about a third expressed an interest in entering the field. For some it is a dream like being a recording or sports star, but among them there are a few who will persevere, put in the work, and break into an industry which will hopefully have made itself ready for them.

Ultimately, skin color may be largely irrelevant because these teens take possession of these characters and appropriate them for their own use and enjoyment. All of the teens interviewed indicated that they identified with characters in graphics. One stated that it was "life's struggles and friendships" which he saw reflected in the books that made a bond for him. Another felt that "teen" stories were an important part of her identification. These young people are finding a resonance in these works which is a part of their own self–identification and which draws them back to the library for more.

In this library, in these circumstances, graphics are clearly an important part of the collection. They are very popular, give good money for budget dollar spent, and act as an entry point for teens to develop pride and ownership in their library. The has used them to great effect. A wide range of libraries and librarians are finding teens responding to graphics in extraordinary ways. This book is an obvious example of that, but a simple lit search shows that librarians in an incredibly wide range of institutions are doing creative and productive work with graphics in their collection. This is not to suggest that graphics are the only thing they are talking about, nor are they a magic bullet to instantly increase circulation and program attendance. Many young people would not be caught dead with a graphic (perhaps preferring to be caught undead with a vampire or zombie book), and establishing and maintaining a graphics collection requires a great deal of work. At its best, this investment can benefit not only the library but ultimately, and more importantly, the patrons.

The teens at Queens Central Library are engaged in dynamic library behavior. They circulate materials, keep their library cards up to date, and are physically present in the brick and mortar library. They engage in literary discussions both casually and as part of a larger library community. They take pride in their library as an institution and engage in discussions about the collection, programming, and room design. It is difficult to estimate whether or not these young people would be in the library were it not for these materials, but graphics certainly dominate the conversation for a good number of these young patrons. Ownership over the graphics collection as teens may very well lead to comfortable and casual lifelong library use.

Endnotes

1. The titles selected were: *Absolute Boyfriend, Arcana, Bleach, Boys Over Flowers, Chronicles of the Cursed Sword, Claymore, D.E.A.R.S., Death Note, Descendents of Darkness, Eerie Queerie, Fruits Basket, Gravitation, Hellshing, Kekkaishi, Moon Child, Naruto, Queen's Knight, Ruroni Kenshin, Skip Beat, Tramps Like Us, Tsubasa, Ultra Cute, Vampire Knight, Zombie Powder,* and *Zatch Bell.*

References

Afzal, Waseem. 2006. "An Argument for the Increased Use of Qualitative Research in LIS." *Emporia State Research Studies* 43: 22–25.

Ching, Allison. 2005. "Holy Reading Revolution Batman! Developing a Graphic Novel Collection for Young Adults." *Young Adult Library Services* 3: 19–21.

Fialkoff, Francine. 2007. "Turf Building." *Library Journal* 5: 132.

"For Marketers, Teens Are a Moving Target." 2003. *Billboard* 45: 60–61.

Heinberg, Allan, and Jim Cheung. 2005. *Young Avengers: Sidekicks.* New York: Marvel Enterprises Inc.

Heinberg, Allan, Jim Cheung, and Andrea Divito. 2006. *Young Avengers: Family Matters.* New York: Marvel.

"Irony Giants." 2003. *Brandweek* 44: 42–44.

"Kids Ain't What They Used to Be." 2003. *Retail Merchandiser* 43: 23–27.

Lyga, Allyson A. W. 2006. "Graphic Novels for (Really) Young Readers." *School Library Journal* 3: 56–61.

McCloud, Scott. 2000. *Reinventing Comics: How Imagination and Technology Are Revolutionizing an Art Form.* New York: Harper Collins.

Morales, Robert, and Kyle Baker. 2007. *Captain America: The Truth.* New York: Marvel.

Mortimore. Jeffrey M., and Amanda Wall. 2009. "Motivating African-American Students Through Information Literacy Instruction: Exploring the Link Between Encouragement and Academic Self-Concept." *The*

Reference Librarian 50: 29–42.

Rivera, Lysa. 2007. "Appropriate(d) Cyborgs: Diasporic Identities in Dwayne McDuffie's Deathlock Comic Book Series." *MELUS* 3: 103–127.

Singer, Marc. 2002. "Black Skins and White Masks: Comic Books and the Secret of Race." *African American Review* 36: 107–119.

Seyfried, Jonathan. 2008. "Reinventing the Book Club: Graphic Novels as Educational Heavyweights." *Knowledge Quest* 36: 44–8.

Stanley, Sarah, and Brian W. Sturm. 2008. "Sequential Art Books & Beginning Readers: Can the Pictures Help Them Decode Words." *Knowledge Quest* 37: 50–57.

Vaughan, Brian K., and Adrian Alphona. 2004. *Runaways, Volume 1: Pride and Joy*. New York: Marvel.

21

The Only Thing Graphic Is Your Mind

Reconstructing the Reference Librarian's View of the Genre

AMANDA STEGALL-ARMOUR

Ruminate about the following phrases: Graphic violence, graphic sex, graphic content, and graphic language. The commonality among the phrases obviously is the word "graphic." Also relative is the connotation each phrase elicits: negativity. These phrases are sometimes seen on labels describing the content of various media formats, such as video games, movies, music, and sometimes graphic novels. With phrases such as the above and the negative connotations, it is no wonder reference librarians may have queries and reservations about graphic novels. So, what does "graphic novel" actually mean? More importantly, what does graphic novel mean to librarians? And, why is it important that reference librarians understand the variety, value, and place of the graphic novel?

The OED states that a graphic novel is "a full-length (esp. science fiction or fantasy) story published as a book in comic-strip format" (Oxford University Press, 1989), and *Merriam and Webster* (online) states the graphic novel is "a fictional story that is presented in comic-strip format and published as a book." Having looked in the *Merriam-Webster's Collegiate Dictionary* (1999 tenth print edition), I found this definition to be a good summation of what many librarians may feel graphic novels are: "a fictional story for adults that is presented in comic-strip format and published as a book" (Merriam Webster, Inc., 1999). Here, the key word that helps spawn negativity and false ideas is "adult." The term adult, many times is associated with adult content, which in turn is associated with sex, violence, harsh language, or pornography. This is not meant to say that graphic novels do not contain this type of material; however, this type of material is not all that graphic novels are comprised of or limited to.

What do the experts say? Graphic novels are considered by their creators, developers, and constituents to be unlimited; however, the term graphic novel is deemed otherwise. Will Eisner, creator of *A Contract with God*, which is considered the first graphic novel, told *TIME* that the term graphic novel is "limited," and he favors the terms "graphic literature" and "graphic story" (Arnold, 2003). Choosing terms literature or story over novel is understandable. The term novel has a specific, derived denotation that librarians and readers alike are already subject to and will not waver far from the established. Whereas, literature or story are less specific and have broader, less limited subjective meanings. Steering librarians, especially reference librarians, away from these boxed in definitions is pertinent. In order for reference librarians to assist patrons in finding appropriate graphic novels, the reference librarian needs to first understand exactly what graphic novels encompass.

Another misconception among librarians is dubbing graphic novels as a "genre," which according to the experts is mistaken. Mark Siegel, an illustrator and the editorial director for *First Second* graphic novel publishing company stated in an interview, hosted by *Booklist*, that the "graphic novel has evolved as a handy term for longer works, often in trim sizes close to the novel. But it's really a format not a genre" (Zvirin, 2006: 66). The term *genre* is too broad; it implies that graphic novels are a single category of book. Frank Miller, famous for his graphic novel *300*, which was recently made into a movie, said in an interview with *Esquire*, "Comic book pages are vertical, and movie screens are relentlessly horizontal. But it's all the same form. We use different tools, but we get the job done" (Esquire, 2007: 52–54).

Graphic novel editor and book artist, Chip Kidd, told *TIME* that he "truly believe[s] that Spiegelman's *Maus* should be shelved next to Elie Wiesel and Primo Levi, not next to *X-Men*" (Arnold, 2003). Basically, these types of books can stand next to related, respectable literature and not be restricted to a lump of unrelated books. Art Spiegelman, as mentioned above, is famous for his non-fiction narrative of his father's life as a holocaust victim and the effect on Spiegelman and the family. He spoke with *TIME* as well and expressed his misgivings about the term graphic novel saying, "The problem with the word graphic novel is that it is an arguably misguided bid for respectability where graphics are respectable and novels are respectable so you get double respectability" (Arnold, 2003). Overall, either graphic novels need to be shifted to shelves containing books of related subject matter (e.g., Spiegelman's *Maus* to non-fiction), or the graphic novel section needs to be subcategorized (e.g., fiction, sci-fi, non-fiction, etc.) to diminish confusion.

To find out what typical public librarians thought about graphic novels, I developed a questionnaire for the staff of the Lee County Library to fill out. The Lee County Library is a public library with approximately 20 staff members, and is located in downtown Tupelo, Mississippi. According to the 2006 U.S. Census Bureau report, the population of the community is approximately 36,000 (U.S. Census Bureau, 2008). The Lee County Library received an LSTA grant to support visual literacy in 2007, so the acquisition of graphic novels is recent and the misunderstandings new. Out of the 20 staff members, I was able to obtain 12 participants from different departments (reference, circulation, and technical services). The questionnaire was distributed and it explained that all results would be anonymous. The results were received anonymously as well. The questionnaire consisted of 3 required questions and 1 optional. The questions were as follows:

1. *What is a graphic novel? (Or define graphic novel.)*
2. *Who reads graphic novels?*
3. *Should* graphic novel*s be considered a form of literature?*
4. **Optional* If you would not mind, please state how many years you have worked as a librarian.*

Participants were advised not to "Google" definitions or answers, and were encouraged to produce individually unique responses.

Upon starting the research, I generated my own assumptions as to what results would be procured; however, I was aware that the results probably would be different than I had expected. Predictions included garbled definitions for graphic novel, teenagers would be listed as primary readers of graphic novels, and I was sure to receive at least a nominal amount of "no" responses to the "form of literature question." The results are shown below through simple charts:

Results from the Lee County Library Graphic Novel Questionnaire:

(All results based on 12 employees' questionnaires.)

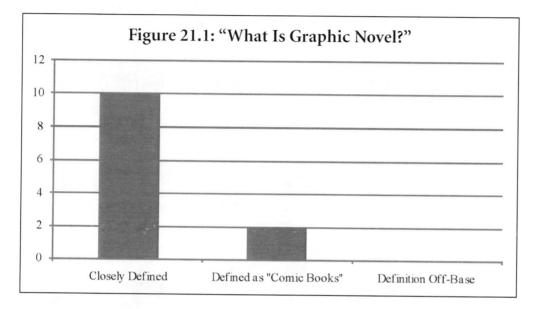

Figure 21.1: "What Is Graphic Novel?"

The results in some instances were different than expected. Starting with question 1 which is represented by Figure 21.1, 10 out of 12 participating librarians had cohesive and cogent definitions for graphic novel. I had expected to read many definitions broken by the words "comics" and "trash." I work with these librarians regularly, and to converse with some of them, one would not have expected the solid responses which were received. In contrast to the aforementioned, I did receive the definition "fancy word for a comic book." At the other end of the spectrum, I received a definition worth highlighting: "Graphic novels are illustrated literature in which the illustrations are as important as the written story. In fact, there are some that do not even have written text and tell the story only with illustrations." This librarian stated that he/she had been a librarian for 32 years. Two key phrases that seize attention in this definition are "the written story" and "to tell the story."

Siegel, who was mentioned earlier, was interviewed in 2007 by Jonathan Hunt, a California "library media teacher." In the interview Siegel stated the "heart of a graphic novel" is "storytelling" (Hunt, 2007: 12–15). And Stefan Petrucha, graphic novel author and illustrator (*Nancy Drew, Wicked Dead, Teen Inc.*), described graphic novels as a fluid concept in his article, "On Writing (and Reading) the Graphic Novel": "Just as a sentence creates a complete thought, a sequence of panels creates a complete movement through time and space" (Petrucha, 2008: 60–63). It is this "movement" that allows the panels to become alive and almost sentient-like. The reader is able to travel in the present and experience this instantaneous moment of "storytelling." Cartoonist Jeff Smith, who participated in an email interview with Jeff Blasingame of the *Journal of Adolescent & Adult Literacy,* stated,

> One of the strengths of working in the graphic novel medium is being able to use pictures to tell part of the story. It's not necessarily better than writing that 'Gran'ma's jaw had a determined set to it,' but it can make the story feel more immediate.... Normal prose, on the other hand, has a slight delay while the action is described, and the reader waits for the end of the sentence to picture the event in his or her mind [Blasingame, 2006: 444–445].

The librarian's definition for graphic novel is very similar to what the two experts described about graphic novels being in the present and drawing the reader into the story by mimicking the act of actual physical storytelling. If graphic novels are *storytelling* then who is listening/reading the most?

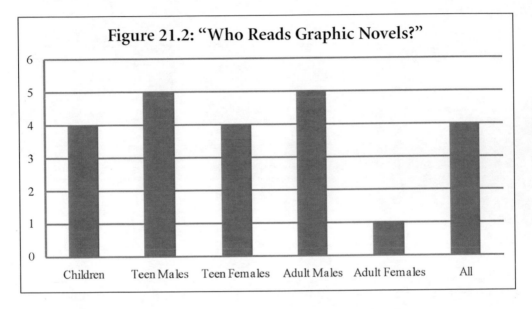

Figure 21.2: "Who Reads Graphic Novels?"

According to Lee County librarians, almost everyone except adult females is reading graphic novels, see Figure 21.2. Many of the librarians' responses consisted of words and phrases such as "young adults," "teens," or "children" somewhere within, and others stated phrases such as "all ages can enjoy," "wide range of readers," "all ages can read these." The latter are very satisfactory responses, and what these responses show us is that librarians do understand that graphic novels do cover a wide variety of interests. As for female readers, one librarian wrote, "I have not seen many females reading these novels." The librarians' notions were acceptable and on target. However, David Saylor, who "is in charge of Scholastic Graphix, which publishes the popular *Bone* series," is hopeful when considering this audience. Hunt, who, as mentioned earlier, interviewed Siegel, also interviewed Saylor in 2007. Hunt and Saylor discussed the relationship of girls with graphic novels. Hunt opened the interview with, "Traditionally, girls have not been as enthusiastic about graphic novels as boys have ..." to which Saylor replied, "My feeling is if you create comics that speak to their audience, they will be embraced. Girls love comics as much as anyone, as long as they find books that interest them" (Hunt, 2007: 8–11).

Female interest, especially adolescent female interest, in graphic novels is growing. As the graphic novel scope broadens toward female curiosities, more readerships will be realized, and reference librarians will need to become more knowledgeable about this group. The particular sphere which females are drawn to is Manga (or Japanese) comics, which "tends to focus on specific groups and sexes ... generalized by *shojo* (female) or *shonen* (male). In doing so, manga has become fairly balanced with regard to sexes" (Fallis, 2005: 16). The gender gap between males and females is becoming smaller thanks to mangas and the writers and artists willing to contribute to creating graphic novels considerate of female interests.

With an even broader scope on the graphic novel horizon, some still have doubts as to whether graphic novels should be considered literature or at the very least a *form* of literature. As mentioned before, I had my doubts about my coworkers' beliefs towards graphic novels due to conversations I have had with them. I expected the inevitable response to graphic novels being considered a form of literature would be several "no" responses; once again, to my delight, my predictions were foiled. Below are the results from question 3.

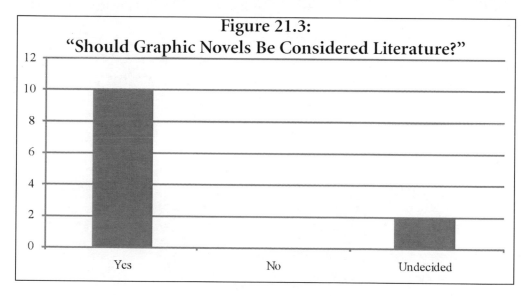

Figure 21.3:
"Should Graphic Novels Be Considered Literature?"

What Figure 21.3 shows is that once again librarians (at least librarians at Lee County Library) give graphic more written, formal credit than verbal, casual credit. At this point, I have to ask, Why? Why do these librarians, who outwardly seem to abhor graphic novels, inwardly recognize graphic novels' place in the library? Being a librarian myself, I could guess it is *because they are librarians*. As a general rule, librarians respect information in all formats, functions, and types. The librarian's job is to protect and provide information, not to oppress and suppress it. Ten replied "yes" and two were "undecided"; however, no one said "no."

One of the undecided librarians wrote, "I have mixed feelings about that. We have one teacher that has encouraged her students to read by starting with the graphic novels. She checks out a variety of books trying to get her students interested in learning." The librarian is probably battling conflict between his/her personal feelings toward graphic novels, and the undeniable fact that these books are helping students gain or further interest in reading. As an example of educational enhancement, consider Jodi Leckbee, who has been teaching for more than a decade. In an article she wrote for *Young Adult Library Services* on the importance of incorporating visual literacy in the classroom, Leckbee wrote that graphic novels are "not to replace, but rather enhance the learning of literary analysis for my students." She also described the graphic novel's function and importance: "Graphic novels, already popular with teen readers, act as a bridge allowing them to transcend the apathy usually felt toward reading assignments" (Leckbee, 2005: 30–31).

The second ambivalent librarian wrote, "Some can be. They have been around for decades." This is the same librarian who designated the term graphic novel as a "fancy word for a comic book." Seemingly, this librarian does not favor graphic novels and deems them less than credible. However, having done research, I find that on the professional end of the spectrum lies the contrary. Siegel, stated in his interview with Hunt, "Librarians have been ahead of the curve and have given us an astonishing welcome" (Hunt, 2007: 12–15). Also, Andy Runton, known for his *Owly* series, affirmed, "[L]ibrarians are some of my biggest fans" (Cart, 2007: 43). The second librarian has had 23 years in the field, which could be cause for the anxiety and doubt. Below is a chart representing how many years the questionnaire participants have worked as librarians. The years represented lead to more theories on why librarians view graphic novels as they do or do not.

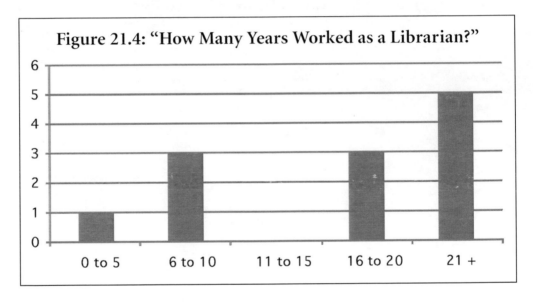

Figure 21.4: "How Many Years Worked as a Librarian?"

More Lee County librarians (5 out of 12) have worked beyond 21 years, which gives them an edge, having seen graphic novels emerge and evolve for over at least 21 years. Graphic novels have not been accepted as readily and widely in the United States as they have been in other countries. European and Asian countries celebrate and have celebrated graphic novels, while the United States has not been so embracing. The French *TinTin*, the Belgian *Asterix the Gaul* and *The Smurfs* have been exceedingly successful and their popularity interminable. Stan Tychinski, 35 year collector of comics and owner of a "pop-culture memorabilia shop" located in Selinsgrove, Pennsylvania, wrote "A Brief History of the Graphic Novel" for Brodart's website. In this brief history, he points to the United States' coyness concerning graphic novels and declares it is time for an amendment: "The time has come for mainstream public acceptance of graphic novels to take their place as valid literature in the United States, as they have been for years in the rest of the world" (Tychinski, 2004).

Some of the negativity towards graphic novels may have arisen from the "underground comics" of the 1960s, which were littered with "sexual themes and drug related culture" (Tychinski, 2004). Possibly a number of these librarians with lengthy tenure as librarians may very well remember those types of comics and label all of today's graphic novels as being the same. One questionnaire participant wrote in answer to Question 1 ("What is a graphic novel?") that "lots of times the story and illustrations are violent with sexual content." This librarian has worked in a library for an extensive period of time, 27 years.

Another theory as to why graphic novels are sometimes met with such disdain is the lessening of language. "In most early civilizations, and well into the current century, the majority of the population was illiterate.... Drawings and cartoons were used as a simple way to convey ideas or sentiments to the working class populace" (Tychinski, 2004). Librarians of long standing may still view graphic novels as mere humoristic novelties for the working masses, and deny graphic novels the right to be anything but simplistic entertainment. Librarians newer to the field may fear that graphic novels are to books as texting has become to writing. Going back to Tychinski's brief history, he opens with, "Since the days of prehistoric man, people have been telling stories using pictures instead of prose. From the cave paintings of the Cro-Magnon to the hieroglyphics of Ancient Egypt, graphic storytelling has been in use as a popular means for communicating thoughts and ideas" (Tychinski, 2004). A fear of language regression may be crossing the minds of both newer and tenured librarians, as well as the scholarly population.

Simple forms of communication dominate today's society. Texting, instant messaging (IM-ing), and icons that represent applications, also known simply as "apps," are prevalent. Where words lead off, images can pick up. If we are bombarded with icons, symbols, and shortcuts, then why not become more literate visually? Gretchen Schwarz wrote the article, "Medial Literacy, Graphic-Novels and Social Issues," which discusses the relevancy of graphic novels in today's social and civil society. Schwarz wrote, "[The Graphic novel] offers excellent opportunities for media literacy education, students learning to ask questions and evaluate information that is communicated through print, image, and technology" (Schwarz, 2007: 1–11). The more technologically advanced we become, the more open and broad the lines of communication become. Thus, understanding visual cues and emblems is now vital to everyday living.

Defining graphic novel is a "slippery slope" that reference librarians must climb when interacting with seasoned and unseasoned readers of graphic novels. However, with a better understanding of where graphic novels came from and where they are going, librarians will be able to welcome graphic novels to the collection more easily and properly put them into the appropriate hands. Not all of the myths and confusion surrounding graphic novels will ever be completely eliminated, but good literature, good reading, and good storytelling always have their complexities. The age of the graphic novel is upon us, whether we librarians like it or not.

References

Arnold, Andrew D. November 14, 2003. "The Graphic Novel Silver Anniversary." *Time*: http://www.time.com/time/columnist/arnold/article/0,9565,542579,00.html.

Blasingame, James. 2006. "Interview with Jeff Smith." *Journal of Adolescent & Adult Literacy* 49, no. 5: 444–445.

Cart, Michael. 2007. "You Go, Graphic!" *Booklist* 103, no. 14: 43.

Fallis, Chris. 2005. "Graphic Generation." *Young Adult Library Services* 3, no. 4: 16

Hunt, Jonathan. 2007. "Taking Comics from Junk Food to Gourmet Meals." *Children & Libraries: The Journal of the Association for Library Service to Children* 5, no. 1: 12–15.

Leckbee, Jodi. 2005. "I Got Graphic." *Young Adult Library Services* 3, no. 4: 30–31.

Merriam Webster, Inc. 1999. *Merriam-Webster's Collegiate Dictionary.* Springfield, MA: Merriam Webster, Inc.

Oxford University Press. 1989. *Oxford English Dictionary graphic, a. and n.* http://dictionary.oed.com.lynx. lib.usm.edu/cgi/entry/50097942/50097942se15?single=1&query_type=word&queryword=graphic++novel& first=1&max_to_show=10&hilite=50097942se15.

Petrucha, Stefan. January 2008. "On Writing (and Reading), the Graphic Novel." *Knowledge Quest*: 60–63.

"Q&A: Frank Miller." 2007. *Esquire* 147, no. 4: 52–54.

Schwarz, Gretchen. 2007. "Media Literacy, Graphic Novels and Social Issues." *Simile* 7, no. 4: 1–11.

Tychinski, Stan. 2004: "Graphic novels." http://www.graphicnovels.brodart.com/history.htm.

U.S. Census Bureau. July 25, 2008. *Quick Facts.* http://quickfacts.census.gov/qfd/states/28/2874840.html.

Zvirin, Stephanie. 2006. "Booklist Interview: Mark Siegel." *Booklist* 102, no. 14: 66.

What's in a Name
Nomenclature and Libraries

Francisca Goldsmith

The history of sequential art publishing has seen the introduction of evolving formats to carry narrative: caricature and single panel cartoon, comic strip, pamphlet-formatted serial comic books, and, 30 years ago, the introduction of the independent, fully formed narrative named "graphic novel."[1] The distinctions among these various formats include qualities of narrative length as well as publishing intention. The comic strip, for instance, is conceived as a mini-story or gag, while the graphic novel is an extended narrative with beginning, middle and end that may go on for hundreds of pages.

One compelling problem with discussing or even announcing graphic novels lies in the current nomenclature used to identify that body of sequential art work, which may or may not be true novels.[2] The term "graphic novel" is an identifier that clarifies the work in question as being a sequential art narrative other than a panel cartoon, comic strip gag, or serial story with multiple and planned-to-be-endless story arcs. "Graphic novel" no longer describes its own content so much as it differentiates the construction of it from other sequential art works.

Those who make use of the term "graphic novel" include publishers, libraries and some booksellers. There are creators in the sequential art field who use the term as well as those who eschew it. Thirty years on from its introduction, the term "graphic novel" has become dangerously close to cant, rather than an edifying phrase. Whether the term strikes a resonant chord with the potential reading and critical audiences, as well as with creators, has become a question. Is "graphic novel" related more to distribution than to creation and consumption?

Library Words

Those for whom libraries are currently created and maintained regularly must cope with jargon created by library staff, as well as those in related fields, such as publishing. Bibliographic classifications naming many types of library materials are not what their users might choose: "periodicals" vs. "magazines and journals," "videodisc" vs. "DVD," and so on. Librarians also try to bridge publishing nomenclature with classification strategies, leading to such positive/negative divides as "fiction" and "nonfiction," instead of a more positive descriptive bifurcation between "tales" and "facts."

Of necessity, bibliographic control includes a controlled vocabulary. Local culture may allow more user-friendly terminology for collection signage and, we hope, in discussions between library users and library staff. There are, indeed, reader's advisers who insist upon discussing bildungsroman with their clients, but probably most allow themselves the luxury of the more popularly understood "coming of age stories" or even "stories about a guy realizing he's become a real adult." However, when we talk professionally, including when we read professional literature and reviews, we utilize a refining and standardized vocabulary. We use this vocabulary to distinguish between publishing cycles and publishing formats, between perhaps closely allied genres, and it would seem, with "graphic novels," in spite of the evidence that bibliographic jargon can fly in the face of true description. We embrace granularity, perhaps at the expense of effective communication.

What's Included in This Catch-All Name?

As we prepare to enter the second decade of the 21st century, the term "graphic novel" has come to include, as far as librarians and the publishing industry seem to presume, any and all of the following distinct narrative types:

- Fiction, including both short stories and those extended and more complex literary pieces we generally call "novels"
- Memoir, poetry and other narratives that may be viewed as "literature," rather than as distinctly fictional or fact
- Journalism, whether reporting fact or opinion
- Interpretive descriptions of aspects of history, science, and other areas of endeavor and factual experience

Each of these narrative types has explicit markings as a genre.[3] In both the Library of Congress Classification System and the Dewey Decimal Classification, each sits in a specific and different range of area-of-knowledge classes. However, in sequential art format, an early professional bibliographic decision to give primacy to the visual aspect of the narrative's framing and expression has led to a conflation of other elements intrinsic to any one example with all other examples. The end result is that, while differentiation is made in provenance, none is made in genre.

Accorded to sequential art books, Japanese comics, manga, have held a large part of bibliographic attention among library audiences and collection developers during the first years of the 21st century. However, their be-all in popularity is beginning to wane somewhat. Since manga includes many serials, and may be brought to American audiences across as many as 25 or 35 volumes, this genre is another awkward match to the term "graphic novel." But, manga publishing is often referenced by critics and librarians as a subset of graphic novel publishing. We have practiced failing to refine terms in this regard, rather than specifying granularity articulately.

Early Confusion of Genre with Format

During the first decade or so of their popularity as library offerings for readers (as opposed to archival efforts to preserve comprehensive collections), both libraries and publishers tended to term graphic novels as representing a genre rather than belonging to a functional format.[4] From the late 1990's more care was taken by critics to remind librarians and readers that this sequential art expression is a format, containing any number of genres, just as the format of "magazine" or "videodisc" may contain content that is representing fact or fancy, addressing niche demographics or general audiences, and so on.

The publishing world has both led and followed the library lead when it comes to naming products for an American collection development audience. Review journals tend to lump graphic novel coverage with either other sequential art coverage, or with fiction.[5] Publishing houses have spent some money and varying degrees of effort in finding or creating sequential art content directed at new comics audiences. Some of these latter have been truly dismal, aiming to catch the bandwagon of format acceptance and merge it with curriculum support material, without care being taken to produce works that respect either the format or the audience.[6] Others substantially help to diversify the modes in which readers can explore topics, offering quality alternatives to straight narrative text reading, broadcast listening or social media information mining.[7]

The Question

Does this distinction of complexity and boundedness, with its concomitant lack of distinction between tale and fact, resolve a semantic question or demonstrate bibliographic coercion of art according to quasi-scientific categorization?

Library science seeks to assert bibliographic control, an effort born millennia before the postmodern publication explosion with which we now live. If we needed control when the physical records people created and promulgated were limited in format and even style, how much more important is it now? Bibliographic control intends to assist in the location of the specifically and immediately wanted among the ubiquitous mass of possibilities. Bibliographic control is asserted through descriptors that categorize, and provide hierarchical bases for comparison and contrast and relationship determination.

What happens then if we "cheat" by pushing things that are not the same, in some of these conditions, into a singular category, or push apart those that share a relationship by virtue of relying on categories that do not show the relationship(s)?

Stance Held by the Library of Congress

Because any science must have standards and a standards developing body, let's note where the Library of Congress has chosen to draw its lines, so to speak, in the nomenclature discussion. As with film, there is a leaning in that body toward categorizing first by format and then by such attributes as provenance and subject.[8] Therefore, all graphic novels are pulled together, in terms of bibliographic mapping, near comic strips and comic books, and at a distance from literature, whether the literature of fiction or narratives that explore any factual area or discipline. The Library of Congress has ruled that graphic novels are related to drawing, not to rhetoric or historiography or mathematics.

Stance Held by Book Industry Study Group

Unlike the Library of Congress, the Book Industry Study Group, the standards developing body who develop and promulgate the Book Industry Standards and Communication (BISAC), recognize Comics & Graphic Novels is a main category, on the same level of division of book output as are such categories as Art, Humor, Political Science and Study Aids[9]. Some public libraries are experimenting with organizing their materials according to BISAC, the systematic now used by publishers and others in the book industry to organize and typify specific titles in relationship to other titles and reader browsing.

Unlike the Dewey Decimal Classification or Library of Congress Classification systems, BISAC does not prescribe the flow of one subject area into the next. The relationships between such subjects as Psychology and Religion are left to the user (the bookstore or publisher's catalog developer). In so doing, BISAC limits its organizational thrust to commonalities that speak to a specific audience, rather than asserting relationships that may or may not seem sensible locally.

How Does Categorization Affect Semantics?

Much of our communication is composed of plain language choices, and is thus unconsidered except in regard to the emotional weight selected terms may intend to transmit or are likely to be heard as suggesting. There is the academic speech of the classroom, the political speech of the arena that governs aspects of our public lives, and so forth. Does bibliographic classification influence these? Perhaps, on occasion. With sequential art, however, very little — beyond the more general terms of "comics" (alternately and meaningfully rendered as "comix" to indicate a type) and manga — has developed in common language. Bibliographic record designers — both catalogers and publishers — are driving the semantic bus.

Let's consider some parallel format semantic issues that have come and gone in recent decades. While the general population called them "movies" or sometimes "films," the industry responsible for their production called them "motion pictures" and catalogers called them that as well. Now that movies/films/motion pictures are available on DVD, Videotape, and Blu-ray, however, catalogers call the format "videorecording." This term is unlikely to cross over into common parlance, but it does describe very specific production packaging (although it doesn't point to the artistic conception with the same specificity as does "movie" or "film" in the common language understanding of these format terms).

"Graphic novel" doesn't go far in describing either format or artistic intent, except to the initiated.

"Graphic Novel" as Bibliotherapeutic Medicine

In addition to the foreclosure on communication threatened by genre classification terminology, publishers and libraries have conspired to reduce aesthetic attention to the sequential art format to a palliative for reluctant readers. Of course, this is hardly all — or even most — publishers, nor is it all libraries. But rare is the press seen against the conceptualizing of the format as a reduction of literary and artistic attributes to fit a demographic whom observing business folk have simplified to the attribute they share: the kid who doesn't like to read, either because he lacks proficiency or because he (and yes, this array of marketers would have us also believe that the demographic is largely male) lacks imagination. This cynical disposition — cynical about both format and untapped potential reader — has spawned books that from a great distance carry some scent of graphic novel, but, in fact, lack many salient features of real sequential art narrative:

- Instead of presenting the narrative art of an individual or several individuals who have come together to create a composition they envision, they tend to be work for hire in which writers and visual artists place are technical experts dealing with preset formulae in both content and style.
- Instead of being original pieces or adaptations that add new depth and meaning, typically, they are recapitulations of curricular material, either factual (geophysical events) or canonical ("classic" literary works).[10]
- Instead of words and pictures "dancing together," text and illustration usually appear disjointed, neither *needing* the other but simply referencing the other — or sometimes not even that.[11]

The problem with such realizations of cynical use of the term "graphic novel" is twofold. On the one hand, poor stuff is taking library dollars that could have been spent on good stuff. Just as wretched a reality, however, is that the target audience for such stuff is quickly taught that what the librarian calls a "graphic novel" is junk; he (or she) may well generalize that realization to decide that (a) the librarian is a poor selector of suitably engaging materials, or (b) graphic novels are junk, or (c) both.

Graphic novels are not vitamin pills any more than are whole grain cereal foods. Both have the potential to deliver something "good for you," but need not bear that as a burden. When libraries cheat their users by offering substandard publications, they put their clientele at real risk; who should know better than the library what is good for you in the way of reading matter? And if the library's offering tripe, is it tripe or is the library cheating?

Adaptations are not, in themselves, a bad thing. Writers and artists often rework ideas, tropes and even full narratives conceived by a predecessor. It is when the artistry of the adaptor falls away, and the new "work" becomes a simplified pass through the original, that the new piece is merely derivative, at best, and hackneyed too often. To pass such "work" off as reader-worthy "graphic novels" hurts the reader and real graphic novel creators, as well as the library's reputation.

How Can We Name a Name That Works?

Well, first off, what needs to work? The need is to call a particular kind of narrative form — specifically that which conveys itself through sequential art — by a name that:

- Accurately describes the delimiters of the format
- Resonates with general audiences rather than merely with either the cognoscenti or marketers
- Holds format aloft but doesn't block the view to such possibilities under that umbrella as fact or fiction

Is it too late to "rescue" the format from the ignominy of a name that confuses and eludes a large part of its potential user group and has been coöpted by some marketers and analysts? If we all started calling graphic novels, of every stripe and on every occasion, pictonarratives, would the tide of general understanding about what is meant change? I doubt it. In truth, almost any term is as much less accurate as it is more accurate when we try to name a body of creativity that extends beyond formula. A sonnet is always a sonnet, but "poem" denotes all manner of possible ingredients and realizations.

Should we do nothing? Should we simply note that the term "graphic novel" has, does, and will cause semantic problems, that it will leave out large numbers of people from what it intends to communicate and move on without further how-do-you-do? It would be better not to be so blithe, but rather to pause and consider how to bring some daylight along with the term that, for now, has shed light only in a few specialized venues.

The project of change may be brought closer simply due to expansions in two related areas of applied technology. On the one hand, social media of more numerous varieties allow increasing venues for "published" use of terms. On the other, by publishing professionals, including librarians and specifically catalogers and reader's advisers, more respect is being awarded the terminologies and languages of book consumers. While these two facts both inform and rely on each other, together they have the capacity to bring us a more utile term than "graphic novel."

Semantics develop because language is set free and observed in action. To collect signatory meaning from terms used by the many involved in graphic novel production and appreciation (through their reviews, blogs, tweets, social catalog tags, fan postings and related verbal output) should move us beyond the misfit between entity and name that has brought us to the question posed at the outset of this essay. Rather than asserting alternative synthetic terms, while standing at one point in the format discussion — no matter which point or how privileged that point — we have the promise of solution through speedy evolution.

Perhaps the many voices and choices will group around a term as difficult and obfuscating as "graphic novel" seems to be for many of us. It seems less likely, given the broader cross section of speakers social media allow. But if they do, or if a term which seems as concretely imperfect rises to the fore of popular use, the choice will be popular, and therefore more broadly understood. And that, essentially, demarks what is a semantic problem from an expression that is idiomatic and readily comprehensible as a pointer. For 30 years, the terminology choice has been undertaken by a few, while the near future holds the likelihood of an agreement among many. With that agreement, any semantic problem slips into obscurity.

Endnotes

1. Arnold, Andrew D. "The Graphic Novel Silver Anniversary," *Time*, 14 November 2003. Discusses when and how Will Eisner adapted the term "graphic novel" and what has flowed from that, since 1978, in terms of bibliographic and marketing confusion.

2. David Hume's 18th century bifurcation of narrative into the realm of belief-instilling and fictional has, of course, undergone refinement and expansion. A variety of media are now vehicles through which creators express and audiences confront narrative works on both sides of the divide. We have televised biographies that utilize archival footage intercut with re-enactment and commentary (often in the form of a "talking head" or a "voice over"). We are familiar with claymation as a medium for full-length movies in which plot and character are as fully developed as print romance novels or serialized dispatches from embedded journalists. "Novel" is a literary descriptor of a fictional narrative, which may but need not be realistic in terms of characters and actions, scenery and physics. It is distinguished from story, or "short story" by complexity as well as length, supporting subplots and minor characters, for which there is no room in a simpler tale.

3. In the lingo of the cataloger, "genre" is not a qualifier denoting type of story, but rather means "form." In common parlance, however — and that is the language of most library users—"genre" refers to a collection of cast markings that are related to specific fiction plots: mystery and detective fiction, fantasy and science fiction, and so on.

4. Just about at 2000, those working closely with readers as well material began a conscientious practice of differentiating between genre (the bibliographic term) and format (the functional term) when describing the publishing and reader typologies into which the graphic novel fits.

5. *Publisher's Weekly* runs a small collection of reviews under the banner "comics" in each issue. The placement of this collection is usually after the grouping under the banner "Fiction" and near the collection under the banners of "Mysteries" and "Mass Market." This "Comics" review collection includes both fiction and nonfiction titles, as well as volumes from manga series and albums of comic strips. *Booklist*, the American Library Association's review organ, on the other hand, places graphic novel reviews in the Fiction category of its reviews, not as a subset but scattered among the other titles under review, in accordance with the alphabetic arrangement of the authors of the books. Review resources for both the comics trade and lay review readers also provide nothing distinguishing about the grouping of graphic novel reviews: in the former, they usually fall into either alphabetic order by primary creator or in publication date order, while in the latter, they appear only sporadically and usually one per issue (or less often).

6. While there are several established graphic novel publishing houses, relevant titles are also brought out by large, general and conglomerate publishers, often but not always under particular imprints. In both these cases, the quality of individual work published may be greater or lesser, but is clearly not work-for-hire. On the other hand, some publishers have tried to establish "graphic novel" series in which they package illustrated work intended as curriculum support; these tend to be imitative but not sufficiently actualized sequential art exemplars. And, almost exclusively, such series treat matters of fact rather than presenting fiction.

7. Hill and Wang has undertaken a number of critical historical examinations of American events through graphic novels. The 2004 publication of Sid Jacobson and Ernie Colón's *The 9/11 Report: A Graphic Adaptation*, maintained the facts of the Commission's voluminous text report while also presenting visual facts that cannot be perfectly stated in words: the concomitancy of flight paths of the doomed airline carriers, markers used to excite race prejudice in the aftermath of the event and so on. Later offerings also provide readers who cannot or will not take up examinations of political or even literary movements with fair and evocative sequential art explorations.

8. In 2005 and 2006, the Library of Congress and OCLC explored how best to subdivide "image-driven texts," but the idea of moving them from being grouped either together or in proximity to sorting them by other salient features of the individual works such as topic being treated through the image-driven text, did not enter the discussion. See the discussion paper at http://www.oclc.org/DEWEY/discussion/papers/graphicnovels.htm

9. The BISAC definition of this category begins "Use subjects in this section for works of sequential illustration in the style commonly associated with 'comic books' or 'comic strips.'" See the full discussion at http://www.bisg.org/standards/bisac_subject/comics.html

10. See, for example Rosen Publications "Graphic Disasters" series which presents earthquakes, tsunamis and other events, or Papercutz "Classics Illustrated" line of adaptations, which are available in both "regular" and "deluxe" editions, the latter boasting "longer, more expansive adaptations."

11. Mark Siegel's definition of a well conceived sequential art work is that in which words and pictures are brought "to that third element of their dance together." See Goldsmith, Francisca. "Words and Pictures Dancing Together: In Conversation with Mark Siegel," *Voice of Youth Advocates*, June 2007: 125.

References

Arnold, Andrew. November 2003. "The Graphic Novel Silver Anniversary." *Time*, 14.

Goldsmith, Francisca. June 2007. "Words and Pictures Dancing Together: In Conversation with Mark Siegel." *Voice of Youth Advocates*.

The Ontology of Art and What Libraries Should Buy

RUTH TALLMAN AND JASON SOUTHWORTH

The Problem for Libraries

Acquisition librarians have to make tough decisions about what to purchase for their collections. Leaving aside issues concerning how poorly funded most libraries are, there is the particular issue of what to do about new editions. While you see this problem creep up from time to time regarding novels (the Library of America reissuing the complete works of Philip Roth, for instance), you see it far more often with graphic novels and trades, as it is the norm for comic books to be printed in a variety of formats. *Batman Dark Victory* comes out monthly in thirteen issues, then it is released as a hardcover volume, then with a soft cover — and lord knows one day we will see it as an Absolute edition. Which of these, and how many, should a library buy?

One way to go about answering this question is to buy only one copy of the work. After all, isn't it better to have one copy of each book before doubling and tripling up? While this might seem like a simple solution, it actually runs head on into a major philosophical problem. It turns out that people have very different intuitions about what makes something a work of art, and if you don't know what a work of art is, you can't know how many art objects there are that need to be purchased. The study of what makes something a work of art is called the ontology of art, and is a growing subfield of philosophy. In this paper, we will explain the most prevalent views in the ontology of art. In doing this, we will pay careful attention to the implications of the theories on how we think about comic books and graphic novels, and the impact this ought to have on library acquisition policy.

Basic Physical Object Hypothesis

The simplest answer to the question of, "what is a work of art?" is that it is a special type of physical object. By "physical object," we mean just what it sounds like — a phone, a cup, a keyboard — all of these things are physical objects. On this account, works of art are just like the phone, the cup, and the keyboard; they are just physical objects which we identify as art (apologies to all phone, cup, and keyboard designers who think what they create is art also).

It helps to think about cases like a single painting or sculpture to understand this view.

The *Mona Lisa* is that physical object comprised of oils and canvas that hangs in the Louvre, and Michelangelo's *David* is that particularly hewn slab of marble displayed in Florence. It would be great if a view as simple as this were correct, but there are some pretty significant problems with it. Think about the case of a comic book. When we talk about a comic, let's say a copy of *Detective Comics 27*, we do talk about that comic as if it were a singular and unique work of art. Collectors have gone so far as to develop the CGC rating system, a one hundred point scale used to judge the physical quality and, as a result, the monetary worth of any comic book. There are people out there who will spend years of their lives looking for a 9.7 copy of *Incredible Hulk 1*, and then turn around and start looking for a 9.8.

It is in this last observation that the major problem with this view can be seen. We also talk about comics like they are not unique at all. They are simply instances of a work of art. When you read your copy of *Batman and Robin 1*, you assume that anyone else who has read a copy of *Batman and Robin 1* will be just as familiar with the work as you are. In fact, the language we used in the last sentence further illustrates the problem with this view, as we referred to the book as a *copy*. If this was not enough to show the problems with this view, it would also commit libraries to a very strange acquisition policy. There would never be such a thing as too many copies of a comic or trade, because in this view they would all be new and unique works. So a collection of thousands of different titles would be just as diverse as a collection of a thousand copies of *The Life and Times of Uncle Scrooge*.

Creation/Performance View

Due to these types of problems with the basic physical object view, some look for alternative understandings of the ontology of art. One route is to view art not as an object, but to see the process of creation/performance as the work of art. Aesthetician David Davies popularized this view, although it is often expressed by artists. On this view, the actual art is the act of the artist drawing, writing, penning dialogue, and so forth. The finished product — what most of us will call the artwork — is merely residue. It is the thing that is left when the art has finished. This view seems most intuitive regarding performing arts. What is there to a ballet or a play other than the performance itself? This is the type of question Davies would ask to try to gain sympathy for this view.

A strange implication of this view, however, is that nothing hanging in a museum and shelved in a library is a work of art. All that museums and libraries have are leftovers from the art. A way to think about the art object is as an artifact, or souvenir from the event which was the actual artwork. The painting, sculpture, or book that you purchase as akin to a t-shirt from a rock concert — but in most cases, it's a rock concert you didn't even attend. The closest a library could come to collecting art would be to acquire videos of artists at work (something like the *Modern Masters* series from Twomorrows Publishing, where they record pencilers and inkers working and explaining their process). Let's hope that administrative bodies in charge of library funding don't find out about this view, or we will see more budget cuts than ever before.

Tolstoy

Rather than viewing art as a performance, Leo Tolstoy, a 19th century Russian writer, argued that art is the point of communication between an artist and viewer. So, what does that mean? Well, Tolstoy saw art as a way for humans to express complex or ineffable ideas and emotions. Everything begins with an artist having a difficult-to-express idea. Since ordinary language has failed him, the artist creates an object of some sort — could be a book, painting, song, or other type of artwork. If everything works right, this object serves to direct viewers' minds to the idea he wants to communicate. The conjunction of the ideas in the heads of the artist and the viewer is the art. When you need to refer to it, the physical object can be called an "artwork," but an artwork is not itself art (Tolstoy). Perhaps the best way to think about the physical object is as a prompt, or catalyst, for stimulating a thought in the mind of the viewer. This process is intended to be analogous to expressing an idea with ordinary language. Say you want a small, black cup of coffee. You tell your barista this is what you want. She complies. What has happened? You had a simple thought in your head — small, black coffee. You put that idea into the barista's head by means of simple language. If you succeeded, in Tolstoy's words, a point of communication occurred — a place where the idea in your mind matched up with the idea in the barista's mind. Because you were thinking of the same object, you succeeded in getting the barista to give you what you wanted.

This model should help explain what Tolstoy thinks is going on in the case of art, which is a lot more complicated. Take one of Tolstoy's own works, *The Death of Ivan Ilyich*. Why, according to his own theory, did Tolstoy write this novella? He had all of these really complicated ideas and emotions raging around in his head about the fear and horror of death. Talking about the fear of one's mortality using ordinary language simply doesn't work. You can't express the full range of emotion and terror through regular exposition. So, Tolstoy told Ivan's story. He created a physical object — a novella — and that object served as a prompt to point the viewers to the collection of emotions and ideas that Tolstoy wants us to think about. What's the actual artwork? The actual artwork is that collection of ideas and emotions that Tolstoy is thinking about, and which his artwork has caused us to think about as well.

In terms of comic books, consider Craig Thompson's *Blankets*. Although the story does have a clear narrative structure (as does *Ivan Ilyich*), the artwork is much more than the simple facts of the story. Thompson had complicated ideas about the feelings and emotions that go along with one's first experience of romantic love, and the tangle of experiences that accompany it. The artwork, according to Tolstoy, is not the physical object, *Blankets*, but is rather the ideas that Thompson put into your head through the medium of *Blankets*.

So, how does this apply to comic books and library acquisitions? Well, for starters, it means that you are never actually acquiring a copy of the work when you purchase a book or trade, since the art is immaterial. Also, strangely, you could make acquisitions without ever buying anything, just by going to another library. If you read a copy of *V for Vendetta* and you have the ideas that Alan Moore (writer), David Lloyd (artist), Steven Craddock (letterer) and Steve Whitaker (colorist) intended for you to have, then you have the art. While this observation is funny, it does not pose a significant problem for the view. A defender of this view could just say that it misrepresents a library's purpose. Libraries are not buildings that hold art which people can come to experience. Rather, libraries merely hold the means by which people can come in contact with the art. As such, it would still be necessary to make acquisitions of physical objects — the prompts which cause people to experience the artwork.

However, comic books and graphic novels cause a pretty serious problem with Tolstoy's view. In a clear majority of cases, comics and graphic novels are the product of several artists. We talk primarily about writers and pencilers, but inkers, colorists, and letterers all contribute important elements to the art. Inkers add depth and detail to the images; coloring greatly affects mood and helps to direct the reader's attention; and anyone who doesn't think lettering contributes important aesthetic qualities to the work should set this book down and go look at any of the *Cerebus* phonebooks.

In cases of artworks with multiple artists, a problem emerges: which artist's ideas are we supposed to come in contact with? The general concepts, themes and dialogue come from the writer. The penciler then puts his own spin on the script when drawing the images. In all cases, artists add details that the writer did not call for, because even a writer who gives lengthy scripts (Alan Moore, for instance, is famous for giving hundred page scripts for 22 page comics.) can't capture every nook and cranny of every object in every panel. The inker manipulates the images in the same way that the penciler manipulates the text. The inker decides which images will stand out and which will even be eliminated (If an inker doesn't ink something, it doesn't get picked up when the page is reproduced. This happens all the time.). The colorist then does the same thing to the work done by the inker. The colorist can enhance what the inker has done, or can make different images stand out in the way that he chooses to apply color. Finally, the letterer gets to put his mark on the work. The letterer must cover parts of the image produced by the penciler/inker/colorist to place the word balloons. These balloons also influence how our eyes move over the page, and this can be different than the penciler, et al., intended. The letters also affect how we read the dialogue. Different fonts imply different tones of voice, and letter size implies how loud a sound is, etc. With all this in mind, it is clear that every artist has something different in mind when he is producing the work, and they all seem to have legitimate claims to it being their thoughts that we should be coming to realize when we come in contact with the art object (see McCloud).

Regardless of how a defender of Tolstoy tries to respond to this problem, there will be interesting consequences for acquisition practices for comic books and graphic novels. Recently, Marvel and DC have begun to sell trade paperbacks of their comics without the color. These *Essentials* and *Showcases*, respectively, have the work of one of the contributing artists removed. On Tolstoy's view, the artwork is the point of communication between artist and viewer. The colorist is one of the artists involved in creating the physical object which prompts understanding of the work. In reproductions of comics in which the color is removed, there is no way for the viewer to reach an understanding about the ideas which the colorist wanted to communicate, so a portion of the artwork is necessarily lost.

Consider the first appearance of the Green Lantern, in *Showcase 22*.[1] Part of what the writer, John Broome, wanted to communicate was that the Green Lantern was vulnerable to yellow. Readers were to be keyed into the fact that the Green Lantern would have particular trouble with certain villains, such as Sinestro, due to the presence of yellow in their costume or weapons. He probably relayed this desire to the colorist, whose name has been lost.[2] When we read the first appearance of the Green Lantern as a reproduction in a *Showcase Green Lantern*, we miss part of the message John Broome and the others intended, because the color, which is clearly very important in this case, has been omitted. Thus, an implication of Tolstoy's view is that it is inappropriate for libraries to acquire Essentials and Showcases in place of colored versions of the books. Presumably, the absence of color will lead to an inability of the reader to reach the appropriate level of understanding of the artists' intended message.

Tolstoy's view implies that libraries should not acquire *Essentials* and *Showcases* if they can get the original, colored versions instead. However, his view also leads us to conclude that sometimes newer versions of comics are better. For example, a double page spread in *Infinite Crisis 7* was left uncolored due to a missed deadline by the colorist. That error was corrected in the hardcover release. In this case, the artists explicitly reported that their initial attempt at communication failed in some way. If that failure was corrected in a later work, we should seek out the version of the art object which the artist reports to be the best route to the abstract artwork.

Sometimes, we run into problems regarding which version of a work is the best, however. Writer Neil Gaiman asked that *Sandman* be re-colored in its absolute version, because he felt the original coloring was a mistake that actually made it harder for the viewer to get to the artwork. Presumably, however, original colorist Robbie Busch would have wanted his coloring kept in the absolute release. The re-coloring of *Sandman* actually forced one of the artists out of the work. One way to respond to this issue is to suppose that, in cases of multiple versions, when there seem to be two different artistic visions, there are two distinct artworks. If you want to reach the point of communication that Neil Gaiman was trying to convey, you should read the absolute. If you want the point of communication Robbie Busch had in mind, stick with the original.

Another implication of Tolstoy's view is that supplemental materials included in printings of works, such as interviews, sketches, and commentaries, might be preferable to the original issues which did not contain that material. If supplementary material is such that it helps the reader reach a more clear understanding of the message the artist intended to communicate, it is preferable to the version that lacks such material. However, some supplementary materials might be completely unneeded. Letters columns, for example, do not contribute to one's understanding of the artist's message, so a library would have no need to ensure that such material was a part of their collection. It is important to remember, also, that even the most helpful commentary would at best be an aid to the viewer's understanding of the work. Commentary is a communication using ordinary language, and Tolstoy's whole point is that art communicates ineffable ideas which cannot be shared through ordinary language.

Abstract Type View

The problems with both the completely physical (like the basic physical object hypothesis) and completely abstract (like Tolstoy's view, and the creation/performance view) accounts of the ontology of art have caused some to look for a compromise position. Richard Wollheim (1971) has attempted to give a theory that balances our intuitions about art being somehow both physical and non-physical by appealing to what philosophers call the type-token distinction. Types are not physical objects at all, but are rather abstract entities by which we categorize things that share many of the same properties. 'Library' is a type, whereas 'Hays Public Library' and 'Bizzell Memorial Library' are two tokens of the type. 'Library' does not exist in any place or time, it does not evolve or decay, but each token of it does these things. Library collections grow and are weeded, and buildings receive face-lifts and additions, yet the type 'library' is unchanging. This distinction accounts for the way in which we are able to continue to refer to something as a library, even when it has undergone such changes, and how the same term can encompass such a wide variety of tokens.

This distinction is especially helpful in understanding particular kinds of artworks. Aestheticians distinguish between artworks which are autographs, and those that are allographs. Autographs are the types of artworks, like paintings and sculptures, in which the common view is that there is only one instance of the work — the original, which was created by the artist, with all other versions being inferior copies or replicas of the one artwork. Allographs, on the other hand, are artworks such as books, CDs and comics, in which the common intuition is that there are multiple instances of the artwork, and there is no one version which is the original, or "real" work, with all others being copies. Wollheim (1971) applies the type-token distinction to allographs, and says that the artwork is the type, while all of the physical instances are tokens. So, the "real" artwork which we call *Identity Crisis* is an abstract entity, a type, and the copy on our shelf, and the one on yours, and the one on the shelf at the Hays Public Library, are all tokens of that type. This explains how the artwork remains the same, even though the library's copy has been rebound and your copy has a coffee ring on the cover.

On this view, the trade paperback, and hardcover reprints of Will Eisner's *A Contract with God* are all tokens of the same abstract type, which is the actual artwork. This view plays to the intuition that destroying a particular copy of *A Contract with God*, though perhaps foolish, would not destroy the artwork, *A Contract with God*. If some foolish patron lets her child rip up the library's copy, we'll be angry, but it can always be replaced. The artwork itself does not cease to exist when particular copies do. Less intuitively, this view also implies that, as the real artwork is an abstract type, even if every single copy of *A Contract with God* was destroyed, the artwork would still exist (though no new viewers could access it).

If the idea that a work could still exist as a type if all its tokens were gone seems crazy, think of one of the most famous comic book panels of all time: Peter Parker's first meeting with Mary Jane Watson, in *Amazing Spider-Man vol. 1, 42*. Even if you haven't seen the image of the red-haired knock-out standing in the doorway, telling Peter "Face it, Tiger, you just hit the jackpot," since you were 12 years old, you can instantly recall it. Would your recollection of this image be any less vivid if every single copy of that comic suddenly poofed out of existence? Wollheim, and other proponents of the abstract type view, don't think so.

The abstract type view speaks to the intuition that some artworks seem to be able to persist as ideas even when they are not physically instantiated. However, this view also carries with it some puzzles. Proponents of this view are divided about when the abstract type that is a particular artwork comes into existence. There seem to be only three options. Either the artwork exists eternally, or it begins to exist when someone thinks about it, or it begins to exist when a token is created. The first view, embraced by Nicholas Wolterstorff (1975), carries with it some pretty obvious problems. Most importantly, if all artworks are eternally existent, it means no artist engages in an act of creation — all artworks are merely discovered.

The second option, that artworks do not exist eternally, but rather come into existence in the mind of the artist, is more attractive. However, it still raises some hairy questions. When, exactly, did *Y: The Last Man* come into existence? The first time the concept of a world with only one remaining male popped into his head (surely he wasn't the first person ever to have that idea!)? The first time he wrote down his idea? The first time his words were paired with Pia Guerra's images? Not until the first issue was completed? Not until the final issue was completed? What does "completed" mean? Published? There seems to be no non-arbitrary answer. This option is susceptible to many of the same objections as Tolstoy's view. If the abstract type's existence is tied to some sort of mental activity on the part of the artist, we are back once again to the question of, which artist? This view also shares a problem with the creation/performance view. If the real artwork is an abstract type, collectors are doing something very strange indeed. They are collecting tokens, but never the real thing. It is strange that someone would pay $35,850 to *not* own the artwork which is *Detective Comics 27*!

So, the view that the abstract type comes into existence before its tokens are created carries with it the combined problems of two other views. Perhaps, then, the most reasonable view is that the abstract type does not come into existence until all tokens of the type have been created. The type is a conjunction of properties which exist within the tokens. This view holds that we should understand the abstract type like the center of a Venn diagram in which each circle is a token, and the type is the place at which each of those tokens overlap. The properties of the type are determined by the properties of the token. The artwork is the ideal which does not exist in any one token. Token A might have a flaw on page 3, but the abstract type does not. This makes sense, given what we know about print runs. The first few and the last few tokens in a fixed run of 10,000 will have imperfect coloring and, though these are tokens of the type, their imperfections do not translate to the artwork itself.

This view avoids many of the previously discussed problems, but invites a new one. If the abstract type is determined when all tokens of the type have been created, we have a problem with second (and subsequent) printings. If the abstract type does not exist until *all* tokens are created, it means the only artworks that exist are those that will never again be reprinted. EC Comics' *Tales from the Crypt 1* was first published in 1950, and has been reprinted many times since. There is no indication that its most recent printing, in 2007, will be the last. Strangely, this means that we can never know if the work exists or not. If the 2007 reprint is the last reprint, then there is a type and an artwork exists. Yet if in 50 years someone gets the idea to print it again, then it will mean that for those 50 years there was never a type or an artwork (even though everyone thought that there was).

A more charitable understanding of this view is that the abstract type comes into existence at the end of each print run. At the end of a print, the type comes into existence with the properties that are the conjunction of properties of the tokens, and this type is the artwork. So, every time a book goes back to print, a new abstract type is created out of the collection of tokens, coming into existence after the print run is finished. However, this also is counterintuitive — the new tokens look just like the old ones, but this view commits us to accepting them as tokens of an entirely new artwork. *The Spirit 1* was first printed for publication in 20 newspapers on June 2, 1940. Twenty separate print runs created 20 separate sets of tokens which, upon completion, resulted in 20 separate (but astonishingly similar!) artworks. This view suggests that libraries ought to acquire tokens from each print run of *The Spirit 1*, which would result in the acquisition of 20 seemingly identical copies of that comic!

Type Physical Object Hypothesis

Thus far we have looked at some of the major views about the ontology of art, and found serious problems with each of them. So, how are we to understand the ontology of artworks? The abstract type view can be combined with the basic physical object view to develop a hybrid position which is more sophisticated and tenable than either of the others on their own. We'll keep the attractive features of both and weed out the aspects of each that raise problems.

What is good about the basic physical object hypothesis? It provides for a unified ontology. Occam's razor advises us to prefer theories that make things less complicated over those that make things more complicated. Unless we have reason to do otherwise, the best way to understand the ontological status of artworks is to use the same rules that we apply to our ontological understanding of everything else. The physical object hypothesis is simple and accords with our understanding of the rest of the world, and is desirable for this reason. It affirms what we already believe. Artworks are not some sort of strange abstraction that floats around in our minds or, even more creepily — independent of our minds. Artworks are just what they look like — physical objects. Sure, we often assign special meaning to artworks, but that is a nonessential subjective evaluative layer added by the viewer. The artwork *David* is a particular piece of marble that has been sculpted in a certain way. The meaning and power which we assign to the work is not part of the ontology of the work itself.

The basic physical object hypothesis is sufficient when dealing with autographs. However, to understand the ontology of comic books and other allographs, something extra is needed. Incorporating elements of the abstract type view into the basic physical object hypothesis leads to a complete and coherent picture. The abstract type view is attractive because it can explain our impulse to understand a comic book as one artwork, even though multiple instances of it exist in the world. This hybrid view retains the understanding of artworks as types, but rejects the abstract element because, remember, understanding artworks as abstract entities led to all sorts of troubles regarding the existence of the work, as discussed above.

On this view, artworks are physical objects, of which there might be multiple tokens of the same type. Rather than hold, as the abstract type view does, that the actual artwork is the abstract type, this view holds that each physical token — each instantiation of the type — is a real art object and an instance of art. Our copy of Ariel Schrag's *Potential* is a real art object, which shares much in common with your copy, the library's copy, and even the photocopied versions she handed out to her classmates back in high school. On this view, the physical instantiations are the real thing, and the type is a linguistic way of classifying groups of artworks which bear a strong family resemblance. This view is preferable to the others because it accords with our common sense intuitions, and it avoids some of the problems of the other views. It explains why grading comics and hunting down particular physical copies of a comic makes sense. Each is an actual, unique artwork, with value in itself, not dependent on an abstraction. This view also explains why we expect people who have encountered the type in a different form to know what we're talking about. If you have read your own copy of *Maus*, you needn't read ours before we can have a conversation about it.

Types are not existent objects, and they are not particularly special — they are just useful. They are our way of understanding allographic artwork, and of labeling works as "the same," even though we understand that they are not really the same. Remember, your copy of *Identity Crisis* has a coffee ring on the cover, but most of them do not. Because types are just a tool we use to classify and communicate, they are somewhat arbitrary. Is the *Showcase Elongated Man* a new type, of which each copy is an artwork? Or is the *Showcase Elon-*

gated Man merely a new collection of a bunch of types that were created in the Silver Age, and have now been bound together in a particular grouping? It doesn't really matter. We know that the re-printings are not identical to the originals, because they lack color, but we also know that even issues from the same print run are not identical — there will be inconsistencies in print color, for example.

This theory admits to drawing arbitrary lines, which might seem like a weakness of the theory, but it's actually a strength. Ambiguity is built into the world. This is not unique to art. We are going to disagree about what falls into the type "library." Does it count as a library if it's in a private home? What about if it is entirely digital? What about video libraries? There is a huge range of things which fall under the type "library." Some people will want to discount certain instances that fall on the fringes. Ludwig Wittgenstein (1953) talked about this using the example of "chair."[3] Chairs can have one leg or many, can have backs or not, can be made of wood, steel, fabric, and more. Perhaps you don't want to call an overturned bucket a chair, but guess what — the guy who is sitting on it will disagree with you! Even if you think he is using the word wrong, however, if, when the guy comes back from the bathroom and finds you sitting on his bucket, and says to you, "Get off my chair!" there is no question that you will know what he means. Concepts can refer, and be meaningful, while having no set boundaries — fuzzy edges are simply a part of the world.

Think about the Fantastic Four. There are radical differences between Stan Lee and Jack Kirby's Fantastic Four, the film adaptations, and the various other runs over the years. In issue *347*, every founding member of the FF was replaced — Ghost Rider, Wolverine, Spider-Man, and Hulk subbed in and saved the day. Yet we still understand what's being talked about when the Fantastic Four is mentioned, because we recognize common elements that exist despite the differences. Given this, there's nothing surprising about calling all of the different versions of the artwork *Fantastic Four 1* — the original issue, its many reprints, its Essential version, its trade versions — the same type.

What, then, does this mean for library acquisitions? It means that each new physical object type is a new work of art, and thus in an ideal world, libraries would obtain a token of each. Practically, however, no library will have the resources to purchase each variant cover of an issue, to buy every reissue with minute changes to coloring, new introductions, and oversized versions. This understanding of artworks offers librarians a rule of thumb by which to make acquisition decisions. If we are to understand each new type as a new work, we will make decisions based on the degree of difference between those works, and will purchase the works which involve enough difference to justify the purchase.

How do we determine how much difference is sufficient to justify purchasing another version of the work? If the viewer could learn something from a new acquisition that couldn't be learned from the closest work in the collection, the acquisition would be justified. Jack Kirby's line work can be seen more clearly in *Essentials* than in the original issues, because the coloring can actually be distracting. Yet, as demonstrated earlier, some elements of the work require the presence of color. This indicates that libraries ought to acquire both versions of the work if possible.

There are salient differences between an *Essential*, an *Omnibus*, a newsprint quality trade, and an issue, so these seem like relevant demarcations. We can learn new things from each, so acquiring each would not be out of line. But the punch line is, because this is just a linguistic distinction, we can argue about which differences are large enough to warrant a new purchase. If someone thinks there's a legitimate difference between the first and second printings of an *Omnibus*, this theory requires that we talk it over. Sometimes we will find that the new edition does not provide enough new material to justify the purchase, but at other times it will.

The first volume of the *Daredevil Omnibus* by Brian Michael Bendis had a printing error on the cover, which resulted in a discoloration on Daredevil's face. This error was corrected in subsequent printings, but the first version is worth more money because people found value in the mistake. So maybe it's worth considering them as different types, both worthy of purchase. It's going to depend on what it is that you find valuable about the art. Someone who cares primarily about getting the story content of a comic will be untroubled by the missing color, and will be happy with *Essentials* and *Showcases*. However, if you are concerned with the effect of color and shading on the work, these will not be appropriate options. They will be too far removed from the work you are looking for to qualify as the same type. Someone who is interested in the historical phenomenon of a fan base and its original reaction to and influence on a comic will see the letters columns as necessary elements of the work — ones that cannot be done without. We have diverging intuitions about where to draw the line regarding "similar enough" and "too different," and that's a strength of the type physical object hypothesis. Where there is wide scale disagreement about a subject, there ought to be an explanation for it, and that is true in this case.

In this paper, we have laid out the major views of the ontology of art, and have explained what each of those views would dictate in terms of library acquisition policies. We have given reasons why the issues specific to comic books would lead you prefer certain views over others. We have argued that one view, the type physical object hypothesis, captures our intuitions most closely, by acknowledging some of the particular features which are important in comic art — features such as the collaborative nature of their creation, and the tendency for the work to be reprinted with sometimes slight, sometimes major, variations. As we tried to make clear in the paper, differing intuitions will give you differing views of the ontology of artwork. This essay is meant to broaden the discussion, not end it.

Endnotes

1. *Showcase #22* was penciled by Gil Kane and inked by Joe Giella.
2. Because we used to think the writer was the only actual artist involved in the creation of comic books.
3. Ludwig Wittgenstein, *Philosophical Investigations*, Remark 59. Blackwell Publishing, 1953.

References

McCloud, Scott. 1994. *Understanding Comics: The Invisible Art.* New York: Harper Paperbacks.
Tolstoy, Leo. 2001. *What Is Art?* Translated by Aylmer Maude. Bridgewater, NJ: Replica Books.
Wittgenstein, Ludwig. 1953. *Philosophical Investigations*, Remark 59. Oxford: Blackwell Publishing.
Wollheim, Richard. 1971. *Art and Its Object: An Introduction to Aesthetics.* New York: Harper Torchbook.
Wolterstorff, Nicholas. 1975. "Toward an Ontology of Artworks." *Nous*, vol. 9: 115–142.

24

Meta-Comics and Libraries
Should Libraries Buy Them?

ADAM J. NOBLE

In an early chapter of his Eisner Award–winning examination of the current state of the comic medium, *Reading Comics: How Graphic Novels Work and What They Mean*, author Douglas Wolk identifies and defines a specific subset of the well-known and frequently maligned superhero comic: the self-referential "superhero metacomic." Superhero metacomics have existed for nearly three decades now. Some have acted as mere vehicles for light-hearted satire, allowing writers to share in-jokes with long time fans, while other metacomics have been among the most socially relevant, personal, artistically unique comics of any genre. Occasionally, metacomics can do both these things at once. In his introduction to the first volume of his epic metacomic, *Astro City*, writer Kurt Busiek offers what he considers to be the greatest merit of the superhero genre:

> [I]f a superhero can be such a powerful and effective metaphor for male adolescence [i.e. traditional comic heroes like Superman and Spider-Man], then what else can you do with them? Could you build a superhero story around a metaphor for female adolescence? Around mid-life crisis? Around the changes adults go through when they become parents? Sure, why not? [Busiek, 1996: 8].

Busiek does all these and more, by creating his own original characters who act as stand-ins for their popularly recognized counterparts. His Samaritan is an obvious ringer for Superman; the First Family is an analogue for Marvel Comics' Fantastic Four, and so on.

However, by their very nature, superhero metacomics assume knowledge of (or at least familiarity with) superhero comics. Can readers approach and enjoy these texts without worrying about being acquainted with decades of comics trivia? Should Collection Development librarians provide them to patrons? This essay will examine these questions, and outline the purposes and theories behind the plethora of mainstream comic books that attempt — with varying degrees of success— to "break down the fourth wall."

To use the broadest possible definition, a "metacomic" is a "comic about other comics" (Wolk, 2008). This self-referencing does not necessarily need to have anything to do with superheroes, or superhero genre conventions, or call-backs to earlier stories featuring familiar characters. It can be something as simple as the sequence in Art Spiegelman's seminal Holocaust memoir *Maus: A Survivor's Tale*, in which Spiegelman discusses the medium and iconography (Germans as cats, Jews as mice) that he is using within the book itself, and the limits/potential of the comics medium (Speigelman, 1992: 41). Or a metacomic can be slightly tongue-in-cheek, like the strip "Are Comics Serious Literature?" from Michael Kupperman's humor comic, *Tales Designed to Thrizzle*, in which two cowboys engage in a ludicrous comic-book-style fight scene to determine whether comics are, indeed, serious literature (Kupperman, 2008).

However, a *superhero* metacomic is, according to Douglas Wolk, "[a comic] whose point is commentary on the conventions of superhero stories or on familiar characters who are represented in a thinly disguised *roman à clef* way" (Wolk, 2007: 105). Wolk continues:

> Metacomics may pay lip service to being universally comprehensible, but they're really aimed at what I call "superreaders": readers familiar enough with enormous numbers of old comics that they'll understand what's really being discussed in the story [Wolk, 2007: 105].

Courtesy of Fantagraphics.

While this is an accurate definition, I take slight exception to Wolk's use of the phrase "lip service. " I think that the best superhero metacomics can serve as more than just parody or nostalgia and are actually *intended* to be accessible to potential "casual readers."

Before proceeding further, it's necessary to explain the matter of comic book "continuity," which has proven to be a major catalyst for the ways that superhero metacomics have evolved. One of the reasons that superhero comics have accumulated the amount of history and experience necessary to start riffing on themselves and have become endlessly self-referential is this notion of "continuity." This might seem an odd notion to non-comics readers, but almost all of the superhero stories that are published by DC Comics (one of the "Big Two" companies that puts out these types of books) take place in a shared universe; all of the stories featuring Batman, Superman, Wonder Woman, The Flash, Green Lantern and the rest of the DC characters have the potential to affect and influence one another. The same goes for superheroes in books published by Marvel (the other "Big Two" company); the X-Men, Spider-Man, Daredevil, The Fantastic Four and so on exist in the same shared "Marvel Universe." A rough equivalent would result if all of the fictional shows on one television network began existing in the same world, and characters regularly appeared on each other's shows, forcing all of the shows' writing staffs to work in conjunction with each other. So, in an "NBC universe," if there was a scandal touching the President on *The West Wing*, it would be expected that the issue would be at least mentioned on *ER*, or that someone on *Friends* would be reading a newspaper about it or chatting about it in a coffee shop.

Unifying storytelling across all of a comic company's titles is a real double-edged sword. As Wolk points out, it's a big part of the genre's appeal: "the thing superhero comics do really well is create this gigantic fictional narrative that's been going on for 70 years. Any comic you pick up is going to be part of this much much bigger story that you can fit it into. In some ways, it's like reading the newspaper every day and fitting it into the big picture" (Wolk, 2008).

On the other hand, as one might expect, making authors share their fictional worlds with hundreds of other writers (past, present and future) can present difficult story-crafting challenges, and some of the metacomics discussed below are direct reactions to the confining nature of DC and Marvel's strict storytelling continuity. As I list the types of superhero metacomics, the ways in which they deal with traditional mainstream comic storytelling will prove to be an important aspect of their creators' agendas.

The most straightforward type of metacomic is one that breaks the fourth wall. In these comics, characters realize that they exist in a comic book. When this is done in "Big Two" comics, it is almost always done for a laugh. Third-tier minor characters may be permitted to become aware of their own fictional existences, but they never share this awareness with other characters, lest the book's main storyline lose all sense of drama and seriousness.

Engaging in author-character dialogue, Scottish comic writer Grant Morrison points out his character, Animal Man, is only a vegetarian because Morrison writes him as such (Morrison and Truog, 2003). Other examples include the self-aware Marvel character Deadpool (recently portrayed by Ryan Reynolds in the *Wolverine* film) and DC's 1980s satirical superhero, Ambush Bug. Marvel's She-Hulk is also often self-aware (particularly when she is written by John Byrne).

These instances are indeed satirical and break the fourth wall — an effort by writers to explicitly satirize the absurdities of the superhero genre, and the business of comics. Similarly, in 2006, the line-wide crossover event *Infinite Crisis* (which involved most of DC Comics' characters) revolved around the notion that the lives of the DC Universe's heroes had become too dark and grisly. This was a rather thinly veiled swipe at the doom-and-gloom DC editorial policy over the course of the 1990s and early 2000s that led to such "events" as the grisly death of Superman and the paralysis of Batman.

However, ham-fisted diatribes like that in *Infinite Crisis* (Johns and Ordway, 2006: 17) are relatively rare, and for the most part, metacomics are at least slightly more subtle than this. For evidence of this, we need look no further than the wellspring of superhero metacomics—the 1980s work of British author Alan Moore.

The opening sequence of Moore's 1982 reboot of the pre-existing British character Marvelman (later re-named Miracleman to mollify Marvel Comics, who officially bought the rights to the character in 2009) handily serves as a microcosm for superhero metacomics as a whole. It begins with a reprint of a 1950s *Marvelman* comic, which concludes, freezing on the main character's face, and then zooming in to his black eyes, while a quote from Nietzsche is superimposed (Moore and Leach, 1985: 11). The dialogue suggests that Moore intends to approach comics with a new level of intellectual and psychological maturity, juxtaposed against adolescent fantasy—a combination that would prove to be fertile ground for at least another three decades of storytelling.

In *Miracleman*, Moore took a pre-existing comic character, a rip-off of DC's Captain Marvel (who himself was a rip-off of Superman), and essentially posed the question, "What would the life of a superhuman be like in the 'real world'?" As a result, Miracleman is forced to deal with the political, sexual, and psychological fall-out of a superhuman living on Earth. By the end of the book, Miracleman and his superheroic brethren have replaced the world's governments with a Utopia (Moore and Totleben; 1987).

Moore's thematic follow-up, 1986's *Watchmen*, took an even more bleak and cynical look at how the world would realistically react to the presence of superheroes within it. There is only one character in the book with super-powers—Dr. Manhattan, who obtains his powers following a botched nuclear physics experiment. He is used by the United States government as a tactical weapon, with one character remarking that the only difference between Dr. Manhattan and the H-Bomb is that "they didn't have to get the H-Bomb laid every once in a while" (Moore and Gibbons, 2005: np). And, in the end of *Watchmen*, just like in *Miracleman*, one of the heroes remakes that the world is a Utopia, albeit a slightly less benign one than in the earlier book.

In his preliminary notes to *Watchmen*, Moore explains that artist Dave Gibbons

> [would] like the world ... the characters exist in to be at once far more realistic in conception than any superheroes' world has been before, and at the same time far different to our own world than the worlds presented [in regular DC Comics' continuity]. To see what I'm trying to get at, you have to try and imagine what the presence of super-heroes would actually do to the world, both politically and psychologically. You can't do that in conventional super-hero comics partly because it would be too difficult to coordinate over more than a couple of books [Moore, 2005: np].

In the Afterword of *Watchmen*'s collected edition, Moore looks back on his completed project and muses,

> In its simplest form, the notion [of *Watchmen*] was simply to take over a whole comic book continuity and all the characters in it, so that one writer could document the entire world without worrying about how his plans could be fitted in with the creators of the other titles his characters were currently appearing in. Regular comics, with their insistence upon rigid, cross-title continuity, present a lot of annoying limitations to the creator [Moore, 2005: np].

In both these statements, we can see how *Watchmen*, which went on to become one of the comics most widely respected and recognized by mainstream literary critics as a masterpiece (witness its placement among *Time* magazine's 100 Greatest Novels), began rather humbly as a narrative experiment for a frustrated superhero writer.

The influence of *Watchmen*, particularly in terms of the way it pushed the boundaries of the superhero genre, began to manifest almost immediately. Moore and his tale of "realistic" superheroes gave birth to a generation of superficial imitators who tried taking a "grim and gritty" approach to characters like Superman and Batman, aping Moore's style, but not his post-modern agenda or literary skill. However, the real successors to *Watchmen*'s literary, satirical and intellectual legacy began to appear in the late 1990s and early 2000s.

In particular, creator-owned series such as *The Boys, Ex Machina, Astro City*, and *Powers* extrapolate certain ideas from *Watchmen* and run with them — primarily the sense of the "street-level" view of fantastic heroic archetypes. *The Boys* is concerned with a branch of the FBI whose job it is to keep tabs on superheroes; its tone is a mix of Capra-esque sentimentality and over-the-top sex and violence, played for laughs. *Ex Machina* tells the story of the world's sole superpowered hero, who successfully becomes mayor of New York after saving one of the twin towers. *Astro City* is a wistful look at the lives of ordinary people who live in a richly realized fictional urban setting. The series examines the ways those people's lives are touched by the everyday presence of bizarre and wonderful superpowered beings, who live in among them. *Powers* is a police procedural, also set in a world where superheroes are a fact of life; it follows two homicide detectives who are responsible for investigating "powers cases" (crimes where super-powers come into play).

Each of these metacomics series has a clear antecedent in *Watchmen*: they are concerned with the role superheroes would play in a "realistic" world; they are self-contained and unfettered by decades of previous comic continuity; and they are free to use adult settings, language and situations. Like *Watchmen*, all the titles mentioned have enjoyed considerable critical accolades, and with good reason.

But while many of the metacomics of the early 2000s have followed the storytelling conventions of *Watchmen*, with their creators setting the stories entirely within self-contained worlds, some truly excellent superhero metacomics have been set within the "Big Two" continuities of Marvel and DC. In the 1990s, both companies released short-lived but admired series that examined their continuity-driven universes from unconventional perspectives: *Chase* and *Young Heroes in Love* at DC and *The Sentry* and *Damage Control* at Marvel. But the two most critically successful metacomics were *Alias* (Marvel, written by Brian Michael Bendis, creator of *Powers*) and *Gotham Central* (DC, co-written by Greg Rucka and Ed Brubaker). *Alias* was the story of an alcoholic former superheroine turned private eye; *Gotham Central* dealt with the homicide detectives of Gotham City, whose lives become enmeshed and entwined with the vigilante Batman and his allies and enemies. Both *Gotham Central* and *Alias* take characters largely known to the general readership via comics, television, merchandising and film (Batman and the Flash; Captain America and the X-Men) and let the reader see them through the eyes of a street-level protagonist. This heightens the experience of the "man on the street perspective," and this added interplay with familiar characters and settings elevates these two books above the creator-owned, self-contained series mentioned earlier (*Watchmen* excluded). Think of it this way: *Powers* and *Gotham Central*, while wildly different in tone, share a similar conceit. The police in the latter express frustration with Batman's interference in their lives; this is bound to have greater resonance with readers than the trials of the officers in the self-contained *Powers,* who grapple with a rogue hero named "Supershock." Any potential *Gotham Central* reader will know going in who the Batman is.

There have been other great metacomics post–Watchmen including Peter Milligan and Mike Allred's media satire *X-Statix,* Alan Moore's *Top 10* and *Supreme,* Warren Ellis' *The Authority, Planetary,* and *Nextwave: Agents of H.A.T.E.* As clever and witty and innovative as many of these books are, they all presuppose that readers pick them up with a knowledge of and interest in superhero comics. But is there any real reason that fans should be the only ones capable of enjoying metacomics? Douglas Wolk himself pointed out that

> *Alias* [for example] has lots of Easter Eggs for the continuity-obsessed, but it probably works even better as a stand-alone story. Someone could potentially come into *Astro City* cold and read it as an adventure story, but thematically it's concerned with the conventions of its genre-in-medium, and that's the juicy part. The question is how well particular comics function as entertainment when the intertextual stuff gets stripped away or isn't visible or comprehensible to the reader [Wolk, 2008].

Undoubtedly, there is something about the superhero concept that resonates with the general public. During their heyday, in the "Golden Age" of the 1930s and '40s, superhero comics circulated in the millions (AC Comics, 2008). Now, superhero movies are an almost uncannily successful phenomenon. But just as superhero comics slowly built up a continuity between titles, now their filmed counterparts are beginning to knit together: Marvel's film studio has an *Avengers* film in pre-production that will link together several of their popular characters from existing franchises (TeaserTrailer.com, 2008). It is reasonable to assume that the storytelling in these entertainments will become more complex and adult as well. Nearly all of the metacomics mentioned above are currently, or were at some point over the past decade, being considered as film or TV projects by major studios. As of this writing, the *Powers* TV series is almost certain to be picked up by cable network FX (ComicBookResources, 2009). (The ur-metacomic, *Watchmen,* was only a modest box office success [Newsarama, 2009], but that can reasonably be attributed to its 3-hour runtime. It is almost guaranteed cult status on DVD.)

With this explosion of the popularity and widespread maturing of the superhero concept, I submit that there is no better time to capitalize on this in public libraries by focusing attention on superhero metacomics.

A number of volunteers from my local library, none of whom were regular graphic novel readers (they had read less than five in the last year), participated in a reading survey, wherein they offered opinions on selected metacomics. Among the responses were:

> "original," "fast-paced," "crisp dialogue," "an interesting political thriller" (on *Ex Machina* vol. 1)
>
> "Mesmerizing" (on *Astro City: Confession*)
>
> "Melancholy," "thoughtful," "resonant" (on *Fantastic Four: Unstable Molecules*—a metacomic that re-imagines the Marvel heroes as 1950s suburbanites)
>
> Favorable reviews for *Gotham Central* vol. 3
>
> An unfavorable review for *Alias* vol. 3, although this was more related to the subject matter (drug addiction, kidnapping) than to the book being impenetrable to non-superhero fans.

A large portion of the questionnaire attempted to elicit from volunteers whether the superhero-based plot elements made the book difficult to understand or alienating—no one responded that they did.

Part of the reason that the best superhero metacomics succeed is that they, like the very best novels, films, and TV shows, are transcendent. They transcend their immediate genre (superhero action-adventure) and their secondary genre (crime/political thriller/family drama) to become something that comments not only on the absurdity of superhero characters, but on the *need* for these characters. Batman, Superman, Spider-Man — these masked, super-powered vigilantes did not become some of the most recognizable global icons by accident. They embody a basal need for a heroic archetype, and the adult need to examine and test those archetypes, that acted as the impetuses for the writers to increase the complexity of these characters and the fictional world they co-inhabit. As to the question of whether or not titles like *Alias, Gotham Central, Astro City* and *Ex Machina* belong in an academic or public library, the answer is yes. The notion that these books are strictly for the most hardcore of comic aficionados is understandable, but misleading.

At their most fundamental level, superhero metacomics are concerned with the critical scrutiny of public figures by the everyman. In other words, they give us new eyes with which to view aspects of our culture that we regularly take for granted — which might serve well as a philosophy for academic and public libraries, as well as for metacomics.

For their assistance and editing I would like to thank Karen and Kit McLeod, Barry Brightman, the members of the New Glasgow Library Book Club, Pat and Beth Avery, and Lindsay McCarney.

References

"Bendis confirms Powers TV Series Heading to FX." 2009. Robot 6 @ CBR (Comic Book Resources). http://robot6.comicbookresources.com/2009/02/nycc-bendis-confirms-powers-tv-series-headed-to-fx/.
Busiek, Kurt, Brent Anderson, and Alex Ross. 1996. *Astro City: Life in the Big City*. La Jolla, CA: Homage Comics.
"Golden Age Overview." 2008. AC Comics. http://www.accomics.com/accomics/goldenage/goldenageover view.html.
Johns, Geoff, Jerry Ordway, et al. 2006. *Infinite Crisis 2*. New York: DC Comics.
Kupperman, Michael. 2008. *Tales Designed to Thrizzle 1*. Seattle, WA: Fantagraphics Books.
Moore, Alan, and Dave Gibbons. 2005. *Absolute Watchmen*. New York: DC Comics.
Moore, Alan, and Garry Leach. 1985. *Miracleman 1*. Guerneville, CA: Eclipse Comics.
Moore, Alan, and John Totleben. 1987. *Miracleman 16*. Guerneville, CA: Eclipse Comics.
Morrison, Grant, and Chas Truog. 2003. *Animal Man: Deus Ex Machina*. New York: DC-Vertigo.
"Newsy notes: 9/24." 2008. The Beat: The News Blog of Comics Culture. PublishersWeekly.com http://pwbeat.publishersweekly.com/blog/2008/09/24/newsy-notes-924.
"Nick Fury Is Assembling the Avengers and Iron Man is Already Helping." 2008. Teaser Trailer.com. http://teaser-trailer.com/2008/10/nick-fury-is-assembling-the-avengers-and-iron-man-is-already-helping.html.
Speigelman, Art. 1992. *Maus II: And Here My Troubles Began*. New York: Pantheon Books
"Watchmen Box Office Watch Week 2: 67% drop." 2009. Newsarama: http://www.newsarama.com/film/090314-watchmen-box-office.html.
Wolk, Douglas. 2008. *Reading Comics: How Graphic Novels Work and What They Mean*. Cambridge, MA: Da Capo Press.
_____. 2008. Personal interview conducted on November 18.

25

Webcomics and Libraries

Amy Thorne

Webcomics have been an important part of the developments in the comics landscape for the last several years. Publishing on the Web has opened many opportunities to would-be comics creators, leading to innovation, experimentation, and the chance to push boundaries. A large body of work on the Web has resulted, and it holds interest for library patrons. Librarians have long accepted a responsibility for seeking out and evaluating resources on the Internet for the benefit of their patrons, and for making their discoveries available in digital subject bibliographies, or pathfinders. Librarians are no strangers to the materials selection process, or to new material formats. A webcomic collection is an appropriate complement to any library's graphic novel collection.

Librarians might have a slight advantage in the area of webcomic familiarity; *Unshelved*, by Bill Barnes and Gene Ambaum, a strip set in a public library, is very popular among library workers. The creators also are active in the library community. They make appearances nationwide at library functions and have even given permission on their site for their full page book club strips to be publicly posted (Barnes and Ambaum, 2009). *Unshelved* is one example of a webcomic that has found a thriving life online when it might not have in print, but it is certainly not the first, nor the only one. Digital comics began almost as soon as the Internet made them possible (Campbell, 2006). Once the Web came into being, so did the first true webcomics. Stafford Huyler's *Netboy*, a computer-based strip, and David Farley's *Doctor Fun*, a one panel humor strip, began within a couple of months of each other in 1993 (Campbell, 2006). These strips were also born digital, illustrating the willingness of some creators to embrace the Web as a distribution method for their work quite early on. The Web offered would-be comics creators an attractive option — relatively quick and easy publication, and a way to gain exposure for their work without having to struggle through luck and limited print runs simply to create an awareness (Usborne, 2009). The Web has also allowed artists, new and established, the chance to stretch creatively. Scott McCloud, an artist and author, became an advocate for embracing digital technologies — arguing that the constraints of the page were no longer necessary (2000). His ideas included the infinite canvas, which meant that the computer monitor, normally a stand-in for a traditional page, could instead "act as a window" for comics that were created for the digital environment (McCloud, 2000: 222). A variety of computer programs have also contributed to the creation of webcomics designed solely for the digital environment. Examples of these types of strips currently available online are math strip *xkcd*'s "The Observable Universe, From Top to Bottom on a Log Scale" (http://xkcd.com/482/) and *PoCom-UK-001*— which is a digital version of a large print piece created for a gallery wall in 2003 (http://e-merl.com/pocom.htm).

Most creators chose to take advantage of the creative freedoms of the Web not in the area of exploring the digital environment but rather for liberation from editorial control. The situation of syndicated strips, where the syndicate partially controls the rights, means emphasis is often on broad appeal and avoiding offense (Colvile, 2007). Creators have no such concerns when self-publishing on the Web. They are immediately freer to push boundaries, and they do. In the very early webcomic *Sluggy Freelance*, by Pete Abrams, one of the main characters tries to summon the devil via Internet connection (Abrams, 1997). *Sluggy Freelance* also starred a talking animal: a rabbit named Bun-Bun, characterized by Campbell as "a tough-as-nails, violent misanthrope" (2006: 35). Bun-Bun would not be the only non-human character with a mean-streak; *Diesel Sweeties* would have Red Robot #C-63, *Goats* added a chicken named Diablo, and *PvP*'s cat, Scratch, had great ambitions and a disdain for any notion of humanity's superiority (Campbell, 2006).

In addition to edgy forms of humor, the creative freedom also gave rise to many different genres. The earlier strips tended to appeal to those who used the early Web the most: computer literate, tech-savvy types—hence the genre name nerdcore (Campbell, 2006). Other genres followed, however. Gamer comics (which include one of the most popular titles on the Web, *Penny Arcade*), fantasy, slice-of-life, mystery, science fiction, even steampunk—as well as more traditionally structured humor (if not always exactly traditional humor)—were all represented. Many webcomics defy easy genre classification. Plenty of creators did not—and still do not—feel bound by genre labels, and many strips moved through these different territories as their writers experimented (Campbell, 2006).

A variety of art styles also developed in webcomics. In addition to the different styles of drawing to be found between artists, some creators used images from video games, creating what came to be known as sprite comics; others used stick figures and still others used photographs (Campbell, 2006). Ryan North's *Dinosaur Comics* used the same set of six images for each strip, and has generated hundreds of strips with this formula. The nature of publishing on the Web has allowed creators to pursue results that were previously unachievable on paper, as well as much more simplified artistic approaches—relying on their writing craft and storytelling skills.

The other major draw to the Web for artists was its ability to archive—something that print syndication could not offer them (Campbell, 2006). That's what drew Bill Holbrook, an artist with two print syndicated strips, to publish *Kevin and Kell*, a strip about an interspecies marriage between a rabbit and a wolf, online (Campbell, 2006). Enabling readers to go back as far as necessary into a storyline allows many creators far greater freedom with their stories than print can.

Libraries have been paying more attention in recent years to comics, although other terms are frequently employed (e.g., graphic novel and manga), normally to denote a longer format, more serious subject matter, or different country of origin. The Young Adult Library Services Association (YALSA), a division of the American Library Association (ALA), publishes a Great Graphic Novels for Teens booklist each year. *Graphic Novels Now*, a collection development guide specifically for graphic novels by Francisca Goldsmith, is currently available in the ALA's online store. These are only a couple of the tools available to librarians for evaluating graphic novels for collection development. The library has come a long way in recognizing the comics arts, both in terms of its own literary and artistic merits and as something patrons want to read.

Webcomics are now playing an important role in comics. *Mom's Cancer*, Brian Fies' autobiographical account of his mother's battle with lung cancer, began as a webcomic in 2004. It won an Eisner Award for Best Digital Comic in 2005 — a new category that year for the awards — and was published by Harry N. Abrams in 2006. The title received attention from the mainstream press, and Fies reported on his Web site that medical professionals were using the story (Fies, 2006). *Mom's Cancer* is not the only webcomic to have found success in print. Fred Gallagher's *MegaTokyo*, a manga-style webcomic, began publishing online in 2000. It is currently published in book form by CMX, and all five volumes are in print and listed as "in stock" on Amazon.com. When Volume 3 of *MegaTokyo*, published in 2005, reached Number 3 on BookScan's list of best selling graphic novels, it achieved the highest sales rank achieved by an original English language manga at the time (ICv2, 2005). Many webcomics' creators print compilations of their strips (some through large publishers, some through smaller ones), while others self publish. Libraries can even find some of these titles through Baker and Taylor, if they wish to hold print versions of popular webcomics on their shelves. The biggest names in webcomics do, obviously, have a print audience — and the books do sell — even though the comics themselves are available for free on the web before, and normally after, the book comes out.

Webcomics' appeal to young adult patrons has already been picked up on by a few libraries. The Hawaii State Public Library hosted Audra Furuichi and Scott Yoshinaga, creators of *nemu*nemu*, during its Teen Summer Reading Program in 2008 (Furuichi and Yoshinaga, 2008). A few others, such as San Antonio Public Library and Internet Public Library Teenspace, have created digital pathfinders for webcomics as part of their teen services web sites. This is a good approach for reaching an age group that is comfortable with the digital delivery of media, but webcomics — like their ink and paper counterparts — are not by any means the exclusive domain of teenagers. Webcomics certainly did not start out for that age group (Campbell, 2006). It is important to bear in mind that creators are not necessarily writing for a younger audience, in the same way that printed comics creators are not. The segment of adult library patrons who are checking out the graphic novels and manga series are also likely to be interested in a webcomic collection, and ignoring this potential audience misses an opportunity to increase library web site traffic at a time when digital services are raising their profile.

For librarians looking to maintain a webcomic collection, there are some tools and starting points available. Of course, librarians are no strangers to evaluating material for the purpose of adding it to a collection. The benefit of evaluating a webcomic is that its entire archive is usually open for examination. There also are some web sites that offer comment and critique of wecomics, but webcomic criticism has historically been a tricky thing to manage, and it is frequently treated with suspicion by both readers and creators (Campbell, 2006). The following is by no means meant to be an exhaustive list of sources — simply a few starting points:

> Eric Burns, who along with Wednesday White runs the web site Websnark (http://www.web-snark.com/) and takes a populist approach;
>
> Comixtalk (http://comixtalk.com/), a webcomics news source;
>
> Fleen (*http://www.fleen.com/*), a webcomics blog;
>
> Kidjutsu (http://www.kidjutsu.com/), a site that focuses on comics for kids that includes some webcomics.

Librarians also can consult the Web Cartoonists' Choice Awards (http://www.ccawards. com/) and the Eisner Awards, which have had a Best Digital Comic entry since 2005.

There are also webcomic collectives, such as Keenspot, which began in 2000 and still hosts popular webcomics today. There are resources for more traditional comics on the Web, too. These include comics that are not born digital, but are available on the web as digital distribution becomes a more popular option for syndicates. GoComics, a comics portal that describes itself as "the Web's largest catalog of syndicated newspaper strips and webcomics," offers users the chance to subscribe to its services, but it also has a great deal of free content available ("About GoComics," 2009). Major comics publishers have also gotten into the digital content act. Marvel has added a subscription service to its web site, but some free comics can be found there, and DC Comics has added a webcomic brand, Zuda Comics. Artists going through Zuda are paid by DC, which has editorial control (Colvile, 2009). This sort of big business presence is unusual for the webcomic community, but the DC and Marvel brands are likely to hold some interest for at least a certain segment of the comic seeking library patron population.

It is clearly possible for a librarian to maintain a digital bibliography, or pathfinder, for webcomics. There is no shortage of titles to choose from or of sources from which to begin the hunt. It also is possible to create webcomics lists that cover many different genres, appeal to many patrons, and address the needs of teen services and adult services, just as many libraries do with their print graphic novel collections. A webcomics guide should also be thought of as a collection by the librarians who maintain it. Webcomic links need to be checked, and the content needs to be evaluated to ensure it is in the appropriate collection (adult or teen). And new webcomics need to be added. It is a service that is worth developing. Much of what is new and innovative in comics is now happening on the Web, and a library with any kind of a graphic novel collection should not be neglecting webcomics.

References

Abrams, Pete. 1997. "Sluggy Freelance." http://www.sluggy.com/daily.php?date=970825.

Barnes, Bill, and Gene Ambaum. 2009. "Unshelved Book Club." *http://www.unshelved.com/bookclub.aspx* .

Campbell, T. 2006. *A History of Webcomics*. San Antonio: Anarctic Press.

Colvile, Robert. September 29, 2002. "Pick of the Webcomics." *Daily Telegraph* (London). *http://www.find.gale group.com/ips/start.do?prodId=IPS* .

Fies, Brian. 2006. "Mom's Cancer." *http://www.momscancer.com/* .

Furuichi, Audra, and Scott Yoshinaga. 2008. "iRead Webcomics!" *http://www.nemu-nemu.com/2008/06/06/ iread_webcomics.php*.

GoComics. 2009. "About GoComics." *http://www.gocomics.com/help/about*.

ICv2.com. 2005. "MegaTokyo Reaches Number 3." *http://www.icv2.com/articles/news/6520.html*.

McCloud, Scott. 2000. *Reinventing Comics*. New York: HarperCollins.

Usborne, Simon. February 4, 2009. "From Pencil to Pixel." *The Independent* (London). http://www.find.gale-group.com/itx/start.do?prodId=SPN.SP00.

26

Cataloging and the Problem of Access

Creativity, Collaboration and Compromise

LAUREL TARULLI

"I just want to pull them out from the rest of the collection and shelve them separately. Why is it so difficult?" Does this sound familiar? If you haven't said this yourself, your colleagues have. Most libraries are struggling with their graphic novel and graphic nonfiction collections. Librarians are attempting to address a variety of issues surrounding these collections. Should they have their own collection codes? What about stickers that identify graphic novel format? Would our collection be more accessible if we got rid of Dewey, or at least moved the graphic novel collection out of 741.5? How do we make sense of the series information in the catalog?

It seems as if, more than any other collection in a library, graphic novels have been difficult to accept, catalog and shelve. Many of the access issues are often considered a cataloging deficiency. What makes graphic novels so challenging to catalog, and as a result, difficult to access?

When a new collection is introduced into the library, the front line is located in the technical services department, not the physical library. As a result, technical services staff, and in particular the cataloging department, are faced with a number of choices that are often made without the benefit of collaborating with the selector or resident expert. When this occurs, catalogers turn to existing cataloging practices and rules, combined with their own expertise, to create a uniform level of cataloging that will provide access to this new collection. Many times, catalogers base cataloging practices on the first items they receive in a new collection, anticipating that the subsequent items will follow the same pattern. However, with the introduction of graphic novels into the collection, and therefore the library catalog, all of our existing rules and precedents are challenged.

Now that the novelty has worn off the graphic novel collections in our libraries, catalogers and front-line staff are beginning to realize that graphic novels behave and challenge our traditional collection models like no other. Many librarians believed that graphic novels were a trend in our libraries that would soon pass. However, this collection continues to grow in popularity, with ever-increasing budgets devoted to their acquisition and circulation statistics reinforcing what a handful of die-hard professionals always knew: graphic novels are here to stay.

With the recognition that graphic novels are becoming high-demand items in our libraries, the problems that were initially hidden by a relatively new and small collection are beginning to surface.

Past and Present Cataloging Challenges

In *Graphic Novels Now*, Goldsmith states, "[G]raphic novels have become so prevalent in libraries that catalogers, as well as collection developers and readers' advisors, are actively working to give the format the professional attention it requires. Nonetheless, current practices remain widely varied" (Goldsmith 2005: 53).

With the growing popularity of graphic novel collections in our libraries, graphic novels are receiving a significant amount of attention from all areas of the library profession. Providing enhanced access both for browsing at the physical library and through finding graphic novels in the library catalog is a priority to many catalogers, readers' advisors and other library professionals. However, to state that it is only because of the prevalence of this collection that we are only now beginning to give the format the professional attention it deserves is, perhaps, not quite accurate. In fact, this increase in attention likely has more to do with a growing familiarity with graphic novels. With the growth of any collection, changes must be made, whether in the form of shelving, signage or cataloging practices. The nature of providing access to our collections is that it is always advancing and evolving. Smaller collections, at least from a cataloging perspective, are treated no differently than larger, popular collections. However, new collections often take longer to evolve, requiring shifts and changes to access issues that long-standing collections do not require. We are seeing and experiencing these "growing pains" with our graphic novel collections.

Cataloging practices always vary to some degree from library to library and this can be seen when examining the variety of cataloging practices applied to graphic novels. As with shelving and borrowing practices that vary from library to library to serve our unique patrons, cataloging rules and practices also vary from library catalog to library catalog. However, maintaining a standard set of core values is ideal for cataloging any format.

It is widely accepted that some of the initial cataloging practices that were first adopted by catalogers and libraries in their handling of graphic novels are no longer satisfactory. The growing pains that we are experiencing with graphic novels are now forcing librarians both in and out of the technical services department to rethink current cataloging and shelving practices.

LOCATION, LOCATION, LOCATION

Graphic novels are both a format and a genre. As such, catalogers needed to decide how such an item was to be treated. For good or ill, many cataloging departments decided to classify all graphic novels in the Dewey classification number 741.5. They did so at a time when a single classification was chosen to represent all graphic novels. Many cataloging departments had yet to be introduced to their kissing cousins, graphic nonfiction.

With the introduction of graphic nonfiction, cataloging practices and policies regarding the classification of graphic novels, as a collection by format, became challenging. Originally, cataloging departments believed that, like comics, the collection would remain a fiction collection. This may have been the result of naïveté, or a lack of communication between acquisitions and cataloging. All the same, this posed a problem in cataloging departments. Should you separate graphic novels from graphic nonfiction? If so, how? This is when catalogers began to re-visit their initial cataloging decisions. Should they continue to catalog graphic novels in the all inclusive 741.5 for both graphic novels and graphic nonfiction? Should format be ignored, opting instead for classification based on subject? What would be involved in a reconnaissance project to reclassify the entire graphic novel collection by subject?

Many catalogers adopted a compromise in their practices. Rather than create a new category and reclassify their graphic novel collections using a wider range of call numbers, they decided to keep graphic *novels* in the 741.5 classification. However, rather than include graphic nonfiction in 741.5, many catalogers decided to treat graphic nonfiction as if it were a nonfiction item and classify them by subject, rather than format. This resulted in graphic novels being shelved together while graphic nonfiction is shelved by its related subject throughout a library's collection. This successfully differentiates graphic novels (fiction) from graphic nonfiction but creates a separate issue: it ignores the format relationship between graphic novels (fiction) and graphic nonfiction. This practice has raised legitimate questions. For instance, why is the format not the first factor for classification, with the items then being sorted by subject? With most other collections in libraries, the practice has always been to sort by format first, and then shelve by subject. Examples of this include our DVD sections, magazine areas and CD bins. This has posed challenges for both browsers and library staff.

WHO'S RESPONSIBLE?

Standard cataloging practices dictate where information should be obtained when cataloging an item. Statements of responsibility, which often include the main author, illustrator, performer or composer, are almost always found on the title page or its verso. This is another challenge with graphic novels. Not only do graphic novels often ignore this common publishing practice, an initial lack of familiarity when cataloging them resulted in access points that are of no relevance to browsers or library catalog users. There has been little dialogue between catalogers and graphic novel experts to resolve questions such as which access points are important to patrons who are trying to find graphic novels in the library collection. Are they most interested in publishers, such as DC or Marvel, or perhaps the illustrator rather than the author of the story?

Once the most relevant access points are identified, the sources of this information must be found. If it cannot be found on the physical item, where do catalogers find this information? While it might be desirable to spend a significant amount of time cataloging a single item, this is simply not practical. Selectors who purchase this material and the acquisitions departments who receive it must look at ways to assist catalogers in providing accurate and enhanced access points that will fulfill our patrons' wants and expectations. This may involve having selectors identify relevant information at the time of purchase or having the information included in the order records supplied by vendors.

LACK OF UNIFORMITY OF SERIES

Series are challenging even among standard book collections. In juvenile collections, stand-alone books are often turned into series because of popularity. Often, the most pressing challenge is whether to cutter the series by author (with the assumption that future books in the series will continue to be written by the same author) or to cutter by series name. In most cases, however, book series are standard and most series names are not repeated among the same publisher or multiple publishers. Graphic novels do not follow the standard series patterns. As a result, catalogers have struggled from the beginning with the cuttering of graphic novels. Often publishers use the same series name, or a new publisher continues a series that a previous publisher started.

Many fans of graphic novels want their graphic novels separated by publisher, rather than series. This poses further challenges for catalogers. While catalogers might appreciate that separating DC from Marvel is indeed useful because of the browsing trends of graphic novel fans, catalogers struggle to balance serving the needs of our patrons with the need for uniformity of cataloging practices. Changing cataloging practices midway or introducing a variety of exceptions into cataloging procedures will result in a lack of access as the collection grows. What is required is a cataloging practice geared toward a long-term view, rather than short-term solutions, particularly when one considers staff turnover, changes in publishing trends and formats. Today, catalogers are dealing with the result of short-term solutions in their juvenile collections, particularly regarding series. Shelving juvenile series separately is a trend being seen throughout public libraries. However, one of the complaints about series is that they lack uniformity and therefore are difficult to shelve. This lack of uniformity is the result of creating multiple exceptions to cataloging rules that are often forgotten, resulting in a variety of cuttering and series tracing practices. Experiencing the difficulties that arise with short term solutions, catalogers do not want to face the same situation in the future with graphic novels. This discrepancy between cataloging practices and front-line staff requests has often resulted in a misunderstanding that we do not share a common goal: to provide enhanced access to collections in the form of browsing and findability in both the physical and "virtual" library (the library catalog).

New Trends and Cataloging Practices

With the understanding that our initial cataloging practices are falling short of our own expectations, we are aware that we are not meeting readers' expectations for accessing our graphic collections.

What do readers want? The dialogue between catalogers and front-line staff in this regard has been limited. We know what front-line staff want; a separately shelved, stand-alone collection that can be browsed based on an intuitive order of classification. Catalogers want this too. However, up until recently, the lack of familiarity with graphic novel collections and their relatively small collections in libraries have allowed professionals to largely ignore or be ignorant of its shortcomings as they relate to cataloging practices and overall access.

With the growth in the popularity of graphic novels, cataloging departments are starting to acquire an expertise in this format that has not been available until recently. In addition, a gap has been bridged in that dialogues have been occurring between graphic novel experts and catalogers, resulting in the development of collaborative relationships. Beyond even these advancements, the cataloging world is currently undergoing changes that allow for the bending of cataloging rules to more descriptive practices and new library catalogs that complement these practices.

EMERGING ACCESS TRENDS

In his article "Graphic Novels in Libraries: One Library's Solutions to the Cataloging Problem," Robert Weiner provides a list of practices implemented at the Lubbock Public Library System for increasing access to their graphic novels collection. Rather than following Dewey classification, the graphic novels were categorized by items. For example, DC comics were separated from Marvel books, with smaller groupings created by like or similar characters (Weiner, 2008). In fact, the reorganization of the materials was taken a step further, pulling in prose novels currently classified under science fiction and shelving them with the graphic novels (Weiner, 2008). He explains that while these books, featuring well-known superheroes, are not graphic novels, users will likely find this new physical proximity, based on character, more useful and accessible, resulting in increased circulation of similar or related items (Weiner, 2008). This is a common philosophy and often considered a take on the "bookstore" model. In fact, Markham Public Library with their new C3 classification system is implementing this practice. Doing away with the Dewey Decimal Classification System, they have created a new classification system that allows for broader classification schemes, shelving items by relationship as well as content. For instance, Italian cooking as well as Italian language materials and travel materials about Italy would all be shelved together in this new classification system. While this concept and practice is worth watching, it is important to note that the classification system was largely created by front-line staff, rather than catalogers. While many believe this is acceptable practice, it's a bit like having a cataloger redesign your reference practices. This fails to take proper advantage of the depths of knowledge each discipline brings to the library. Mutual respect and collaboration are essential in creating a classification scheme that works in both the physical library and the virtual library, which ultimately serves the user's needs. In the end, while alternative classification systems are being explored in libraries, examination into these new systems must be undertaken in order to prove that they offer any benefit over the Dewey Decimal Classification System and its flexibility. Many times, it is the increased signage or new shelving that results in easier access to our collections. As a result, what must be addressed at this point deals more with shelving practices than cataloging practices.

Where does the cataloger's role end and the front-line staff's role begin? There are many arguments about the impact classification has on shelving practices of graphic novels. While most professionals will agree that some form of classification is necessary, it is the way in which the classification is being applied that has been the topic of many discussions among professionals, and a source of frustration for all players.

One of the steps catalogers have taken to make graphic novels more recognizable is to apply a GN prefix to the call number. While many libraries are adding this prefix to all items with graphic novel formats (graphic novels and graphic nonfiction), others have decided to apply this by content, thereby not applying it to, for example, their graphic nonfiction. Halifax Public Libraries in Halifax, Nova Scotia, has attempted to make the pulling out and sorting of graphic novels even simpler. In addition to assigning the GN designation to all call numbers in the graphic *novels* collection (not graphic nonfiction), they have also implemented a practice whereby all graphic novel formatted items receive a graphic novel sticker. Therefore, regardless of whether the item is a graphic novel, classified in 741.5 or a graphic nonfiction item, they will be recognizable by the sticker which adorns them.

With respect to classification, while the GN prefix has been introduced into some libraries, most cataloging departments have unilaterally decided to continue to classify their graphic nonfiction collections according to Dewey designations. The rationale is that the graphic novel collection should continue to be treated as all other collections, including traditional books, DVDs, books on CD and so on. In all cases, fiction is separated out from nonfiction and, to the professional opinion of catalogers, graphic nonfiction should follow suit because it is a practice users are familiar with. It is assumed that these nonfiction collections will grow, and as they do, separating these titles out by subject, rather than format, will make access easier for both staff and users of these collections. Many graphic novel fans continue to argue that while it is acceptable to continue to do this, by taking it one step further and pulling out the entire collection, and then shelving it separately as we do with feature and non-feature DVDs, this practice will be enhanced.

Recently, many libraries have improved upon this practice. Collection codes offer a compromise for making the existing classification schemes work with new shelving practices. Creating a graphic novel collection code and graphic nonfiction collection code allows staff to pull materials out of the traditional book collection to shelve all graphic novels, including graphic nonfiction, in one place. This assists in aiding front-line staff in shelving their graphic novel collections separately, while maintaining the existing level of uniformity and findability in current classification practices.

While the original classification systems and practices remain in place and shelving by publisher or character may still pose challenges, this does make the graphic novel collection more browseable. And, with the increased practice of cuttering graphic novels by series, cataloging practices and shelving needs are beginning to merge. The difficulty with cuttering by character is that some graphic novels feature more than one superhero. Catalogers cannot spend the time reading the item to determine who the *main* superhero is, and therefore how the item should be cuttered. However, if there is a series, the cataloger can, in short order, provide a cutter number that allows for a sequential shelving system that appears intuitive and browseable.

To deal with online access issues, new subject headings are also being introduced into the bibliographic records of graphic novels. Catalogers, with the assistance of selectors, are recognizing the need to insert geographic locations into their genre headings. Manga is a good example of this. Although it originated in Japan, other countries are now copying the manga style. Rather than using the broad genre heading "manga" for all graphic novels, cataloging practices are also subdividing these headings by country of origin, distinguishing between Korean, Japanese or American manga.

Cataloging departments are also attempting to apply detailed descriptive information into their catalogs, including changes in series names, information on parent series, style and content. In some cases, catalogers are even attempting to add target audience information if given by the publisher. This is not a common practice, however, because it can be seen as a form of censorship, should it appear as if the library is choosing the target audience. In addition, the inclusion of this information must follow the library's standard practices. If movies or music in the library also follow rating systems and include this information in the library catalog, it may be seen as an acceptable practice. However, many libraries shy away from adding any age range or advisory warnings, leaving the judgment of appropriate content to users and the traditional use of juvenile, young adult and adult. As a result, those libraries including this information in their catalogs are only doing so if it is provided by an outside agency. Overall, increased attention to descriptive information is a growing practice and one that is recognized as an area of improvement.

LOCALIZED PRACTICES ARE BECOMING NATIONAL PRACTICES

As discussed briefly at the beginning of this article, cataloging practices may not be uniform, but they are developing to meet the needs of their users. If cataloging practices are examined on a national or even international level, a degree of uniformity for sharing records will follow. However, as many professionals who have experience in copy cataloging are aware, all cataloging departments vary in their cataloging practices. What needs to be examined is the standardization of core values in cataloging practices. Active listservs, online wikis and conference sessions have provided a forum for catalogers and graphic novel experts to share their expertise and cataloging practices globally. A general search of the web will reveal numerous results that outline local cataloging practices at any given library throughout North America. The accessibility of this information and the ability to contact other professionals has increased the level of uniformity and standard cataloging practices in graphic novel cataloging. These standard practices will continue to grow and improve.

SOCIAL CATALOGS AND RDA

While there is literature available on the cataloging of graphic novels, the development of next generation catalogs and the new Rules for Descriptive Access (RDA) have not been mentioned in relation to how these advancements in cataloging will assist in promoting and accessing graphic novels. However, they do bear exploring.

Many graphic novel fans bemoan the fact that the classification of graphic novels and subject content do not pull together relationships or similarities between items. However, with the development and, with any luck, implementation of RDA into cataloging practices in the near future, these relational values will soon be available. RDA is meant to recall all items that share a relationship. For instance, the structure of RDA will allow books by Shakespeare to be retrieved, as well as books about Shakespeare, movies about or based on Shakespeare's plays and so on. This would all be retrieved in one search and sorted by relevancy based on the type of search performed. For example, was format the most important search component, or character? These levels of relationship and relational values should excite graphic novel enthusiasts. Not only will graphic novels with the main superhero be retrieved, but additional graphic novels about that character will be recalled, as will other works of fiction and nonfiction, regardless of format. This will bring together relevant items, including those not shelved in close proximity, with an effort to promote the entire collection and increase circulation. While many professionals may still present the argument that this does not solve the browsing problem at the physical library, it can be answered with a most basic question: "Will we ever really be able to shelve all like things together?" As many catalogers and librarians are only too well aware, relevance is in the eye of the beholder and what is relevant to one individual is not relevant to another. As a result, many of our attempts to shelve all similar items together may seem rational to us, while a user may not understand the relationships that we have drawn.

The emergence of next generation catalogs, often called discovery tools or social catalogs, is also notable when discussing graphic novels in the library catalog. Discovery tools allow for faceted searching and browsing of cover images within the library catalog. With an increased number of our patrons accessing our libraries remotely, emphasis is being placed on discovering and browsing through the catalog, rather than in the physical library.

One unique feature that is available in these social catalogs is the ability to sort by format. If your library has created unique collection codes for their graphic novel collections, this format can be pulled and presented to a user as a facet. For instance, if a patron uses the general keyword search and types in "Superman," he will not only retrieve the usual list of items in the catalog, now ranked by relevancy, but will be provided with a list of facets in which to narrow his search. He will also be provided with tags, a tag cloud or something similar in which to explore by related subjects.

The facets, which are usually located on a side toolbar, will give the patron an option of choosing "graphic novel" or "graphic nonfiction" should he so desire. He will also be given the option of choosing Superman as a topic, series, or personal topic. In addition to this, there is the ability to choose other formats, such as books on CD, downloadable audio or an ability to narrow down by year or geographic location. Without the need for creating long and convoluted search strings, this can all be done with the click of a user's mouse.

These new catalogs are meant to allow for easier access to collections and exploring relationships that have currently been unavailable in a library catalog. With the increasing popularity of next generation catalogs, enhancement of summaries and descriptive information in the catalog, as well as the creation of unique collection codes for graphic novels, many of the concerns regarding access to graphic novel collections can be addressed. This is where the development of collaborative partnerships between graphic novel experts and catalogers becomes important. Opening a dialogue to enhance what users want and what staff need to assist in their workflow can only be accomplished by working together. Taking advantage of these new technologies in cataloging and the changing cataloging practices of graphic novels places this collection in a desirable position. With the need for change in graphic novel cataloging practices acknowledged, building partnerships that share expertise during this time will benefit catalogers, readers' advisors, library staff and users.

Conclusion

Much of the literature regarding the cataloging of graphic novels has been written by graphic novel experts, and not cataloging or classification experts. While catalogers have agreed that their rules for the cataloging and classification of graphic novels should be revisited, it is not widely acknowledged that front-line staff have also fallen short of their professional responsibilities. The professional literature often discusses how librarians have attempted to change shelving practices only to be hindered by a collection's classification. Rarely does the literature or personal practice reflect on attempted collaborative relationships between cataloging and front-line staff. Nor does the literature reflect on the role front-line staff took in working with catalogers when they were first introduced to graphic novels.

While there are promotional and access issues with every collection, graphic novels have especially demonstrated that our current practices are not sufficient to maintain a growing and thriving collection. This can only be accomplished through collaborative relationships, communication and compromise.

While catalogers need to be made aware of the special needs and wants of users for any given collection, front-line staff must also educate themselves on why specific cataloging or classification decisions have been made. This can be done through many professional channels, but more importantly, communication must be encouraged at the local level. What many graphic novel experts will find is that catalogers are more than willing to work together because they share the same goal: to enhance access to our collections.

References

Goldsmith, Francisca. 2005. *Graphic Novels Now: Building, Managing and Marketing a Dynamic Collection*. Chicago: American Library Association.

Weiner, Robert G. "Graphic Novels in Libraries: One Library's Solution to the Cataloging Problem." *Texas Library Journal*. Spring 2008: 8–16.

27

An Example of an In-House Cataloging System

Robert G. Weiner

*A number of people have asked me to publish the system that we used at the Lubbock Public Library (LPL) for classifying and cataloging graphic novels. This is the basic plan that we developed for LPL, but please note that this "system" is **MEANT** to be modified as conditions change. Thus, it can be modified to meet the conditions that exist at other libraries.*

I am publishing this document for those librarians who are struggling with the classification of graphic novels, and want to see what one library did as an in-house classification system. I hope that they will find this system useful.

While I have not been employed at LPL for the past several years, apparently the system is still in place.

Lubbock Public Library System
Graphic Novel Classification Policy

*Classification scheme designed by Robert G. Weiner
with input from various Mahon Public Library Staff*

Graphic Novels or photo novels are generally a combination of graphic images and text. Examples range from superhero stories to adaptations of literature, from humorous segments to Japanese comics like Manga, from general comics to memoirs and histories. The Lubbock Public Library has in recent years significantly expanded its Graphic Novel collection to include these types of books. Examples include superhero novels, drawing books, comic related books, history of comics, specific comic artists, comic price guides, anything relating in some way to superheroes, comic books writers, etc.

The classification system for LPL's Graphic Novel collection is designed to be both general and specific. It is primarily a browsing collection, but we also want to have the ability to shelve and organize the collection in a "loosely" coherent way in order to make materials easier for staff to shelve and find. We tried to avoid over classifying the collection, but there should be enough detail to make the collection accessible. Characters that have 20 or more titles in the main library will be considered to have their own call number and category. Those categories that we have already assigned will remain in place. If a title has two characters listed, the first character will determine the call number and category.

If a novel is related to a character that started out as a comic character (e.g., the Hulk, Batman, Spider-Man) then those novels will be included in the Graphic Novel collection and shelved with the appropriate character. If a novel is related to a series or character that did not start out in the comics, then those novels (like Star Wars) will be shelved in the regular library collection, despite the fact that there are Graphic Novels in the collection which are related in some way. These Graphic Novels will be shelved in the Graphic Novel collection.

Graphic novel call numbers are composed of two or three lines. The first line of the call number is always "GN," clarifying the collection (Graphic Novels) in which the title belongs. The second line is generally a four letter abbreviation for the category into which we are placing the title. DC is the only exception to the four character abbreviation rule. Here is an example of a basic call number for an Elfquest Graphic Novel:

> GN
> ELFQ

Occasionally there are three lines in a call number. Since we decided to keep all of the DC and Marvel comic books together, in these particular circumstances, the second line of the call number represents the publisher (DC or Marvel). Here are some examples of DC and Marvel call numbers:

> GN   GN
> DC   MARV
> SUPE   XMEN

Non-fiction Graphic Novels are another exception. The first line of the call number will be "GN." The second will be the Dewey Decimal number for the book. The third line will be the first four letters of the author's last name. Here is an example:

> GN
> 940.5315
> SPIE

Categories

Listed below are the categories into which we divided our Graphic Novels.

Non-Fiction: These are books, which include history/memoirs/philosophy/science etc., that combine both narrative and graphic text and will have the designation GN-Call#

Classics Illustrated: These are Graphic Novel versions of classic literature or are related in some way, e.g. *Tom Sawyer, The Sea Wolf, War of the Worlds* etc. GN-CI

Comic Related: These include narrative books that are related to comics or the industry in some way. Books about comic book writers (Stan Lee) or artists are also included. They can include books like the *Science of Superheroes, Overstreet Price Comic Book Price Guide,* or the *Encyclopedia of Super Heroes.* GN-COMI

Conan: Any Graphic Novel or guide to comics about the character Conan. We would not include the regular novels in this particular case. GN-CONA

DC: We have chosen to separate the two biggest comic book companies, DC and Marvel, and their materials into their own categories. This makes sense because most of the users of the collection like to find the various DC characters and titles together in one section. This also includes the Vertigo and Wildstorm imprints as DC publishes them. The categories are as follows:

> *Batman:* anything related to Batman including novels/Graphic Novels/movie books/or academic study with Batman in the title. This also includes Batgirl and Robin (who are mostly associated with Batman and some children/young adult books). GN-DC-BAT
>
> *Flash:* anything related to the Flash (novels, movie books, etc.). GN-DC-FLAS
>
> *Green Lantern/Green Arrow:* anything related to these two characters. GN-DC-GREE
>
> *Heroes:* anything related to DC heroes that does not have its own separate designation, e.g. Teen Titans/Legion of Superheroes etc. GN-DC-HERO
>
> *Justice League/Justice Society:* any JLA/JSA book, including novels and children's books as well as guides. GN-DC-JUST
>
> *DC-Miscellaneous:* material that does not necessarily fit into a general superhero category or is geared more toward older readers. This includes *Books of Magic*, DC history, horror etc. GN-DC-MISC
>
> *Superman:* any books related to Superman, including novels, movie books, *Smallville*, Supergirl etc. GN-DC-SUPE
>
> *DC Women:* many books featuring female characters. It was decided that they should have their own category. This includes Wonder Woman, Birds of Prey, Catwoman, etc. GN-DC-WOMA

Drawing Books: books that focus on how to draw comics, superheroes, manga, etc. GN-DRAW

Elfquest: anything related to Elfquest, including books, novels, and Graphic Novels. GN-ELFQ

Funny and Newspaper Strips: a WIDE range of materials from Walt Disney and *Peanuts* to *Doonesbury, Tintin, Flash Gordon, Calvin and Hobbes,* and *The Far Side.* GN-FUNN

Independents: a wide range of materials that are basically not within the confines of our other designations and are not published by Marvel and DC. Many of these books are geared toward alternative press material and older readers. Their content is fiction. GN-INDP.

Manga: These are Japanese/Asian books that are very popular. They are alphabetized by title and series. GN-MANG

> *Manga-Miscellaneous:* materials that don't fit into any general category or are geared toward older readers such as AKIRA and Death Note. GN-MANG-MISC
>
> *Manga-Related:* includes histories of Anime or Manga/Trivia/or anything remotely related to Manga and Japanese comics. GN-MANG-REL

Marvel: As previously mentioned Marvel gets its own special section as it is also one of the biggest collections we have. The categories are as follows:

> *Avengers:* Anything related to the group the Avengers and the Ultimates. GN-MARV-AVEN
>
> *Captain America:* Anything related to the Golden Age of Marvel and Captain America which features this character. GN-MARV-CA
>
> *Cosmic:* Marvel published many supernatural/cosmic/alien type books. These characters get this designation, e.g. the Silver Surfer, Ghost Rider, Dr. Strange, Dracula. GN-MARV-COSM

Daredevil/Elektra: These include any books related to Daredevil and Elektra (who was created in the DD comic). GN-MARV-DD/EL

Fantastic Four: These include any items related to the FF and its offshoots, including the Human Torch and the Thing. GN-MARV-FANT

Heroes: These include other characters that don't fit into the other categories, such as Iron Man, Iron Fist, Squadron Supreme etc. GN-MARV-HERO

Hulk: These include any items related to the Hulk. GN-MARV-HULK

Miscellaneous: These include material which doesn't fit into any of the above. Subjects include Marvel history, and non-hero related material. GN-MARV-MISC

Spider Man: This includes any Spider Man related titles including Venom, Toxin, Carnage, Spidergirl, Spiderwoman, and Arena. Spider-Man is probably the most popular character we have in the collection. GN-MARV-SPID

Thor: These include any books related to Thor. GN-MARV-THOR

Wolverine: The X-Men's most popular character, this category also includes Weapon X, Sabretooth, etc. GN-MARV-WOLV

X-Men: These are any materials with the title *X-Men*, including novels, guidebooks, academic works and Graphic Novels. GN-MARV-XMEN

X-Men Related: These include those books which feature mutants or members of the X-men such as Captain Britain, Excalibur, New Mutants, Cable, Rogue, Gambit etc. GN-MARV-XMRL

Movies and Television: These are any Graphic Novels related to movies and television and include subjects such as Spawn, Kiss, Tomb Raider, Dark Shadows, Hellboy, Buffy, etc. These can include novels and movie guides. GN-MOVI

Religious: This section includes those Graphic Novels that have obvious religious connections such as *Left Behind,* and the *Comic Book Bible* and *Graphic Bible.* GN-RELI

Star Trek: These ONLY include Graphic Novels relating to Star Trek. GN-STRE

Star Wars: These ONLY include Graphic Novels relating to Star Wars and its characters. GN-SWAR

Transformers: This section includes novels, Graphic Novels, children's books and guides relating to Transformers. GN-TRAN

Zorro: This section only includes Graphic Novels related to Zorro. GN-ZORR

28

Drawing Comics into
Canadian Libraries

RACHEL COLLINS

The Comic Problem

Comics (including graphic novels, trades, and comic books) are by no means a new medium, but the level of intensity with which libraries write, present, and organize information about them has exploded over the past six years. The new library comic collections, which have been popping up with great frequency and growing with great speed, appear to be matching this interest. Library comic collections and their comic collection practices are still in their infancy, yet libraries are not alone in their recent interest and general acceptance of comics. Lately, they have appeared on everyone's radar. In the article "Graphic Novels by the Number," *Publishers Weekly* revealed that revenues for graphic novel sales have more than quadrupled from 2001 to 2006, with sales expected to continue growing over the next few years (*Publisher's Weekly,* 2007).[1] In 2003, Dark Horse Comics, a major comic book publisher, reported libraries as significant purchasers of graphic novels, and said that over the past few years comic sales to libraries had increased 400 percent (MacDonald, 2002).

Despite libraries frequently professing their interest and their growing collections of this newly noticed medium, the library literature that deals with these burgeoning comic collections commonly overlooks an integral part to the cycle of collection management: collection evaluation. Collection evaluation can be the final step in the collection management cycle; ideally it allows libraries to gain a greater understanding of gaps or strengths in their collection, which they can then bring back into the cycle of collection management by making changes in their collection policy or selection of titles. Libraries can later use this knowledge when looking into downsizing or expanding their collections, which would ensure the best and brightest future for these newly forming collections. This new attention on the comic format has given libraries a very interesting task, as they cannot yet be sure for whom they are collecting this material.

Recently, comic publishers have begun to capture ever-more-specific and varied demographics for potential comic buyers. At the same time stigmas associated with the format are beginning to break down. Therefore, libraries cannot be sure of the patrons who will frequently use their new comic collections, and should carry a varied selection of subjects and material for all age-levels. If comics succeed in sustaining the greater public's interest, the public library comic collections, which are being started today, will become permanent and evolving collections within the library. If they remain as a permanent part of libraries' collections, rather than a trend, then the ways we are beginning these collections and establishing our selecting and collecting habits will have long-term consequences for future collections. Thus, we, as a profession, should reflect on them through an evaluation of our current collections.

Comic Formats

Before further exploring the challenges of collecting comic material and the methods and results of this study, it may be best to clarify the different formats of comics commonly referred to in this study. While the term *graphic novel* was coined over forty-four years ago by American comic critic Richard Kyle (Gravett, 2005), it has recently come under fire by comic theorists like Douglas Wolk, as can be seen in his book, *Reading Comics: How Graphic Novels Work and What They Mean,* or by famous writer/illustrator and theorist Art Spiegelman, as can be seen in his exhibitor's notes for the 2008 exhibit *KRAZY!: The Delirious World of Anime + Comics + Video Games + Art* (which he co-curated with fellow artist/writer Seth, at the Vancouver Art Gallery). Common criticisms are that the term *graphic novel* disregards any work of graphic journalism, biography, history or poetry and is used as a catch-all phrase for all comic works, including trades and individual comic books. Thus, for the purposes of this study, these terms will refer to the various forms of comics:

Comic Book: the approximately thirty-page, pamphlet-sized floppy booklets, which have a tendency to be periodicals which are published at different intervals throughout the year, and are commonly part of a greater series (e.g., *Echo* by Terry Moore or *Rasl* by Jeff Smith).

Trade: the compilation of several comic books, most often from a run in a series, which are bound together to form a single-bound book (e.g., The first few issues of *Echo* have already been bound together to form a trade called *Echo: Moon Lake,* and there is a second trade to follow after Moore produces a few more comic books for the series).

Graphic novel: a single story-line completed in a single volume (e.g., *Black Hole* by Charles Burns or *SpiralBound* by Aaron Renier). These stories were written to be published as a single volume rather than in installments, and are not part of a greater series.

Comic: a broad term used to encompass all three previously defined formats.

At this point, it also should be noted that this study does not intend to explore the history or collections of manga, as it draws from a different tradition and therefore requires its own focus.

The Study

As important as collection evaluation is, it is often overlooked because it requires a great deal of time, which often correlates directly to a drain on the library's budget (Emmanuel, 2002). Howard White has developed two quick, quantitative methods for evaluating collections as a way to remedy this problem and allow libraries an efficient way to evaluate their collections for the overall greater good: Brief Tests of Collection Strength, and Power Tests of Collection Strength. For libraries who participate in OCLC WorldCat, Power tests allow an individual to recall a body of literature from a selected subject held by that library and then compare it to all of OCLC's holdings in that subject. Thus, this study tests the entire comic collection of several of Canada's most populous English-speaking cities (Victoria, Vancouver, Edmonton, Winnipeg, Ottawa, Toronto) against the entire comic literature in OCLC WorldCat. This is done using the keyword searches, or call number searches available through WorldCat, and then limiting the search by the number of libraries that hold the item. Howard White's Brief Tests of Collection Strength were also used to measure the individual age-based comic collections (children's, young adults,' and adults') in four Canadian Public Libraries (Vancouver, Edmonton, Winnipeg, and Toronto). Like power tests, you measure the "difficulty" of holding titles and rank a library's collection according to RLG levels. However, brief tests are a random sampling and testing of the collection through its OPAC, rather than an extensive comparison of all the holdings within that subject's section compared through that library's available listings in OCLC WorldCat. Brief tests were performed alongside the power tests because they allow you to look at the three separate age-based collections in greater detail by allowing you to analyze them separately.

I chose to adopt Howard White's methods because they provide a framework to test whether libraries are going beyond the most popular and current titles to find a range of comic works from a variety of subjects, presses, and time periods. (I mention time periods because many classic titles are being made available again through reprints.) Comics have a rich history and appeal to many different subjects and all age ranges, thus the idea was that as comics have a very broad potential audience, which is currently on the rise, libraries may also wish to collect a broad range of titles to appeal to the widest audience. At the very least, we should be analyzing our collections to understand patterns in our current collections before reassessing and tailoring them for these future potential users.

Research Problems

AGE APPROPRIATENESS

In his article, "Beyond Superheroes: Comics Get Serious," Stephen Weiner claims that the average comic reader is twenty-nine years old (Weiner, 2002). Weiner's statistic may be out of date when one considers the growth occurring in the comic industry, but he is not alone in pointing a finger at adults as the main consumers of the format. Michael Pawuk, a Young Adult librarian, claims the average age of comic readers is thirty (Pawuk, 2007). Olivier Charbonneau, who conducted a survey in the Octagone Public Library, in the LaSalle borough of Montreal, found that:

- 38 percent of graphic novel users, and respondents to the survey, were aged fifteen years and younger;
- 22 percent were sixteen to twenty-one;
- 21 percent were twenty-two to thirty-nine;
- and 19 percent are forty and older (Charbonneau, 2005).

His study suggests that while at least half of comic users are over 18, the collection receives patrons across all age groups fairly equally. From these numbers one could assume the adult comic sections would be bursting off library shelves, or at least were as developed as the teen section. Yet the trend of library literature tends to focus on teenagers and, more recently, children as the target audience for comic collections. Writers such as Michele Gorman and David Serchay have created whole books on the collection of graphic novels and trades for children and teens, and even the American Library Association has demonstrated a focus on graphic novels and trades for young adults through the Young Adult Library Services Association (YALSA), which hosts a top ten best graphic novels of the year list called "Great Graphic Novels for Teens" (*www.ala.org/yalsa/booklists/gn*).

TARGET AUDIENCE

It is impossible to know which age section of the comic collection to develop most fully because the number of comic readers is increasing so dramatically. While only ten years ago comics toted the labels of "nerdy" or "childish," they are now increasingly "hip" or even "Bohemian," with many aspiring artists and writers choosing this medium in which to express themselves (Dominus, 2008). As a medium, comics encompass all subjects, age ranges, and levels of artistic and literary merit. Publishers are recognizing the potential customer base available for comics and are expanding to try and entice this new clientele. Scholastic, which is traditionally not a comic book publisher, began an imprint for kids, called Graphix, that publishes original fiction, such as Jeff Smith's *Bone*, and adaptations of chapter books like *The Baby-sitter's Club* (Serchay, 2008). Christian publisher Zondervan has also jumped into the fray, and begun producing graphic novels through its Zonderkidz line (Serchay, 2008). Until the stigma previously attached to comics no longer prevents people from reading them, libraries should aim to hold well-rounded graphic novel collections to entice these potential patrons.

There is little information available about the current state of comic collections and few suggestions for comic collection evaluation. If libraries were to evaluate their comic collections, they could gain an understanding of the current quality of their collections and get a clearer perspective for the future shaping and direction of their collection.

DIFFICULTIES OF COLLECTING COMICS

Libraries routinely deal with serialized texts in the form of magazines, journals, or paperbacks. The decision to carry a serial carries much weight because serials are ongoing and as such they pose long-term budgetary and space commitments as they slowly expand across the library's shelves (Evans, 2001). Most serials, like magazines and journals, are typically available through subscription, whether in a physical or digital form, and this binds the library to receiving a set number of issues over a set amount of time before they can re-evaluate the worth of each title. Comic serials are different because they tend to be bound together into trades before libraries purchase them for their permanent trade and graphic novel cataloged collections. They are available for purchase as individual volumes rather than subscriptions.

Comics' unique nature creates many issues that librarians must work through before pursuing a serial title for their comic collections. Libraries must first decide whether they wish to commit to following a serial and purchasing all volumes within the series, including back issues or replacement issues. Comic serials can be rather short, encompassing only a few trades, such as Alan Moore's *Promethea* (which represented a complete series within five trade volumes), or they can continue in a seemingly endless fashion, such as Bill Willingham's *Fables* (which started in 2002, and is already up to eleven trade paperback volumes with no apparent end in sight). Maintaining the complete series is essential to serials that have ongoing storylines. Just as it would disrupt a patron's reading experience if a library omitted a chapter from Todd Babiak's serialized novel, *Garneau Block*, so too it would confuse (and perhaps devastate) a reader if the library failed to carry Volume 2 out of four from Bryan Lee O'Malley's series *Scott Pilgrim vs. The World*. Either absence would leave holes in the storyline, and would make it impossible to fully understand and appreciate subsequent installments.

Librarians must also consider the tendency for series to have comic specials, which are published out of sequence and relate to the storyline and characters, but are not essential to the overall story arc, such as *Fables' 1001 Nights of Snow* or *Sandman's Endless Nights*. Cross-overs, in which characters from one comic serial are featured in a completely separate serial and story-line, are another popular aspect of many comic publications. While not integral to the overall storyline, dedicated readers may feel left out by references to the cross-over, or feel they have an incomplete view of the greater character development for their favorite character, if not presented with the opportunity to read it. *Runaways,* a comic about six children who discover their parents are super villains, participates in a cross-over with Marvel's *Civil War* series. The storylines were separate, but are alluded to in *Runaways* comics. Cross-overs are especially complicated because one would ideally start collecting the other series from the very beginning to make it easier for readers to make sense of the overall story.

The availability of complete comic serials contributes to the patron's experience of comics. Carefully collecting complete comic series shows a respect for comics in that the library respects the importance of each story and its characters as a whole, much in the same way that libraries collect complete series of monographs and their side projects. Libraries commonly collect the entire *Harry Potter* series along with Rowling's related works, such as *Quidditch Through the Ages* or the recent release of *The Tales of Beedle the Bard*. This kind of collecting respects the fans' desire to know more about Harry's world. Libraries must consider the complex characteristics of comic serials and the possible ramifications their collection patterns will have on patrons when developing their collection's development policy, goals, and guidelines for dealing with comics.

Methods

Brief Tests of Collection Strength

Brief Tests of Collection Strength: A Methodology for All Types of Libraries was written by Howard D. White in 1995. White modeled his quantitative collection evaluation on the Research Library Group Conspectus' collection levels, a system that began in the 1980s, and attempted to inventory existing library collections (Bendetto Beals 2006). White developed his new system of evaluation, in part, because he felt the criteria present in the Conspectus approach for assigning RLG levels to collections was too vague, and led to subjectivity and error in the evaluations (White, 1995). His brief tests are a collection-centered method "intended for assessing the collection-building activity of the past-perhaps the entire past of the collection" (White, 1995: 13); from this, librarians can understand the state of their collection in relation to other collections. David Lesniaski supports brief tests and believes they "assist the librarian in obtaining a good understanding of the library collection's range and depth with accuracy and a minimal investment of time and effort" (Lesniaski, 2004: 22). This allows librarians to plan future goals for their collections. Ideally, "it would be better to measure serviceability, since notions of strength or depth are idle if the collection fails to respond to customer demands" (White, 1995: 7). This is especially true because this study deals with public libraries, which are heavily focused on satisfying user needs. However, user demand is difficult to measure at this point in the development of comic collections because the audience continues to grow exponentially. Thus it is fitting for librarians to collect a broad spectrum of material to appeal to a diverse user groups, and then later, after attracting potential users, measure the collection's serviceability to those users.

White's method analyses lists of works that represent RLG levels one through four of the RLG on OCLC WorldCat by ranking the "difficulty" of holding a title and determining the level of collection achieved by the library, based on the number of titles it holds. OCLC WorldCat reveals the number of libraries that hold each title, and White explains that,

> Titles held by more than 750 libraries are items of the sort that a library would buy if it collects anything at all in a given subject; they are, in words from the book, "popular, standard, indispensable, classic." But that does not necessarily mean they are easy to read ... while at the other extreme, titles held by fewer than 150 libraries have only small, specialized readerships because they may be "advanced, localized, foreign, academic, obscure, old." But they are not necessarily hard to read [White, 2008: 159].

White stresses that all levels are equally worthy to aspire to for collection goals because some libraries may have a patron population that only needs best-sellers falling into level 1 (White, 1995: 43). However, libraries cannot be certain of the crowd their comic collections will appeal to, so it is wise to collect titles that fall into the "harder" range to collect simply because they are lesser known, not due to availability.

Table 28.1: Suggested Values for Assigning Titles to Levels

Counts	Levels
751 to highest	1 Minimal
401 to 750	2 Basic
151 to 400	3 Instructional
1 to 150	4 Research

The Brief Test methodology is primarily meant to analyze subject collections in academic libraries. Selectors choose forty titles to represent levels one through four on the RLG scale and then search these titles in OCLC WorldCat, record the number of libraries holding the title, reorder the original forty title list accordingly, and divide it into groups of ten. The group comprised of the highest number of library holdings corresponds to the Minimal level and so forth. Then the selector searches for the individual titles at their library and records the holdings. For every five or more titles held in a group of ten, the library receives that level of collection. Although primarily done as subject searches defined by a specific LC call number, White claims that "brief tests are, in fact, usable by librarians in any setting as long as they are interested in defining their collections by level on a scale such as the one developed by the RLG" (White, 1995). Brief tests' adaptability makes them an ideal objective evaluation for comic collections. White even suggests a numerical range for holding counts that a researcher should logically expect to correspond to the various RLG levels (See Table 28-1). However, this distribution is based on experience evaluating well established subject areas. Comics represent a newly discovered area of interest and thus are unlikely to match this distribution. Consideration was made into collecting a balance of titles that fit into the four RLG levels by drawing from: award lists, thought to represent levels 1 and 2; library bibliographies and periodicals, thought to represent levels 2 and 3; and old comic bibliographies and non-library publications, thought to hold titles from level 4 and 5. However, in the end the test was simply divided along every thirtieth title in the popularity ranking created on OCLC WorldCat, as had occurred in Thomas Twiss' study of brief tests (Twiss, 2001).

There has been some dispute over the choice of ten titles per level (Bendetto Beals, 2006), but White assures readers that the original choice of ten titles was to save the evaluator's time, thus longer tests can be used to prevent a single item from becoming a deciding factor in a test, due to its heavy weighting (White, 1995). This study will increase the number of titles to thirty per RLG level in the hopes of decreasing the margin of error. Jennifer Bendetto Beals also suggests that the titles chosen for brief tests should thoroughly represent all areas (Bendetto Beals, 2006) and thus, whenever possible (e.g., as in bibliographies divided by genre or historical period) a similar number of titles will be drawn from each genre section.

The study evaluates the children's, young adults,' and adults' comic collections. This means that three lists of 120 titles, comprised of thirty titles at each RLG level, are required to perform the test. Thus the children's section will have a different list of 30 comic titles for the Minimal, Basic Information, Instructional Support, and Research RLG levels. The teen and adult section will also have four unique lists for each of their four different RLG levels. After all tests are created, there will be three final lists of 120 titles, making 360 titles for the whole brief test, and once the master test list is compiled, it can be used to test every selected library's online public access catalog (Vancouver, Edmonton, Winnipeg, Toronto).

Table 28.2: Children's Section
Level 1: Pass (21/30)

Titles	Library Count	EPL Holding
The Boy, The Bear, The Baron, The Bard	3051	yes
Time Warp Trio	2658	yes
The Strongest Man in the World: Louis Cyr	2329	yes
Ug: Boy Genius of the Stone Age	1881	yes
Robot Dreams	1511	yes
Babymouse	1292	yes
City of Light, City of Dark: A Comic Book Novel	1225	yes
Graphic Universe: Graphic Myths and Legends	1212	no
Creepy Creatures adapted by Gabriel Hernandez	917	no
Alia's Mission	895	yes
Akiko	893	yes
Bone	883	yes
Artemis Fowl: The Graphic Novel	841	yes
Polo: The Runaway Book	818	yes
Captain Raptor and the Space Pirates	770	yes
Sardine in Outer Space	712	yes
Redwall: The Graphic Novel	701	yes

Selections for the brief test lists were made from library and comic literature in order to create a well-balanced list of items. These award lists, bibliographies, and periodicals hosting comic reviews were the main sources consulted in compiling the lists

Award Lists

• Harvey Awards (http://www.harveyawards.org/awards_current.html)
• Eisner Awards
• YALSA Top Ten

Bibliographies

• Mike Benton. *The Comic Book in America: An Illustrated History.* Dallas, Texas: Taylor Publishing Company, 1989.
• Kempkes, Wolfgang. *International bibliography of comics literature.* New York, R. R. Bowker, 1974
• Gravett, Paul. *Graphic Novels: Everything You Need to Know.* New York: HarperCollins, 2005.
• Gorman, Michele. *Getting Graphic! Comics for Kids.* Columbus, Ohio: Linworth Publishing, 2008.
• Kurtzman, Harvey. *From Aargh! to Zap!: Visual History of the Comics. Toronto:* Byron Preiss Book, 1991.
• Serchay, David S. *The Librarians Guide to Graphic Novels for Children and Tweens.* 2007.

Journals

• *School Library Journal*
• *Publisher's Weekly*

The completed lists of titles were divided according to the library holdings count in OCLC WorldCat, with the 30 titles held by the most libraries making up level one and the thirty next most popular titles making up level two and so on. These reordered lists were then used to test each library's collection strength through searching their OPAC. A search for each title was performed based on title, author, or sometimes in a final attempt a list of keywords. Any item held by the test library would receive a check. The library achieved a research level by owning 15 or more of the titles on the list for that level. So, for example, the partial image of the children's list for level 1 shows which titles the library held and also that after tallying the list, the library held 21 out of 30 titles on the list, so they received a pass on level one of their children's section. This test was performed in May, 2009 and only pertains to the graphic novel and trade collection, as the comic book collection was not available through the test group's OPACs.

Coverage Power Tests of Collection Strength

White published the methodology for brief tests in 1996. Since that time, membership in OCLC WorldCat has grown exponentially and OCLC has expanded and refined the services it provides to the public. In 2008, White released a new method of collection evaluation called coverage power tests, which he discusses in detail in his article, "Better Than Brief Tests: Coverage Power Tests of Collection Strength." White claims that his new method "defines both collections and literatures in such a way that libraries may be validly compared" (White, 2008: 155) by extracting complete literatures. White and his students performed a search for a complete literature, broke the titles in this subject apart according to the WLN levels,[2] for collection evaluation, and then compared a chosen library's collection to the literature's distribution of titles. White's new method is feasible because WorldCat now provides access to the detailed collection information for more than 69,000 libraries in over 112 countries (OCLC WorldCat About, 2009). It also provides the tools necessary to extract whole literatures based on LC subject headings, LC classes, or Dewey classes and then to limit this information by individual libraries or map this information according to the number of libraries holding a particular work. These tools give anyone with access to OCLC WorldCat the ability to compare an enormous number of collections based on a whole literature, according to the principles of Conspectus and brief tests, quickly and objectively. (A more complete tool to analyze your library's collection is also offered from OCLC WorldCat for a fee.) Working with such a large scale of items removes doubts over the seemingly arbitrary forty items customarily used in brief tests of collection strength (White, 2008).

Table 28.3

Libraries Studied	OCLC Library Code
Edmonton Public Library	CNEDM
Vancouver Public Library	VP@
Greater Victoria Public Library	G8V
Toronto Public Library	TOH
Ottawa Public Library	OTP
Winnipeg Public Library	CNWPU

Coverage power tests are ideal because White claims they are equally easy to perform when using LC classes, LC subject headings, or Dewey classes (White, 2008). Comics are not a subject, but they are a medium, which divides them from other mediums such as film or literature. It is their unique format that allows the multiple genres that comprise the comic medium to be grouped together under the LC subject heading *graphic novels* or *comic books, strips, etc* — (Library of Congress Authorities). White cautions that there are several margins of error present in his new form of testing and points to several issues that arise when using subject headings as a means to extract a whole body of literature. LC subject headings are not mutually exclusive. Thus books about comics, such as Scott McLeod's *Understanding Comics,* or comic strips pulled up because of their tie to the older indexing term *comic books, strips, etc.,* get lumped into the same body of works when the whole collection on OCLC is pulled. However, White promises that regardless of this the test results will appear intelligible (White, 2008).

Power tests can be used to quickly compare several public libraries' comic collections and discover the state of the individual libraries' collections, while also gaining insight into trends of graphic novel collection across multiple public libraries. Power tests will be used to view the trend in comic collection in Canadian public libraries (although only in Victoria, Vancouver, Edmonton, Winnipeg, Toronto, and Ottawa because of to the limited selection of major Canadian public library collections in OCLC WorldCat). The power test is performed in OCLC WorldCat by using the keyword searches or the call number searches that are available through WorldCat to extract your selected body of literature. In this case, the terms "graphic novel*" and "comic books, strips, etc" were limited to a genre/form search and joined with the Boolean operator "or." Because thousands of manga titles were retrieved with the initial search string, the search was narrowed by using the addition of the "not" operator and the keyword "Japan*."[3] Each library was searched individually by using its unique OCLC Library Code. After retrieving the library's comic holdings in OCLC WorldCat, the items were divided into their research levels through OCLC's "limit" option, which is available in the top-left side of the search results page. Next, the "Limit Your Results by Number of Libraries" feature was used This feature provides a breakdown of the titles held by the test library according to the frequency of them being held by other library members of OCLC WorldCat.[4] It should be mentioned that, while OCLC contains records for comic books, trades, and graphic novels, none of the libraries catalog these selections; this would lead to an inaccurate evaluation of a libraries' holdings, as these tests only measure what is online. Also, there is a delay, typically of a few months, between a library getting a comic title and it being accessible in OCLC WorldCat, which again would lead to a lower score.

Results

POWER TESTS

After completing a power test on each of the six libraries, I discovered that none of them had extensive comic collections, but they were succeeding in creating collections of material from the minimal to basic level of collection. Winnipeg, Edmonton, and Ottawa are most actively collecting the majority of material in the basic level of collection, while Ottawa houses the only collection that holds a significant amount of comics that are uncommon (more diverse). Successfully collecting a large percentage of popular material suggests that libraries are succeeding in their collections. However, libraries' comic collections are new and are less developed and diverse in age, publishers, and overall uniqueness than a staple collection that has been around for decades. Power tests analyze libraries' collections by those standards set up by other libraries, and thus a further analysis of the material comprising the levels was needed to further understand how libraries were collecting comic material.

All of OCLC WorldCat's comic titles were retrieved using the aforementioned search string minus the limiting factor of an individual library code. The titles retrieved, sans collections of comic strips that were accidentally included through the use of the descriptor "comic books, strips, etc.," were analysed for the date of publication. Only titles at the minimal level of the collection were analysed because all the libraries achieved this level. The minimal level is defined by Howard White to be items that are held by 750 or more libraries. According to WorldCat, the majority of titles that are held at the minimal level were published after 2004. Only 10 comics published before 2000 were held in the minimal level of library collection and include seminal classics like *Watchmen* by Alan Moore, *Maus* by Art Spiegelman, and *Bone* by Jeff Smith. The list of older titles included on the list was problematic because it included *Maus* and *Watchmen*, but it ignored classics like Frank Miller's *The Dark Knight*, which along with *Watchmen* and *Maus*, is a part of the triumvirate of life-altering comic titles that were published in 1987, and are considered by many to have ignited the whole revolution of serious comics over the past twenty years.

Other popular titles in the comic community are also overlooked simply because they were originally published before the recent library interest in comics. Mike Allred's work is one example, and I can attest to his popularity, as at the Calgary comic con in late April, 2009, he had an almost never ending line of fans coming to get things signed and to chat. Allred is well known for working with big DC series and names like Sandman and Fables. Now, despite the popularity of Mike Allred in the comic community, his books likely will come only to the attention of the library community until film director Robert Rodriguez brings Allred's comic superhero Madman (who has been around since 1992) to the general public's attention. Currently, Allred's *Madmen* and *the Atomics* titles are in the hardest level to collect, up there with titles that are no longer being printed or are only available in the original comic book form and held by specialty libraries. Collection developers cannot be expected to be experts in everything. However, one trend I noticed while interviewing a member of the centralized collection development team from a Western Canadian city, was that her collection resources, while quite diverse, differed greatly from any used by local comic merchants who also were interviewed for selection tools and practices used when selecting titles for library collections. Both library and comic stores considered employee and customer suggestions to be important selection tools, but they differed completely on the print and online resources used as selection tools. The library relied heavily on professional journals like *Library Thing, Booklist, VOYA*, and *School Library Journal*, while comic stores focused solely on periodicals produced by the comic industry as selection tools. They consulted *The Comics Journal, Wizard Magazine* and *The Comics Buyer Guide* for reviews, and both consulted Previews as a fairly definitive list of items available for purchase. Perhaps libraries need to consider the inclusion of industry based periodicals as a way to pick up on titles outside the library realm that are reviewed specifically by and for a public already interested in comics.

BRIEF TESTS

Brief tests were performed through the OPACs for Vancouver, Edmonton, Winnipeg, and Toronto public libraries in August, 2008, and only pertain to the graphic novel and trade collection, as the comic book collections were not available through the OPACs. The results for the brief tests are comparable to the results from the earlier power tests. All three age sections pass the first level, but the young adults' and children's sections are the most common to pass the second level of collection strength. One thing that comes out of the brief test is the fact that the adult collection has fallen behind the children's and young adults' trade and graphic novel collection. This division could be greater than it appears in the brief tests, as the test merely evaluates whether the library holds the item or not. It does not explore which section of the library the item was located in, which has the potential to change the idea of the size of the adult, young adult, or children's collection.

The tendency to place titles in the teen section does not apply to all libraries, but it does speak to a noticeable trend in library literature that places an emphasis on teenagers or young adults as the primary user-group for this collection. This tendency has also become evident in the library literature devoted to policies and practices for comics in the library. The American Library Association's publication *Booklist* provides reviews of adult-centered graphic novels, but far more prevalent is the tendency to provide reviews and recommendations for children and young adult sections, with a great deal of emphasis placed on the young adult section. Young Adult Library Services (YALSA) provides an annual top ten list[5]; the ALA provides a list of resources on their website that is primarily geared towards the Young Adult sections[6]; and periodicals such as *Voice of Youth Advocates* and *School Library Journal* provide regular reviews of graphic novels. Even books like Steve Miller's *Developing and Promoting Graphic Novel Collections,* which appear unbiased, are part of a greater series for young adult librarians called *Teens @ the Library.* Even more common, though, are the bibliographies and comic guides for librarians that are specifically targeted at young patrons. Even YA books like the first edition of *Young Adult Liter-*

ature: Exploration, Evaluation, and Appreciation by Kathleen Bucher and M. Lee Manning, which are not specifically about comics, feature a few panels of Spider-Man comics as the cover art.

As mentioned earlier, there is a tendency to focus on teen comic material in library literature devoted to policies and practices for comics in the library. According to a western Canadian library that was interviewed for their selection practices with comics, a customer-driven comic collection was top priority. But by serving the existing user-base, libraries are missing out on users who already feel the current collection is not for them, or for all future potential users that are created as this medium grows in popularity and cultural capital. One must question why the majority of comics are shelved in the teen section and what image this propagates for the medium. By emphasizing the young adult section, libraries could be alienating adult patrons who may potentially be interested in comics, but are put off by the image the library creates for them as teen literature. Is this in fact any better than the older stereotype, sarcastically mentioned by Michael Pawuk that, "aren't comic books just made for kids?" (Pawuk xviii).

As my dad is a collector, I have always had comics in my life, so it has been quite interesting for me to see the change in attitudes surrounding the medium as negative images of the format break down. For instance, my mom has never shown any interest in my father's collection, but after hearing reviews and author interviews on the CBC she has read *Persepolis* and has put Lynda Barry's works on her "need to read" list. We might trust that our users will always check the OPAC for the location of material, but it is also likely that if a woman, like my mother, heard a book reviewed for adults on an adult program, she would walk into her local library branch and promptly head towards the adult section thinking to find that title there. We have shown a tendency to place the majority of comic titles in the young adult section almost as a default location for comic titles. This cuts down on the browsability of the section, and sends the message that the material is for children or teenagers, not adults.

It is important to remember that comics are becoming more mainstream, and as such are making it into many places they were previously neglected. Comics are being picked up by educators and used in the classroom, even at the university level. University of Alberta professors use *Maus* in their introductory English courses, and *The Amazing "True" Story of a Teenage Single Mom*, by Katherine Arnoldi was used in a graduate level English course about biography. The U of A even devotes whole graduate courses to comics in the English Department and the School of Library and Information Studies, and could well offer further courses in upcoming years. One could argue that comics' presence in university coursework, outside of children's lit classes, marks titles as targeted at adults. *Connecting Young Adults and Libraries* argues that many librarians may still live under the assumption that the average comic book reader is a "semiliterate juvenile delinquent who isn't smart enough to read 'real books'" (Jones 54). Librarians must be mindful of their role in creating the idea of the book for their public because promoting the teen comic section at the expense of the adult and children's sections can reinforce negative stereotypes.

Comics are currently being celebrated in many culturally elite fields like universities or art galleries, for example: last summer's blockbuster exhibit KRAZY!; The Delirious World of Anime comics video games and art; and a newly opened exhibit on comic art at the Louvre. The coming years are definitely a formative time in comic history. Hopefully libraries will continue to actively involve themselves in comic related events and continue to collect this material for their publics.

Appendix

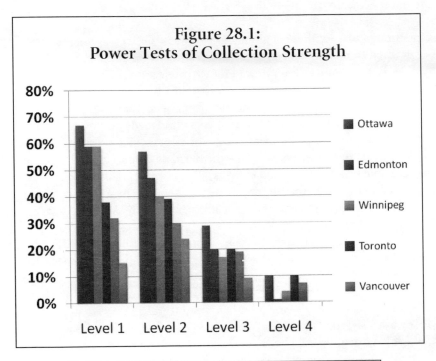

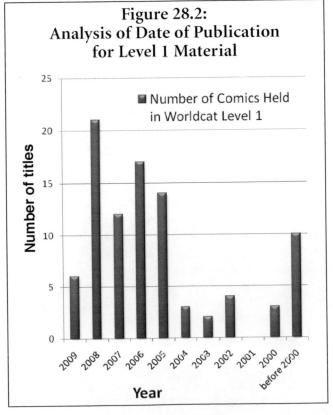

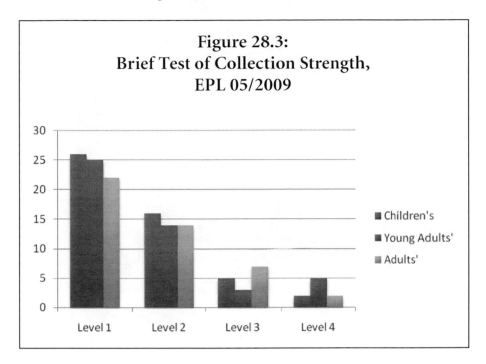

Figure 28.3:
Brief Test of Collection Strength,
EPL 05/2009

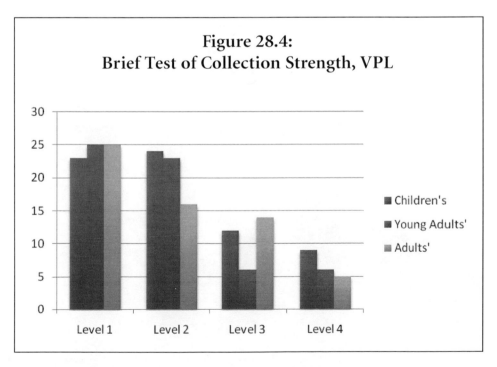

Figure 28.4:
Brief Test of Collection Strength, VPL

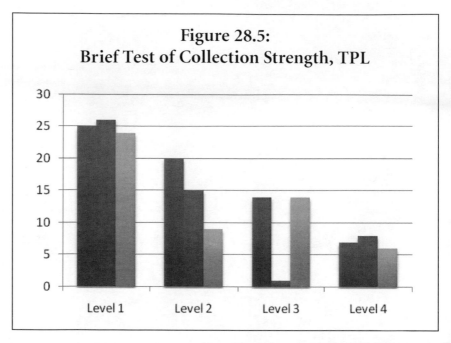

Figure 28.5:
Brief Test of Collection Strength, TPL

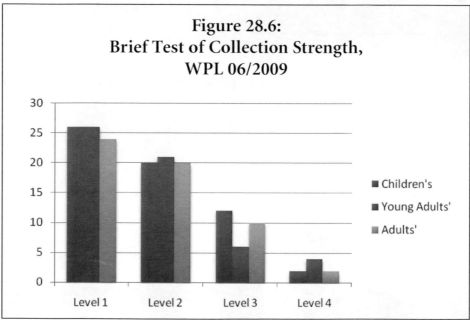

Figure 28.6:
Brief Test of Collection Strength,
WPL 06/2009

Endnotes

1. While the jump over recent years has not been quite so drastic, comic sales have again risen from $375 million in 2007 to $395 million in 2008, which may have been in part driven due to popularity surrounding the release of the Dark Knight movie, and also the buzz around the Watchmen movie (ICv2, Feb 2009). As of April 2009, sales of comic books, trades, and graphic novels in the first quarter of 2009 were down by only 5 percent from the first quarter of 2008 (ICv2, April 2009). Editors at ICV2, a website that houses many stats on the comic industry, feel this is quite good considering the recession.

2. White adapted the RLG scale associated with the WLN Conspectus, formerly the Pacific Northwest Conspectus, to better reflect the gradations of non-research collections (White, 1995: 78). The WLN Conspectus

is an adaptation of RLG conspectus and is meant for smaller libraries and uses either Dewey or LC classification system and can be used as an internal assessment tool that communicates the strengths and weaknesses of a collection (Loken, 1994: 31). The added levels are meant to balance the relatively few titles used to calculate brief tests and allow public libraries claim uneven coverage of subject in higher levels (White, 96: 80–81). The additional levels are comparable to standard letter grading, like the difference between receiving a C or a B-.

3. The term Japan or Japanese finds its way into the description of many manga items, but its inclusion is not necessary to mark an entry of manga and the exclusion of all Japan related items can also weed out comics about Japan.

4. Please see Howard White's article "Better Than Brief Tests: Coverage Power Tests of Collection Strength." *College & Research Libraries* 69 (2): 155–174 for a more detailed and comprehensive plan for performing a power test.

5. The Top Ten lists have been produced for 2007 and 2008 and are available online at http://www.ala.org/ala/yalsa/booklistsawards/greatgraphicnovelsforteens/08ggnt.cfm.

6. ALA Graphic Novel list available at http://www.ala.org/ala/booklist/speciallists/speciallistsandfeatures3/referenceonweb/graphicnovels.cfm.

References

Beals, Jennifer Benedetto. 2006. "Assessing Library Collections Using Brief Test Methodology." *Electronic Journal of Academic and Special Librarianship* 7 (3): http://southernlibrarianship.icaap.org.login.ezproxy.library.ualberta.ca.

Charbonneau, Olivier. 2005. "Adult Graphic Novels Readers: A Survey in a Montréal Library." *YALSA* 3 (4): 39–42.

Dominus, Susan. 2008. "Young, Hip and Wild About Comic Books." *The New York Times*: B2 (L).

Emanuel, Michelle. 2002. "A Collection Evaluation in 150 Hours." *Collection Management* 27 (3): 79–93.

Evans, G. Edward, and Margaret Zarnosky Saponaro. 2005. *Developing Library and Information Center Collections.* 5th ed. Westport, CT: Libraries Unlimited.

Gravett, Paul. 2005. *Graphic Novels: Everything You Need to Know.* New York: HarperCollins.

ICv2. 06 Feb 2009. "Graphic Novels Up in 2008 Manga Down." *ICv2.* http://www.icv2.com/articles/news/14239.html.

ICv2. 15 April 2009. "Not Bad, Considering ... Comic Sales Down Just 5% in Q1." *ICv2.* http://www.icv2.com/articles/news/14746.html.

Kim, Ann, and Michael Rogers. 2007. Librarians out Front at Comic Con. *Library Journal* 132 (6): 15.

Lesniaski, David. 2004. "Evaluating Collections: A Discussion and Extension of *Brief Tests of Collection Strength*." *College & Undergraduate Libraries* 11 (1): 11–24.

Library of Congress. "Cataloguing and Acquisition: Collection Levels." http://www.loc.gov/acq/devpol/cpc.html .

Library of Congress. "Library of Congress Authorities." http://authorities.loc.gov/.

Loken, Sally. 1994. "WLN Conspectus." *Cooperative Collection Management.* New York, Neal-Schuman Publishers: 31–35.

MacDonald, Heidi. 2002. "Year of the Graphic Novel." *Publisher's Weekly* 249 (51): 21–24.

OCLC WorldCat. "OCLC WorldCat:" About. http://www.oclc.org.login.ezproxy.library.ualberta.ca/about/default.htm.

Pawuk, Michael. 2007. *Graphic Novels: A Genre Guide to Comic Books, Manga, and More.* Westport, CT: Libraries Unlimited.

Publisher's Weekly. 2007. "Graphic Novel by the Numbers." *Publisher's Weekly* 254 (10): 9.

Serchay, David S. 2008. *The Librarians Guide to Graphic Novels for Children and Tweens.* New York: Neal-Schuman Publisher.

Twiss, Thomas M. 2001. "A Validation of Brief Tests of Collection Strength." *Collection Management* 25 (3): 23–37.

Weiner, Steve. 2002. "Beyond Superheroes: Comics Get Serious." *Library Journal* 127, no 2: 55–58.

White, Howard D. 2008. "Better Than Brief Tests: Coverage Power Tests of Collection Strength." *College & Research Libraries* 69(2): 155–174.

_____. 1995. *Brief Tests of Collection Strength: A Methodology for All Types of Libraries.* Westport, CT: Greenwood Press.

29

Graphic Novel Holdings in Academic Libraries

Eric Werthmann

Comic books have become increasingly popular in the past several years, both on university and college campuses and in the wider world. They are read for pleasure by people across the social spectrum, and they are also studied by college students for their classes and used by faculty in their research. In particular, graphic novels — comics that are produced in a more durable, book-like format — have seen rapid growth in both status and sales in recent years. However, this growth has been tremendously swift, and some academic librarians still retain biases against the format. In addition, even those who see it as worth collecting may lack the knowledge to do so effectively. Because of these factors, it is unclear if the graphic novel collections of academic libraries have grown to become substantial enough to support the needs of their patrons.

In America, despite their widespread popularity, comic books have been perceived, since their beginnings in the 1930s, as being, at best, sub-literary dross meant for children and the uneducated, and, at worst, as a threat to public morality. This last view was embodied by Dr. Frederic Wertham, whose crusade against comics reached its pinnacle with the 1954 publication of *Seduction of the Innocent*. Wertham felt that the sex and violence filling the comic books of his day were having a negative psychological effect on the nation's children. His work led to Senate hearings on the matter, as well as to the creation of the Comics Code Authority. The seal of this organization, which could only be used if the work followed strict guidelines, was ubiquitous on the covers of comic books for several decades. The result of all this was that, for most of the last half-century, "comic books were greeted with disdain and outright hostility by many of the (largely self-appointed) arbiters of American cultural tastes and values. Numbered among these anti-comic book cultural elitists were many members of the library community" (Ellis & Highsmith, 2000: 39). It would take a significant amount of effort for comics to be thought worthy of serious consideration, especially in academia.

A re-evaluation of the role of comic art began to take place among the cultural changes of the late 1960s and early 1970s. A community of "underground comics" creators that was connected to the burgeoning counterculture began to grow in places like San Francisco and New York City. Robert Crumb is by far the most famous of these creators, but there were dozens of others. The work they produced was filled with sexuality and drug use, and was thus aimed squarely at an adult audience. These artists were followed in the next two decades by other creators of "alternative comics," such as Harvey Pekar, Will Eisner, Jaime and Gilbert Hernandez, and Art Spiegelman. Titles like *Fax from Sarajevo*, an account of the 1990s Bosnian War, deal with subjects of such immense seriousness that it was difficult not to view them with some respect. In addition, these works explored all types of stories, from autobiography to magical realism to war stories, thus making extremely clear that "comics" are a medium, not a genre. In the late 1980s, even the superhero comic was brought to a new level of maturity with the publication of such dark, postmodern landmarks as *Watchmen* and *Batman: The Dark Knight Returns*.

The new respectability of the comics medium was aided by a new form which could be presented to audiences, the graphic novel. Will Eisner's *A Contract with God, and Other Tenement Stories*, published in 1978, is often considered to be the first graphic novel, and it is certainly the one that made the term fairly well-known in the comics world and beyond. Eisner, who had been working in the comics industry for decades, used the term because he was trying to create something more substantial than his previous work, something of more lasting value. And in its early years, this is how the term graphic novel was generally used — to refer to comics that had literary value and that often had adult themes. It was also often used to refer to an "original graphic novel," i.e. a book that was not a collection of work that had been first published in comic book form. However, today the term graphic novel is used much more loosely, generally to refer to any work of comic art that is bound as a book. This new format, with its similarity to "real" books and its durability, added an additional air of refinement and permanence to the medium.

These advances in comic art were rewarded with more widespread recognition for the form, and graphic novels began to win mainstream awards and to be reviewed in mainstream publications. For instance, Art Spiegelman's holocaust memoir *Maus* won a Pulitzer Prize in 1992,[1] and *Watchmen* was chosen for *Time* magazine's list of the "100 best English-language novels from 1923 to present" in 2005.[2] In addition, reviews of graphic novels now appear regularly in such esteemed publications as the *New York Times* and the *New Yorker* (as well as in library publications like *Booklist* and *Library Journal*). And, while graphic novels in the past were mostly released by specialized publishers, today, many of the most visible comics are published by mainstream companies (Pantheon, in particular, seems to be embracing graphic novels as a viable format). In 2007, Houghton-Mifflin even added a *Best American Comics* to its annual line of *Best American* anthologies. This attention has paid off — graphic novels are slowly replacing comic books as the most popular expression of the medium, and sales of graphic novels hit $395 million in 2008, a 5 percent increase from the year before.[3] In 2008/2009, comics have made significant progress towards the goal of being accepted as legitimate by mainstream society.

Graphic novels and comics have also, in recent years, found a greater prominence on college and university campuses. This prominence was partly due to a new attitude towards popular culture materials that began in the 1960s, an attitude in which even the most lowly examples of popular culture are seen as acceptable subjects of artistic expression and of academic inquiry. This collapsing of the dichotomy between high and low culture was perhaps most apparent in the visual art movement of Pop Art. Of particular relevancy here is the work of Roy Lichtenstein, whose famous paintings such as *Whaam!* and *Drowning Girl* adapted comic book art to the concerns of high art. These new attitudes quickly spread into academia; today various forms of popular culture are studied at academic institutions across the country and Bowling Green State University in Ohio even has a Department of Popular Culture. This new paradigm has allowed the study of comics to thrive, as they have benefited from the enhanced status being afforded popular culture materials in general ... scholars in the field have marshaled an imposing array of arguments in favor of the serious study of popular culture materials—and, by extension, the importance of such materials to library collections [Ellis & Highsmith, 2000: 39].

As the *Journal of Popular Culture*'s website says, "the popular culture movement was founded on the principle that the perspectives and experiences of common folk offer compelling insights into the social world."[4] The proponents of popular culture studies view all products of a given culture as valid subjects for academic study.

There are also many within academia who recognize that comics are capable of making their own unique contribution to art, narrative art in particular. This type of thought has meant that graphic novels have worked their way into all types of academic endeavors, from required undergraduate classes to research done by professors. Because of the unique nature, both socially and aesthetically, of comic art, graphic novels are used in a wide variety of disciplines, from comparative literature to graphic design, and from education to library science. As Bussert (2005) writes, "Many in the fields of history, sociology, and arts and literature realize the unique and valuable insight inherent in studying comic books and graphic novels" (103). There are now two scholarly journals entirely devoted to comics—the *International Journal of Comic Art*[5] based at Temple University and *ImageTexT*[6] based at the University of Florida. In addition, there are several academic conferences on comics held annually, including the International Comic Arts Forum[7] and the University of Florida's Conference on Comics.[8] However, while all this is impressive, it is still certainly true that the place of comics in academia is still rather tenuous. As Bart Beaty (2004) writes, "the scholarly study of comic books and comic strips (collectively, comics) is, to provide the generous reading of the situation, in a state of infancy" (403). While graphic novels have obviously not reached the same level of prestige as painting, prose, or cinema, they are becoming increasingly prominent in scholarly life.

It is still not entirely certain how well the academic library community has responded to these changes in the status of graphic novels. It is the mandate of these libraries to serve the institutions of which they are a part, but there has long been a certain amount of prejudice among academic librarians against comic books. Writing about the form and librarians in 1984, Randall W. Scott lamented that "the profession's stance has been seen as blanket disapproval for so many years" (25). This attitude has obviously affected the quality of academic graphic novel collections. Lavin (1998) notes that, "aside from a few dozen specialized, non-circulating research collections, retrospective comic book holdings remain virtually unknown as a library resource. Browsing collections of current comic books are equally rare in public, school, and college libraries" (31).

It is the aim of this study to provide a general picture of the current quantity and quality of graphic novel holdings in academic library general collections. As of now, there has not been a study attempting to gauge graphic novel resources in these types of institutions. Such data will be extremely valuable if libraries wish to build successful collections in this area, and if they wish to understand where their weaknesses might be found. Because of the recent, swift rise to prominence of this form, and because of lingering prejudices against it in the library community, it is expected that many of the libraries' collections will be weak. In addition, this paper will provide some analysis regarding the types of graphic novels collected by academic libraries and the types of institutions that have strong or weak collections.

Literature Review

Given the marginalization that comic books and graphic novels have long suffered in academia, it is perhaps not surprising that the literature focusing on these forms in academic libraries is not particularly broad or deep. While there is a fairly significant body of literature dealing with graphic novels in school and public libraries, very little of this relates directly to the concerns of this study. This is especially true because school and, to a slightly lesser extent, public librarians seem to largely regard graphic novels as children's literature. Still, there have been several excellent articles dealing with different facets comics in academic libraries and these will be covered here. However, none of these articles present any quantitative data regarding graphic novels in academic libraries.

Comic Books and Special Collections

Most of the earliest articles on this subject focused on non-circulating special collections of comic books. Randall W. Scott is the Comic Art Bibliographer at Michigan State University, which has the biggest and best known comics special collection in the country. Scott's article "The Comics Alternative" (1984) was written just as comics were beginning to gain some acceptance among the academic community. He details the neglect that librarians have shown to comics, noting that "the Library of Congress has never provided cataloging for comic books, which may have discouraged librarians from keeping what they had acquired" (23). However, he details the reasons why "comic books are maturing as a medium" (24), and proposes that librarians therefore begin to take them more seriously. In "Comics and Libraries and the Scholarly World" (1993), he advocates building collections such as the one at MSU, even in the face of opposition or indifference from administrators or faculty members. He sees librarians as both scholars and leaders, and he believes that "the library profession is in a unique position to contribute to the future of scholarship by preserving 20th century popular communication artifacts, and making roadmaps through them" (84). Scott's 1998 article "A Practicing Comic-Book Librarian Surveys His Collections and His Craft" is an in-depth profile and history of the MSU Comics Art Collection. Particular attention is paid to the cataloging and indexing of the collection, though he also discusses preservation and storage.

Highsmith (1992) discusses collection development tools and tactics for an academic librarian who is building a comic book collection. Particular emphasis is placed on developing relatively narrow criteria for the collection, since there are far too many comic books out there for all but the largest libraries to attempt to collect comprehensively. Savage (2003) is mostly concerned with describing the various tools of the comic researcher's trade, but he also makes several salient points regarding comic research collections. He laments the "paucity of research collections available to investigators," which "suggests the low esteem in which most libraries have held comic books" (85). He does list two high quality research collections, those at Michigan State University and Bowling Green State University. Serchay (1998) profiles fourteen special collections with focuses that relate to comic books, including several academic libraries. Serchay also includes a directory of more than 50 notable comic research libraries in an appendix.

Graphic Novels and Academic Libraries

It is only within the last few years that a literature relating specifically to graphic novels in the general collections of academic libraries has emerged. While the library literature relating to this still-emerging field consists of only a few works, it nonetheless gives a good picture of the problems and opportunities that graphic novels can create for academic libraries. Chris Matz, Collection Development Librarian at the University of Memphis, shares his experiences with the medium in "Collecting Comic Books for an Academic Library" (2004), and though he uses the term "comic book," he is explicitly referring to graphic novels. His library was asked by this university's Department of English to attempt to improve its graphic novel resources in order to support doctoral level research in the area. A donation of funds from the university's Friends of the Library allowed them to amass a significant collection in a short time. While this source of money was temporary, Matz predicts demand for graphic novels among faculty and students will only increase and will spur the further growth of the collection. He also discusses selection tools and provides a list of "ten important creators" whose work academic libraries should consider collecting (all of whom are represented on this study's list of core titles). Matz follows up this article with another in 2006. Here, he delineates the reason why the rosy future predicted in his previous article did not come true (mostly, as would be expected, because of budgetary concerns).

Behler (2006) also offers a survey of important titles and collection development tools. Though the article is about libraries in general, Behler is an academic librarian (at Pennsylvania State University) and therefore particular emphasis is placed upon titles that would be useful in an academic setting. Similarly, Bussert (2005) offers collection development resources, including bibliographies, journals and databases.

One of the most recent, and best, library science articles relating to graphic novels is by O'English, Matthews, & Lindsay (2006), all librarians at Washington State University. These authors discuss the myriad ways in which graphic novels are used in academic libraries, ways connected both to the scholarly endeavors of the larger institution and to the recreational needs of students. They go into great detail about the history of the form and the types of graphic novels available. They also examine some of the reasons graphic novels may not be especially prevalent in academic library collections, including difficulties with cataloging and classification. In addition, they advocate for increased internal and external promotion of graphic novel collections, since "library staff may need to be convinced of the appropriateness of a graphic novel collection, while faculty, students and non-academic campus units may need to be made aware of the scholarly, creative, entertainment, and marketing opportunities that can arise" (178).

Collection Analyses

There are several studies in the library literature that examine the presence of marginalized materials in library collections. Rothbauer and McKenchie (1999) attempt to discern the extent to which Canadian public libraries are collecting young adult novels with homosexual themes. They examined the holdings of 40 such libraries, and noted what percentage of a random sample of 40 relevant novels were owned by each. They found that the average number of titles held was 16.2 or 40.4 percent. They conclude that "access to gay and lesbian fiction for young adults ... is somewhat limited and certainly inconsistent even when one accounts for size of library" (36).

Mulcahy (2006) performs a study on science fiction novels in Association of Research Libraries academic libraries. It is after his study that the current one is largely patterned. He attempts to find "evidence for either the canonization or continued marginalization of science fiction" (16). He develops a core list of science fiction novels from titles that have won major awards or have been cited in "best-of" lists. He then looks at what percentages of these books are in the collections of individual academic ARL libraries. He finds the mean percentage of novels owned by the libraries is 50 percent, with a range from 9 percent to 97 percent. Mulcahy finds this result disappointing, and he concludes by saying, "if science fiction continues to be studied in colleges and universities ... ARL libraries will need to consider their collection practices, committing a larger amount of their budgets and perhaps more aggressively pursuing gift collections" (33). He also wonders "how do collections of science fiction compare with collections of other genre fictions ... or with formats such as comic books or graphic novels?" (33).

Methodology

In order to gauge the quality of graphic novel collections in academic libraries, it was decided to examine the holdings of all academic members of the Association of Research Libraries in the U.S.[9] Of the 123 current members of the ARL, 114 are academic libraries and 99 of these are in the U.S. (the rest being in Canada). ARL libraries were chosen because they are large, prestigious libraries whose resources are theoretically deep enough to have potentially constructed significant graphic novel collections in the relatively small amount of time that the form has been considered appropriate for academic libraries. Also, these institutions' focus on research means that they have even greater cause to collect graphic novels, in addition to the curricular and recreational needs present at all academic institutions.

The quality of these libraries graphic novel collections was judged by comparing their holdings with a core list of titles. This core list of graphic novels was constructed largely from titles that had won the two major awards in the comics field, the Eisner Awards[10] and the Harvey Awards.[11] Both awards were begun in 1988, and the core list incorporates winners from that year until 2007. This is a relatively brief time span, but it also roughly parallels the period in which graphic novels started to receive increased attention from mainstream and academic sources. An attempt was made to include all winning titles from the most relevant categories. An exception was made for *Acme Novelty Library 13*, which won a Harvey Award in 2000. This was left off the list, since it is included *in Jimmy Corrigan: The Smartest Kid on Earth*, which won both Eisner and Harvey awards the following year. The author, while constructing this list, defined a graphic novel as simply a work of comic art that is bound as a book.

For the Eisner Awards, the winners of the category "Best Graphic Album" were included for the years 1988 and 1989. After these years, this category was split into "Best Graphic Album: New" (denoting a graphic novel of newly published material) and "Best Graphic Album: Reprint" (denoting a collection of material previously published in comic book format). The winners of both of these categories from 1990–2007 were included. Similarly, for the Harvey Awards, the category "Best Graphic Album" was used for 1988–1990, while

"Best Graphic Album of Original Work" and "Best Graphic Album of Previously Published Work" were used thereafter.

In addition, numerous titles that won mainstream awards were also included. Finally, the list was supplemented with several works that, while they have not won any significant awards, are generally considered to be classics of the form. The final list contained 77 titles. It is hoped that the method used to create the list will result in a varied group of titles that embody the most important and critically acclaimed graphic novels of the last several decades. The full list can be seen in Appendix A.

While the list, as developed, certainly has its idiosyncrasies, it does, at the least, include representatives from most of the different genres and artists that have dominated graphic novels in America during the time period under discussion. Among these idiosyncrasies is the presence of nine Batman titles on the list. This does make the list somewhat unbalanced; however, these titles are good representatives for the "superhero" genre — the medium's dominant type of story, which is otherwise rather sparse on the list.

The collections of the libraries were surveyed to see how many of the titles on the core list they own. This data was primarily collected through the libraries' online public access catalogs, though WorldCat was also occasionally used to supplement them. The catalogs were consulted from March to June 2008. An attempt was made to ensure that a title was counted "owned" as long as any edition or printing of it was found to be present in a library's catalog. Though the focus of this study is libraries' general collections, titles in special collections were counted as owned if they were found in an institution's online catalog.

Certain peculiarities of the comic book publishing industry created some challenges in discovering which titles were owned. Many of the works that won awards have been repackaged in different forms several times, often with different names. For example, 1989's *Blood of Palomar* by Gilbert Hernandez is a collection of material originally published in various issues of the quarterly *Love & Rockets* comic book series. The material in *Blood of Palomar* was also later collected in 2003's *Palomar* and 2007's *Human Diastrophism*. In instances such as this, a title was counted as "owned" regardless of the format the work was in or the title it was under. Other titles on the list, such as *The New American Splendor Anthology,* basically function as a "best of" for a certain artist, and the work therein has often been anthologized several times. In these instances, the presence of any comparable book in the catalog meant that the title was counted as "owned."

Results

The aim of this study was to determine the quality of the holdings of graphic novels in the collections of members of the Association of Research Libraries. In general, the results indicated that these holdings were not particularly strong. The full results are available in Appendix B and Appendix C. The mean number of titles from the core list held by the libraries examined was 25.93, which is 34 percent of the total number of titles. The median was 23, or 30 percent. There was a wide range in the numbers of titles held, with the top institution (Michigan State University) owning 69 (90 percent) and the bottom institution (Howard University) owning none. Only five institutions owned more than 70 percent of the list, while four owned less than 10 percent. Figure 29.1 shows the general distribution of titles among the libraries. As can be seen, the libraries' holdings do not follow a normal distribution, but instead they skew heavily to the left.

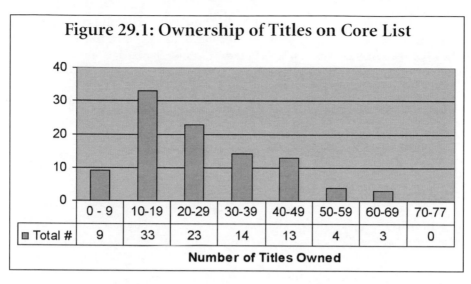

Figure 29.1: Ownership of Titles on Core List

■ Total #	0 - 9	10-19	20-29	30-39	40-49	50-59	60-69	70-77
	9	33	23	14	13	4	3	0

Number of Titles Owned

In terms of the ownership numbers for graphic novels, the mean was 33.34 (34 percent). The median was 25 (25 percent). There was a wide range here as well, with the two titles tied at the top (*Maus* and *Maus II*) held in 98 libraries (or 99 percent of the total), and the bottom title (*Batman and Superman Adventures: World's Finest*) held in only 1 library (1 percent of the total.). However, it is worth nothing that there was a particularly steep drop-off after the top four titles, all of which were held in more than 90 percent of libraries. After this, the two titles tied for number five fall to 76 percent. Figure 29.2 displays the general distribution of the titles at the libraries. Most of the titles are in the bottom half of the chart. In fact, over 44 percent of titles were found in nineteen or less libraries (approximately the bottom fifth of the data set).

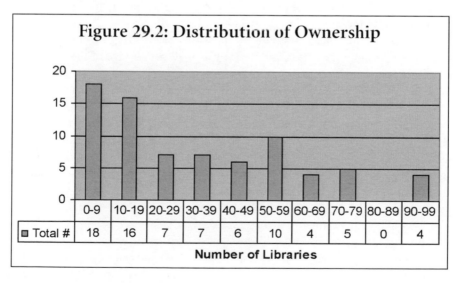

Figure 29.2: Distribution of Ownership

■ Total #	0-9	10-19	20-29	30-39	40-49	50-59	60-69	70-79	80-89	90-99
	18	16	7	7	6	10	4	5	0	4

Number of Libraries

Institutional Characteristics

Certain characteristics of institutions with higher quality graphic collections become apparent upon examination of the data collected for this study. In general, it seems that, as might be expected, the libraries with the highest number of graphic novels in their hold-ings are generally those with the largest overall collections according to ARL statistics.[12] Of the top 10 libraries in these results, six of them (Illinois, Harvard, Columbia, Wisconsin, Michigan, and Yale) are among the top ten libraries studied in terms of total volumes held. The top two libraries, Michigan State and Ohio State, are only medium-sized in terms of holdings, but, as previously noted, they both have extremely large special collections related to comics. Presumably this has led them to invest heavily in graphic novels in their general collections in order to support these special collections.

At the same time, collection size cannot entirely explain the quality of an institution's graphic novel holdings. The libraries with the five smallest total collections according to the ARL statistics (Colorado State, Louisville, SUNY-Albany, George Washington, and Houston) all, with the exception of SUNY-Albany, had graphic novel holdings well above the median, with the University of Houston notably so. It would seem that those institutions that came out on the bottom of this study did so for reasons not entirely related to collection size or resources available (e.g. an institutional focus on science and technology, or faculty indifference to the medium).

Graphic Novel Characteristics

Next, the author examined what characteristics might make a title more or less likely to be owned by an academic library. This examination focused on two major characteristics: type of publisher and genre. A large percentage of graphic novels are published by specialty comic publishers. The two largest of these are Marvel and DC (often times referred to as "the big two"), who have dominated the industry for decades and who have largely focused on publishing superhero stories. In addition, there are a host of smaller, independent comic publishers, often devoted to publishing more experimental or literary stories. The foremost among these include Fantagraphics, Dark Horse, and Drawn & Quarterly. In recent years, mainstream publishing houses have also begun to publish graphic novels in greater numbers, though they still produce only a small percentage of the total number of titles released each year.

The make-up of the core list constructed for this study does not match particularly well with that of the industry as a whole. As can be seen in Figure 29.3, almost half of the titles on the list were put out by independent comics publishers. This makes some sense, considering that the types of stories that these companies publish are more likely to be sophisticated enough to win major awards. The same is true for the high (relative to the small number of tiles they produce) number of titles put out by mainstream publishers.

However, it is when examining how these three different types of publishers fared in the final results of this study that the real discrepancies between the market and academic library collecting policies show up. Figure 29.4 shows the average percentage of ownership for works on the list, sorted by these different types of publishers. As figure 29.4 makes immediately apparent, mainstream publishers have an average rate of ownership (62.65 percent) that is considerably higher than those of comics specialty publishers. In fact, Pan-theon, the mainstream publisher whose graphic novel line is most visible, has an average ownership rate of 74.86 percent. The rates are both significantly higher than the mean ownership rate for this study, 34 percent. Conversely, the two major comic book publish-ers have an average rate of only 23.24 percent, while the average for independent publish-

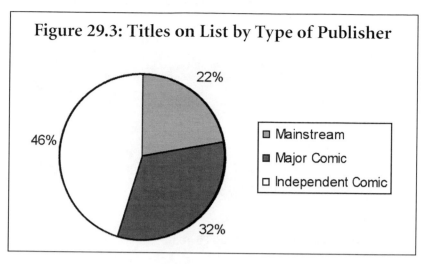

Figure 29.3: Titles on List by Type of Publisher

ers is not much higher at 26.97 percent. Undoubtedly this is partially due to the higher marketing budgets and visibility being produced by mainstream publishers affords the relevant titles. In addition, the work put out by these publishers may be more in sync with these libraries' collecting goals. However, while Marvel and DC focus largely on publishing superhero stories, independent publishers also put out a substantial body of comics with literary value. The fact that these publishers are extremely small, that their work may not be available via the regular suppliers libraries use for their acquisitions, and that their titles can sometimes go out of print quickly may explain why their ownership average is so low.

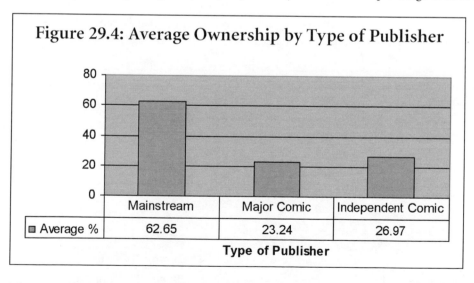

Figure 29.4: Average Ownership by Type of Publisher

The researcher also wished to investigate whether or not genre had an effect on ownership rates. The titles on the list were divided into six different types of works: Superhero, Memoirs, History/War, Genre Fiction (e.g. crime, fantasy, etc.), General Fiction, and Other. The distribution of these genres in the core list genres can be seen in Figure 29.5. While works of the superhero genre and of genre fiction make up a respectable 21 percent and 19 percent, respectively, much of the list consists of more "serious" genres, such as memoirs, history, and "literary" fiction.

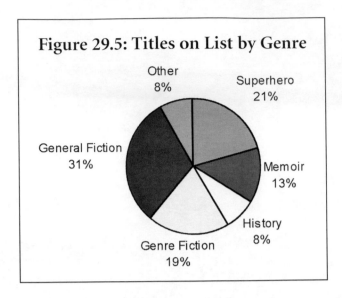

Figure 29.5: Titles on List by Genre

It was expected that the genres that ARL members might normally collect would have higher ownership percentages, and an examination of the data bore this out. As can be seen in Figure 29.6, both the memoir and history categories had average ownership rates significantly higher than the mean for the study as a whole, at 59.70 percent and 40.67 percent, respectively. General Fiction and Other had ownership rates very close to the mean at 34.58 and 34.5 percent, respectively. Genre Fiction was several points below the mean at 28.8 percent, while Superhero was less than half the mean at 17.38 percent. It is particularly notable that the Superhero category is so low, since that is generally considered to be the dominant genre of the comics medium, at least in the U.S.

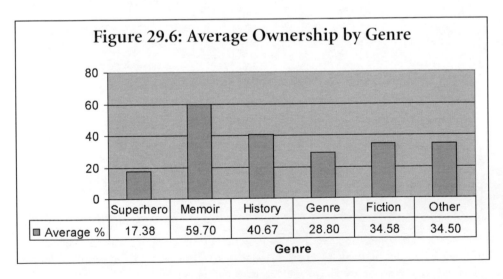

Figure 29.6: Average Ownership by Genre

A general picture of what types of graphic novels are being collected by academic libraries can be gleaned from the above data. Librarians are selecting works from mainstream publishers over those from comics specialty publishers, and they are selecting memoir and history titles over titles relating to other genres. While collection development decisions must always place greater emphases on certain aspects of a collection over others, it is worth taking notice of these emphases to see what their underlying causes might be.

Conclusion and Suggestions for Further Research

In general, while the results of this study indicate that the ARL libraries do not yet have strong collections of even prize-winning graphic novels, this is perhaps not extraordinarily surprising considering the relatively new status of graphic novels as an acceptable form in academia. If libraries want to be able to support the needs of their students, faculty, and staff, they must attempt to collect newly prominent forms such as graphic novels at an acceptable level.

Of particular note are this study's findings regarding the types of graphic novels collected by ARL members. Libraries have a particular deficit in terms of collecting both comics not put out by mainstream publishers and those focusing on storylines not relating to mainstream genres. Librarians should pay special attention to the low ownership rates for independent comics publishers, since these publishers are producing serious works in fields such as fiction, memoir, and history. While these failures may simply be a reflection of these libraries' selection policies, it may also be a failure to satisfactorily explore different collection development avenues.

In a future study, it would be worth examining the reasons behind the relatively poor results of some of the libraries. A number of suppositions as to these reasons seem likely to have some validity. Presumably some of these libraries are not facing an especially high demand for graphic novels, especially those with a focus on science and technology. Other librarians may still harbor some prejudices against the form, or they may feel that they do not have adequate collection development tools to make adequate selection choices. A survey of academic librarians' perceptions and knowledge of the format would be invaluable while attempting to see to what extent these suppositions are true.

In addition, such a survey could also look into the reasons why librarians responsible for collection development make their graphic novel selection decisions. Are they attempting to provide students with appealing leisure reading material? Are they supporting a curriculum where graphic novels are often included on reading lists? Are they supporting faculty members who are doing research related to the form? Do they simply have a personal affinity for them? Answers to these questions could provide librarians with knowledge of where their weaknesses lie, and their strengths.

It seems that the importance of the graphic novel format will only continue to grow rapidly for the foreseeable future, and so the need to evaluate and enhance these collections will only become more important. To those who might say that comics are not suitable materials for an academic library collection, it can be said that "comics are not a mindless but a mindful form of escapism that uses a unique kind of language — 'graphic language' — to invite us into different worlds in order to help us better understand our own" (Versaci, 2007: 6). Academic libraries should embrace this new language and build the collections that will be needed to allow both faculty and students to master it.

Appendix A

Core List of Graphic Novels

Title	Author(s)	Year	Award
A Contract with God and Other Tenement Stories	Will Eisner	1978	
Batman: the Dark Knight Returns	Frank Miller & Klaus Janson	1987	
Watchmen	Alan Moore & Dave Gibbons	1988	Hugo, Eisner, Harvey
Batman: the Killing Joke	Alan Moore & Brian Bolland	1989	Eisner, Harvey
Blood of Palomar	Gilbert Hernandez	1989	
The Death of Speedy	Jaime Hernandez	1989	
Ed The Happy Clown	Chester Brown	1990	Harvey
Sandman: Dream County	Neil Gaiman et al.	1991	World Fantasy Award
Elektra Lives Again	Frank Miller & Lynn Varley	1991	Eisner
Sandman: the Doll's House	Neil Gaiman et al.	1991	Eisner
Why I Hate Saturn	Kyle Baker	1991	Harvey
Warts and All	Drew Friedman	1991	Harvey
The New American Splendor Anthology	Harvey Pekar et al.	1991	Booklist
Maus	Art Spiegelman	1992	Pulitzer
Maus II	Art Spiegelman	1992	Eisner, Harvey
To the Heart of the Storm	Will Eisner	1992	Eisner, Harvey
The Playboy	Chester Brown	1992	
Signal to Noise	Neil Gaiman & Dave McKean Dave McKean	1993	Eisner
Sin City (The Hard Goodbye)	Frank Miller	1993	Eisner
Fairy Tales of Oscar Wilde	P. Craig Russell	1993	Harvey
Hey Look!	Harvey Kurtzman	1993	Harvey
A Small Killing	Alan Moore & Oscar Zarate	1994	Eisner
Cerebus: Flight	Davis Sim and Gerhard	1994	Eisner
Understanding Comics	Scott McLoud	1994	Harvey
Bone: Out From Boneville	Jeff Smith	1994	Harvey
Paul Auster's City of Glass	Paul Karasik & David Mazzucchelli	1994	
Fairy Tales of Oscar Wilde, Vol. 2	P. Craig Russell	1995	Eisner
Hellboy: Seeds of Destruction	Mike Mignola	1995	Eisner
Our Cancer Year	Harvey Pekar et al	1995	Harvey
Marvels	Kurt Busiek & Alex Ross	1995	Harvey
Stuck Rubber Baby	Howard Cruise	1996	Eisner, Harvey
The Tale of One Bad Rat	Bryan Talbot	1996	Eisner
Hellboy: the Wolves of St. August	Mike Mignola	1996	Harvey
Fax From Sarajevo	Joe Kubert	1997	Eisner, Harvey
Stray Bullets: Innocence of Nihilism	Dave Lapham	1997	Eisner
Astro City: Life in the Big City	Kurt Busiek & Brent Anderson	1997	Harvey
The R. Crumb Coffee Table Art Book	R. Crumb	1997	
Ghost World	Daniel Clowes	1998	
Batman and Superman Adventures. World's Finest	Paul Dini, Joe Staton & Terry Beatty	1998	Eisner
Sin City: That Yellow Bastard	Frank Miller	1998	Eisner
Sin City: Family Values	Frank Miller	1998	Harvey

Title	Author(s)	Year	Award
Batman: Black and White	Various	1998	Harvey
Cages	Dave McKean	1999	Harvey
Superman: Peace on Earth	Paul Dini & Alex Ross	1999	Eisner
Batman: The Long Halloween	Jeph Loeb & Time Sale	1999	Eisner
You Are Here	Kyle Baker	1999	Harvey
Ethel & Ernest	Raymond Briggs	1999	
The Fatal Bullet	Rick Geary	1999	
The Jew of New York	Ben Katchor	1999	
From Hell	Alan Moore & Eddie Campbell	2000	Eisner, Harvey
Batman: War On Crime	Paul Dini & Alex Ross	2000	Harvey
Alec: The King Canute Crowd	Eddie Campbell	2000	
Safe Area Gorazde	Joe Sacco	2001	Eisner
Jimmy Corrigan: The Smartest Kid on Earth	Chris Ware	2001	Eisner, Harvey
Last Day in Vietnam	Will Eisner	2001	Harvey
Palestine	Joe Sacco	2001	
The Golem's Mighty Swing	James Sturm	2002	Harvey
The Name of the Game	Will Eisner	2002	Eisner
Batman: Dark Victory	Jeph Loeb & Time Sale	2002	Eisner
Lone Wolf and Cub	Kazuo Koike & Goseki Kojima	2002	Harvey
One! Hundred! Demons!	Lynda Barry	2003	Eisner
Batman Black & White vol 2.	Various	2003	Eisner
The Cartoon History of the Universe: From the Rise of Arabia to the Renaissance	Larry Gonick	2003	Harvey
Twentieth Century Eightball	Daniel Clowes	2003	Harvey
Persepolis	Marjane Satrapi	2003	
Blankets	Craig Thompson	2004	Eisner, Harvey
Batman Adventures: Dangerous Dames and Demons	Paul Dini et al	2004	Eisner
Louis Riel	Chester Brown	2004	Harvey
The Originals	Dave Gibbons	2005	Eisner
Blacksad 2	Juanjo Guarnido & Juan Diaz Canales	2005	Harvey
American Born Chinese	Gene Luen Yang	2006	Michael L. Printz, Eisner
Tricked	Alex Robinson	2006	Harvey
Black Hole	Charles Burns	2006	Eisner, Harvey
Top 10: The Forty-Niners	Alan Moore and Gene Ha	2006	Eisner
DC: The New Frontier	Darwyn Cooke	2007	Eisner, Harvey
Pride of Baghdad	Brian K. Vaughn & Niko Henrichon	2007	Harvey
Fun Home	Alison Bechdel	2007	Eisner

Appendix B

American ARL Academic Libraries Ranked by Holdings of Core List of Graphic Novels

Rank	School	Number of Titles	Percentage of Titles
1	Michigan State University	69	90%
2	Ohio State University	68	88%

Rank	School	Number of Titles	Percentage of Titles
3	University of Illinois— Urbana-Champaign	64	83%
4	Harvard University	59	77%
5	Columbia University	54	70%
6	University of Wisconsin — Madison	51	66%
7	Yale University	50	65%
8	University of Michigan	49	64%
9	Pennsylvania State University	47	61%
	Texas A&M University	47	61%
11	University of Iowa	45	58%
	University of North Carolina — Chapel Hill	45	58%
13	University of Washington	44	57%
14	University of Virginia	43	56%
15	Indiana University — Bloomington	42	55%
	Massachusetts Institute of Technology	42	55%
	University of Missouri — Columbia	42	55%
	University of Pittsburgh	42	55%
19	University of California — Berkeley	41	53%
20	University of Texas	40	52%
21	University of Cincinnati	39	51%
22	University of California — Los Angeles	38	49%
	University of Nebraska — Lincoln	38	49%
24	Dartmouth University	36	47%
	New York University	36	47%
26	University of California — Davis	35	45%
27	University of Houston	34	44%
	University of Pennsylvania	34	44%
29	University of Utah	33	43%
30	University of Delaware	32	42%
	Washington State University	32	42%
32	Duke University	31	40%
	University of Florida	31	40%
34	University of Minnesota	30	39%
35	Cornell University	29	38%
36	University of California — Riverside	28	36%
	University of Louisville	28	36%
38	University of Chicago	27	35%
	Colorado State University	27	35%
	Florida State University	27	35%
	George Washington University	27	35%
42	University of California — San Diego	26	34%
	University of Georgia	26	34%
	North Carolina State University	26	34%
	Northwestern University	26	34%
46	University of Massachusetts— Amherst	25	32%
	Rutgers University	25	32%
48	Arizona State University	24	31%
	University of South Carolina	24	31%
50	University of Ohio	23	30%
51	Iowa State University	22	29%
	Notre Dame University	22	29%
	Southern Illinois University — Carbondale	22	29%
	Temple University	22	29%
55	University of California — Irvine	21	27%
56	University of Alabama	20	26%
	Emory University	20	26%
58	University of California — Santa Barbara	19	25%
59	Georgetown University	18	23%
	Louisiana State University	18	23%
	Texas Tech University	18	23%

Rank	School	Number of Titles	Percentage of Titles
62	Brigham Young University	17	22%
	University of Kentucky	17	22%
	Princeton University	17	22%
	University of Southern California	17	22%
	Washington University in St. Louis	17	22%
67	Boston College	16	21%
	University at Buffalo—SUNY	16	21%
	University of Miami	16	21%
	Virginia Tech	16	21%
71	University of Colorado—Boulder	15	19%
	Stony Brook University—SUNY	15	19%
	University of Tennessee—Knoxville	15	19%
74	University of Connecticut	14	18%
	University of Oregon	14	18%
	Rochester University	14	18%
	Vanderbilt University	14	18%
78	University of Arizona	13	17%
	Brown University	13	17%
	Johns Hopkins University	13	17%
	University of Kansas	13	17%
	Rice University	13	17%
83	Auburn University	12	16%
	University of Hawaii—Manoa	12	16%
	Syracuse University	12	16%
	Wayne State University	12	16%
87	Kent State University	11	14%
	University of New Mexico	11	14%
	Oklahoma State University	11	14%
90	Case Western Reserve University	10	13%
91	University at Albany—SUNY	9	12%
	University of Illinois—Chicago	9	12%
	University of Maryland	9	12%
94	University of Oklahoma	8	10%
95	Boston University	7	9%
	Purdue University	7	9%
97	Tulane University	6	8%
98	Georgia Tech	3	4%
99	Howard University	0	0%

Appendix C

Core List of Graphic Novels Ranked by Holdings in American ARL Academic Libraries

Rank	Title	Number of Libraries	Percentage of Libraries
1	*Maus*	98	99%
	Maus II	98	99%
3	*Persepolis*	94	95%
4	*Understanding Comics*	93	94%
5	*Watchmen*	75	76%
	Palestine	75	76%
7	*American Born Chinese*	73	74%
	Fun Home	73	74%
9	*Jimmy Corrigan: The Smartest Kid on Earth*	72	73%
10	*The R. Crumb Coffee Table Art Book*	69	70%
11	*Blankets*	65	66%
12	*American Splendor*	64	65%
13	*Safe Area Gorazde*	62	63%

Rank	Title	Number of Libraries	Percentage of Libraries
14	*A Contract with God*	58	59%
	Ghost World	58	59%
16	*Batman: the Dark Knight Returns*	57	58%
	The Jew of New York	57	58%
18	*The Death of Speedy*	56	57%
	Sandman: the Doll's House	56	57%
20	*Blood of Palomar*	55	56%
21	*One! Hundred! Demons!*	54	55%
22	*Sandman: Dream County*	52	53%
23	*Ethel & Ernest*	50	51%
24	*Black Hole*	49	49%
25	*Stuck Rubber Baby*	48	48%
26	*Bone: Out From Boneville*	43	43%
	Louis Riel	43	43%
28	*From Hell*	42	42%
29	*Sin City*	41	41%
30	*Our Cancer Year*	36	36%
	Pride of Baghdad	36	36%
32	*City of Glass*	35	35%
33	*The Golem's Mighty Swing*	32	32%
	The Cartoon History of the Universe: From the Rise of Arabia to the Renaissance	32	32%
35	*The Tale of One Bad Rat*	31	31%
36	*Sin City: That Yellow Bastard*	30	30%
37	*Sin City: Family Values*	26	26%
	Twentieth Century Eightball	26	26%
39	*Marvels*	25	25%
40	*Last Day in Vietnam*	24	24%
41	*To the Heart of the Storm*	22	22%
42	*Astro City: Life in the Big City*	21	21%
	Lone Wolf and Cub	21	21%
44	*Fax from Sarajevo*	19	19%
	DC: The New Frontier	19	19%
46	*Fairy Tales of Oscar Wilde*	17	17%
	Hellboy: Seeds of Destruction	17	17%
	Cages	17	17%
	Tricked	17	17%
50	*Batman: the Killing Joke*	16	16%
	Fairy Tales of Oscar Wilde, Vol. 2	16	16%
52	*The Name of the Game*	15	15%
	Top 10: The Forty-Niners	15	15%
54	*Why I Hate Saturn*	14	14%
55	*The Originals*	13	13%
56	*The Playboy*	12	12%
57	*Stray Bullets: Innocence of Nihilism*	11	11%
	Batman: The Long Halloween	11	11%
	The Fatal Bullet	11	11%
60	*Hellboy: the Wolves of St. August*	9	9%
	Batman: Dark Victory	9	9%
62	*Signal to Noise*	8	8%
	Cerebus: Flight	8	8%
64	*A Small Killing*	7	7%
	Superman: Peace on Earth	7	7%
66	*Ed the Happy Clown*	6	6%
	Elektra Lives Again	6	6%
	Warts and All	6	6%
	You Are Here	6	6%
	Blacksad 2: Arctic Nation	6	6%
71	*Batman: Black and White*	5	5%

Rank	Title	Number of Libraries	Percentage of Libraries
72	*Hey Look!*	4	4%
	Batman: War On Crime	4	4%
	Batman Black & White Vol. 2	4	4%
75	*Alec: The King Canute Crowd*	2	2%
	Batman Adventures: Dangerous Dames and Demons	2	2%
77	*Batman and Superman Adventures: World's Finest*	1	1%

Endnotes

1. See "The Pulitzer Prizes for 1992" at http://www.pulitzer.org/cgi-bin/year.pl?year=1992 for a full list of winners from that year.
2. Watchmen's entry is available at http://www.time.com/time/2005/100books/0,24459,watchmen,00.html.
3. Figures from "ICv2 — Graphic Novel Sales Up in 2008" at http://www.icv2.com/articles/news/15117.html.
4. From http://www.blackwellpublishing.com/aims.asp?ref=0022–3840&site=1.
5. More information available at http://www.ijoca.com/.
6. *ImageText* is an open access journal; all content is available at http://www.english.ufl.edu/imagetext/.
7. The Forum's website is at http://www.internationalcomicartsforum.org/.
8. See http://www.english.ufl.edu/comics/conference.shtml for more information.
9. A full list of ARL member libraries is available at http://www.arl.org/arl/membership/members.shtml.
10. The Eisner Awards' website is available at http://www.comic-con.org/cci/cci_eisners_main.shtml.
11. The Harvey Awards' website is available at http://www.harveyawards.org/.
12. ARL statistics can be viewed at http://www.arl.org/stats/annualsurveys/arlstats/index.shtml. Statistics used here are for 2007–08, the last years for which they were available.

References

Beaty, Bart. 2004. "Review Essay: Assessing Contemporary Comics Scholarship." *Canadian Journal of Communication* 29 (3): 403–409.

Behler, Anne. 2006. "Getting Started with Graphic Novels: A Guide for the Beginner." *Reference & User Services Quarterly* 46 (2): 16–21.

Bussert, Leslie. 2005. "Comic Books and Graphic Novels: Digital Resources for an Evolving Form of Art and Literature." *College & Research Libraries News* 66 (2): 103–113.

Ellis, Allen, and Doug Highsmith. 2000. "About Face: Comic Books in Library Literature." *Serials Review* 26 (2): 21–43.

Highsmith, Doug. 1993. "Developing a 'Focused' Comic Book Collection in an Academic Library." In *Popular Culture and Acquisitions,* Allen Ellis ed. New York: Haworth.

Lavin, Michael R. 1998. "Comic Books and Graphic Novels for Libraries: What to Buy." *Serials Review* 24 (2): 31–45.

Matz, Chris. 2004. "Collecting Comic Books at the University of Memphis: A Beginning." In *Charleston Conference Proceedings 2003,* Katina Strauch, Rosann Bazirjian & Vicky Speck eds Westport, CT: Libraries Unlimited.

Matz, Chris. 2004. "Collecting Comic Books for an Academic Library." *Collection Building* 23 (2): 96–99.

Mulcahy, Kevin P. 2006. "Science Fiction Collections in ARL Academic Libraries." *College & Research Libraries* 67 (1): 15–34.

O'English, Lorena, J. Gregory Matthews, and Elizabeth Blakesley Lindsay. 2006. "Graphic Novels in Academic Libraries: From Maus to Manga and Beyond." *The Journal of Academic Librarianship* 32 (2): 173–182.

Rothbauer, Paulette M., and Lynne E. F. McKechnie. 1999. "Gay and Lesbian Fiction for Young Adults: A Survey of Holdings in Canadian Public Libraries." *Collection Building* 18 (1): 32–39.

Savage, William W. 1993. "Research and Comic Books: A Historian's Perspective." *Popular Culture in Libraries* 1 (1): 85–90.

Scott, Randall W. 1984. "The Comics Alternative." *Collection Building* 6 (2): 23–25.

_____. 1993. "Comics and Libraries and the Scholarly World." *Popular Culture in Libraries* 1 (1): 81–84.

_____. 1998. "A Practicing Comic-book Librarian Surveys His Collection and His Craft." *Serials Review* 24 (1): 49–56.

Serchay, David S. 1998. "Comic Research Libraries." *Serials Review* 24 (1): 37–48.

Versaci, Rocco. 2007. *This Book Contains Graphic Language: Comics as Literature.* New York: Continuum.

Weiner, Robert G. 2008. "Graphic Novels in Libraries: One Library's Solution to the Cataloging Problem." *Texas Library Journal* 84 (1): 8–14.

Afterword

STEPHEN WEINER

Public Libraries, Graphic Novels and Me

As a young librarian I was very concerned with literacy, particularly literacy among boys. Books, after all, had saved my life on more than one occasion. So I set out to collect and promote books appealing to teenage boys. I visited the four local schools within walking distance from the branch library where I worked, and book talked to classes. I book talked *Interstellar Pig* by William Sleator and *Scorpions* by Walter Dean Myers. I book talked *The Hardy Boys* books and *Something Upstairs* by Avi. Most of the time I was met with blank faces. One day I book talked *Tin Tin* by Herge and got no response. But after school that day a boy came by to check the book out. I had stumbled onto the allure of comics.

Not that I should have been surprised. I'd learned during my teenage years that people sat up straighter and paid more attention when I argued that comic books were better and more literate than they were reputed to be. I got as much mileage out of this idea as I could; in high school I wrote my thesis on "comic books as literature" and taught a course to my peers on the history of American comics. As an undergraduate my most successful short story was about a young man selling his comic book collection. In graduate school I wrote papers defending the place of Art Spiegelman's *Maus* in the public library.

There was no money in the library budget for comics, so I donated a few boxes of my own. My boss, a newly minted librarian, was skeptical. My co-worker was aghast. We sent the comics to the main branch to be cataloged, and we hoped they would be back sometime during the next week. We waited. After some weeks I called the cataloging office. The books were still in a box, as the department head refused to catalog them. I called the Library Director who invited me up to his office, and sat me in a comfortable chair. "Comic books are outside our collection development policy," he told me.

I gave him my reasons for keeping them.

He gave me his.

The conversation ended as he handed the box of comics back to me. I went back to my branch, and complained to my supervisor. He went up to the main library and spoke to the big boss, and my comics were cataloged and put out for kids to take out.

The comics were a hit. I had boys coming into the library after school looking for them. Some of them got cards just to read comics, and others paid overdue fines. It became clear that soon we'd run out of new comics. I had to get more, but none of the book vendors we used carried them. I called the local comic book specialty shop, *The Million Year Picnic*.

The owner invited me over and recommended books with public library appeal. We were onto something!

We started a club for trading comics. The first meeting went on for 3 hours. This led to the idea of sponsoring more programs around comic books. I invited a friend in who could draw superheroes. The kids attending the program were disappointed. "I thought he was a *real* comic book artist," one of them complained.

I called *The Million Year Picnic* again and they arranged for a cartoonist to call me. "My name is Scott McCloud," the cartoonist told me. McCloud came in and did a program on comics which was very well attended. Afterwards, we talked. McCloud was skeptical that libraries should collect comics. "The same argument can be made for collecting *Playboy*," he said.

There were several problems with collecting graphic novels. There was an obvious stigma against them. They weren't reviewed in library literature, and book jobbers didn't carry them. When they were available they were hard to catalog. I might have been deterred, but the circulation numbers were staggering. People were walking in to the library from surrounding towns because they'd heard of the comic book collection, and other libraries were requesting them from our branch for their patrons to read. Scott McCloud and I met several times. Fairly quickly, he was won over to the value of libraries collecting graphic novels. Not only by our discussions, but because he was a library user and saw patrons checking them out.

"You have to tell people about this," he said.

I tried to. My first article appeared in *Voice of Youth Advocates* in December 1992. I thought I'd found a forum for bringing the virtues of comics to librarians. But I was wrong; *VOYA* had a regular reviewer who wanted the job. I sent out query letters to over a dozen library publications, offering to review graphic novels for them, but every publication I had approached declined my offer.

If I couldn't review for magazines, I'd write a book. Highsmith, the publisher of my guide, *Bring an Author to Your Library*, wanted a second book. I proposed one on comics. Highsmith was enthusiastic and told me a contract would be forthcoming. A few weeks later, I opened the envelope from Highsmith with great excitement. Instead of a book contract I had received a thoughtful rejection letter; the editors had consulted with experts in the library field, and had concluded that, although graphic novels added value to library collections, the bias against them was so great that it could not be overcome.

I was against the wall. Maybe comic book publishers would be interested. They had a vested interest in placing graphic novels in library collections. I revamped my book proposal, and sent it out to comic book publishers. A small press, NBM, commissioned me to do a promotional insert for the 1994 edition of *Books in Print*. Big companies such as Marvel and DC did not return my query letters. In 1993, Kitchen Sink Press published Scott McCloud's seminal book, *Understanding Comics*. I called Kitchen Sink repeatedly. Finally, with McCloud's urgings, a meeting was arranged. The outcome of the meeting was this— Kitchen Sink would publish a special catalog for librarians, and I would write the copy. Although I wrote the copy and was paid, the catalog was never produced. Meanwhile, McCloud's book, *Understanding Comics*, broke out of the comics world into the larger world of trade publishing and landed in library collections. The success of that book convinced Kitchen Sink to try a follow up, and my graphic novel guide, *100 Graphic Novels for Public Libraries*, was released in Winter, 1996. It included a Foreword by Neil Gaiman and an interview with Scott McCloud. Although the book was purchased primarily by librarians frequenting comic book shops, the word about graphic novels was beginning to get out.

I still hoped to appeal to the library field directly, and offered to review graphic novels for *Library Journal*. The journal deliberated for months, and then sent me some review copies. I reviewed for them from 1997–2002. In 2001, NBM published the follow up book on graphic novels, *The 101 Best Graphic Novels*. By this time graphic novels were becoming accepted in libraries and many library publications, notably *VOYA* and *Booklist*, regularly included them in their reviewing columns. Programs on graphic novels were beginning to pop up at state library conferences.

Also, in 2001, YALSA, the Young Adult division of the American Library Association, began planning a day long national conference on graphic novels to be held in 2002, complete with cartoonists and librarians as presenters. Although I wasn't a young adult librarian, I was asked to help arrange the programming and present at the conference. Many cartoonists' names were bandied about as potential speakers, and after much debate, Neil Gaiman, Art Spiegelman, Colleen Doran and Jeff Smith were identified as the premier candidates. My assignment was to bring Jeff Smith to the national YALSA conference.

That was easily said but difficult to do. Gaiman, Spiegelman, and Doran all had the backing of a publisher to pay their way and help them prepare. Jeff Smith was one of several self-published cartoonists, who set up small publishing houses to produce their own work. Because YALSA wasn't paying Smith's expenses, he and I discussed the merits and the costs of attending the conference. At length. What began as a simple programming assignment evolved into a year long discussion between Jeff Smith and me; he educated me on the various aspects of cartooning and I recommended ways to promote his work in the library field. The Graphic Novel conference was a success, as eager librarians listened to Smith, Gaiman, Doran, and Spiegelman on the virtues of bringing comics to libraries, and librarians offered practical advice on how to manage and promote the collections. 2002 was a big year for comics in other ways as well. That year the Public Library Association also held a major conference on graphic novels. The first *Spider-Man* movie was released and became a mega-hit, and Manga began its trek into bookstores and libraries, where girls who might never venture into a comic book specialty shop could read them. Chris Ware's ground-breaking graphic novel, *Jimmy Corrigan: The Smartest Kid on Earth*, was awarded the prestigious Guardian "first novel" prize. Graphic novels were making noises in many different places.

Nowhere was it more noticeable than in public libraries. Graphic novels were now acknowledged as one of the fastest growing areas of library collection development. Review columns focusing on them appeared in every major library collection development publication, helping librarians build credible collections; conferences were sponsored at the state and national levels, and books on the subject were being published. The long wait was over; graphic novels had arrived.

Since 2002, several graphic novel handbooks have been published, giving librarians more tools in collecting and promoting graphic novel library collections. I'm delighted to say the book that you hold in your hands is unique in that it covers such a wide array of topics related to graphic novel collecting and use. Use this book; go forth and strengthen your library!

About the Contributors

Ruth Boyer was born in Shanghai, China. She developed a love of reading even as she was learning the English language. She received her BA in history from UCLA and her MLIS at San Jose State University. Her husband introduced her to world of American comics and she's been a fan ever since.

Rachel Collins is a recent MLIS graduate from the University of Alberta. Shortly after finishing her program she moved to Toronto and continues to explore the collection practices of comics from her new city surrounded by her husband, cat, and shelves full of comics.

Charlotte Cubbage is the humanities coordinator and subject specialist for English, comparative literatures, and the performing arts at Northwestern University Library, Evanston, Illinois. She provides research assistance to faculty and students, and offers instruction in research techniques. She also serves as a fellow for Northwestern's Fine and Performing Arts Residential College and is an adjunct professor in the Department of English.

Anne-Marie Davis is the anthropology librarian and collection development coordinator for the Odegaard Undergraduate Library at the University of Washington. She received her MLIS from the University of Washington in 2001.

Gwen Evans is an assistant professor and coordinator of library information and emerging technologies at the University Libraries, Bowling Green State University, and the library instruction liaison to the School of Art. She has a MS from the University of Illinois Graduate School of Library and Information Science and an MA in cultural anthropology from the University of Chicago.

William T. Fee has been with the State Library of Pennsylvania for 15 years. During this time he founded the State Library's Digitization program, and was the first library technician promoted to librarian without a degree in several decades, though he did finally earn an MLIS. He recently published, in *Serials Review* (vol. 34, no. 3, Sept. 2008), the first practical article on the art of comic book cataloging since Randall Scott's seminal volume *Comics Librarianship*. He is now the leading member on the library's team on Resource Description and Access (RDA), which they are beta-testing.

Elizabeth Figa is an associate professor in the College of Information Department of Library and Information Sciences at the University of North Texas. Her PhD is from the University of Illinois at Urbana-Champaign. A reader and lover of Sunday comics and comic books since her childhood, she now teaches the popular master's course, Graphic Novels and Comics, to hundreds of library and information sciences students each year.

Karen Gavigan, a former media specialist, is the director of the Teaching Resources Center at the University of North Carolina at Greensboro. She is a PhD candidate in curriculum and instruction with a concentration in teacher education and development. She is currently conducting research examining the ways in which male adolescents respond to graphic novels.

Francisca Goldsmith has been working with graphic novels and comics in libraries for more than 20 years. She regularly reviews them for a variety of professional journals and is the author of *The Readers' Advisory Guide to Graphic Novels* (ALA Editions, 2009) and other publications on the subject of graphic novels and libraries.

Liorah Anne Golomb is an assistant professor and humanities librarian at University of Oklahoma. She holds advanced degrees from Washington University in St. Louis, the University of Toronto, and Pratt Institute, and has written about the work of author Will Self and playwrights Sam Shepard, David Hare, and Peter Barnes. She is constantly amazed at the cynical brilliance of *Peanuts*.

Richard Graham is an assistant professor at the University of Nebraska–Lincoln. In addition to overseeing a growing comics collection, he is in charge of the microforms area. In his spare time, he rescues feral cats and contemplates educational philosophy.

Heidi K. Hammond received her PhD in education from the University of Minnesota. She has taught graduate courses in children's and young adult literature and has been a K–12 media specialist as well as a language arts teacher. Currently she is the media specialist of a suburban high school near St. Paul, Minnesota.

Amy Hartman is currently a humanities librarian at the Toledo–Lucas County Public Library in Ohio. She most recently presented "Et tu, Ironman? The latest assassination of feminist hope: Pepper Potts as the Marvel idealized woman" at Bowling Green State University's 2008 Comics in Popular Culture conference.

David Hopkins is associate professor of American studies at Tenri University in Nara, Japan. His main interests are popular music, movies, comics, and comparative study of the popular cultures of Japan and the United States.

Alicia Holston is a 2009 graduate of the MLS program at the University of North Texas. She was instrumental in the creation of the Maverick Graphic Novel List Committee for the Texas Library Association, and is an active member of the Comic Book Legal Defense Fund. She promotes literacy and liberty through the promotion of graphic novels in libraries.

Vivian Howard is an assistant professor at the School of Information Management at Dalhousie University, Halifax, Nova Scotia. She teaches classes in services and resources for teens and children, as well as collections management. She is also the editor of the *YA Hotline Newsletter*.

Rachel Kitzmann discovered her love of graphic novels in middle school with *Bone* by Jeff Smith, and has been a devoted manga Otaku since her second year of college, after reading *From Eroica with Love* by Yasuko Aoike. She graduated from Dominican University in River Forest, Illinois, in 2007, and works for the Los Angeles Public Library as a young adult librarian in Teen'Scape, the Central library's teen department.

Diana P. Maliszewski is a teacher-librarian at Agnes Macphail Public School in Toronto, Canada. She is completing her master of education degree with the University of Alberta, and is also the editor-in-chief of *The Teaching Librarian*, the official magazine of the Ontario School Library Association. She was chosen as Canada's Teacher-Librarian of the Year in 2008 and is a popular speaker and presenter.

Adam J. Noble has performed Shakespeare, hosted radio shows, written music criticism and worked Drive-Thru. His love of comics dates to his 1986 purchase of *Peter Porker: The Spectacular Spider-Ham 8*. He took a BA degree in 2005 from St. Thomas University in New Brunswick after which he attended Dalhousie University's MLIS program in Halifax, Nova Scotia. He works as the supervising librarian at the public library in New Glasgow, Nova Scotia, and is at work on his first novel.

Amy Kiste Nyberg is the author of *Seal of Approval: The History of the Comics Code*, as well as many book chapters, articles and conference papers on various aspects of comics. She is a three-time Popular Culture Association winner of the Thomas M. Inge Award for Comics Scholarship. An associate professor, she teaches media studies and journalism in the Department of Communication at Seton Hall University in South Orange, New Jersey. She has a PhD in mass communication from the University of Wisconsin–Madison and two master's degrees from Northern Illinois University. She lives in Madison, New Jersey.

Derek Parker Royal is professor and chair of the Department of English & Journalism at Western Illinois University. He is also the founder and executive editor of *Philip Roth Studies*. His essays on American literature and graphic narrative have appeared in such journals as *Contemporary Literature, Modern Fiction Studies, Modern Drama, Studies in the Novel, Critique, MELUS, Shofar,* the *Mark Twain Annual, Poe Studies/Dark Romanticism,* and the *International Journal of Comic Art*. He is the editor of *Coloring America,* a special issue of the journal *MELUS* devoted to race and ethnicity in comics, and an upcoming special issue of *Shofar* devoted to Jewish comics.

Randall W. Scott is in charge of the international comic art collection at Michigan State University. He grew up on a farm reading Batman and Superman. He didn't discover Marvel comics until he went to college in 1965. By 1971 he was working in a comic book store, and has been cataloging comics at MSU since 1974. He wrote the ground-breaking book *Comics Librarianship: A Handbook* (McFarland, 1990).

Erica Segraves is a young adult librarian at the Mamie Doud Eisenhower Public Library in Broomfield, Colorado. She earned her MLS and an information management certification from Emporia State University.

Jason Southworth is an ABD graduate student in philosophy at the University of Oklahoma, Norman, and a philosophy instructor at Fort Hays State University, Hays, Kansas. His research interests include the philosophy of language and the philosophy of mind.

Amanda Stegall-Armour works at the Lee County Library in Tupelo, Mississippi, in reference and technical services. She received her BA in English from the University of Mississippi and is currently working on an MLIS degree from the University of Southern Mississippi.

Ruth Tallman is an ABD graduate student in philosophy at the University of Oklahoma, Norman, and an adjunct philosophy instructor at Fort Hays State University, Hays, Kansas. Her research interests include aesthetics, ethics, and the philosophy of religion.

Laurel Tarulli is the collection access librarian at Halifax Public Libraries in Halifax, Nova Scotia. She received a BA in music from Ithaca College and an MLIS from the University of Alberta. She is the author of the blog *The Cataloging Librarian,* which focuses on day-to-day cataloging issues in libraries, with an emphasis on the future of cataloging. She is the 2009 recipient of the Esther J. Piercy Award.

Amy Thorne has a BA in history from Texas A&M University and an MLIS from Florida State University. She currently works as a children's and teen services librarian for the San Antonio (Texas) Public Library.

Robert G. Weiner is an associate humanities librarian for Texas Tech University, and librarian for sequential art. He has written numerous books and articles on popular culture topics including music, film, and sequential art. He is the author of *Marvel Graphic Novels: An Annotated Guide* and co-author of the *The Grateful Dead and the Deadheads: An Annotated Bibliography,* and is editor of *Captain American and the Struggle of the Superhero* and *Perspectives on the Grateful Dead*. He has been published in the *Journal of Popular Culture,* the *Texas Library Journal,* the *West Texas Historical Association Journal* and the *International Journal of Comic Art*.

Stephen Weiner is director of the Maynard Public Library in Maynard, Massachusetts. He holds an MA degree in children's literature and an MLIS, and has been a pioneering advocate for the inclusion of graphic novels in libraries and other educational settings. His articles and reviews have appeared in *The Boston Globe, Voice of Youth Advocates, Library Journal, School Library Journal, The Shy Librarian, Public Libraries, Comic Buyer's Guide, The Graphic Novel Review, Comic*

Book Artist, and *The English Journal.* His books include *Bring an Author to Your Library* (1993), *100 Graphic Novels for Public Libraries* (1996), *The 101 Best Graphic Novels* (2001; second edition, 2005), *Faster Than a Speeding Bullet: The Rise of the Graphic Novel* (2003). He is the co-author (with N.C. Christopher Couch) of *The Will Eisner Companion* (2004), *Using Graphic Novels in the Classroom including* Bone: *A Guide for Teachers and Librarians* (with Philip Crawford, 2005), and *The Hellboy Companion* for Dark Horse Comics.

Eric Werthmann is a reference librarian at the Acorn Public Library in Oak Forest, Illinois. He holds a bachelor's degree from Boston College and a master's degree in library science from the University of North Carolina at Chapel Hill.

Nicholas Yanes, who has written two theses focused on graphic literature, created and teaches American Comic Book History, a junior level course in the American Studies Program at Florida State University. His first publication is the essay "Graphic Imagery: Jewish American Comic Book Creators' Depictions of Class, Race, Patriotism and the Birth of the Good Captain" (in *Captain America and the Struggle of the Superhero: Critical Essays).* He is writing an essay on African religion in mainstream American comic books, editing a collection of essays on Obama in popular culture; and writing a documentary script about women and comic books.

Christian Zabriskie is a young adult librarian at Queens Library in New York City. He is also the founder of Urban Librarians Unite, a public speaker, and a Samurai librarian.

Sarah Ziolkowska holds an MLIS from the School of Information Management at Dalhousie University, Halifax, Nova Scotia. She is currently the youth services librarian at Vaughan Public Libraries in Ontario.

Index